HIDEYUKI FURUHASHI

In American superhero
movies, I love the scenes
where the protagonist starts
coming into his or her own
as a hero. They're usually
kind of full of themselves at
that point, which I also like.

BETTEN COURT

This is volume 2.
There's a truckload of
American superhero movies
and TV shows that I want to
watch, but when I put them
on in the background while
I'm working, it all goes in
one ear and out the other.

It sucks.

MY HERO ACADEMIA VIGILANTES

VOLUME 2
SHONEN JUMP Manga Edition

STORY: HIDEYUKI FURUHASHI
ART: BETTEN COURT
ORIGINAL CONCEPT: KOHEI HORIKOSHI

Translation & English Adaptation/Caleb Cook
Touch-Up Art & Lettering/John Hunt
Designer/Julian [JR] Robinson
Editor/Mike Montesa

VIGILANTE -BOKU NO HERO ACADEMIA ILLEGALS-
© 2016 by Hideyuki Furuhashi, Betten Court, Kohei Horikoshi
All rights reserved.
First published in Japan in 2016 by SHUEISHA Inc., Tokyo.
English translation rights arranged by SHUEISHA Inc.

Printed in the U.S.A.

Published by VIZ Media, LLC
P.O. Box 77010
San Francisco, CA 94107

10 9 8 7 6 5 4 3 2
First printing, October 2018
Second printing, October 2018

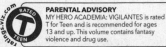

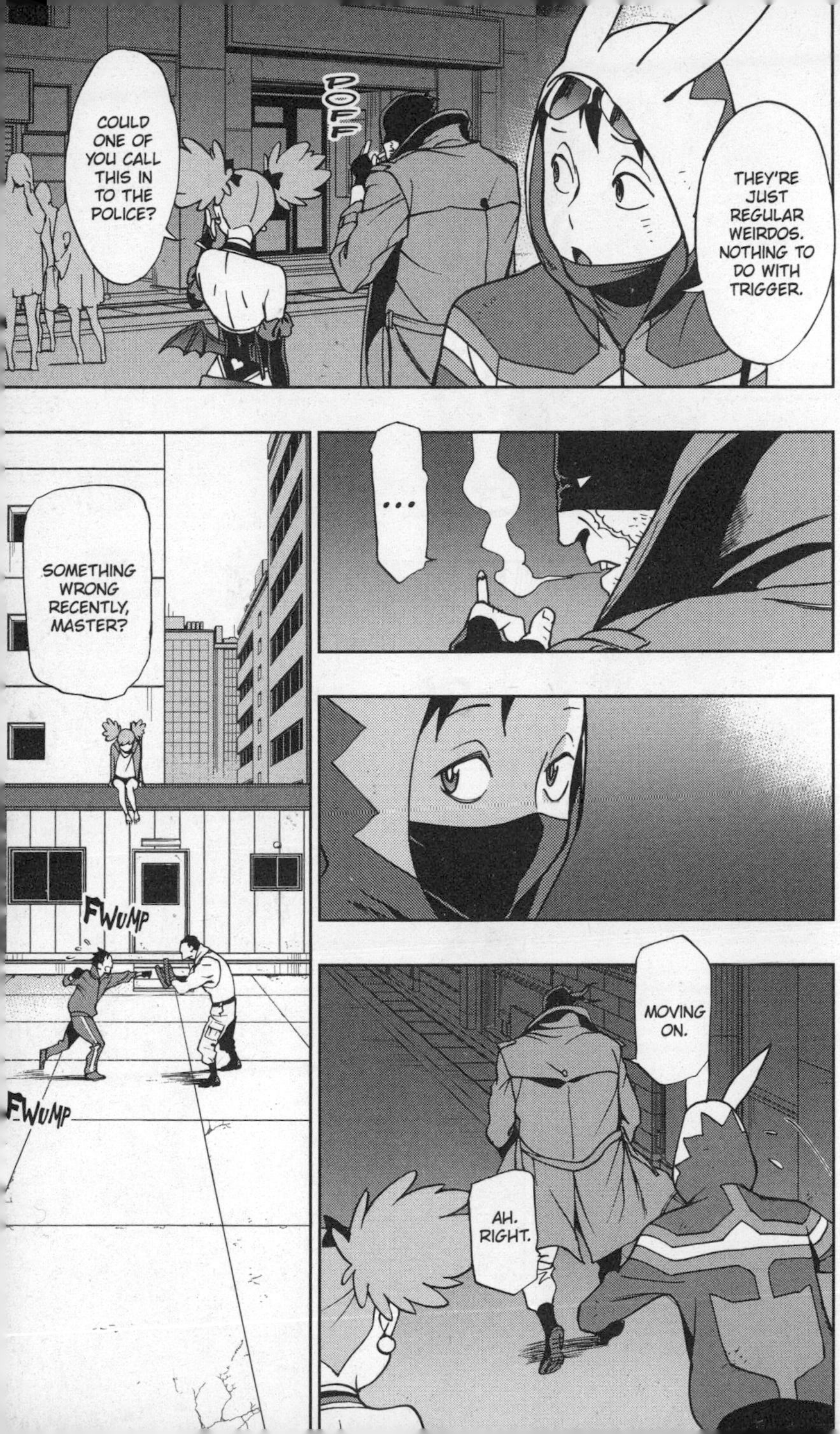
THEY'RE JUST REGULAR WEIRDOS. NOTHING TO DO WITH TRIGGER.
POFF
COULD ONE OF YOU CALL THIS IN TO THE POLICE?
...
MOVING ON.
AH. RIGHT.
SOMETHING WRONG RECENTLY, MASTER?
FWUMP
FWUMP

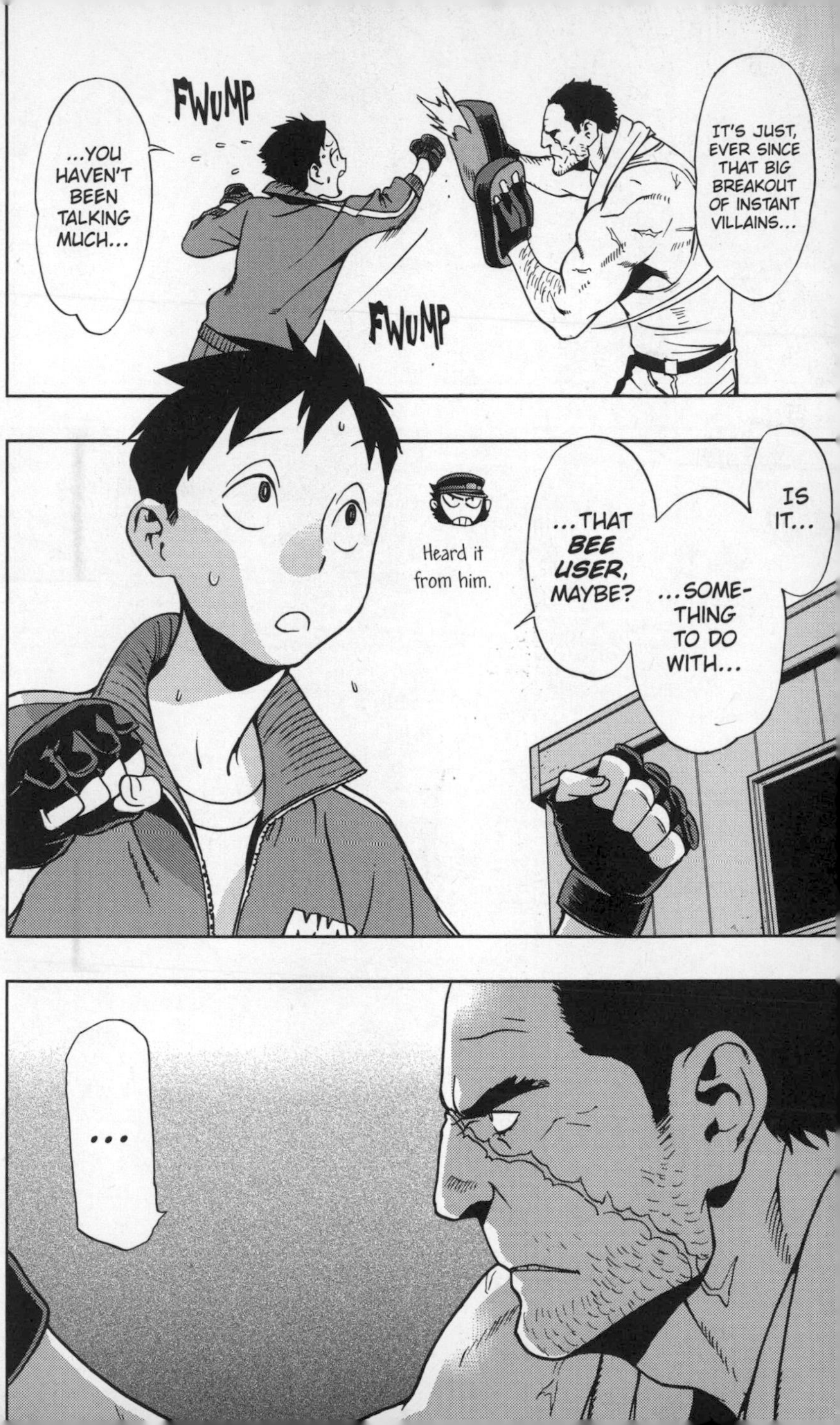
IT'S JUST, EVER SINCE THAT BIG BREAKOUT OF INSTANT VILLAINS...
FWUMP
FWUMP
...YOU HAVEN'T BEEN TALKING MUCH...
IS IT...
...SOME-THING TO DO WITH...
...THAT BEE USER, MAYBE?
Heard it from him.
...

MY HERO ACADEMIA
VIGILANTES

2

Writer / Letterer
Hideyuki Furuhashi

Penciller / Colorist
Betten Court

Original Concept
Kohei Horikoshi

【villain】

noun | vil · lain

: a character in a story or play who opposes the hero; a deliberate scoundrel or criminal; one blamed for a particular evil or difficulty

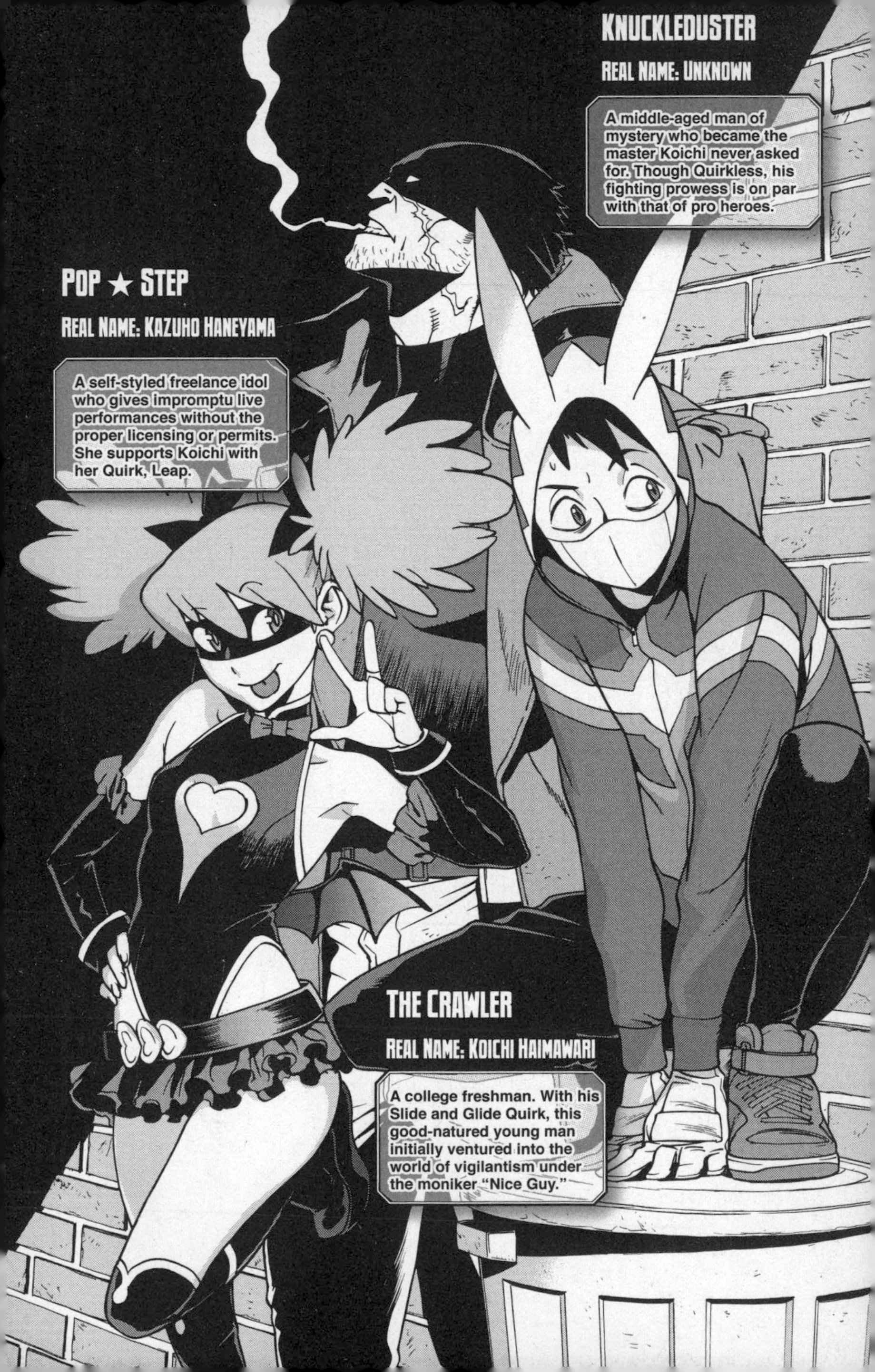
KNUCKLEDUSTER
REAL NAME: UNKNOWN
A middle-aged man of mystery who became the master Koichi never asked for. Though Quirkless, his fighting prowess is on par with that of pro heroes.
POP ★ STEP
REAL NAME: KAZUHO HANEYAMA
A self-styled freelance idol who gives impromptu live performances without the proper licensing or permits. She supports Koichi with her Quirk, Leap.
THE CRAWLER
REAL NAME: KOICHI HAIMAWARI
A college freshman. With his Slide and Glide Quirk, this good-natured young man initially ventured into the world of vigilantism under the moniker "Nice Guy."

CHARACTERS

NAOMASA TSUKAUCHI

A justice-driven detective hot on the trail of Trigger, a dangerous drug linked to the rash of pop-up villain incidents. Always shrewd and insightful.

KUIN HACHISUKA

A second-year high school student and part-time villain. Her Quirk, Queen Bee, has thrown the neighborhood into chaos.

STENDHAL

A masked man who suddenly showed up in Naruhata, the neighborhood Koichi and friends call home. His goals and background are complete mysteries.

INGENIUM/TENSEI IDA

The Turbo Hero whose Tokyo-based agency employs a large number of sidekicks. His Quirk is Engine.

STORY

What is "justice" anyway? Get ready for a PLUS ULTRA spin-off set in the world of *My Hero Academia*!!

Heroes. The chosen ones who, with explicit government permission, use their natural talents, or Quirks, to aid society. However, not everyone can be chosen, and some take action of their own accord, becoming illegal heroes. What does justice mean to them? And can we really call them heroes? This story takes to the streets in order to follow the exploits of those known as vigilantes.

MY HERO ACADEMIA VIGILANTES

2

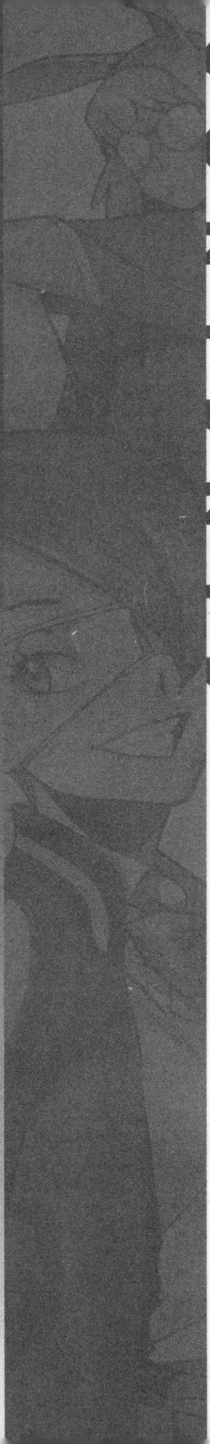

CONTENTS

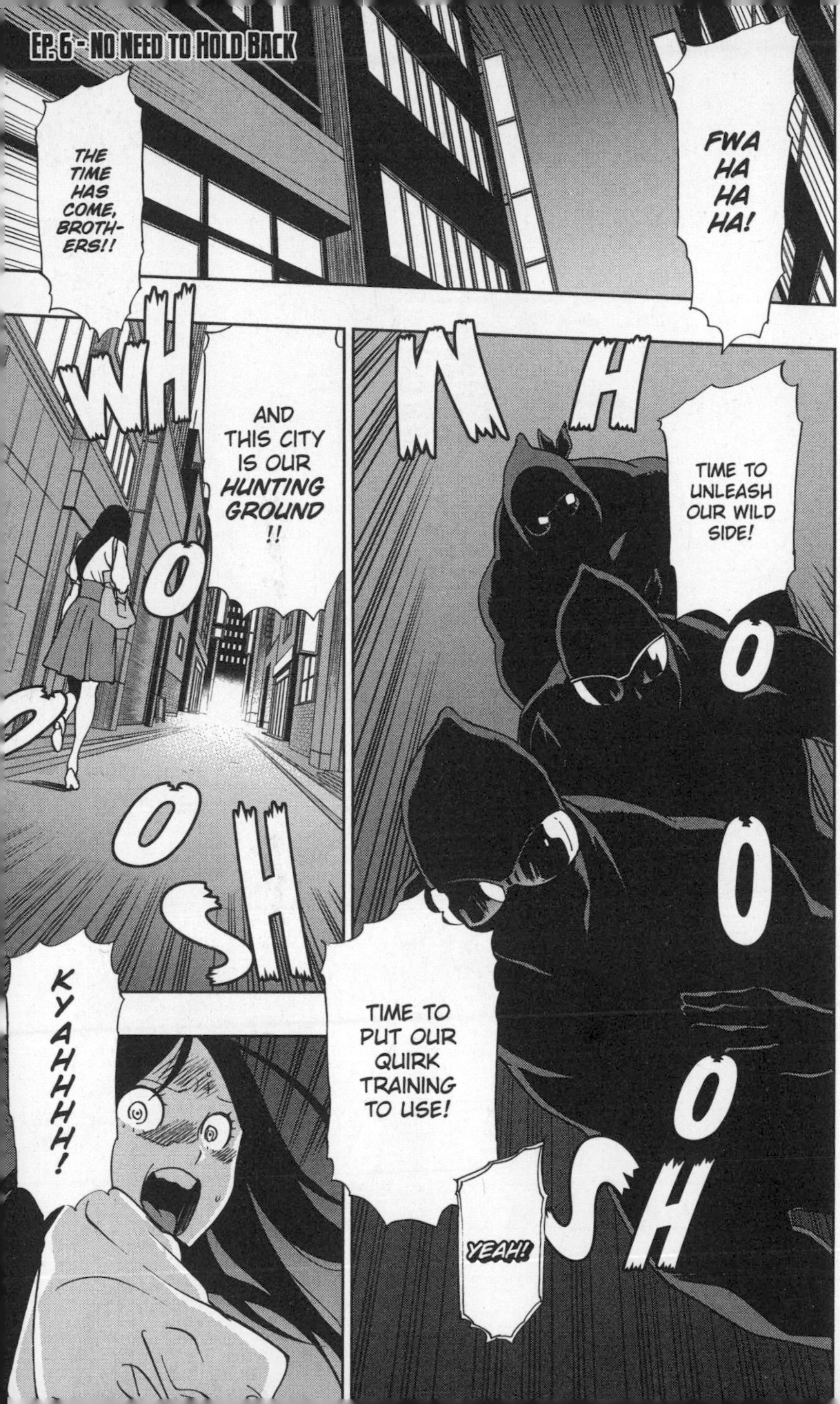

Ep. 6 - No Need to Hold Back
FWA HA HA HA!
THE TIME HAS COME, BROTHERS!!
TIME TO UNLEASH OUR WILD SIDE!
WHOOOSH
AND THIS CITY IS OUR HUNTING GROUND!!
WHOOSH
TIME TO PUT OUR QUIRK TRAINING TO USE!
YEAH!
KYAHHHH!

EP. 6 - NO NEED TO HOLD BACK

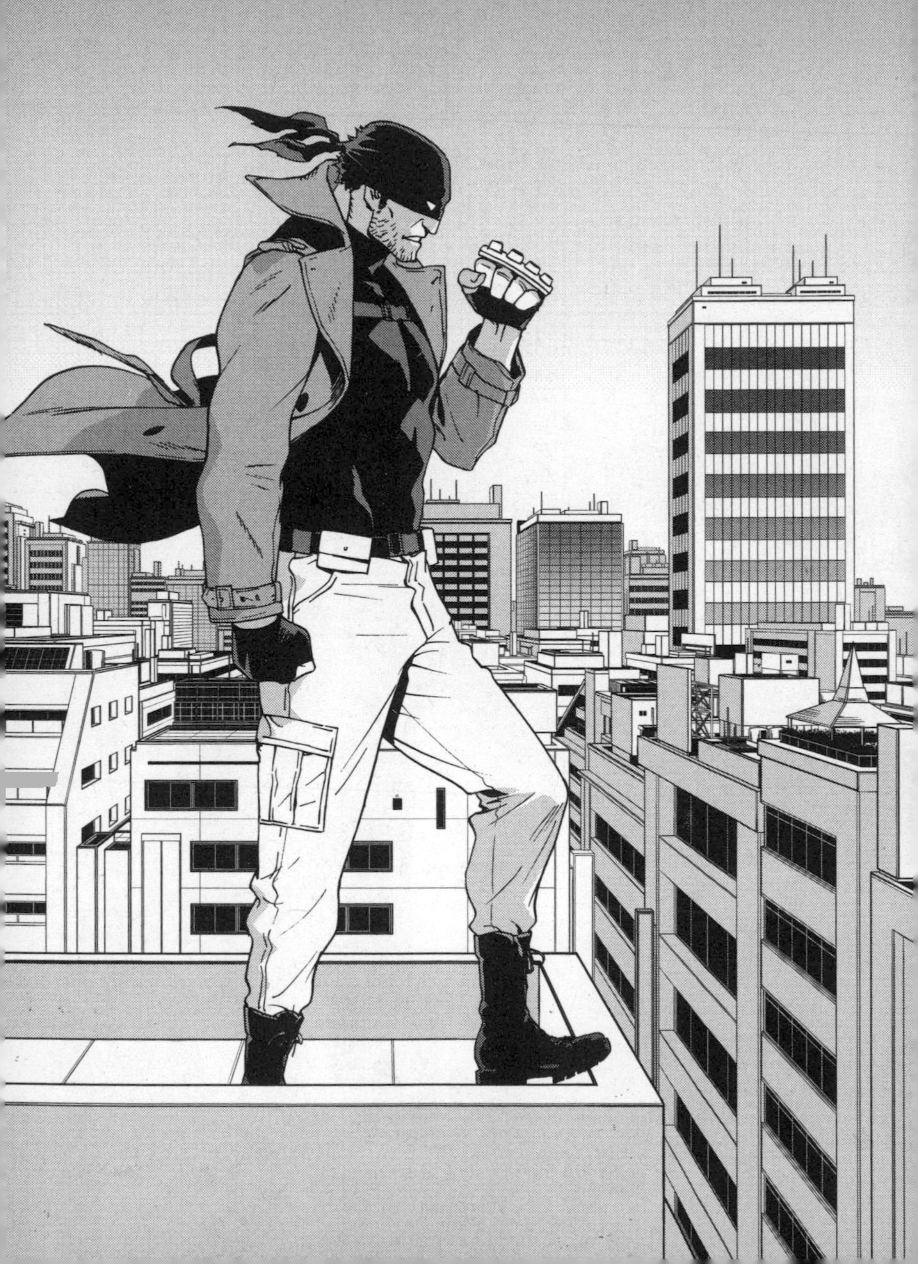

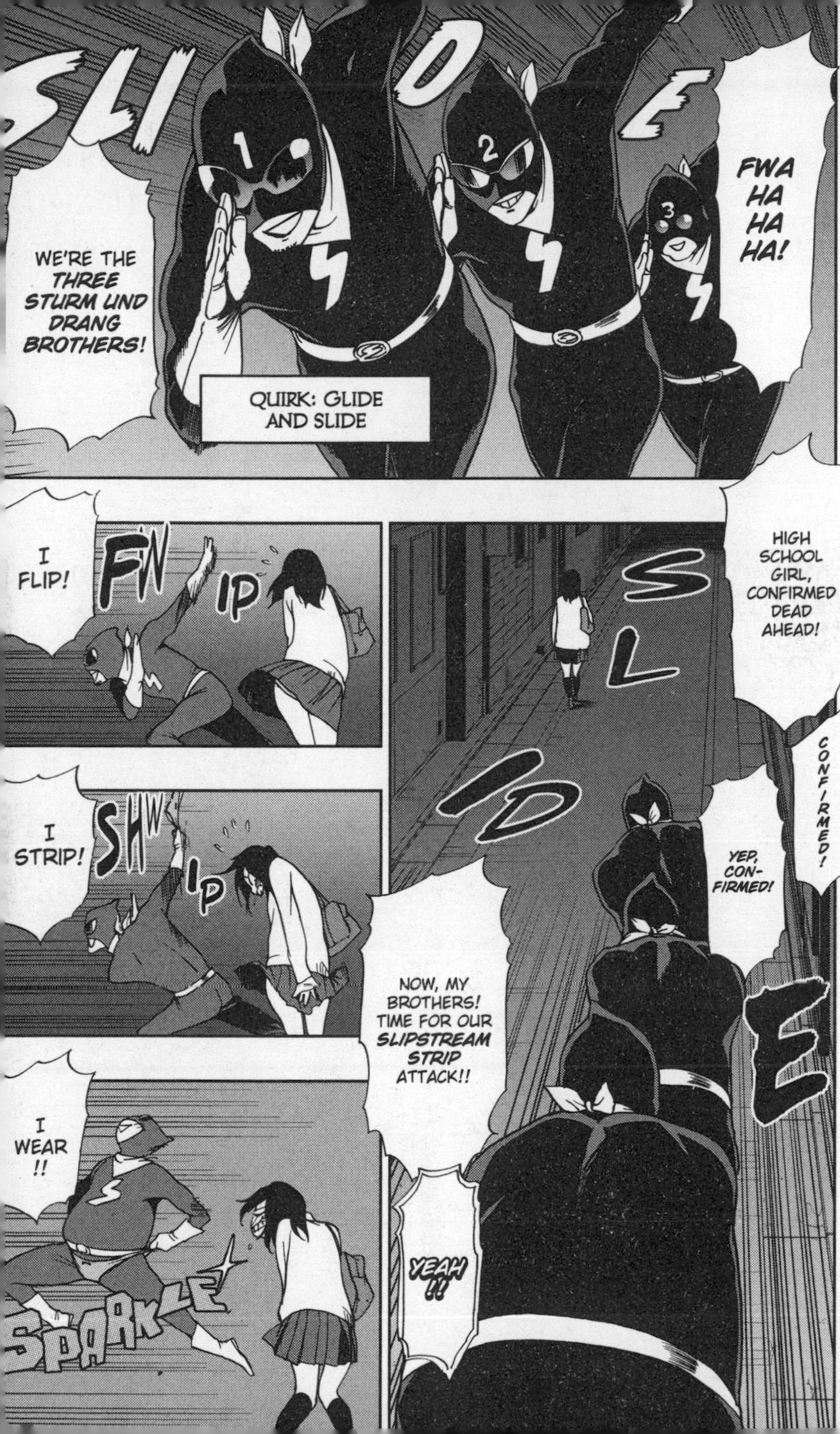
SLIDE
FWA HA HA HA!
WE'RE THE THREE STURM UND DRANG BROTHERS!
QUIRK: GLIDE AND SLIDE
HIGH SCHOOL GIRL, CONFIRMED DEAD AHEAD!
CONFIRMED!
YEP, CONFIRMED!
SLIDE
NOW, MY BROTHERS! TIME FOR OUR SLIPSTREAM STRIP ATTACK!!
YEAH!!
I FLIP!
FWIP
I STRIP!
SHWIP
I WEAR!!
SPARKLE

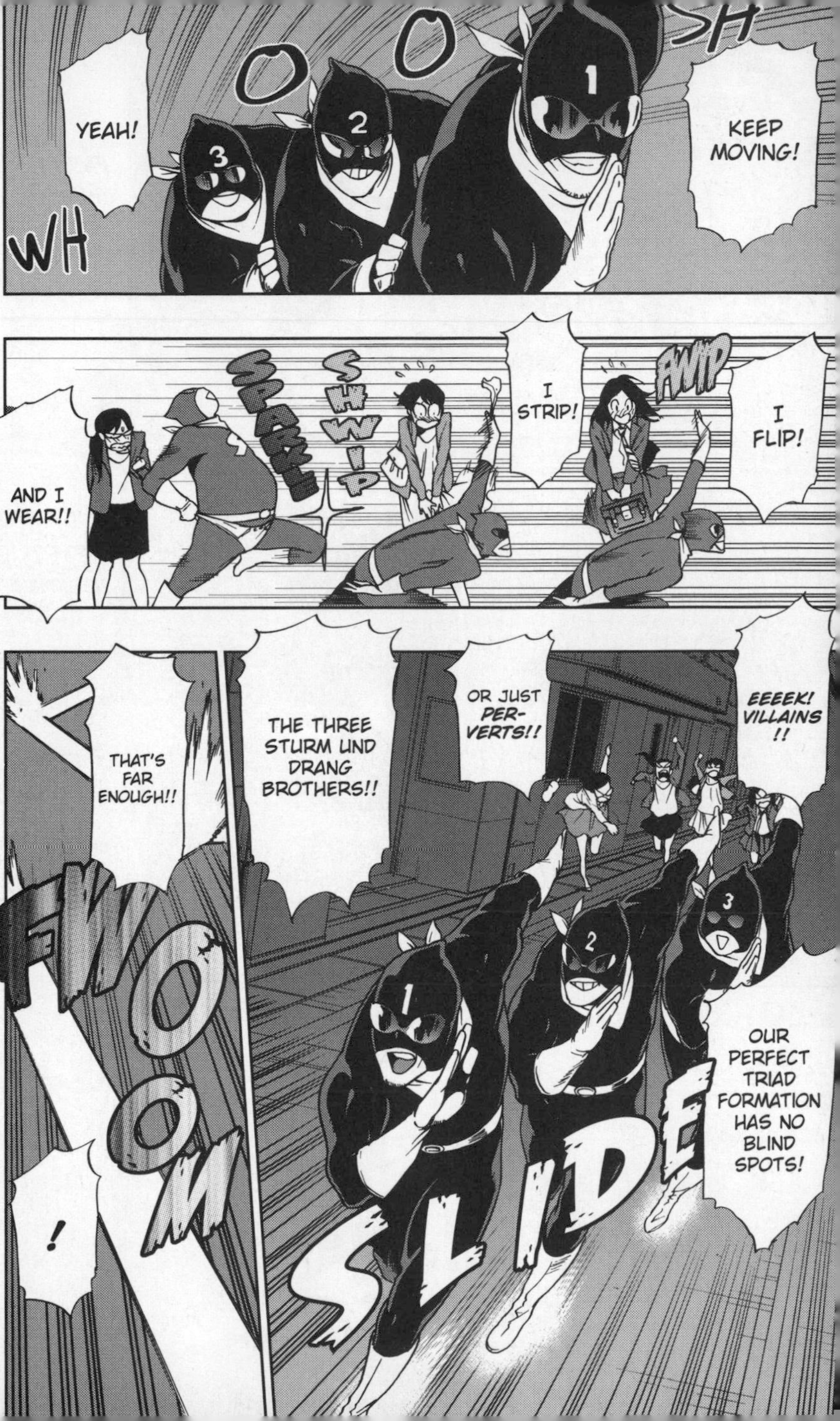

KEEP MOVING!
YEAH!
WH
OO
SH
I FLIP!
AWIP
I STRIP!
SHWIP
AND I WEAR!!
EEEEK! VILLAINS!!
OR JUST PER-VERTS!!
THE THREE STURM UND DRANG BROTHERS!!
OUR PERFECT TRIAD FORMATION HAS NO BLIND SPOTS!
SLIDE
THAT'S FAR ENOUGH!!
FWOOM
!

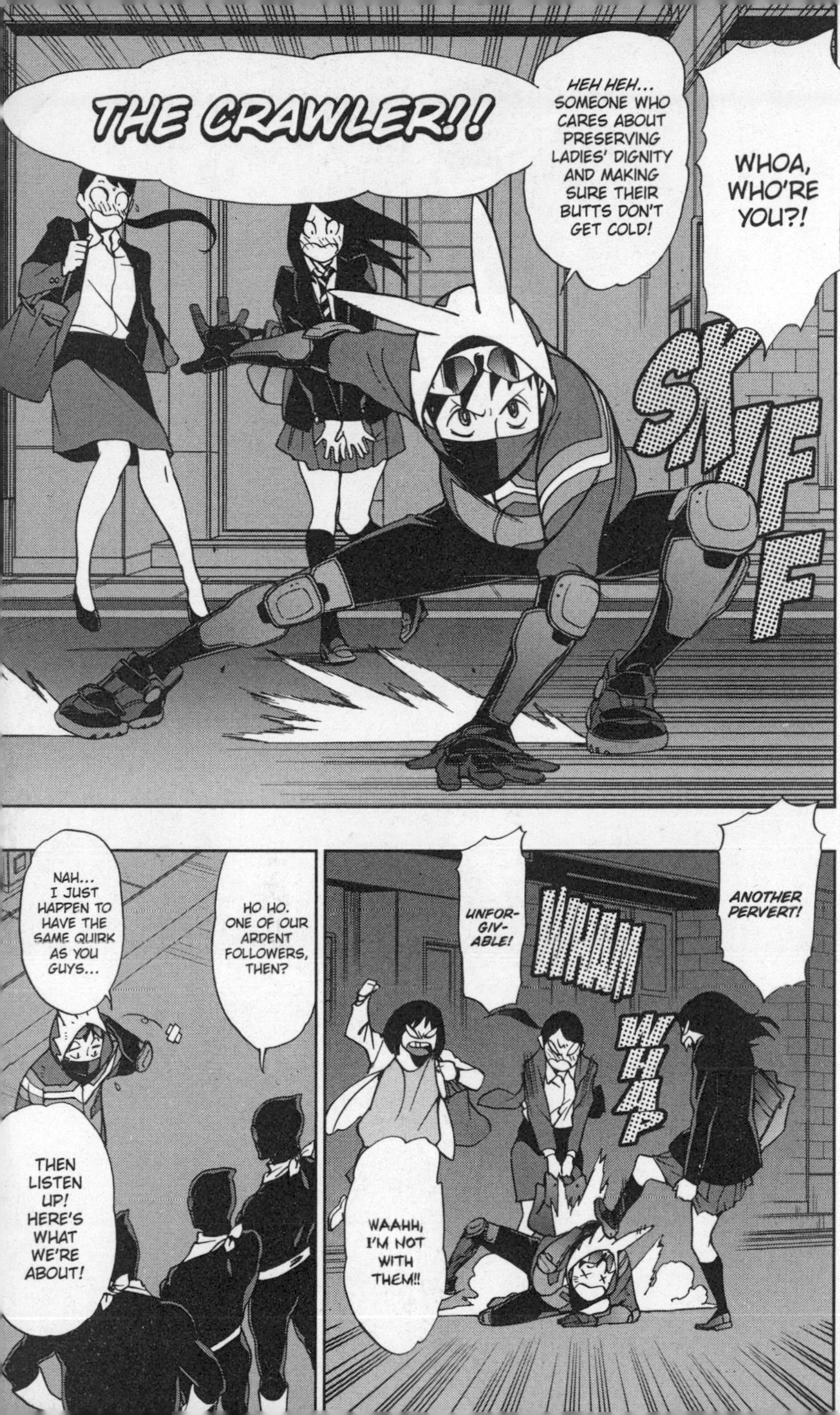
WHOA, WHO'RE YOU?!
HEH HEH... SOMEONE WHO CARES ABOUT PRESERVING LADIES' DIGNITY AND MAKING SURE THEIR BUTTS DON'T GET COLD!
THE CRAWLER!!
SKIFF
ANOTHER PERVERT!
UNFOR-GIVABLE!
WHAM
WHAP
WAAHH, I'M NOT WITH THEM!!
HO HO. ONE OF OUR ARDENT FOLLOWERS, THEN?
NAH... I JUST HAPPEN TO HAVE THE SAME QUIRK AS YOU GUYS...
THEN LISTEN UP! HERE'S WHAT WE'RE ABOUT!

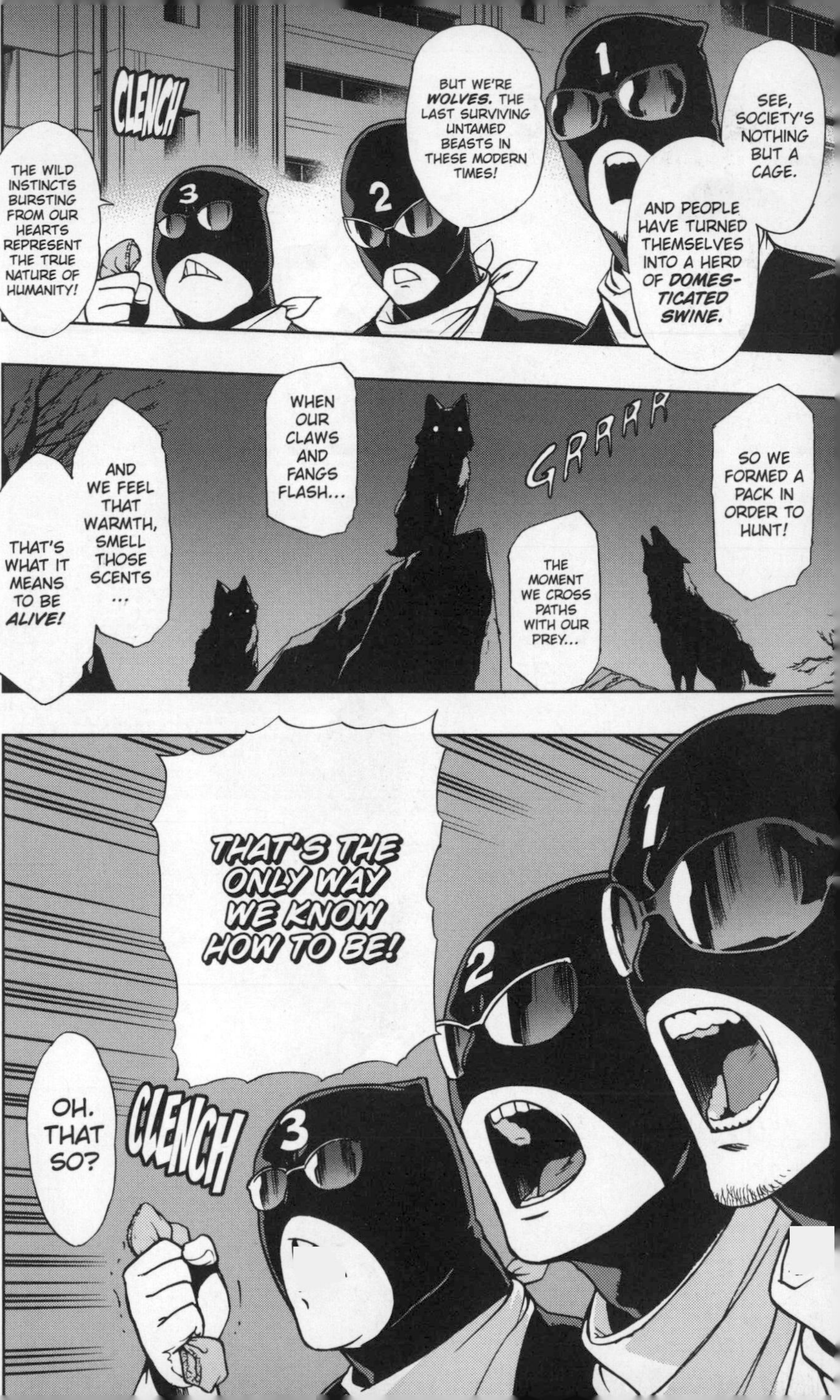
SEE, SOCIETY'S NOTHING BUT A CAGE.
AND PEOPLE HAVE TURNED THEMSELVES INTO A HERD OF DOMESTICATED SWINE.
BUT WE'RE WOLVES. THE LAST SURVIVING UNTAMED BEASTS IN THESE MODERN TIMES!
CLENCH
THE WILD INSTINCTS BURSTING FROM OUR HEARTS REPRESENT THE TRUE NATURE OF HUMANITY!
SO WE FORMED A PACK IN ORDER TO HUNT!
GRRRR
THE MOMENT WE CROSS PATHS WITH OUR PREY...
WHEN OUR CLAWS AND FANGS FLASH...
AND WE FEEL THAT WARMTH, SMELL THOSE SCENTS...
THAT'S WHAT IT MEANS TO BE ALIVE!
THAT'S THE ONLY WAY WE KNOW HOW TO BE!
CLENCH
OH. THAT SO?

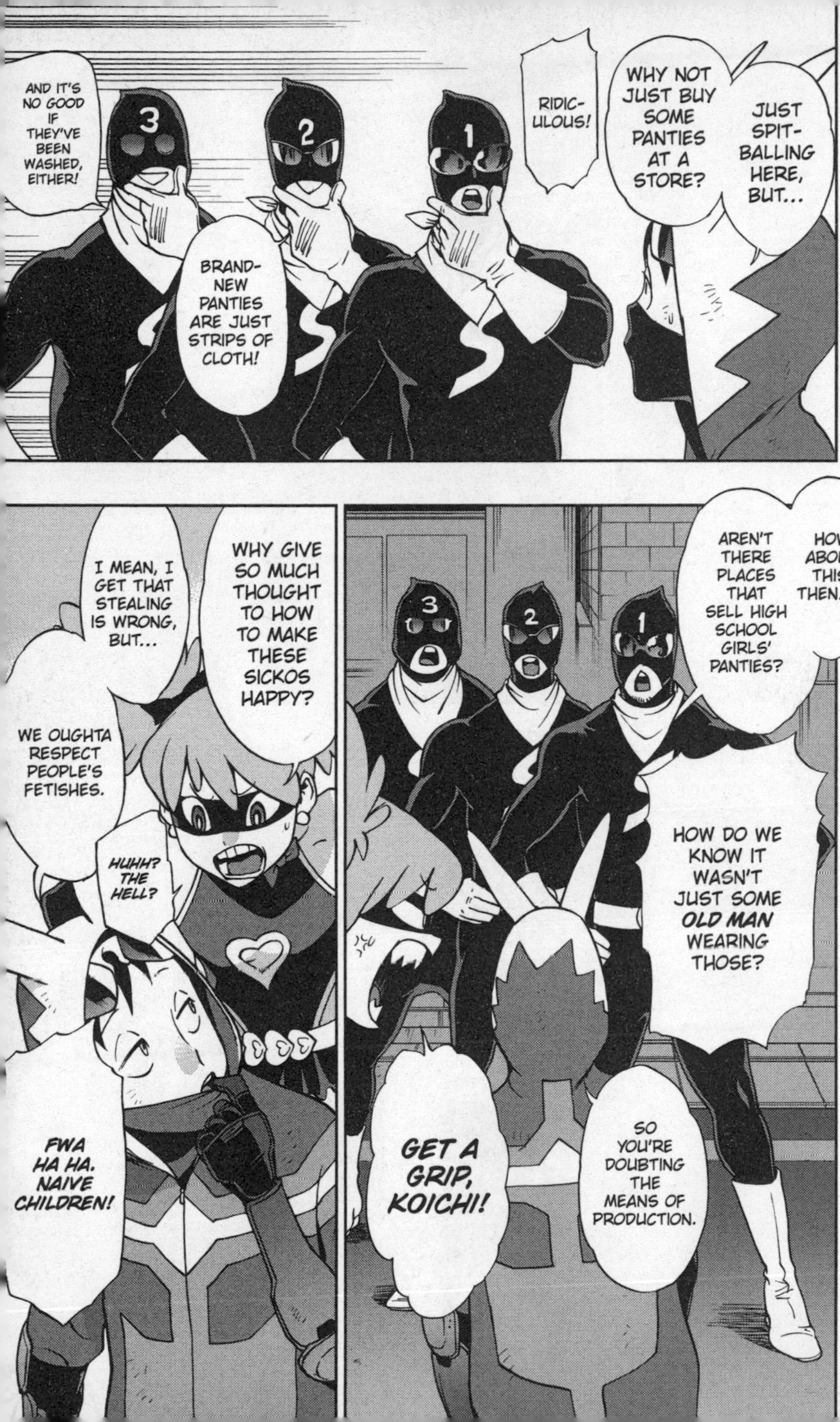

JUST SPIT-BALLING HERE, BUT...
WHY NOT JUST BUY SOME PANTIES AT A STORE?
RIDIC-ULOUS!
BRAND-NEW PANTIES ARE JUST STRIPS OF CLOTH!
AND IT'S NO GOOD IF THEY'VE BEEN WASHED, EITHER!
HOW ABOUT THIS, THEN...?
AREN'T THERE PLACES THAT SELL HIGH SCHOOL GIRLS' PANTIES?
HOW DO WE KNOW IT WASN'T JUST SOME *OLD MAN* WEARING THOSE?
SO YOU'RE DOUBTING THE MEANS OF PRODUCTION.
GET A GRIP, KOICHI!
WHY GIVE SO MUCH THOUGHT TO HOW TO MAKE THESE SICKOS HAPPY?
I MEAN, I GET THAT STEALING IS WRONG, BUT...
WE OUGHTA RESPECT PEOPLE'S FETISHES.
HUHH? THE HELL?
FWA HA HA. NAIVE CHILDREN!

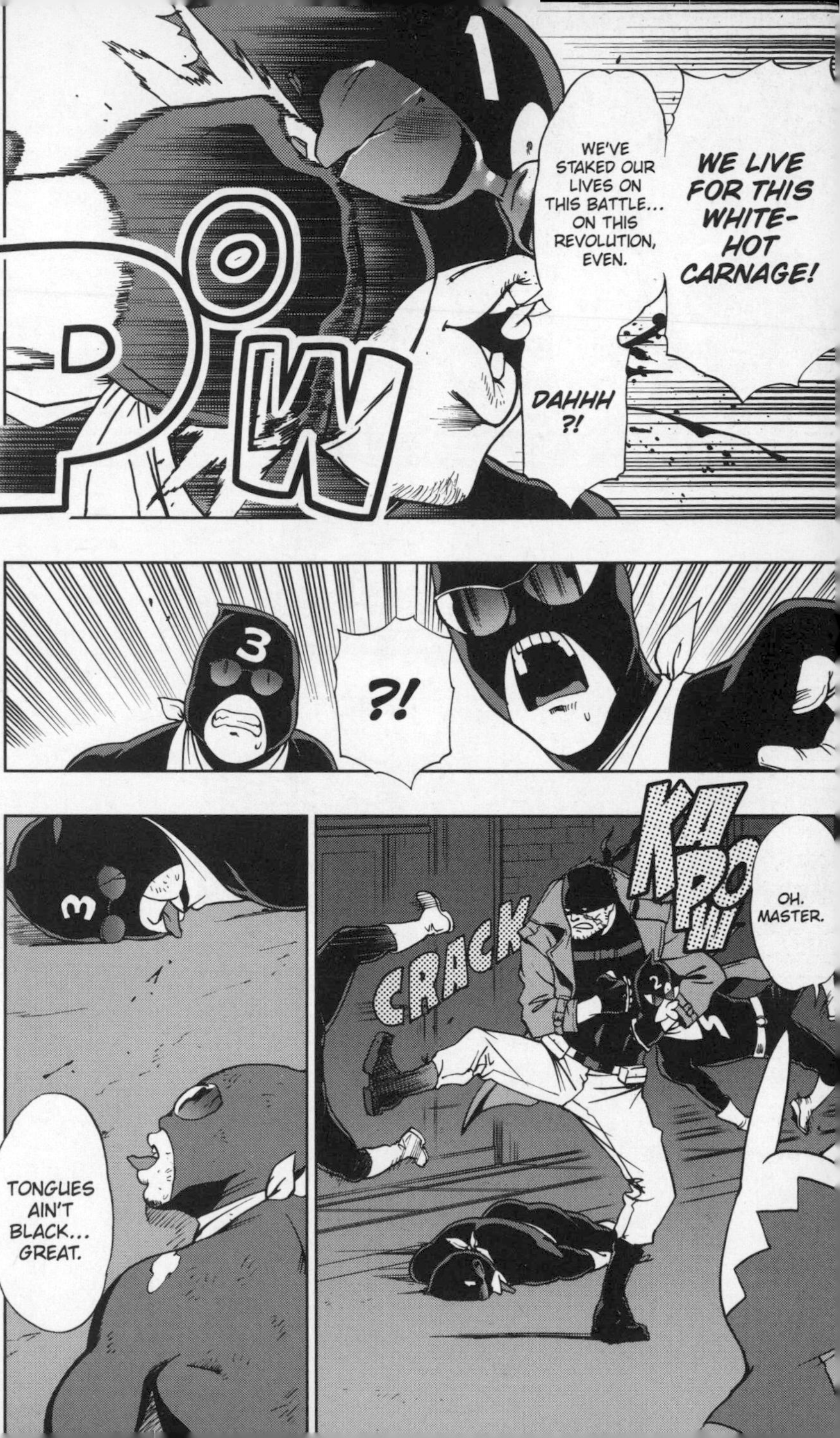
WE LIVE FOR THIS WHITE-HOT CARNAGE!
WE'VE STAKED OUR LIVES ON THIS BATTLE... ON THIS REVOLUTION, EVEN.
DAHHH ?!
POW
?!
OH. MASTER.
KAPOW
CRACK
TONGUES AIN'T BLACK... GREAT.

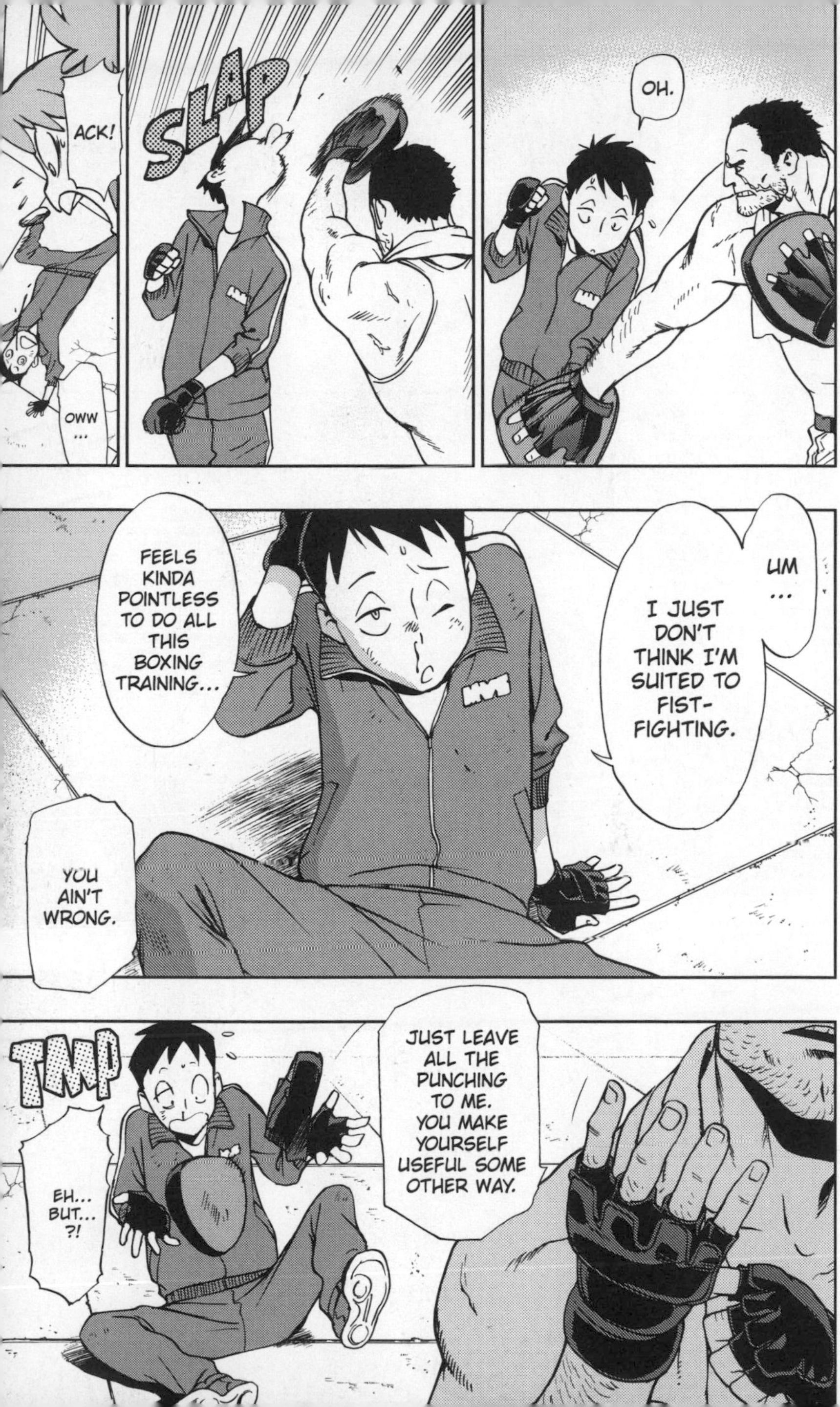
OH.
SLAP
ACK!
OWW...
UM...
I JUST DON'T THINK I'M SUITED TO FIST-FIGHTING.
FEELS KINDA POINTLESS TO DO ALL THIS BOXING TRAINING...
YOU AIN'T WRONG.
JUST LEAVE ALL THE PUNCHING TO ME. YOU MAKE YOURSELF USEFUL SOME OTHER WAY.
TMP
EH... BUT...?!

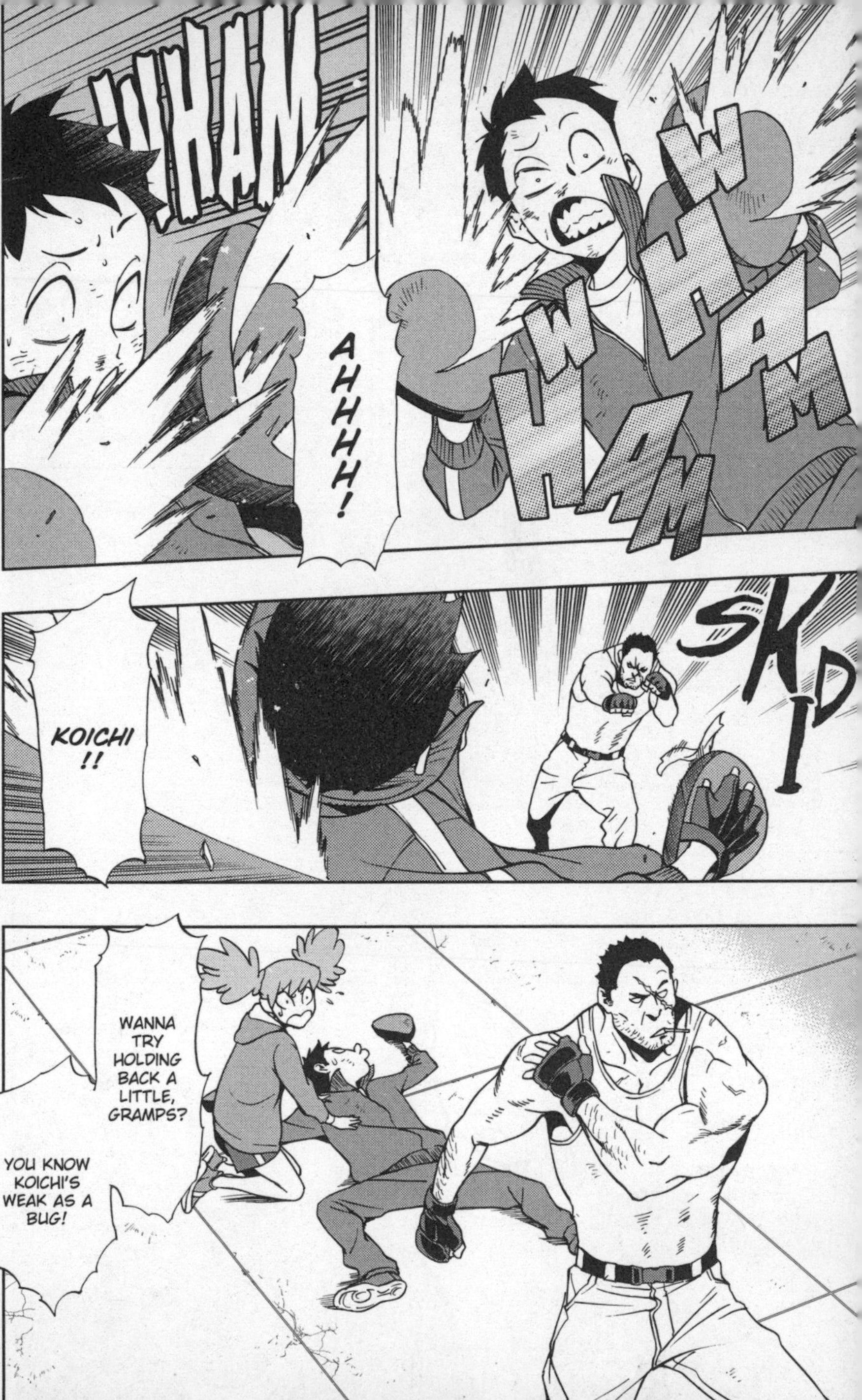
WHAM
WHAM
AHHHH!
WHAM
SKID
KOICHI!!
WANNA TRY HOLDING BACK A LITTLE, GRAMPS?
YOU KNOW KOICHI'S WEAK AS A BUG!

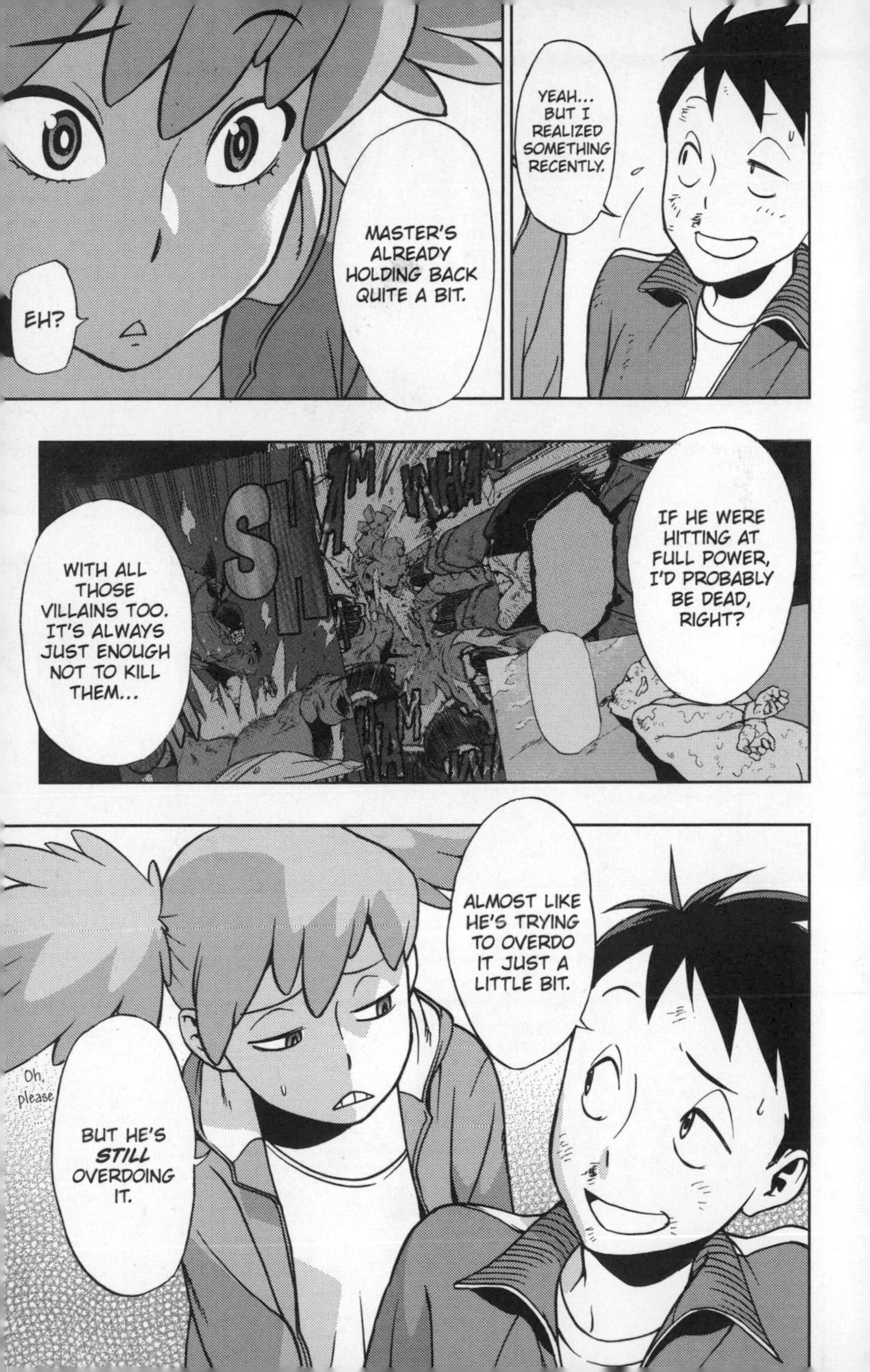
YEAH... BUT I REALIZED SOMETHING RECENTLY.
MASTER'S ALREADY HOLDING BACK QUITE A BIT.
EH?
IF HE WERE HITTING AT FULL POWER, I'D PROBABLY BE DEAD, RIGHT?
WITH ALL THOSE VILLAINS TOO. IT'S ALWAYS JUST ENOUGH NOT TO KILL THEM...
ALMOST LIKE HE'S TRYING TO OVERDO IT JUST A LITTLE BIT.
Oh, please
BUT HE'S *STILL* OVERDOING IT.

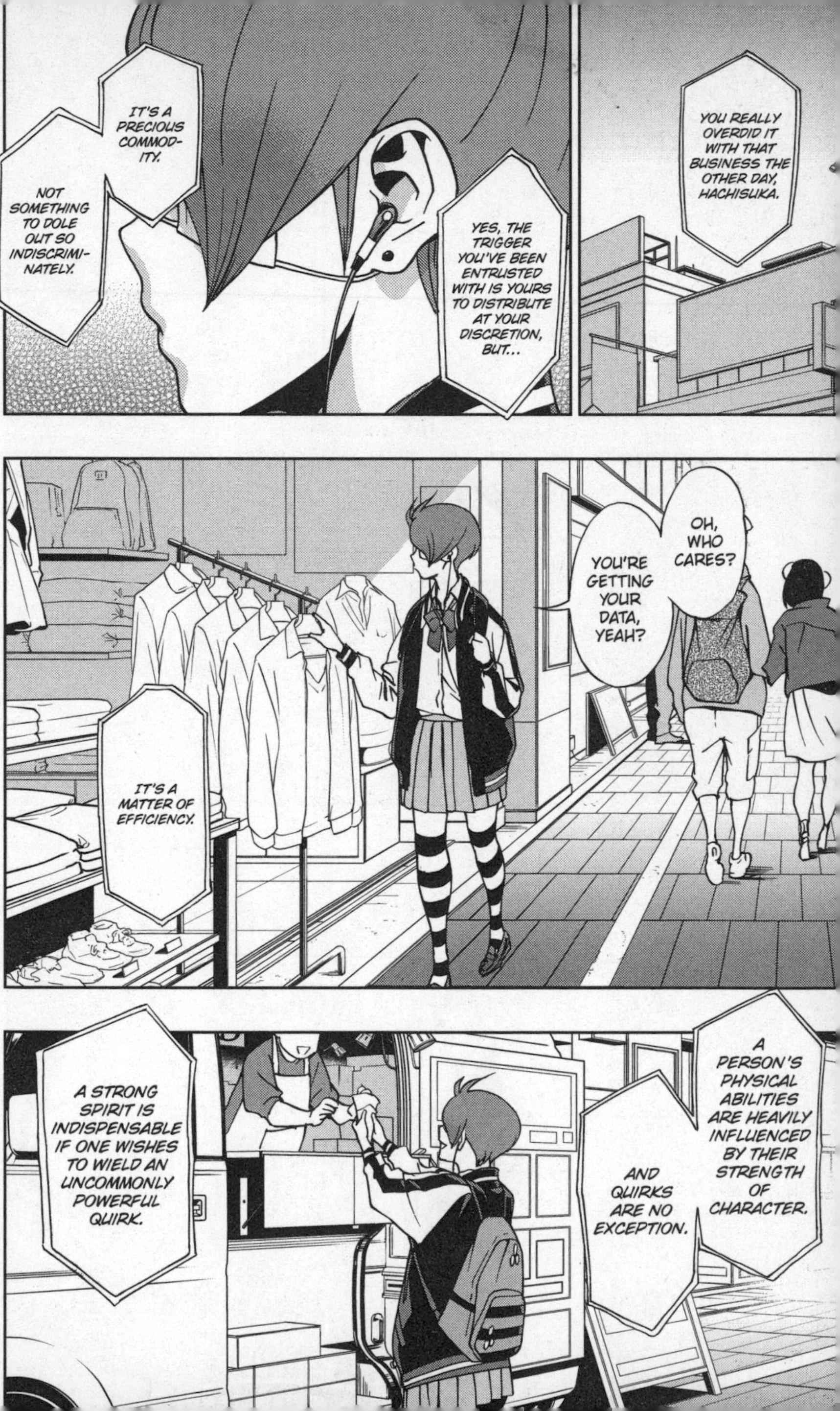
YOU REALLY OVERDID IT WITH THAT BUSINESS THE OTHER DAY, HACHISUKA.
YES, THE TRIGGER YOU'VE BEEN ENTRUSTED WITH IS YOURS TO DISTRIBUTE AT YOUR DISCRETION, BUT...
IT'S A PRECIOUS COMMODITY.
NOT SOMETHING TO DOLE OUT SO INDISCRIMINATELY.
OH, WHO CARES?
YOU'RE GETTING YOUR DATA, YEAH?
IT'S A MATTER OF EFFICIENCY.
A PERSON'S PHYSICAL ABILITIES ARE HEAVILY INFLUENCED BY THEIR STRENGTH OF CHARACTER.
AND QUIRKS ARE NO EXCEPTION.
A STRONG SPIRIT IS INDISPENSABLE IF ONE WISHES TO WIELD AN UNCOMMONLY POWERFUL QUIRK.

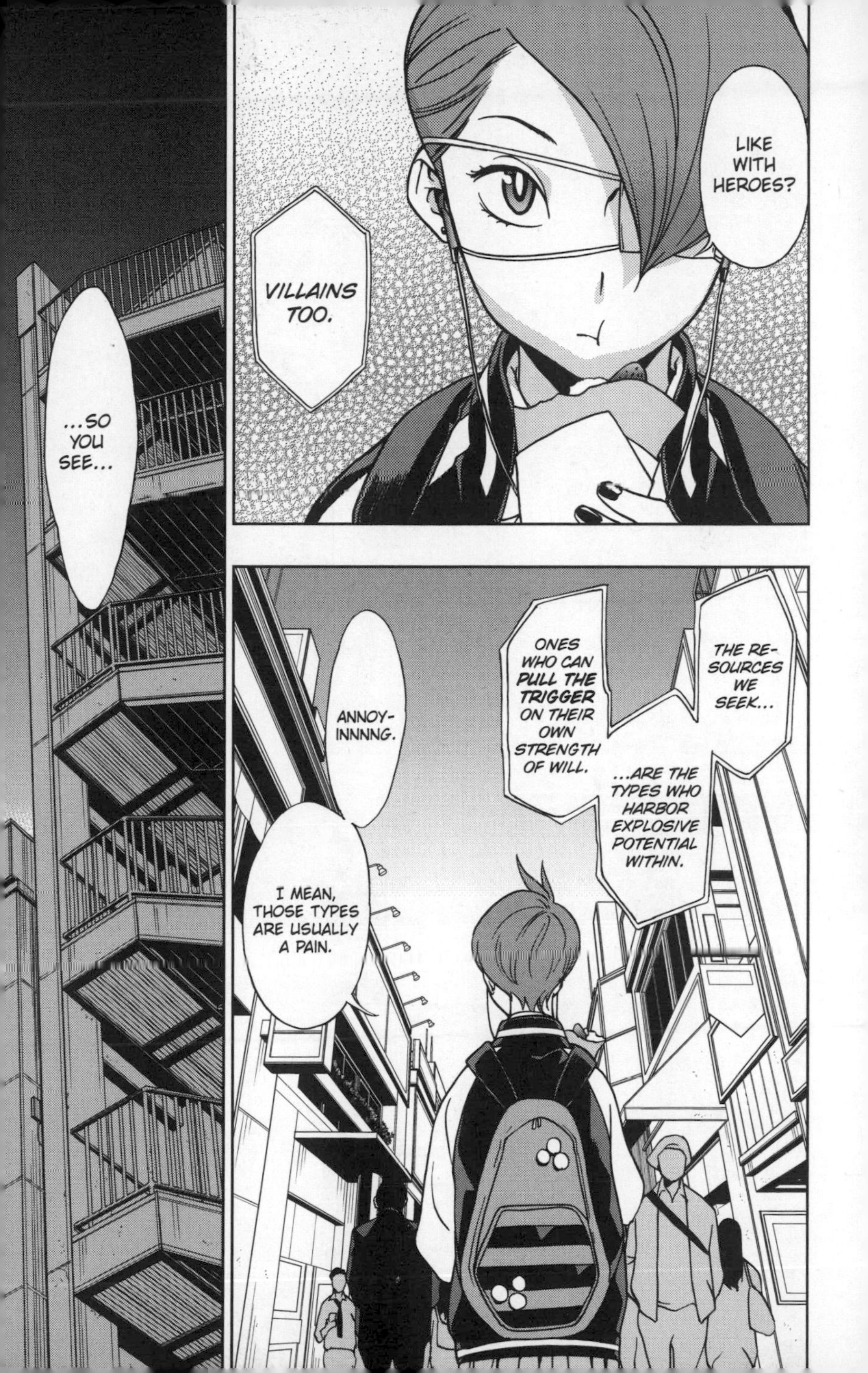
LIKE WITH HEROES?
VILLAINS TOO.
THE RE-SOURCES WE SEEK...
...ARE THE TYPES WHO HARBOR EXPLOSIVE POTENTIAL WITHIN.
ONES WHO CAN PULL THE TRIGGER ON THEIR OWN STRENGTH OF WILL.
ANNOY-INNNNG.
I MEAN, THOSE TYPES ARE USUALLY A PAIN.
...SO YOU SEE...

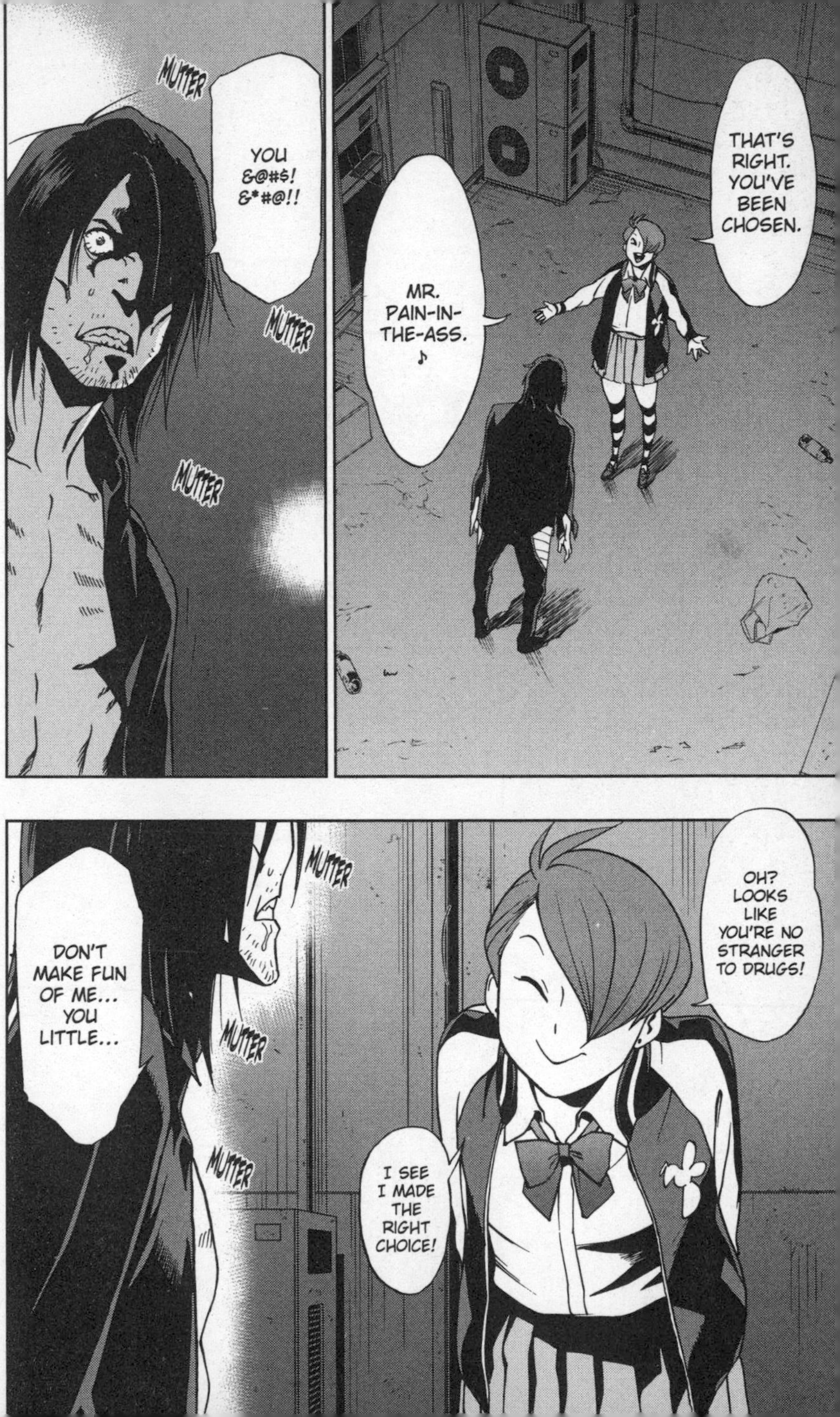
THAT'S RIGHT. YOU'VE BEEN CHOSEN.
MR. PAIN-IN-THE-ASS. ♪
MUTTER
YOU &@#$! &*#@!!
MUTTER
MUTTER
OH? LOOKS LIKE YOU'RE NO STRANGER TO DRUGS!
MUTTER
DON'T MAKE FUN OF ME... YOU LITTLE...
MUTTER
I SEE I MADE THE RIGHT CHOICE!
MUTTER

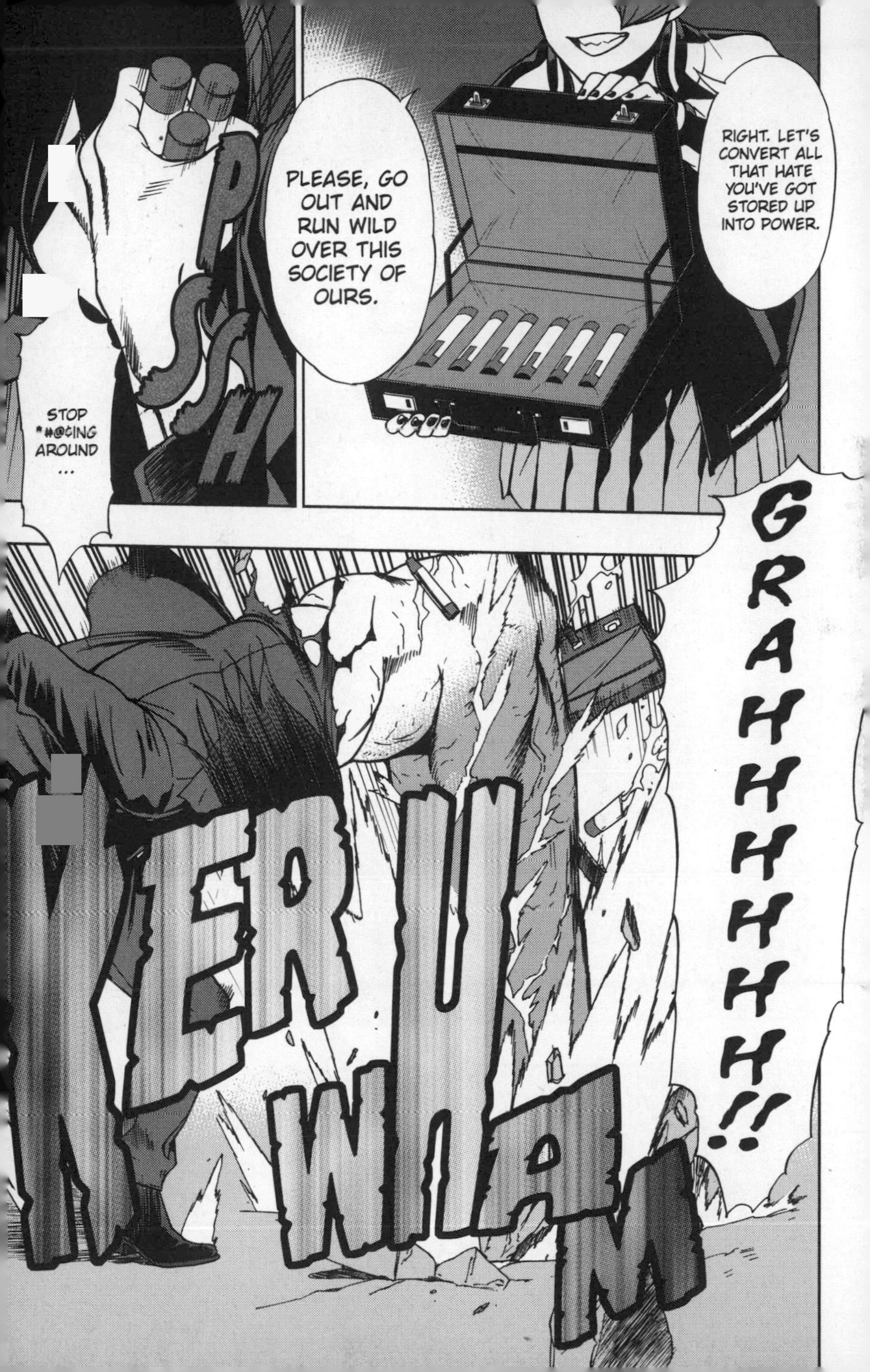
RIGHT. LET'S CONVERT ALL THAT HATE YOU'VE GOT STORED UP INTO POWER.
PLEASE, GO OUT AND RUN WILD OVER THIS SOCIETY OF OURS.
PSSH
STOP *#@¢ING AROUND...
GRAHHHHHHH!!
WHAM

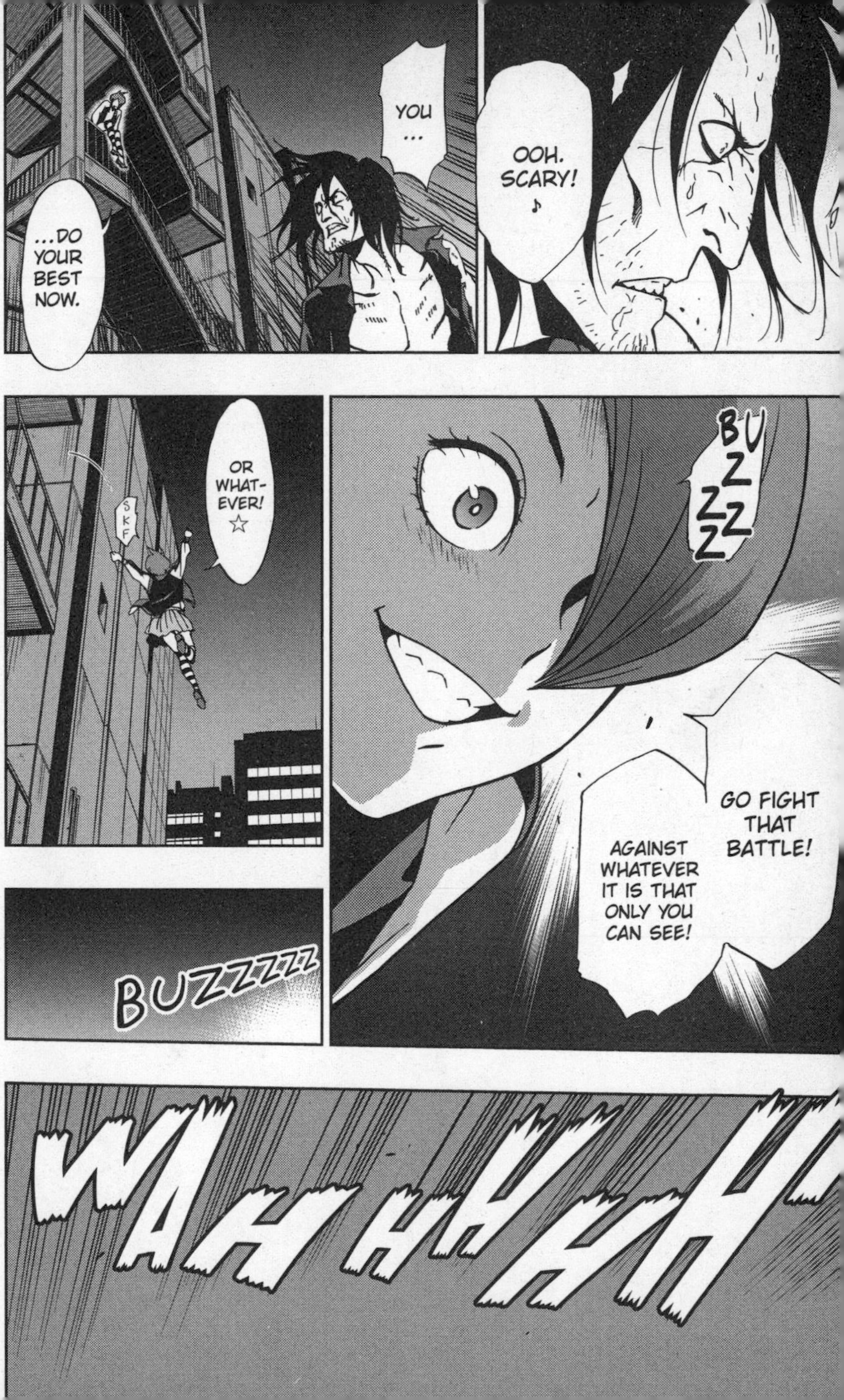
OOH. SCARY! ♪
YOU ...
...DO YOUR BEST NOW.
BUZZZZ
GO FIGHT THAT BATTLE!
AGAINST WHATEVER IT IS THAT ONLY YOU CAN SEE!
OR WHAT-EVER! ☆
SKF
BUZZZZZZ
WAHHHHH

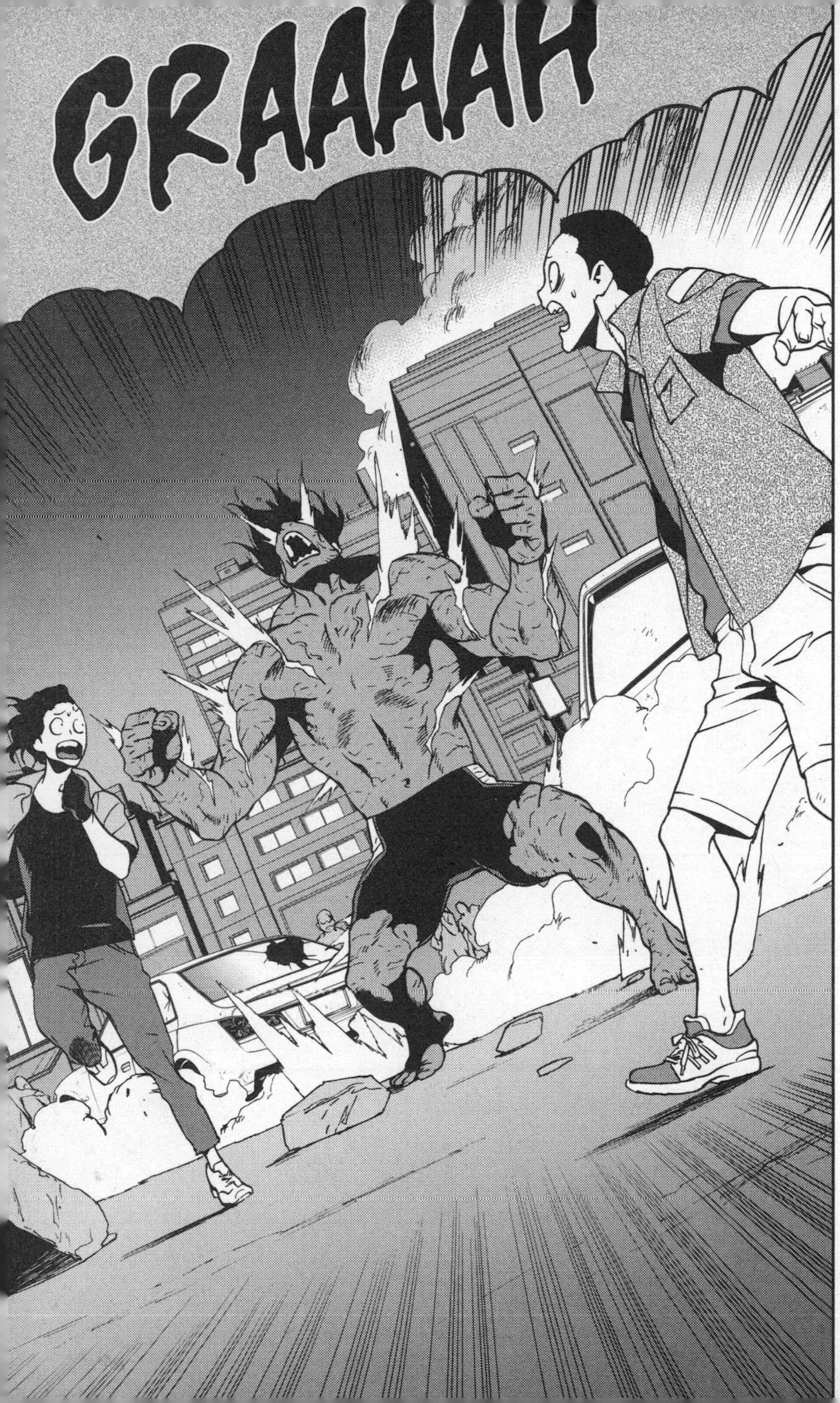
GRAAAAH

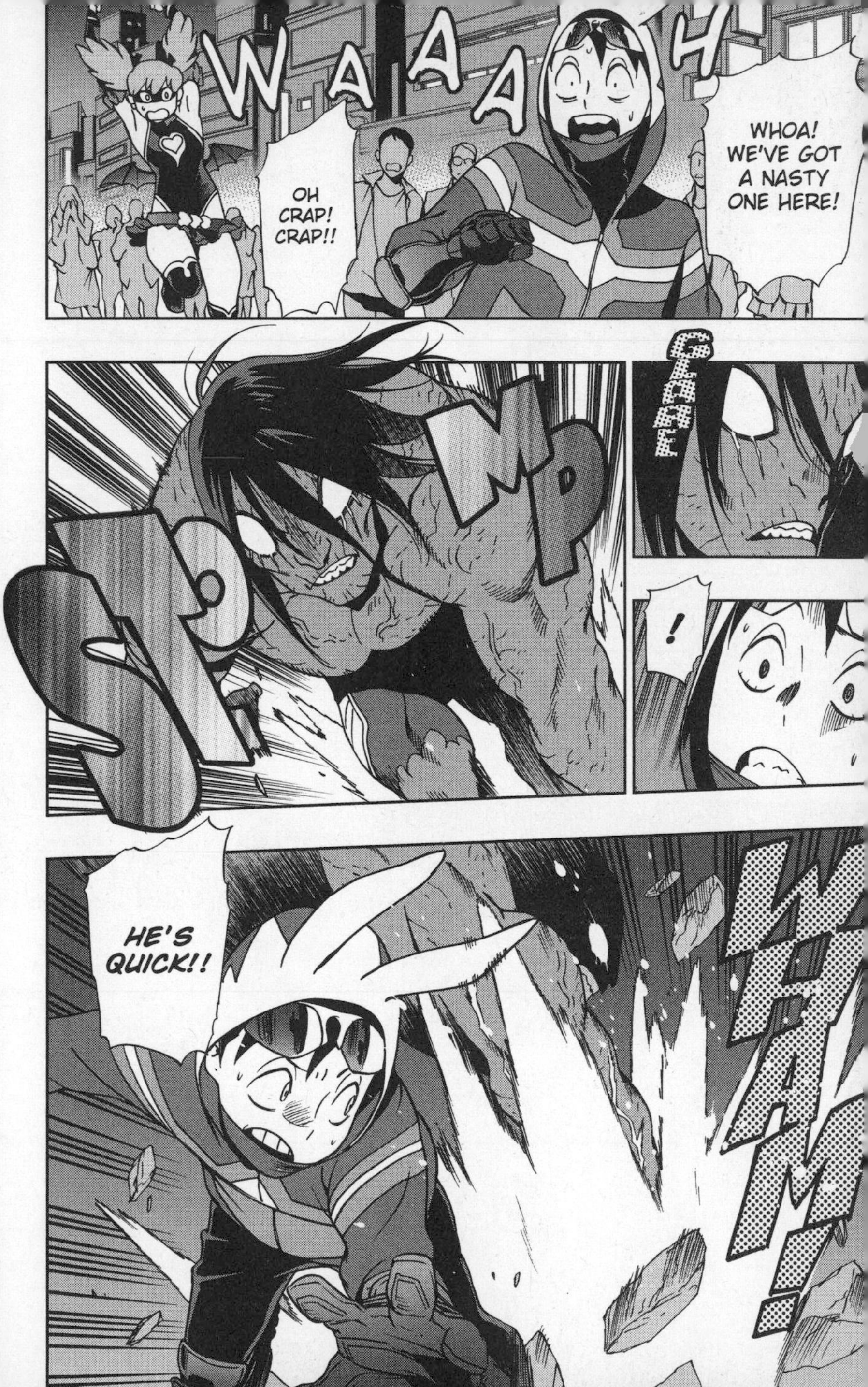
WAAAAH
WHOA! WE'VE GOT A NASTY ONE HERE!
OH CRAP! CRAP!!
GLARE
!
STOMP
WHAM!!
HE'S QUICK!!

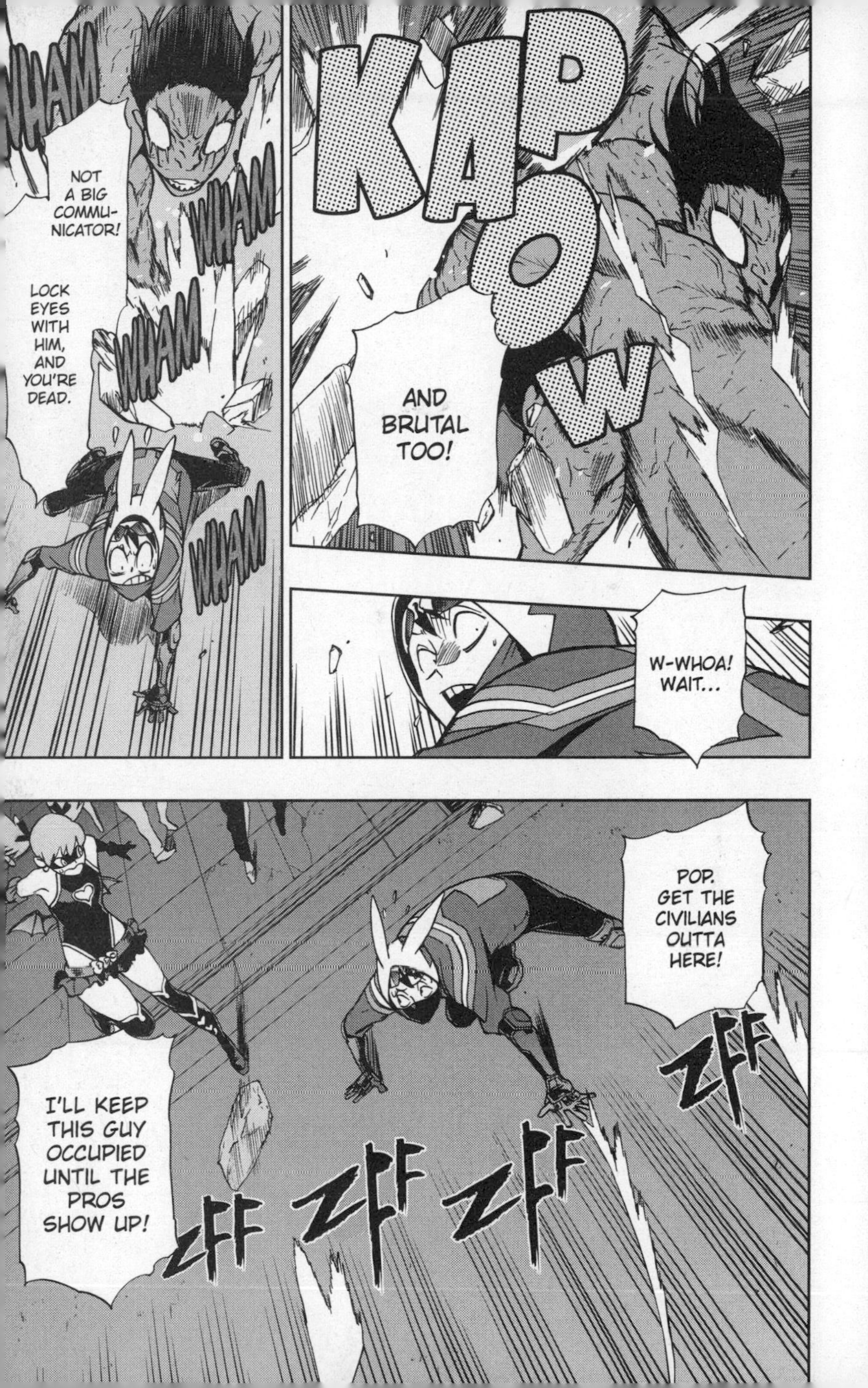
KAPOW
AND BRUTAL TOO!
W-WHOA! WAIT...
WHAM
NOT A BIG COMMUNICATOR!
WHAM
LOCK EYES WITH HIM, AND YOU'RE DEAD.
WHAM
WHAM
POP. GET THE CIVILIANS OUTTA HERE!
ZFF
ZFF
ZFF
ZFF
I'LL KEEP THIS GUY OCCUPIED UNTIL THE PROS SHOW UP!

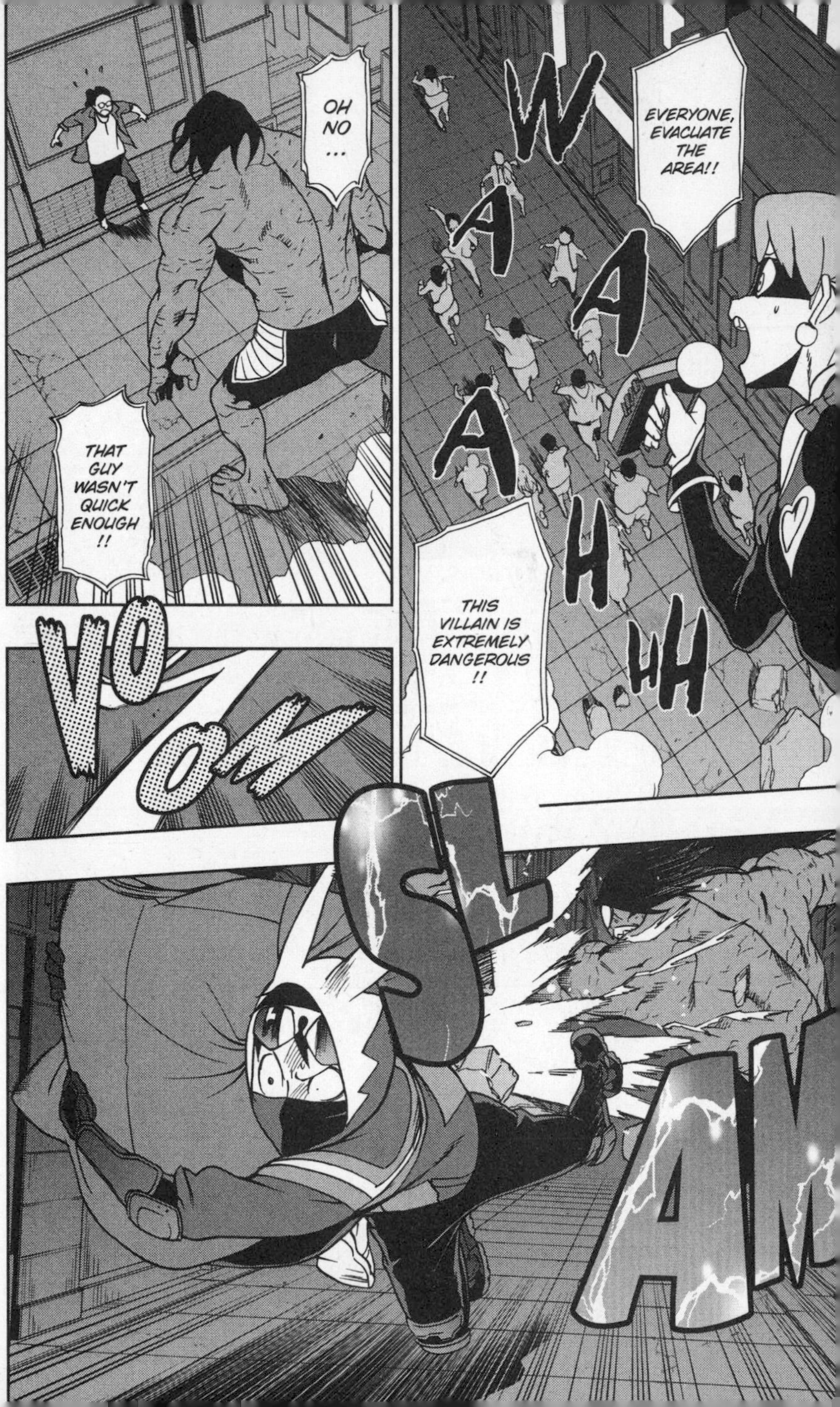
EVERYONE, EVACUATE THE AREA!!
WAAAHHHH
THIS VILLAIN IS EXTREMELY DANGEROUS!!
OH NO...
THAT GUY WASN'T QUICK ENOUGH!!
VOOM
SLAM

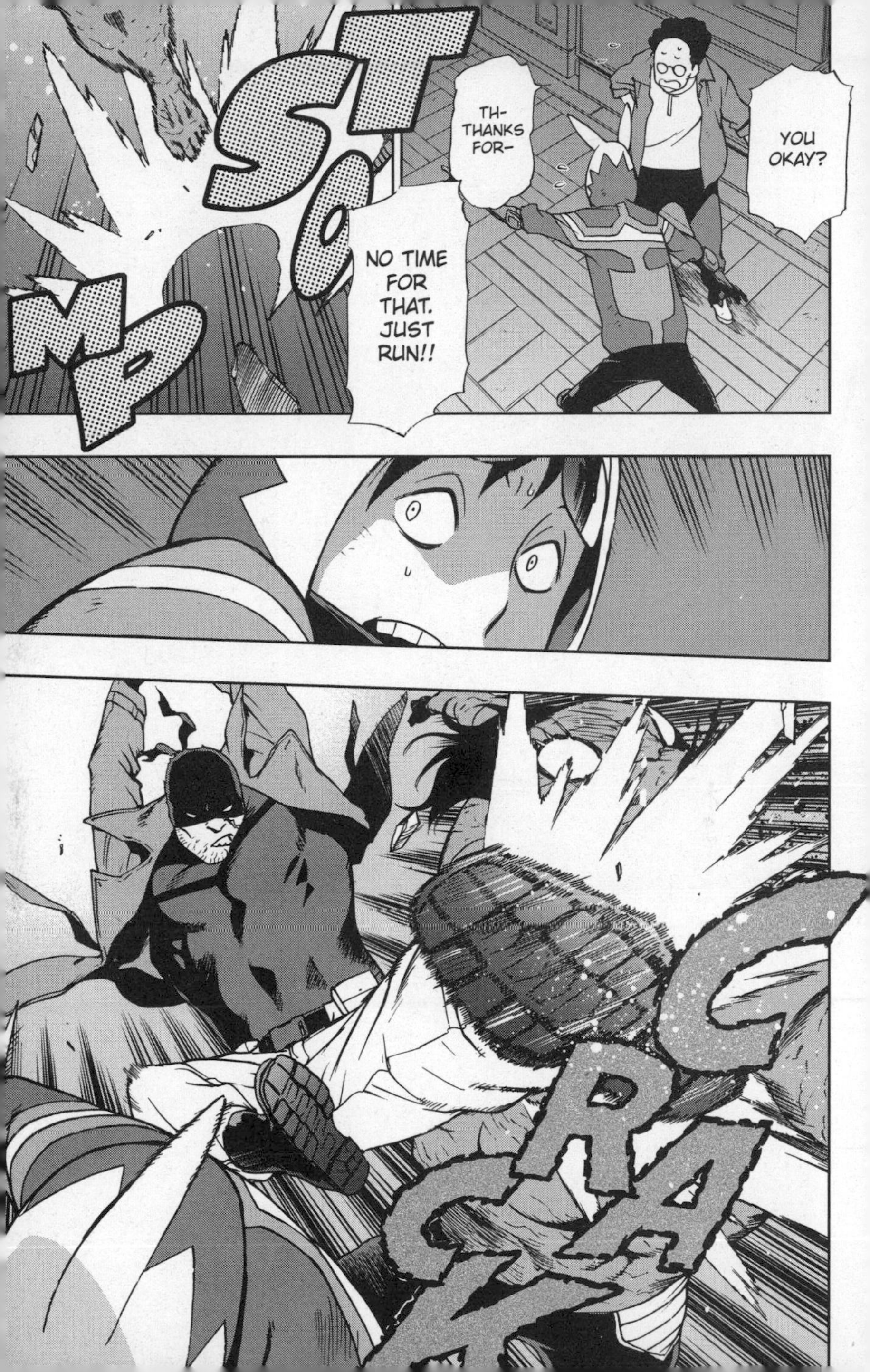
YOU OKAY?
TH- THANKS FOR-
STOMP
NO TIME FOR THAT. JUST RUN!!

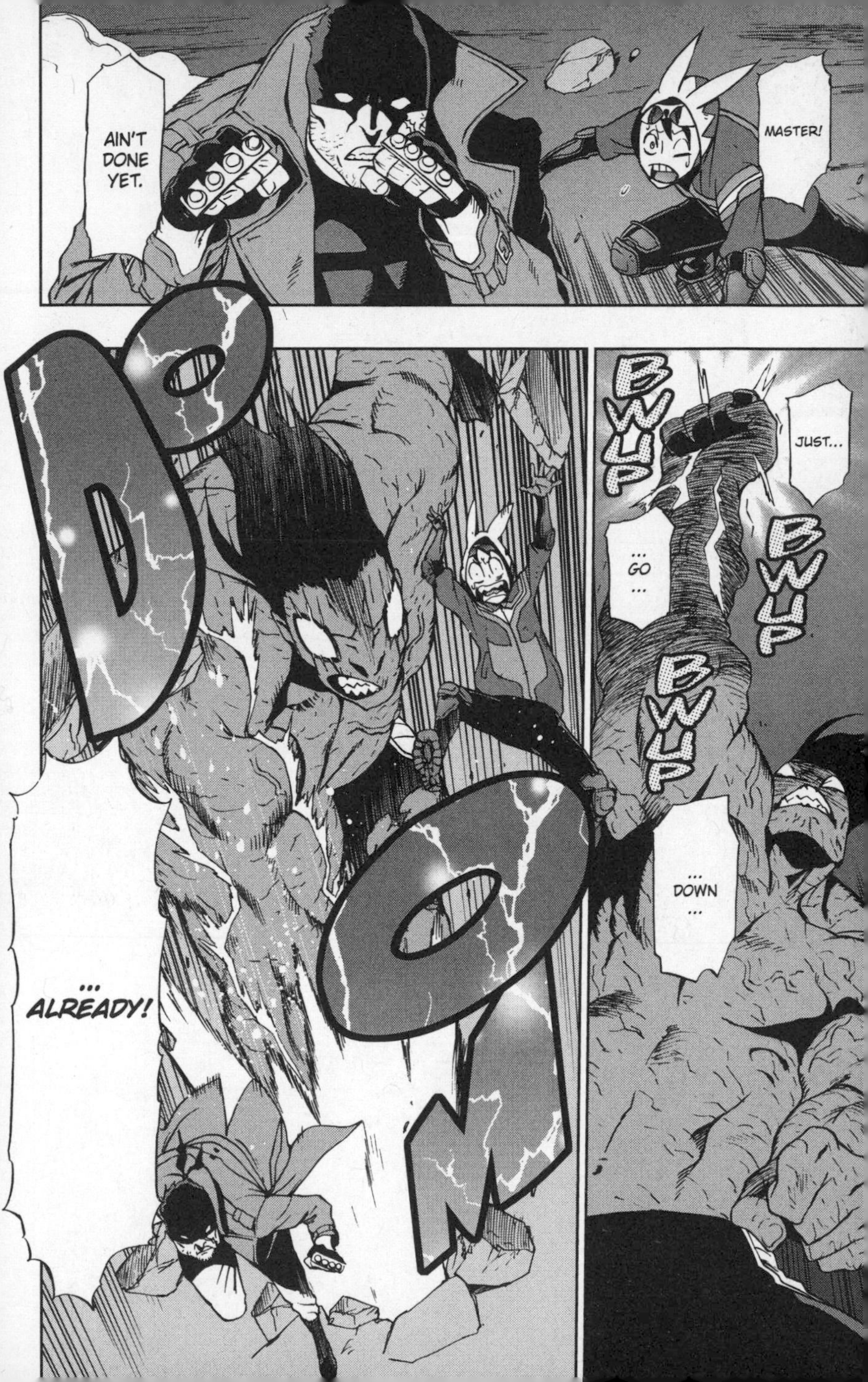
MASTER!
AIN'T DONE YET.
BWUP
JUST...
BWUP
... GO ...
BWUP
... DOWN ...
DOOM
... ALREADY!

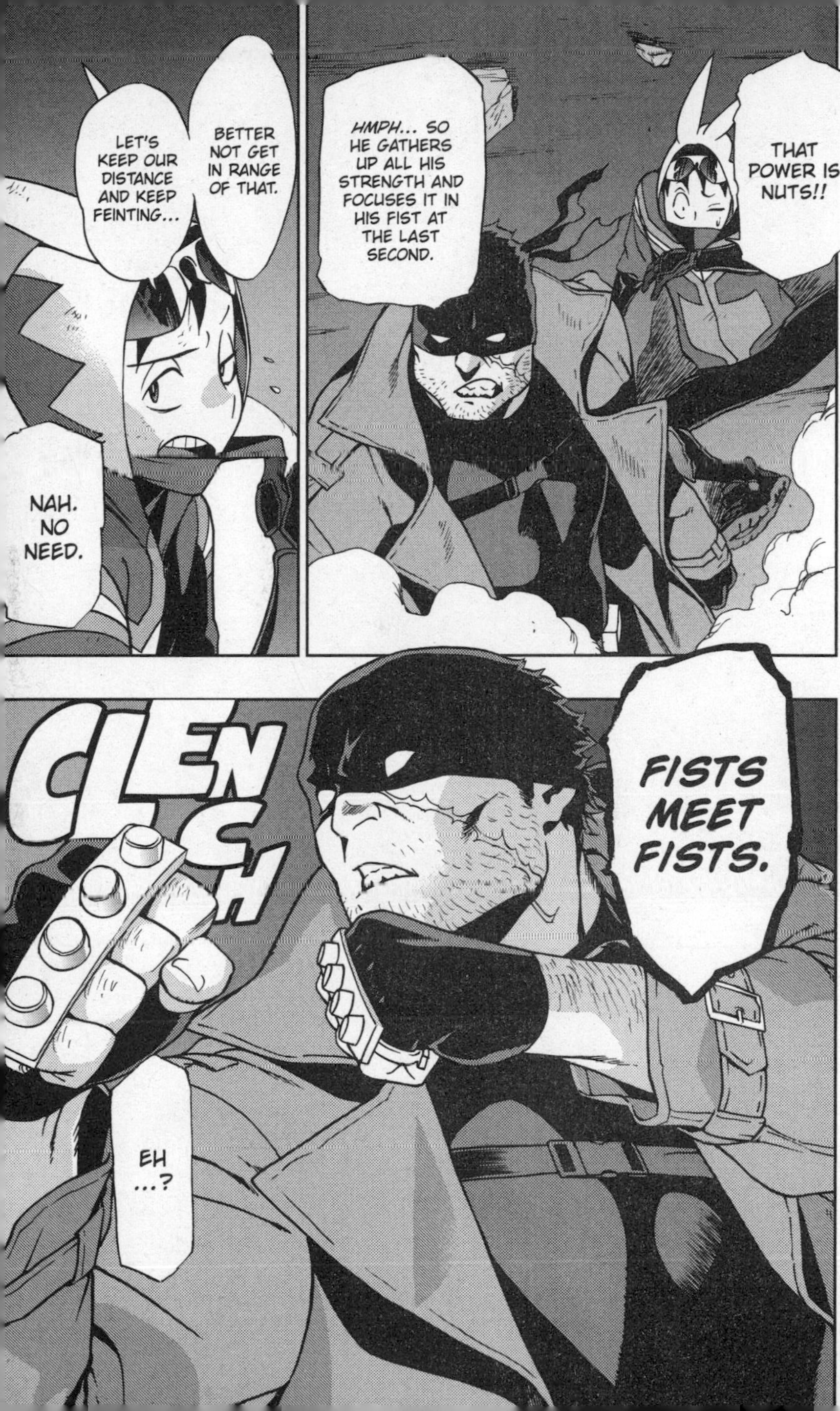
THAT POWER IS NUTS!!
HMPH... SO HE GATHERS UP ALL HIS STRENGTH AND FOCUSES IT IN HIS FIST AT THE LAST SECOND.
BETTER NOT GET IN RANGE OF THAT.
LET'S KEEP OUR DISTANCE AND KEEP FEINTING...
NAH. NO NEED.
FISTS MEET FISTS.
CLENCH
EH ...?

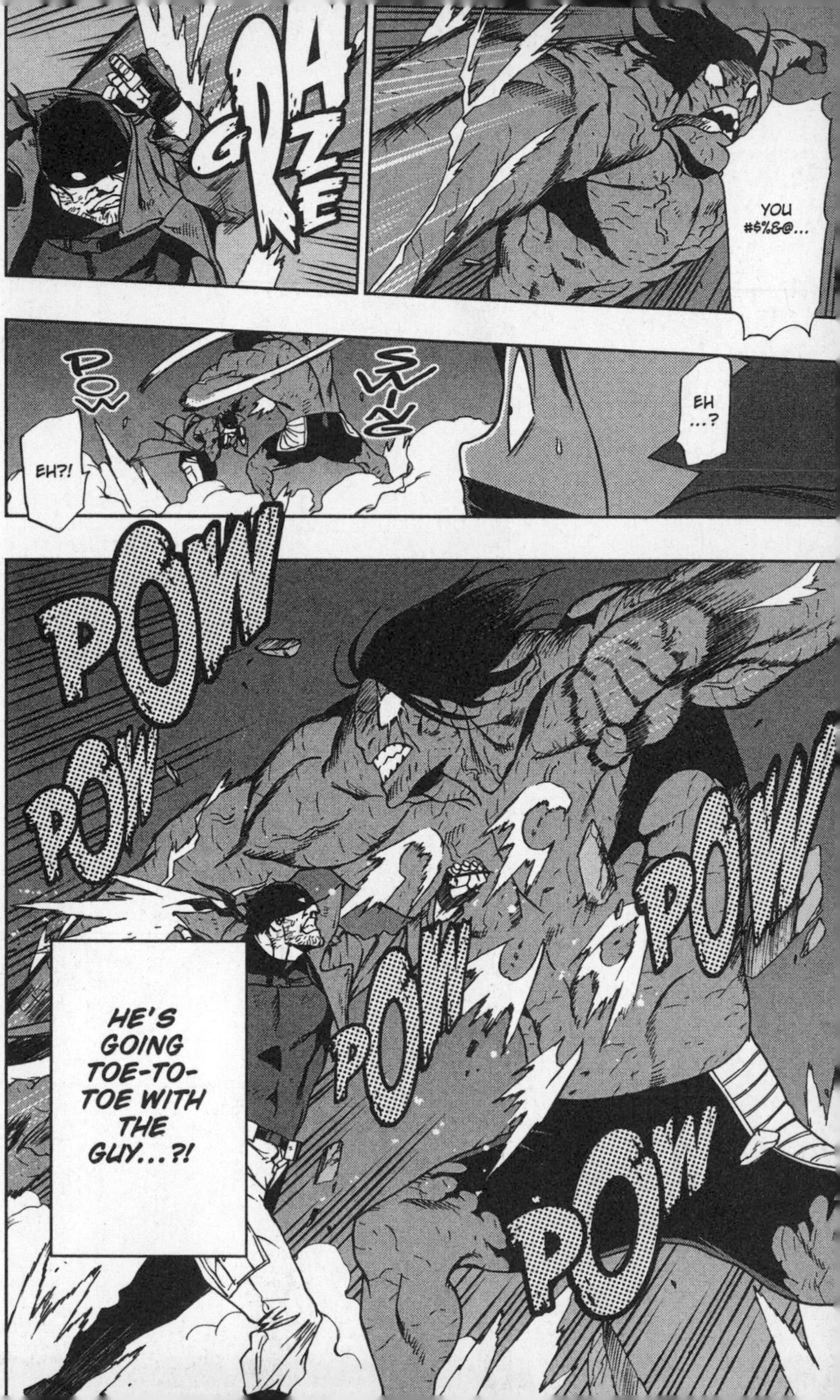
YOU #$%&@...
GRAZE
EH ...?
SWING
POW
EH?!
POW
POW
POW
POW
POW
HE'S GOING TOE-TO-TOE WITH THE GUY...?!

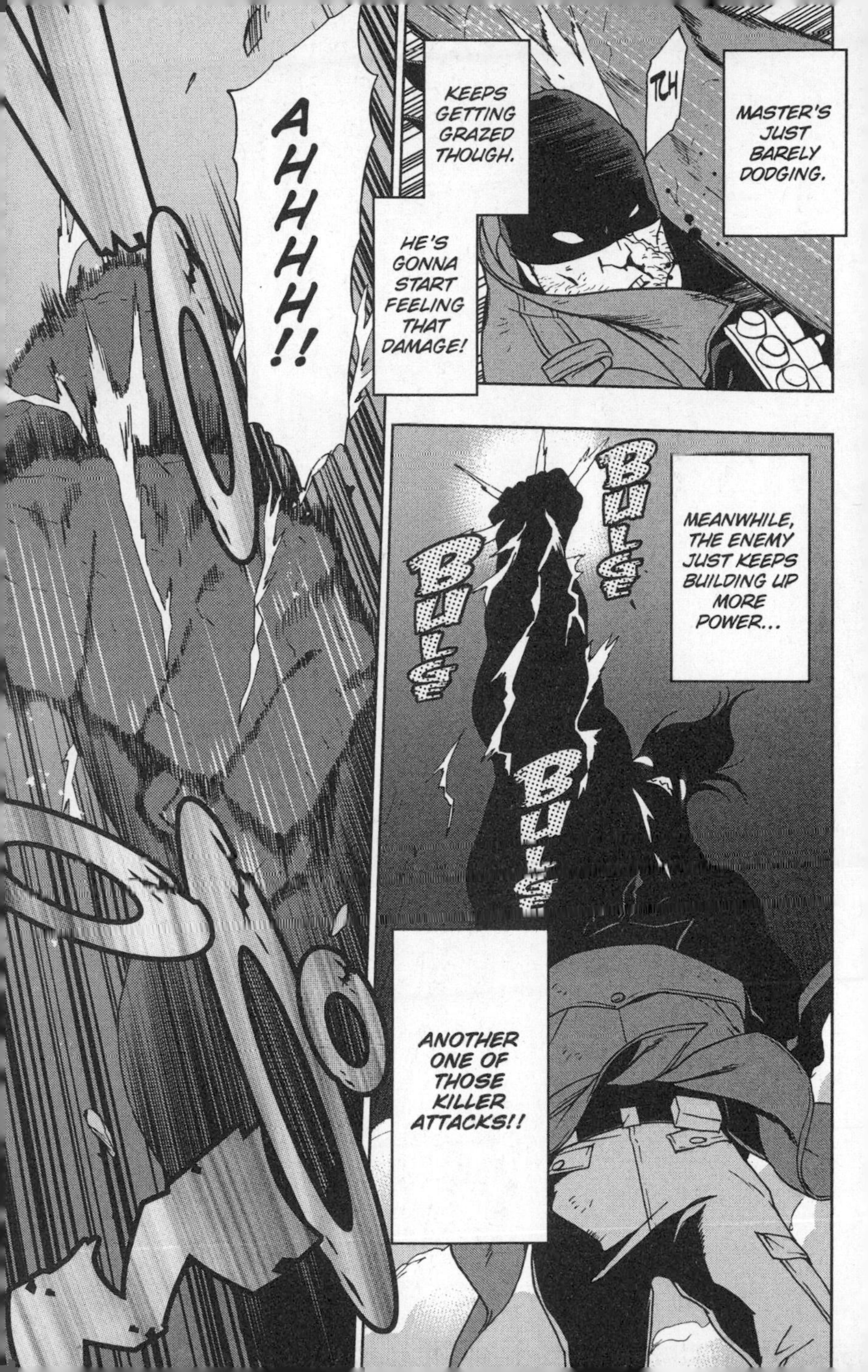
MASTER'S JUST BARELY DODGING.
TCH
KEEPS GETTING GRAZED THOUGH.
HE'S GONNA START FEELING THAT DAMAGE!
BULGE
MEANWHILE, THE ENEMY JUST KEEPS BUILDING UP MORE POWER...
BULGE
BULGE
ANOTHER ONE OF THOSE KILLER ATTACKS!!
AHHHHH!!

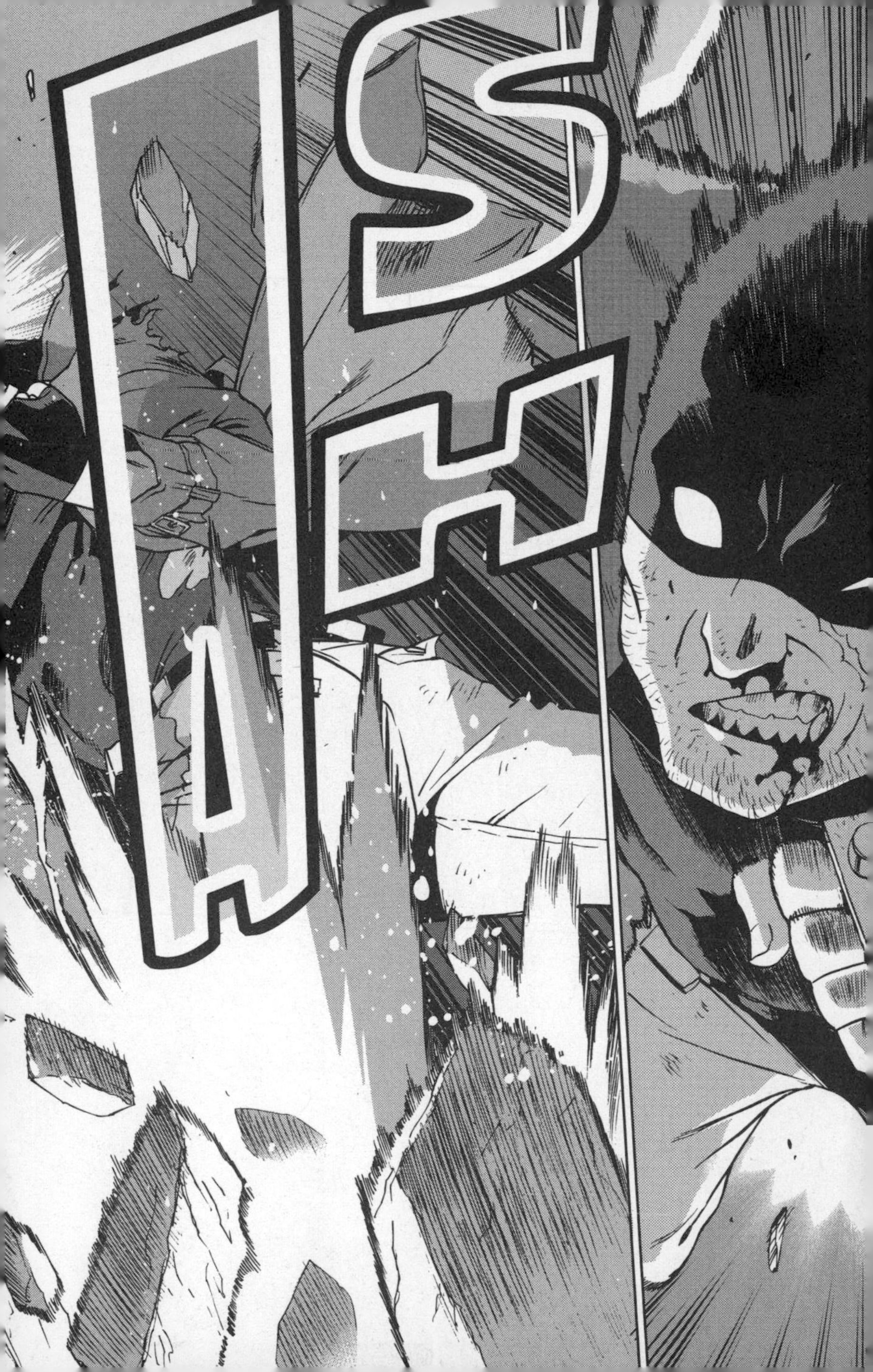
SHA

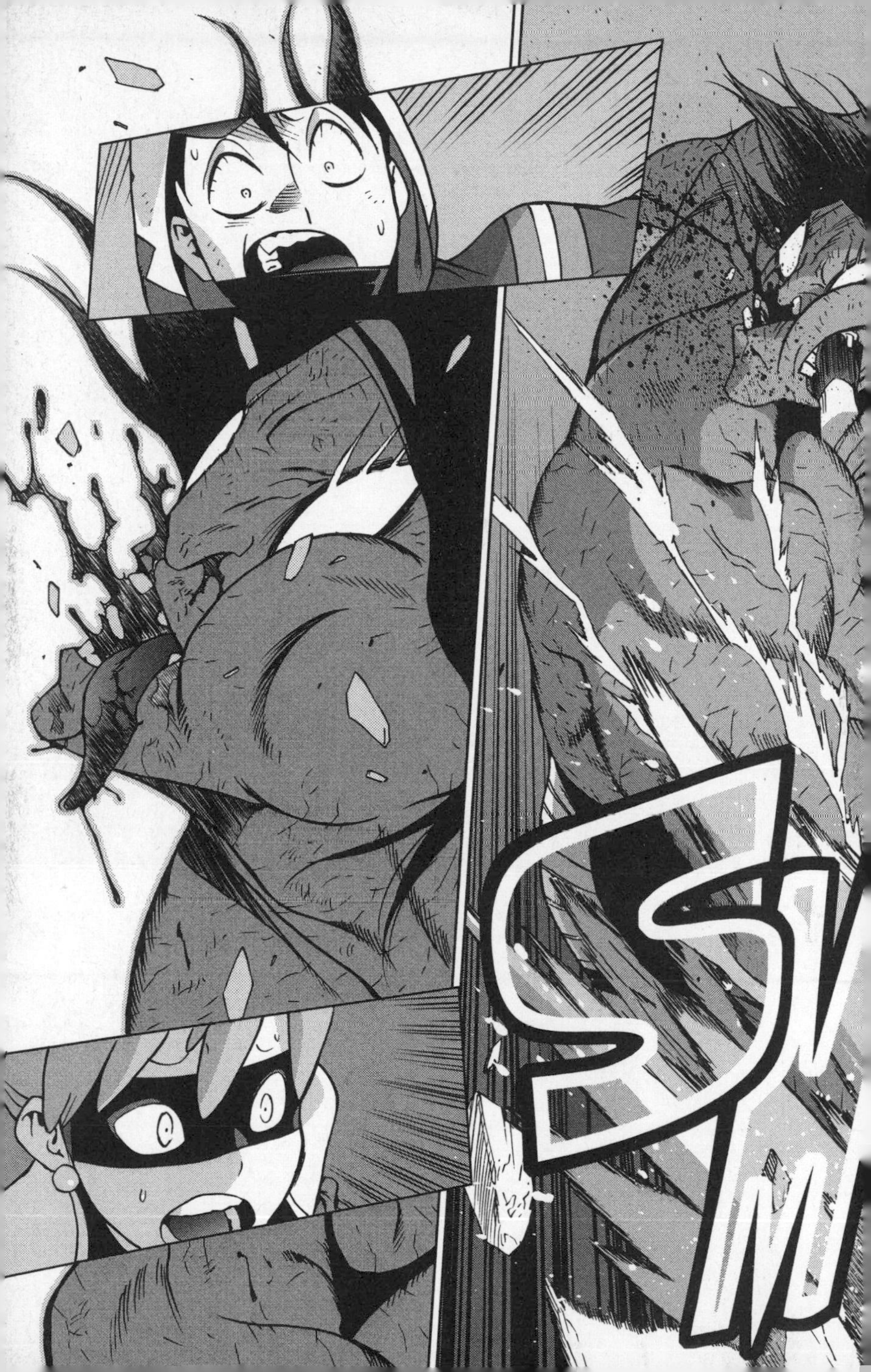

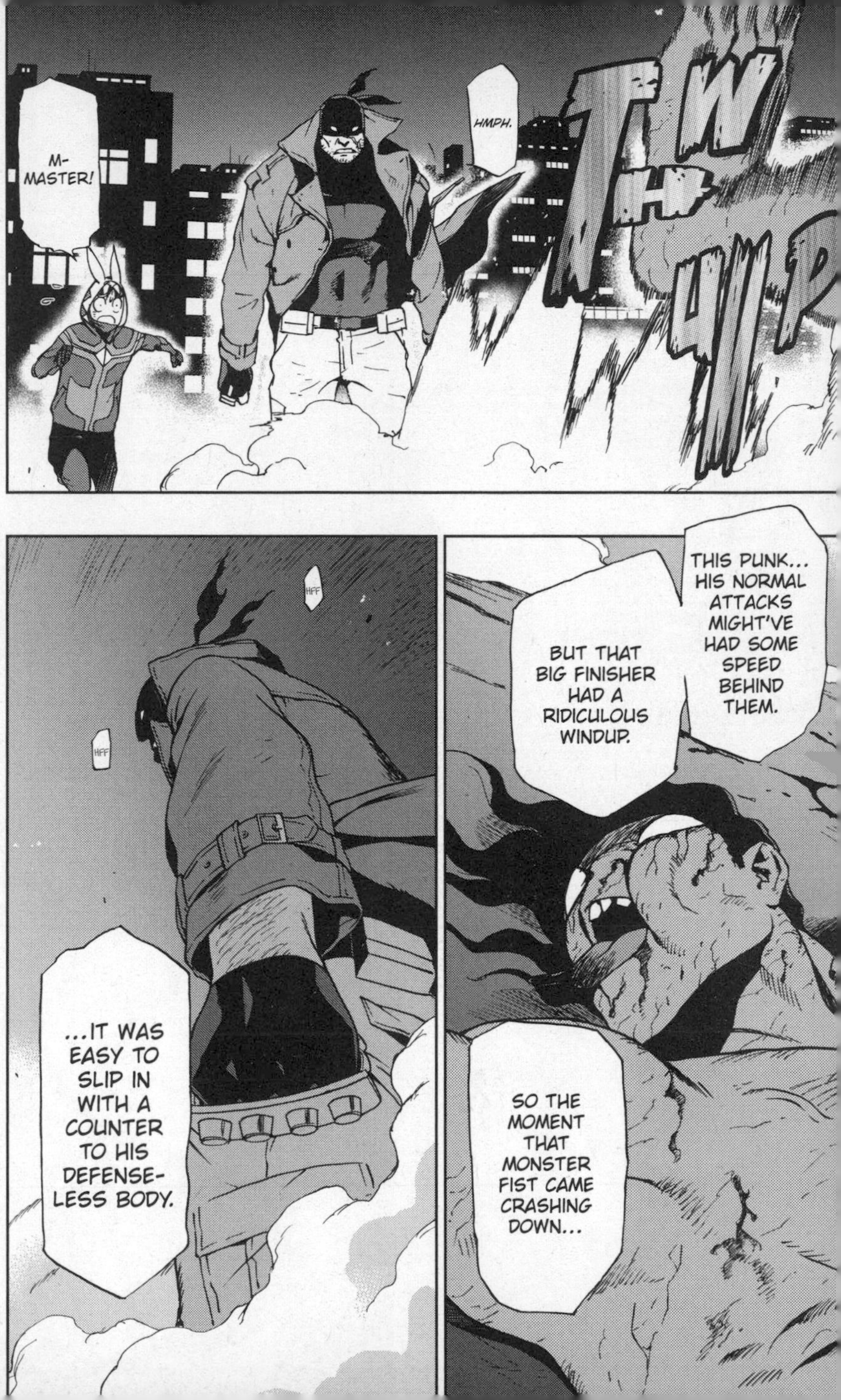
HMPH.
M-MASTER!
THIS PUNK... HIS NORMAL ATTACKS MIGHT'VE HAD SOME SPEED BEHIND THEM.
BUT THAT BIG FINISHER HAD A RIDICULOUS WINDUP.
SO THE MOMENT THAT MONSTER FIST CAME CRASHING DOWN...
HFF
HFF
...IT WAS EASY TO SLIP IN WITH A COUNTER TO HIS DEFENSE-LESS BODY.

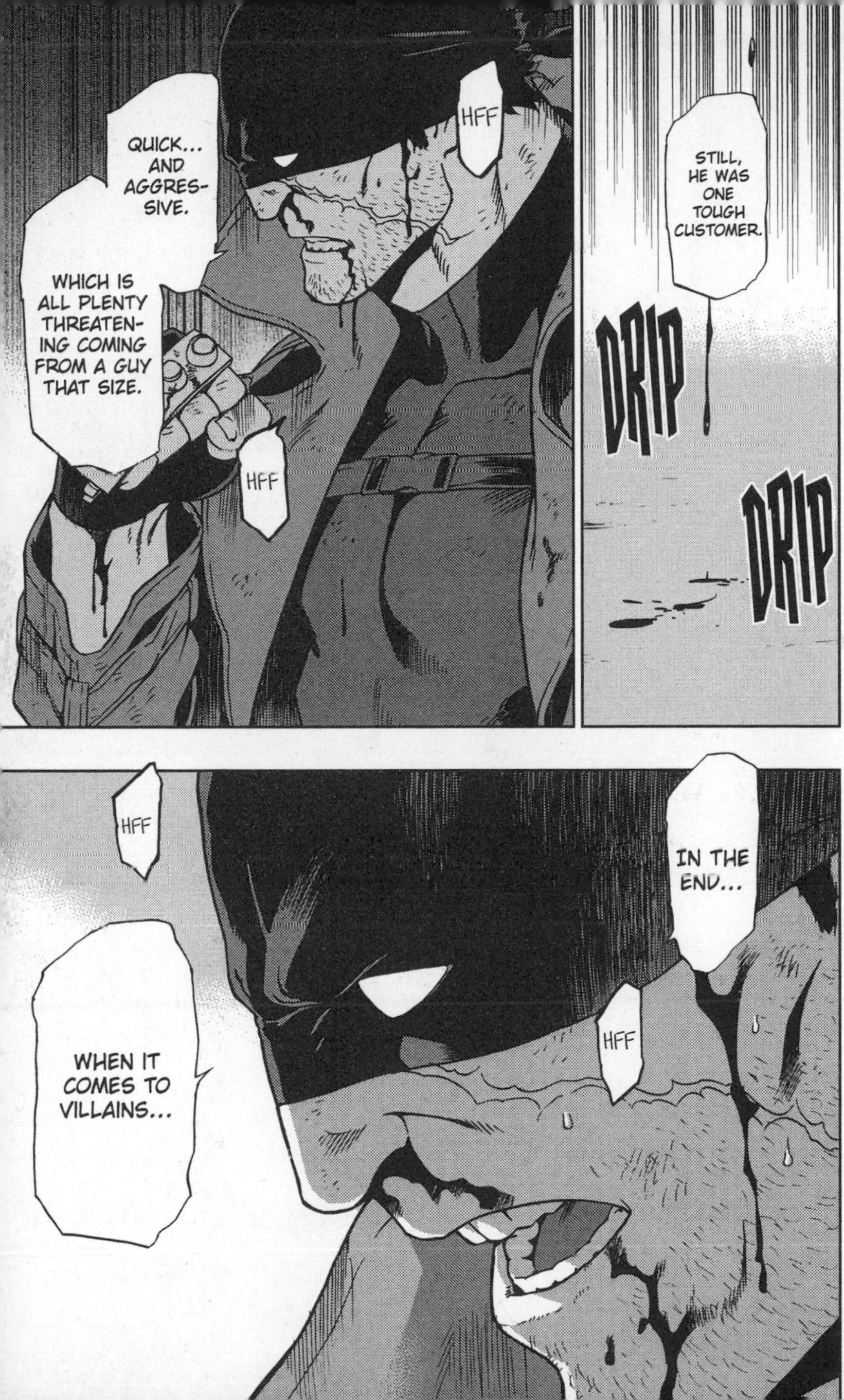
STILL, HE WAS ONE TOUGH CUSTOMER.
DRIP
DRIP
HFF
QUICK... AND AGGRES-SIVE.
WHICH IS ALL PLENTY THREATEN-ING COMING FROM A GUY THAT SIZE.
HFF
IN THE END...
HFF
HFF
WHEN IT COMES TO VILLAINS...

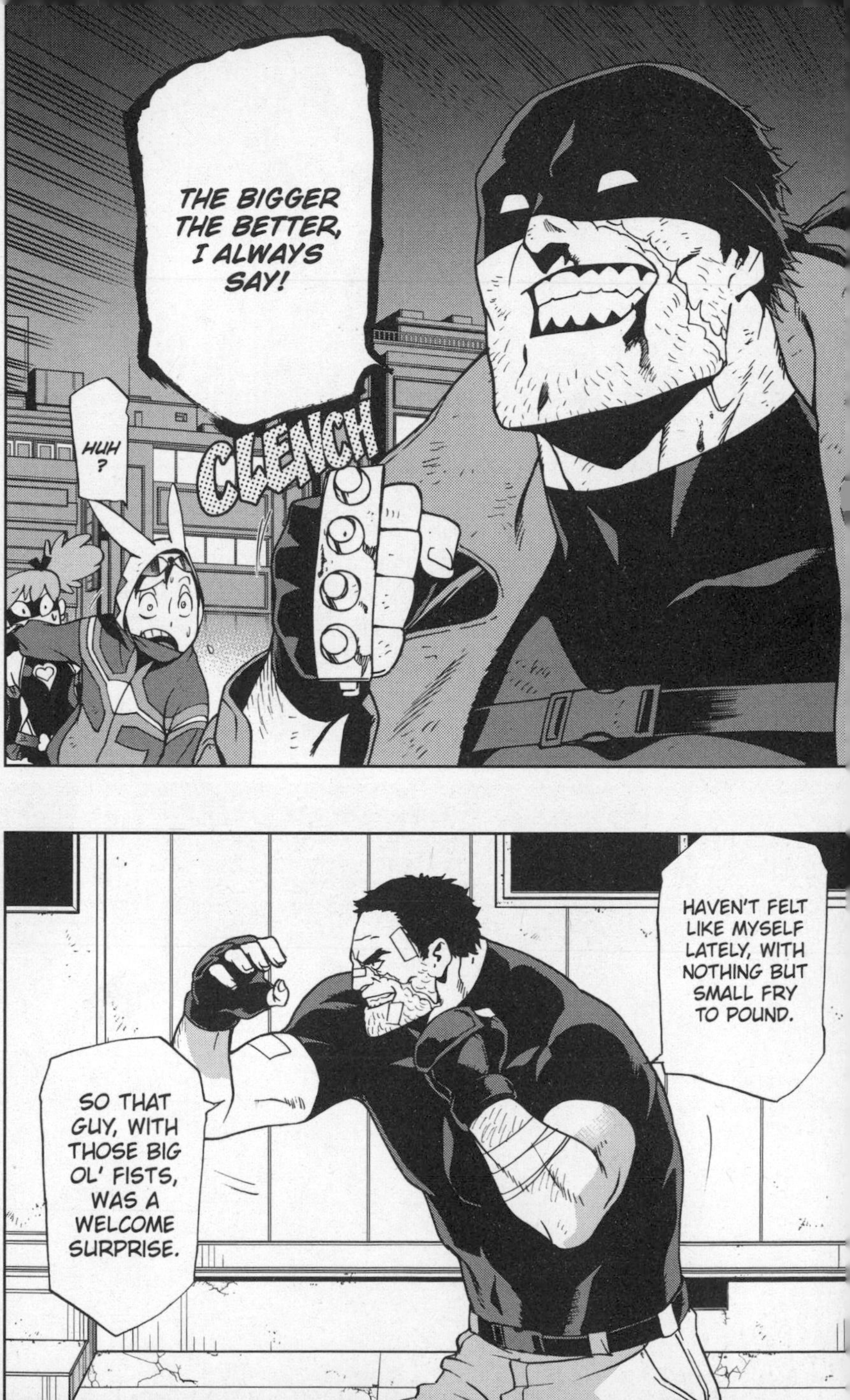
THE BIGGER THE BETTER, I ALWAYS SAY!
CLENCH
HUH?
HAVEN'T FELT LIKE MYSELF LATELY, WITH NOTHING BUT SMALL FRY TO POUND.
SO THAT GUY, WITH THOSE BIG OL' FISTS, WAS A WELCOME SURPRISE.

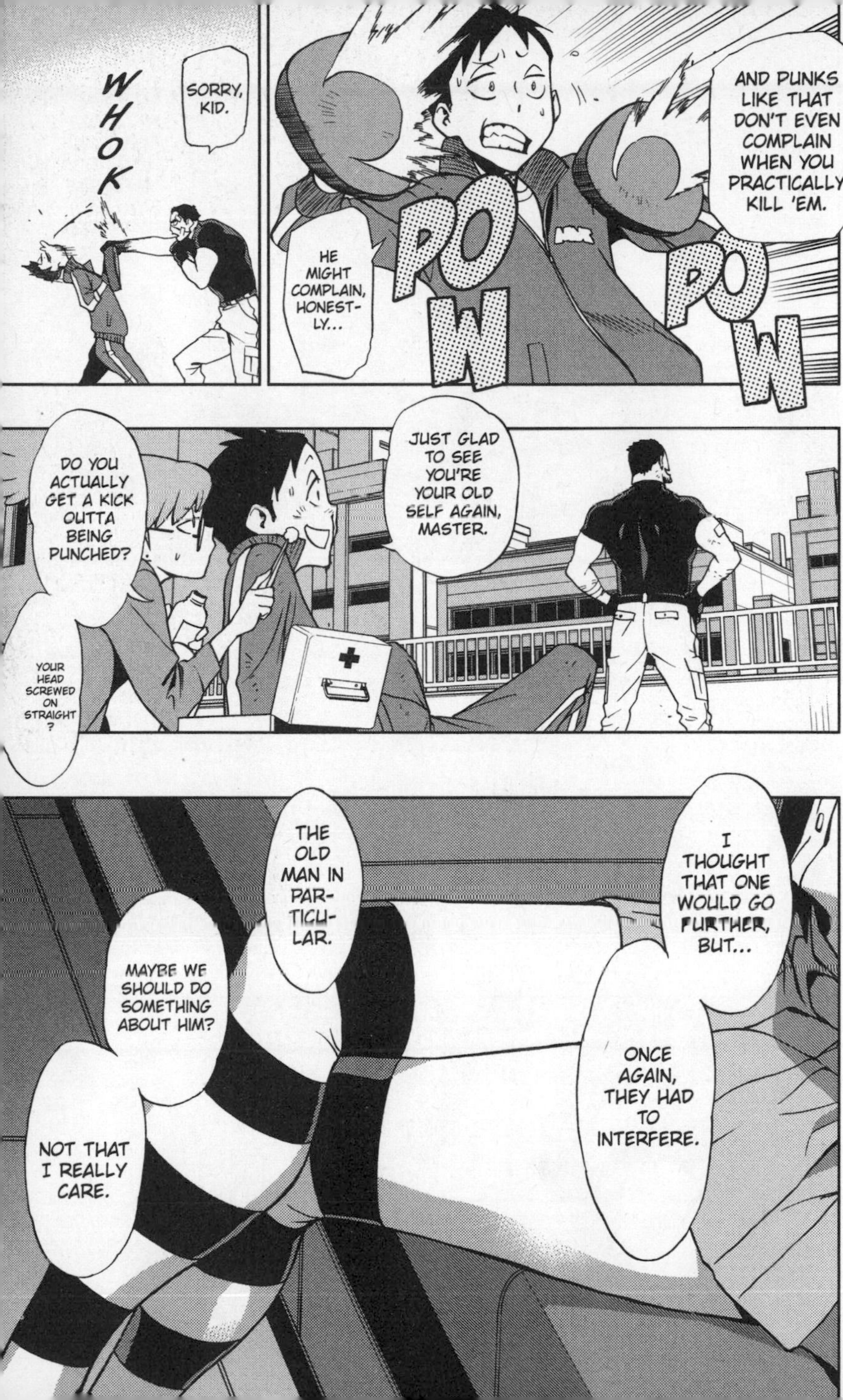
AND PUNKS LIKE THAT DON'T EVEN COMPLAIN WHEN YOU PRACTICALLY KILL 'EM.
POW
POW
HE MIGHT COMPLAIN, HONESTLY...
SORRY, KID.
WHOK
JUST GLAD TO SEE YOU'RE YOUR OLD SELF AGAIN, MASTER.
DO YOU ACTUALLY GET A KICK OUTTA BEING PUNCHED?
YOUR HEAD SCREWED ON STRAIGHT?
I THOUGHT THAT ONE WOULD GO FURTHER, BUT...
ONCE AGAIN, THEY HAD TO INTERFERE.
THE OLD MAN IN PARTICULAR.
MAYBE WE SHOULD DO SOMETHING ABOUT HIM?
NOT THAT I REALLY CARE.

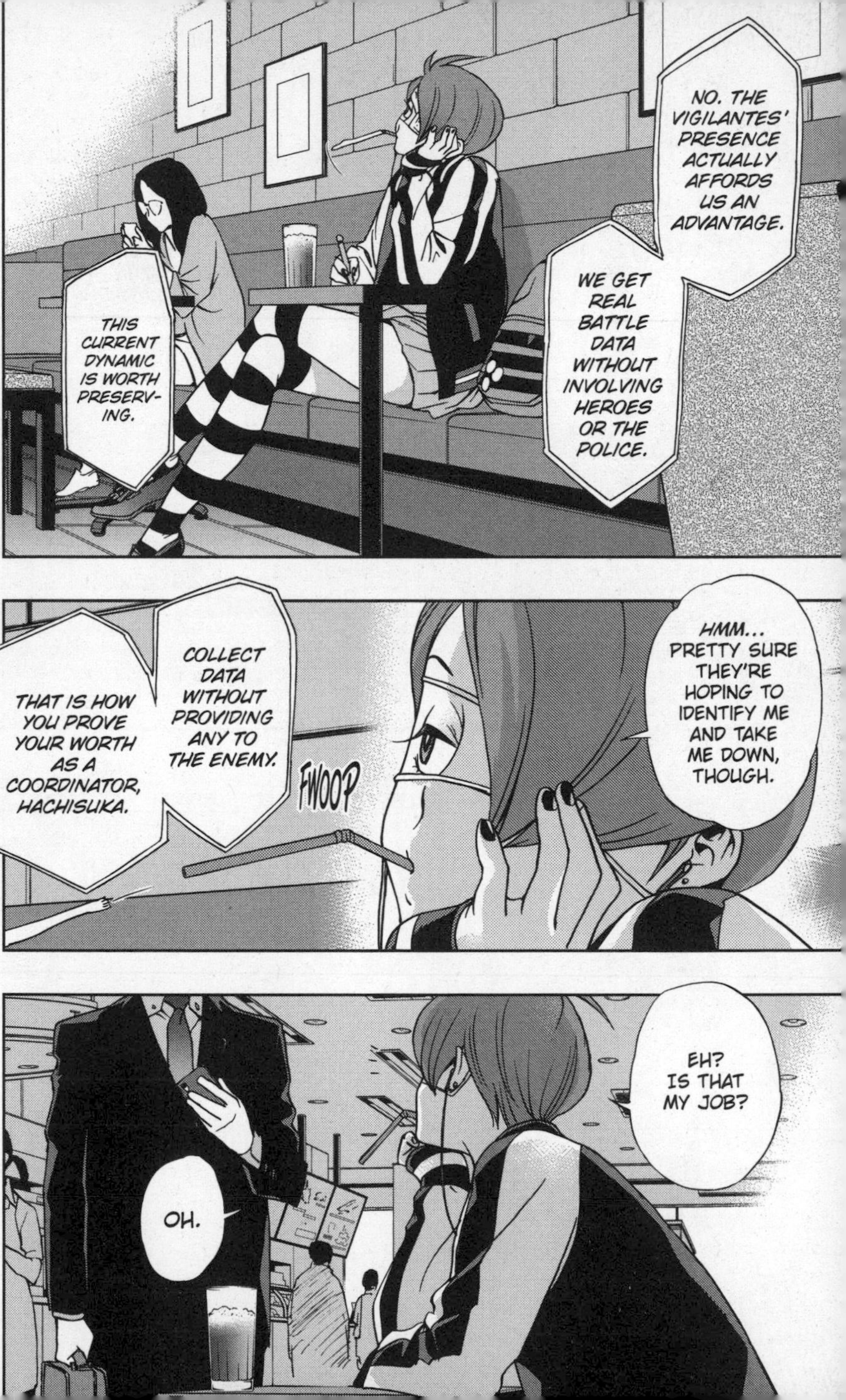
NO. THE VIGILANTES' PRESENCE ACTUALLY AFFORDS US AN ADVANTAGE.
WE GET REAL BATTLE DATA WITHOUT INVOLVING HEROES OR THE POLICE.
THIS CURRENT DYNAMIC IS WORTH PRESERVING.
HMM... PRETTY SURE THEY'RE HOPING TO IDENTIFY ME AND TAKE ME DOWN, THOUGH.
FWOOP
COLLECT DATA WITHOUT PROVIDING ANY TO THE ENEMY.
THAT IS HOW YOU PROVE YOUR WORTH AS A COORDINATOR, HACHISUKA.
EH? IS THAT MY JOB?
OH.

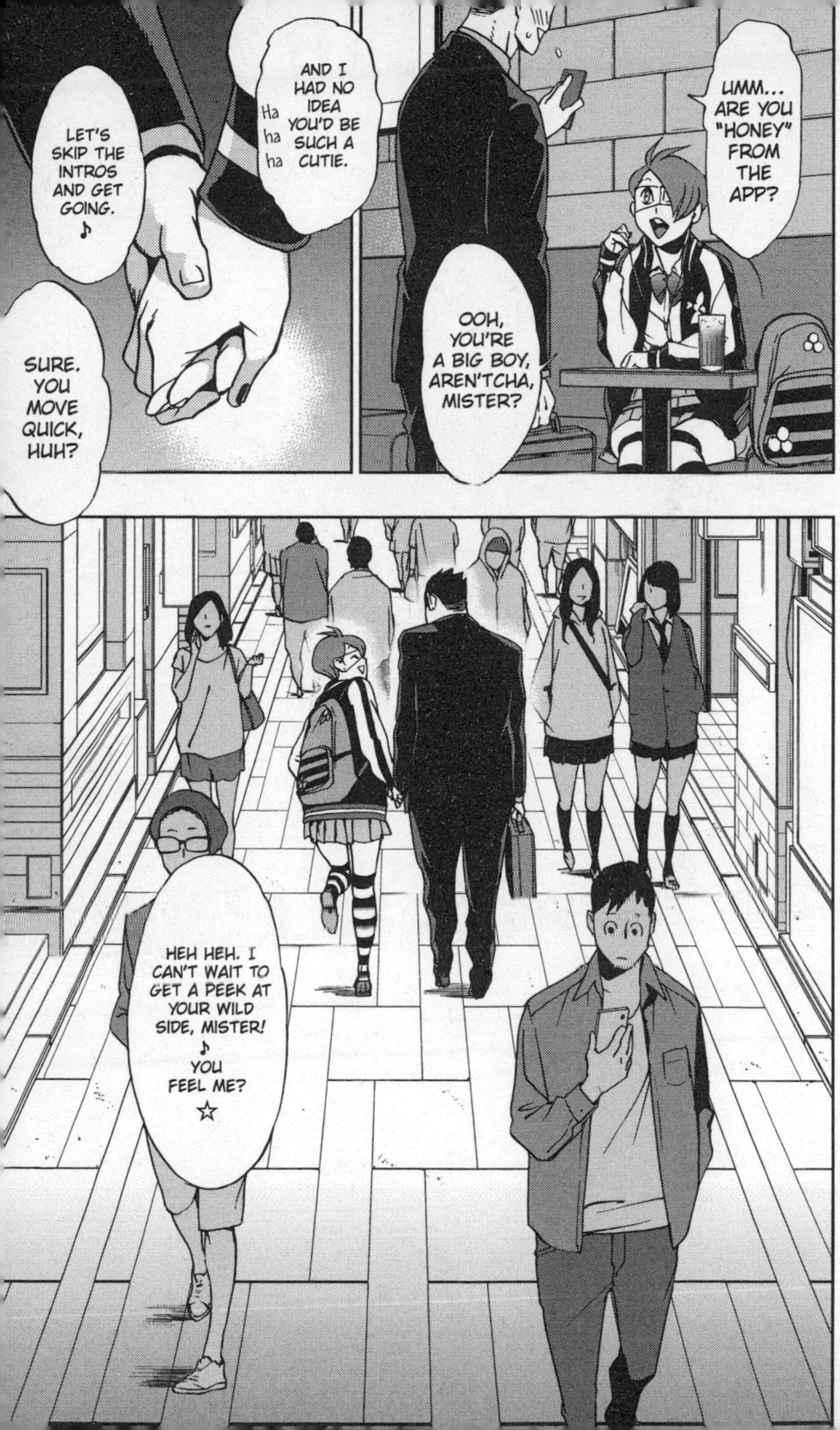
UMM... ARE YOU "HONEY" FROM THE APP?
OOH, YOU'RE A BIG BOY, AREN'TCHA, MISTER?
AND I HAD NO IDEA YOU'D BE SUCH A CUTIE.
Ha ha ha
LET'S SKIP THE INTROS AND GET GOING. ♪
SURE. YOU MOVE QUICK, HUH?
HEH HEH. I CAN'T WAIT TO GET A PEEK AT YOUR WILD SIDE, MISTER! ♪ YOU FEEL ME? ☆

JUNKIE VILLAIN

THE ROUGH DESIGN

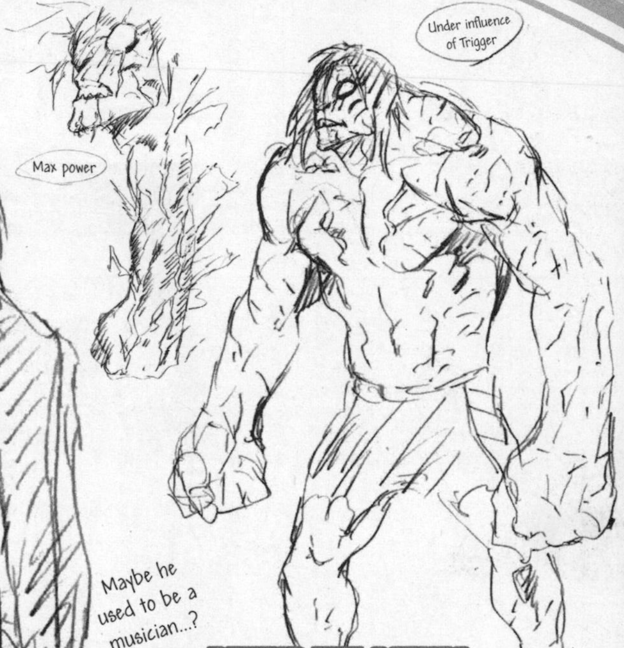
Under influence of Trigger
Max power

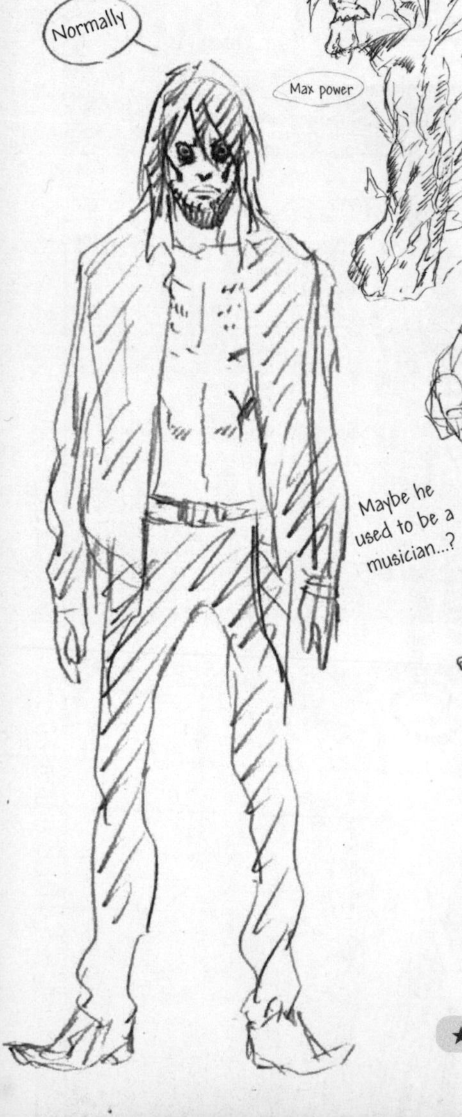
Normally
Maybe he used to be a musician...?

BEHIND THE SCENES

Unlike the pervy trio and their endless sophistry, this guy can't hold much of a conversation. My request to Betten was "A real bad dude!"

When he loses his senses and turns into a monster, he's basically just a wrecking ball who can't be reasoned with...

—Furuhashi

I'm relatively pleased with the design for this guy, but I regret that the gimmick Furuhashi came up with didn't come across in the story that well... Drawing him was tough, in a mundane way.

—Betten

★ See page 205 for more on the Three Pervy Brothers.

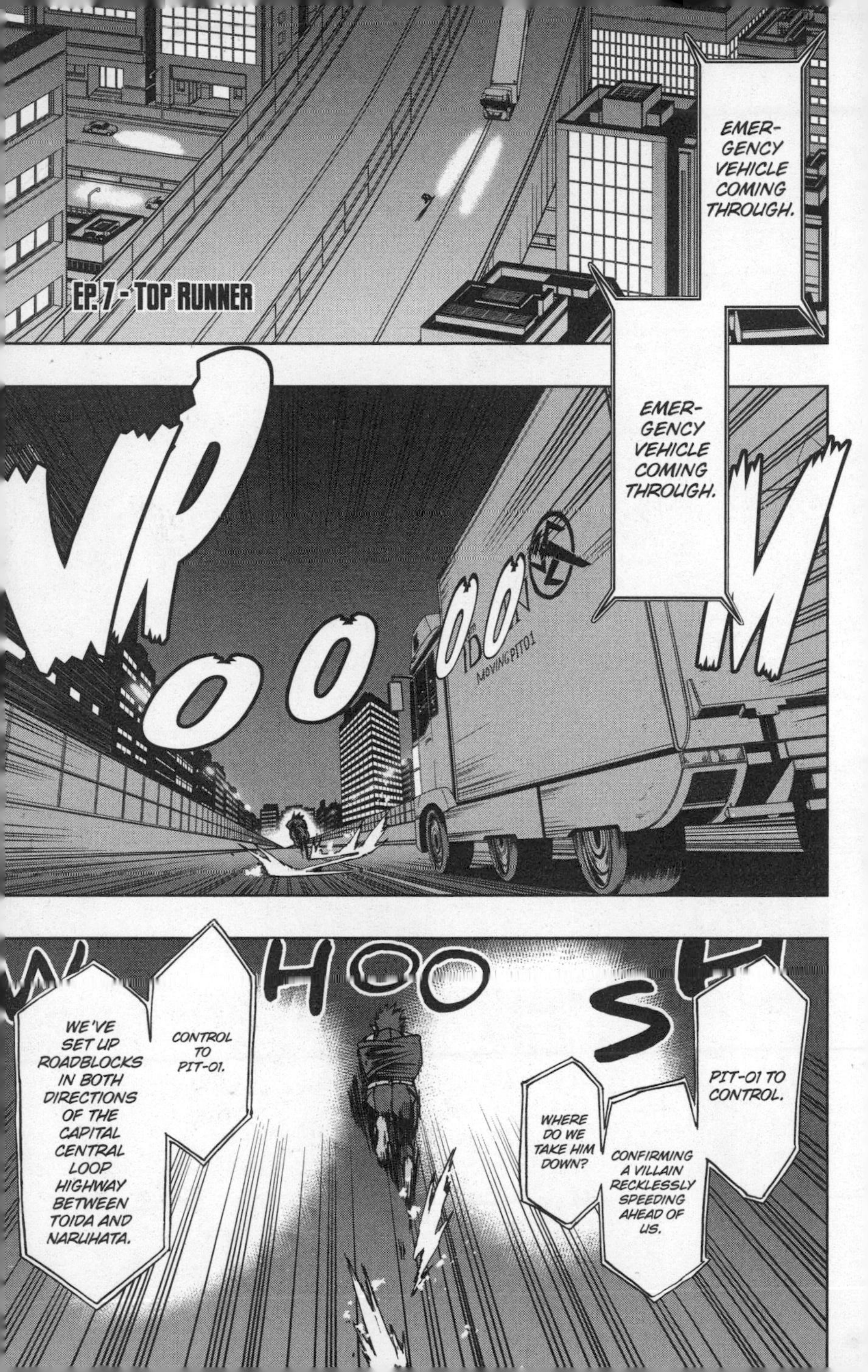
EMERGENCY VEHICLE COMING THROUGH.
EP. 7 - TOP RUNNER
EMERGENCY VEHICLE COMING THROUGH.
VROOOOOM
WHOOSH
PIT-01 TO CONTROL.
CONFIRMING A VILLAIN RECKLESSLY SPEEDING AHEAD OF US.
WHERE DO WE TAKE HIM DOWN?
CONTROL TO PIT-01.
WE'VE SET UP ROADBLOCKS IN BOTH DIRECTIONS OF THE CAPITAL CENTRAL LOOP HIGHWAY BETWEEN TOIDA AND NARUHATA.

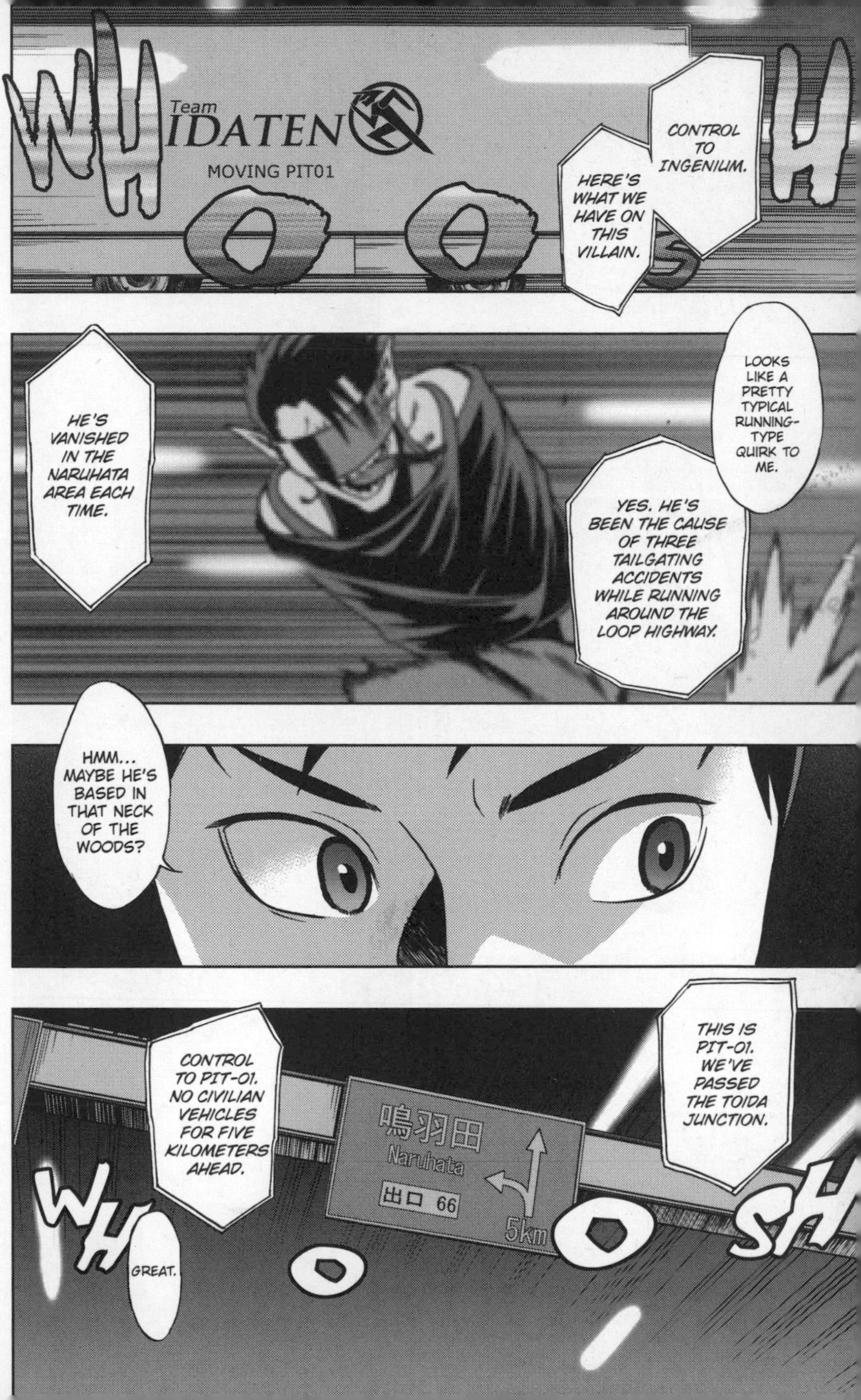
WHOOSH
Team IDATEN
MOVING PIT01
CONTROL TO INGENIUM.
HERE'S WHAT WE HAVE ON THIS VILLAIN.
LOOKS LIKE A PRETTY TYPICAL RUNNING-TYPE QUIRK TO ME.
YES. HE'S BEEN THE CAUSE OF THREE TAILGATING ACCIDENTS WHILE RUNNING AROUND THE LOOP HIGHWAY.
HE'S VANISHED IN THE NARUHATA AREA EACH TIME.
HMM... MAYBE HE'S BASED IN THAT NECK OF THE WOODS?
THIS IS PIT-01. WE'VE PASSED THE TOIDA JUNCTION.
CONTROL TO PIT-01. NO CIVILIAN VEHICLES FOR FIVE KILOMETERS AHEAD.
鳴羽田
Naruhata
出口 66
5km
WHOOSH
GREAT.

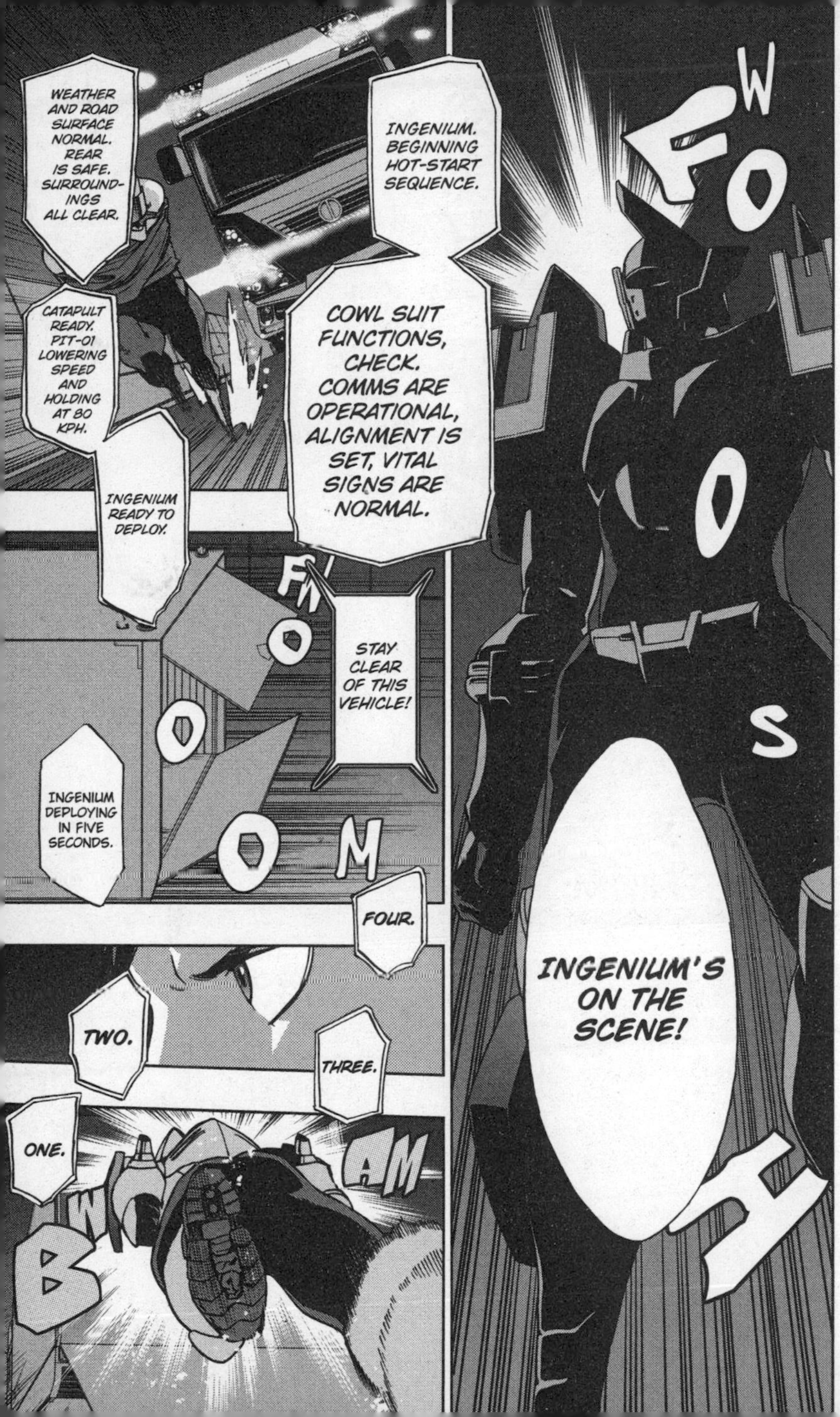
INGENIUM. BEGINNING HOT-START SEQUENCE.
COWL SUIT FUNCTIONS, CHECK. COMMS ARE OPERATIONAL, ALIGNMENT IS SET, VITAL SIGNS ARE NORMAL.
WEATHER AND ROAD SURFACE NORMAL. REAR IS SAFE. SURROUNDINGS ALL CLEAR.
CATAPULT READY. PIT-01 LOWERING SPEED AND HOLDING AT 80 KPH.
INGENIUM READY TO DEPLOY.
STAY CLEAR OF THIS VEHICLE!
FWOOOM
INGENIUM DEPLOYING IN FIVE SECONDS.
FOUR.
THREE.
TWO.
ONE.
BWAM
FWOOOSH
INGENIUM'S ON THE SCENE!

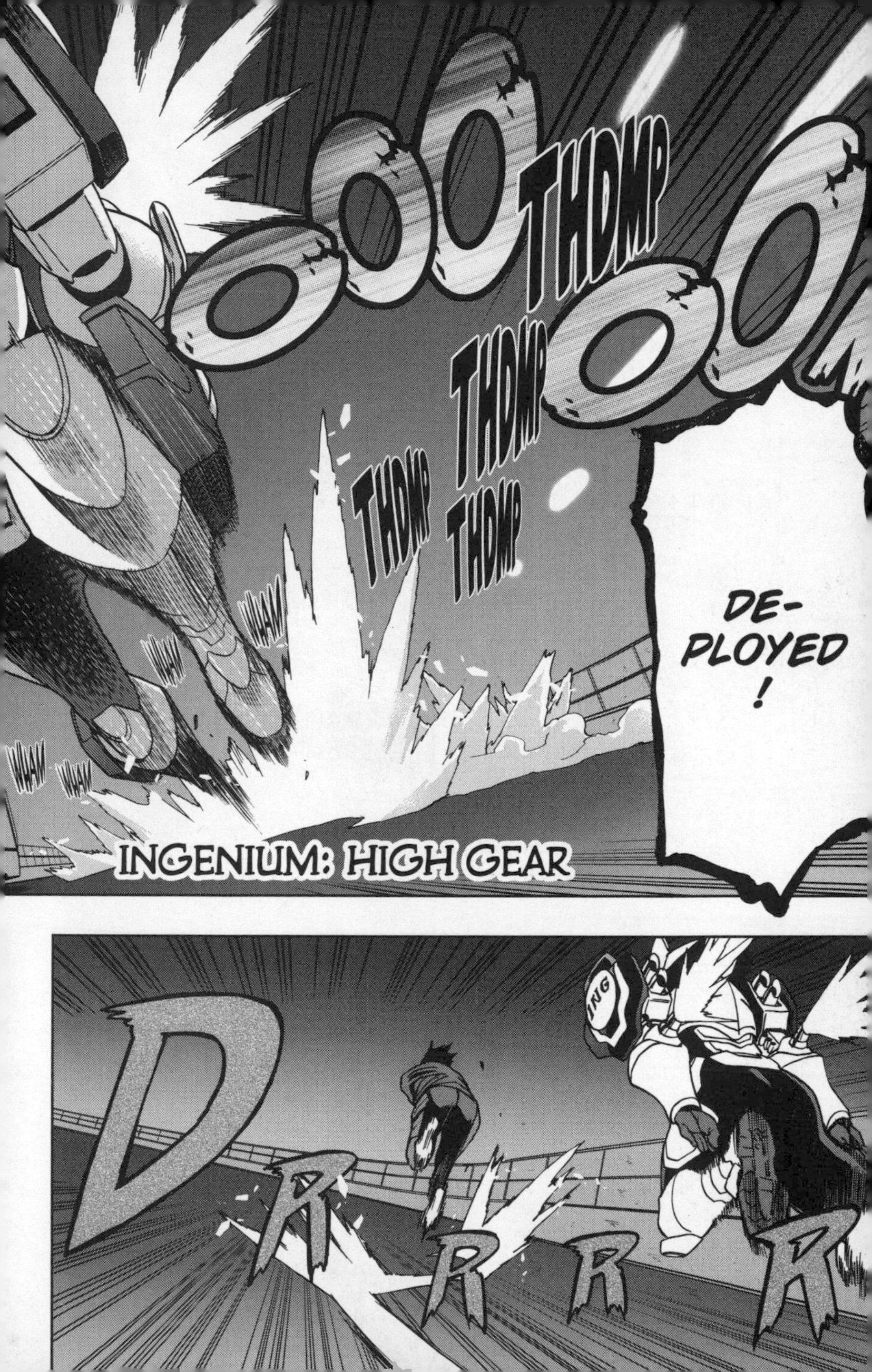
DE-
PLOYED
!
THDMP
THDMP
THDMP
THDMP
THDMP
WHAM
WHAM
WHAM
WHAM
INGENIUM: HIGH GEAR
DRRRR

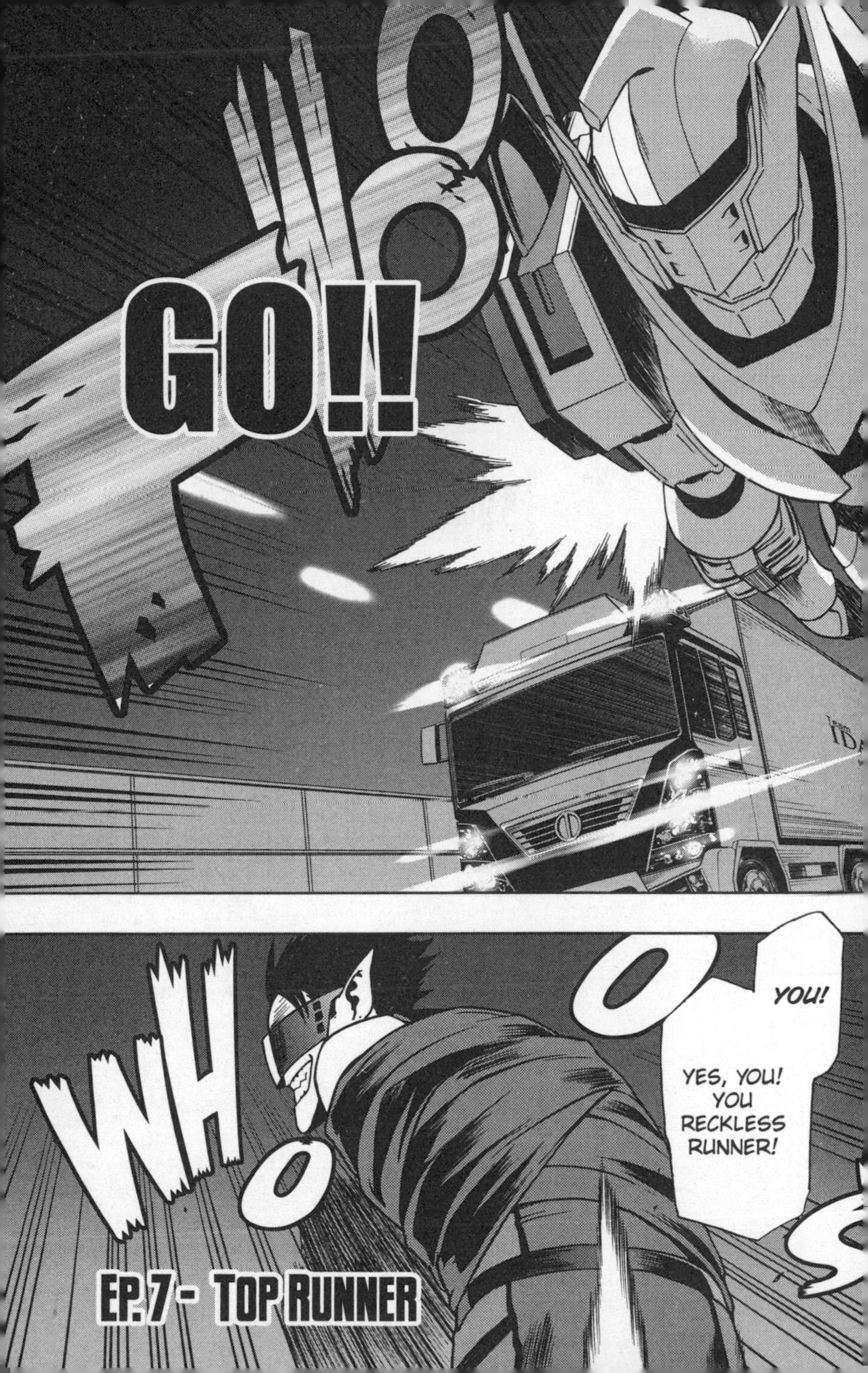
GO!!
WHOO
YOU!
YES, YOU! YOU RECKLESS RUNNER!
EP. 7 - TOP RUNNER

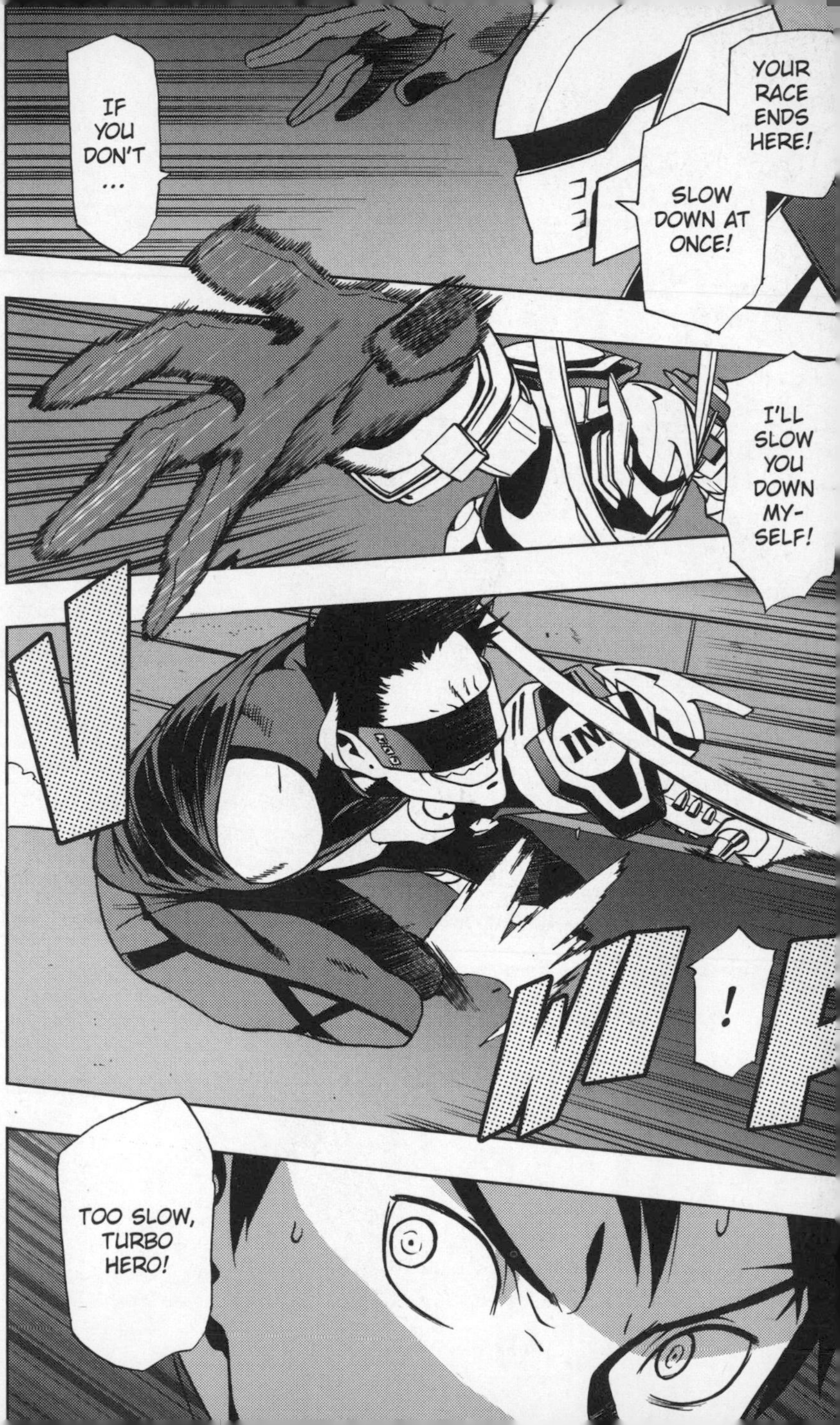
YOUR RACE ENDS HERE!
SLOW DOWN AT ONCE!
IF YOU DON'T ...
I'LL SLOW YOU DOWN MYSELF!
VWIP
!
TOO SLOW, TURBO HERO!

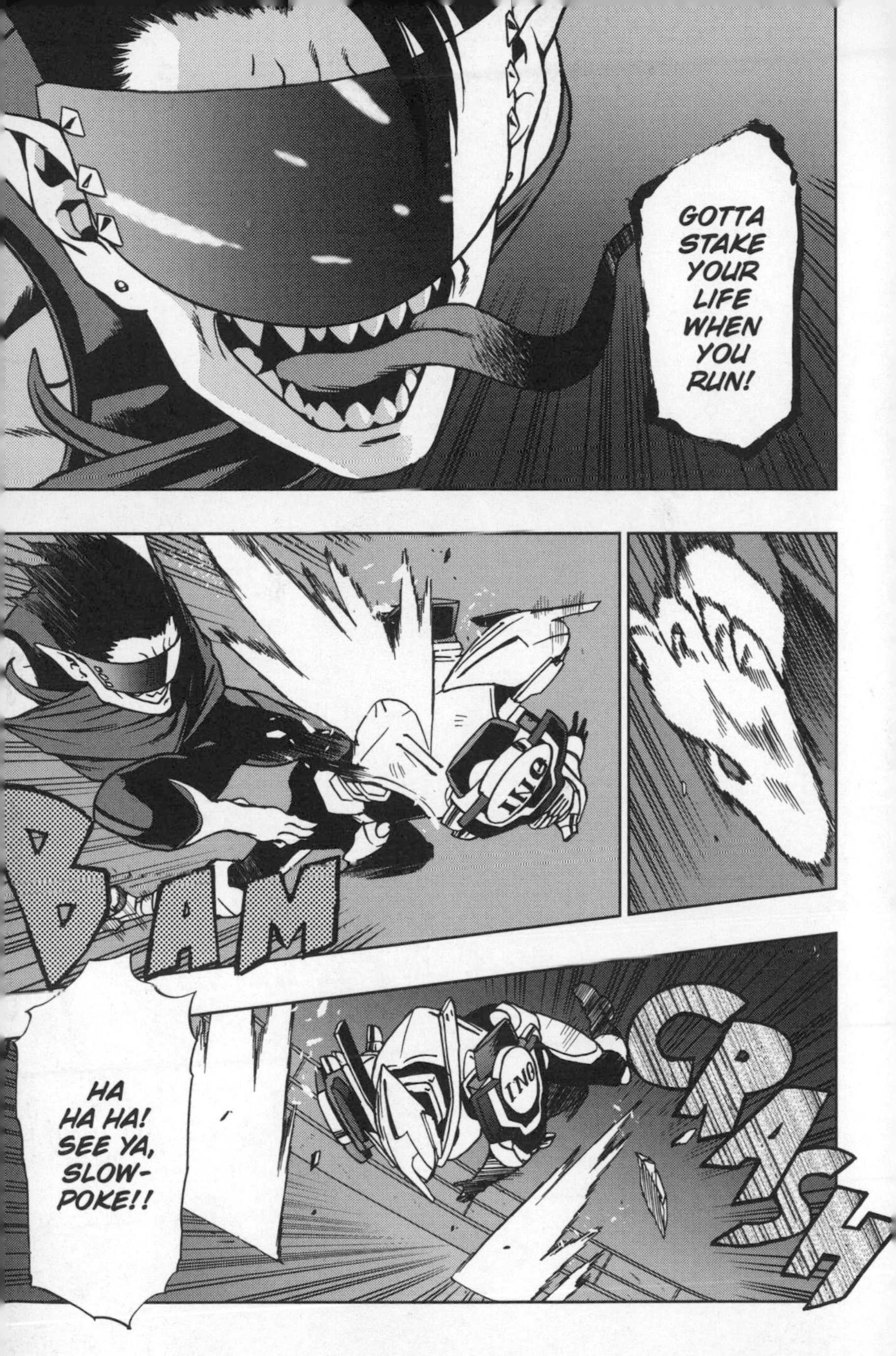
GOTTA STAKE YOUR LIFE WHEN YOU RUN!
BAM
CRASH
HA HA HA! SEE YA, SLOW-POKE!!

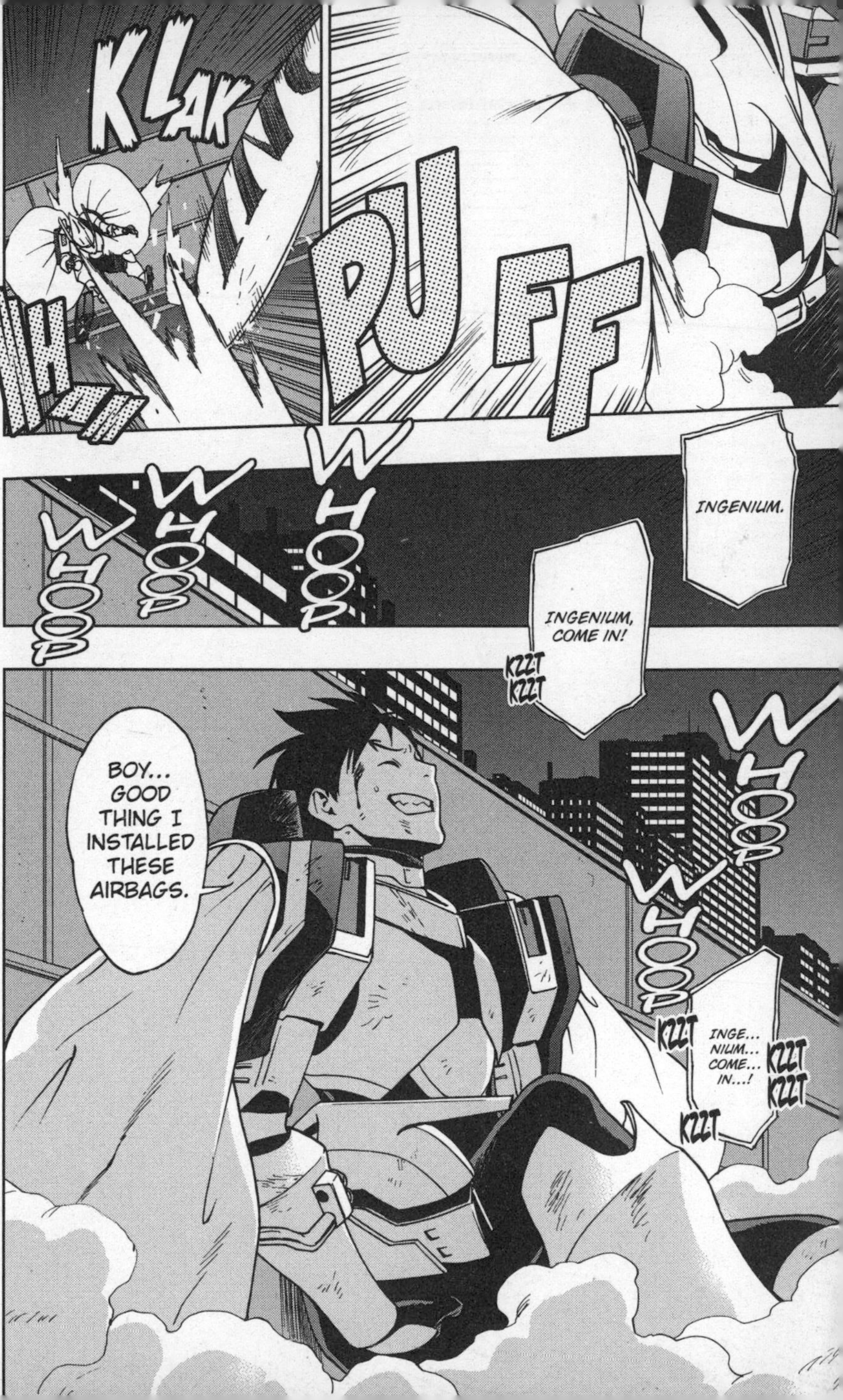
PUFF
KLAK
INGENIUM.
INGENIUM, COME IN!
KZZT KZZT
WHOOP
WHOOP
WHOOP
WHOOP
WHOOP
INGE... NIUM... COME... IN...!
KZZT
KZZT KZZT
KZZT
BOY... GOOD THING I INSTALLED THESE AIRBAGS.

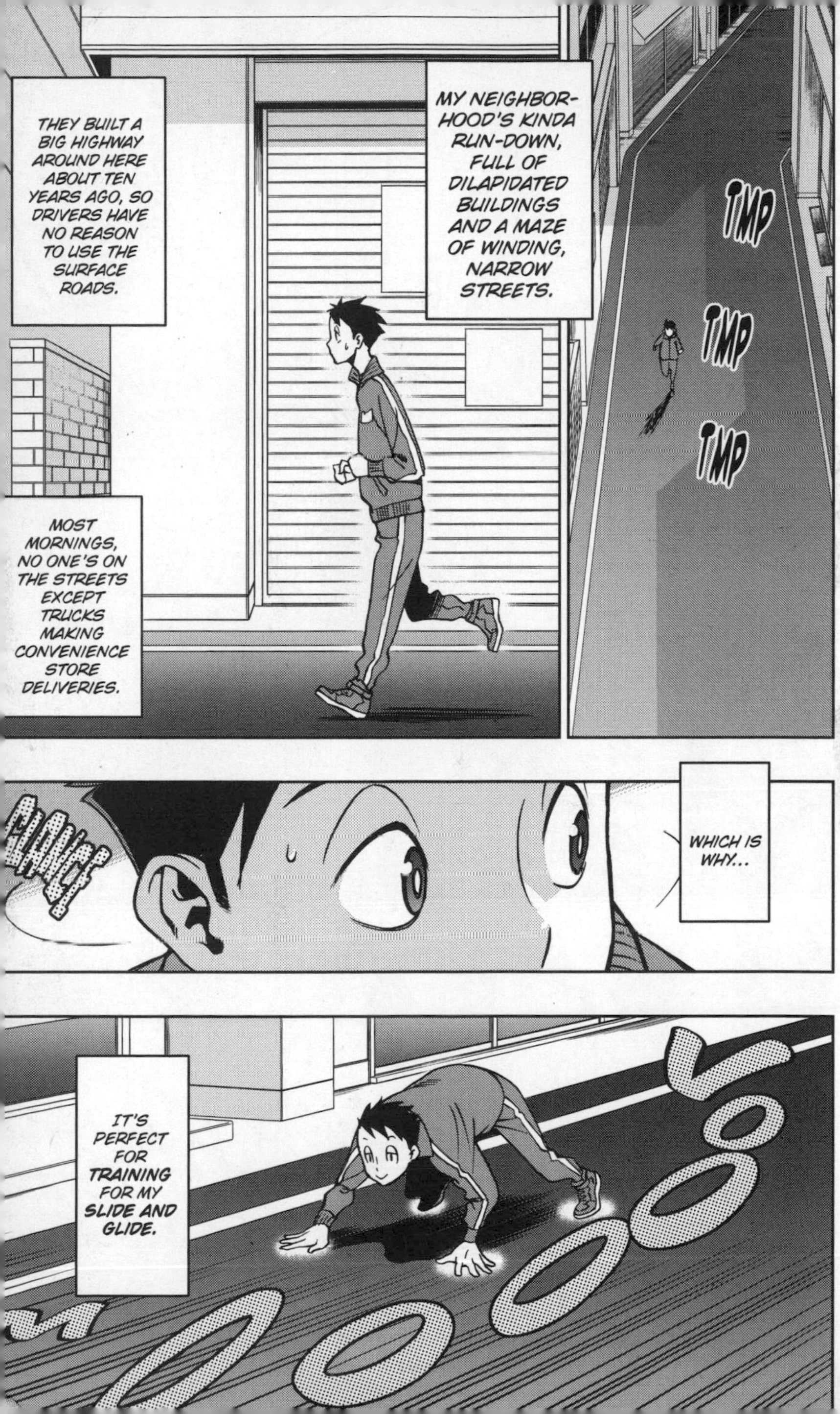
MY NEIGHBORHOOD'S KINDA RUN-DOWN, FULL OF DILAPIDATED BUILDINGS AND A MAZE OF WINDING, NARROW STREETS.
TMP
TMP
TMP
THEY BUILT A BIG HIGHWAY AROUND HERE ABOUT TEN YEARS AGO, SO DRIVERS HAVE NO REASON TO USE THE SURFACE ROADS.
MOST MORNINGS, NO ONE'S ON THE STREETS EXCEPT TRUCKS MAKING CONVENIENCE STORE DELIVERIES.
WHICH IS WHY...
IT'S PERFECT FOR TRAINING FOR MY SLIDE AND GLIDE.

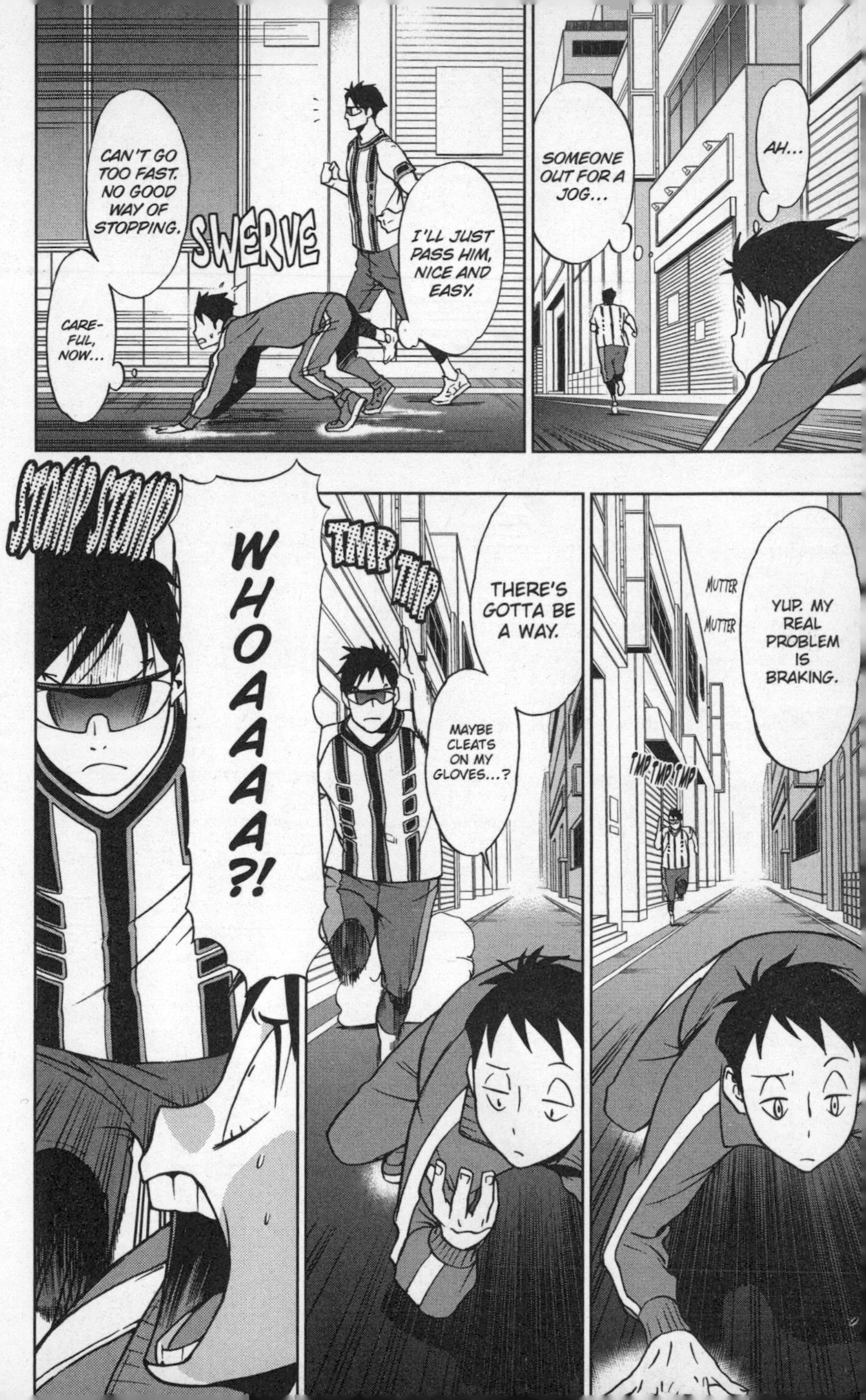
AH...
SOMEONE OUT FOR A JOG...
I'LL JUST PASS HIM, NICE AND EASY.
SWERVE
CAN'T GO TOO FAST. NO GOOD WAY OF STOPPING.
CARE-FUL, NOW...
MUTTER
MUTTER
YUP. MY REAL PROBLEM IS BRAKING.
TMP TMP TMP
THERE'S GOTTA BE A WAY.
TMP TMP
MAYBE CLEATS ON MY GLOVES...?
STMP STMP
WHOAAAAA?!

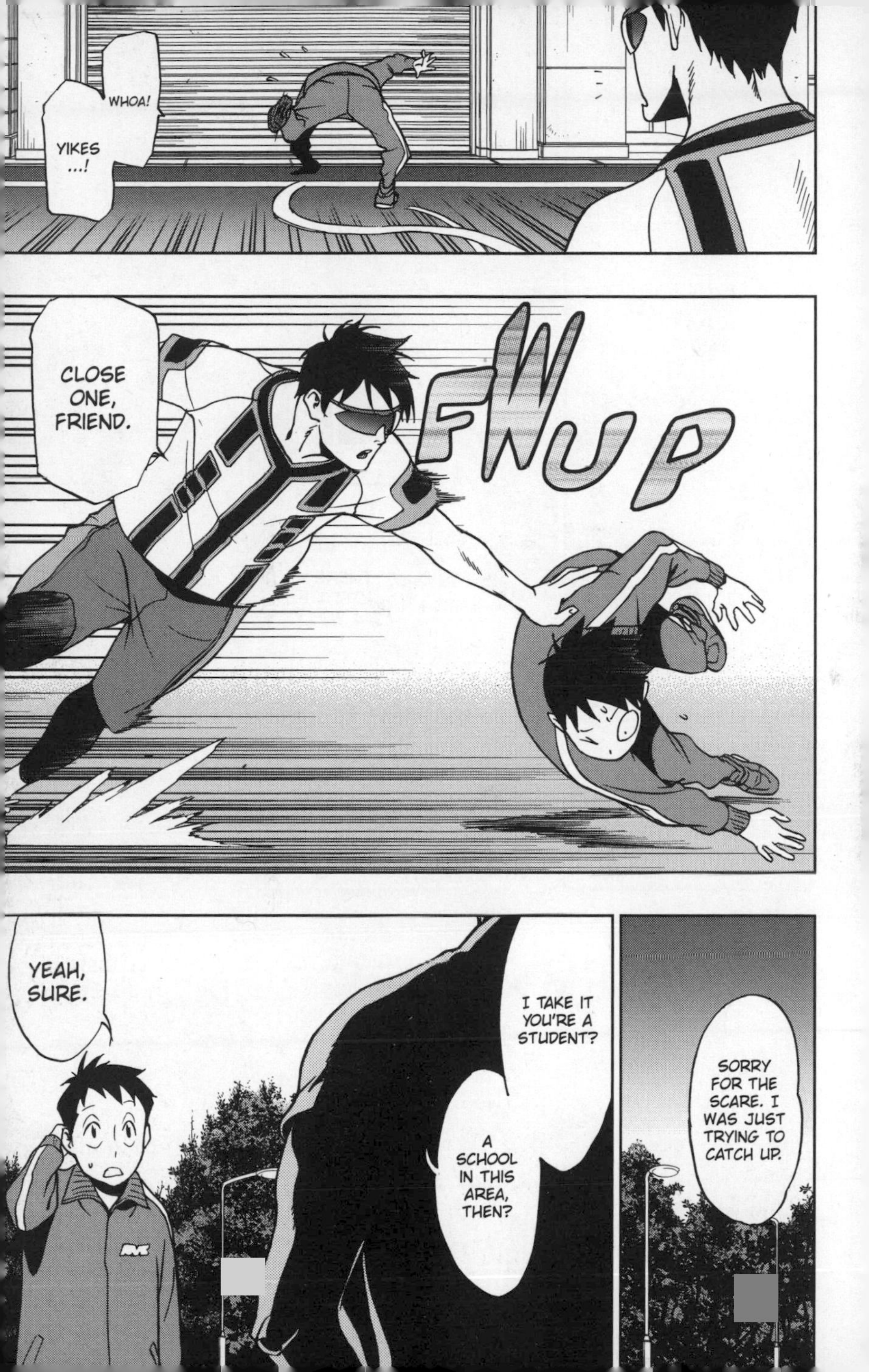
WHOA!
YIKES ...!
FWUP
CLOSE ONE, FRIEND.
SORRY FOR THE SCARE. I WAS JUST TRYING TO CATCH UP.
I TAKE IT YOU'RE A STUDENT?
A SCHOOL IN THIS AREA, THEN?
YEAH, SURE.

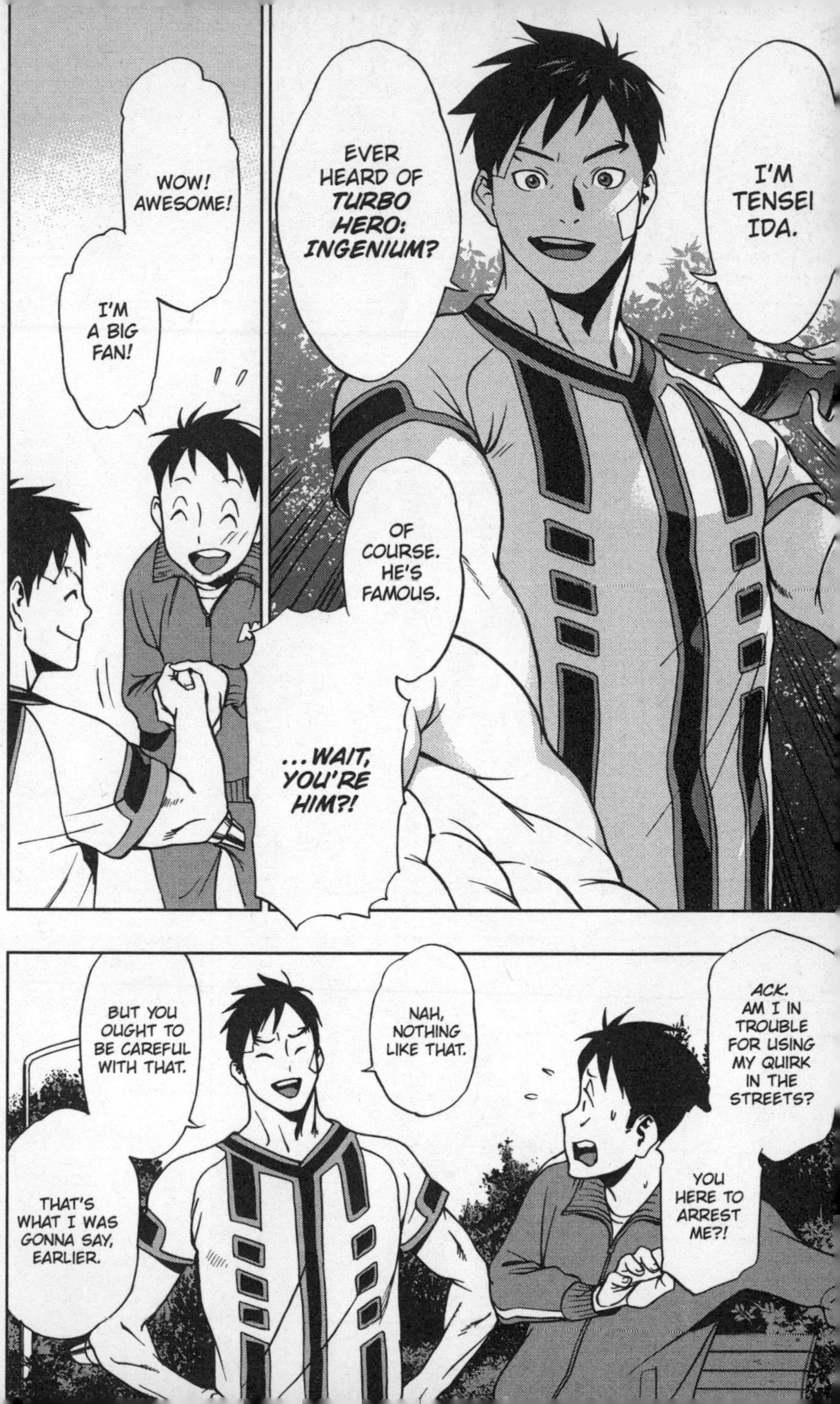
I'M TENSEI IDA.
EVER HEARD OF *TURBO HERO: INGENIUM?*
OF COURSE. HE'S FAMOUS.
...WAIT, YOU'RE HIM?!
WOW! AWESOME!
I'M A BIG FAN!
ACK. AM I IN TROUBLE FOR USING MY QUIRK IN THE STREETS?
YOU HERE TO ARREST ME?!
NAH, NOTHING LIKE THAT.
BUT YOU OUGHT TO BE CAREFUL WITH THAT.
THAT'S WHAT I WAS GONNA SAY, EARLIER.

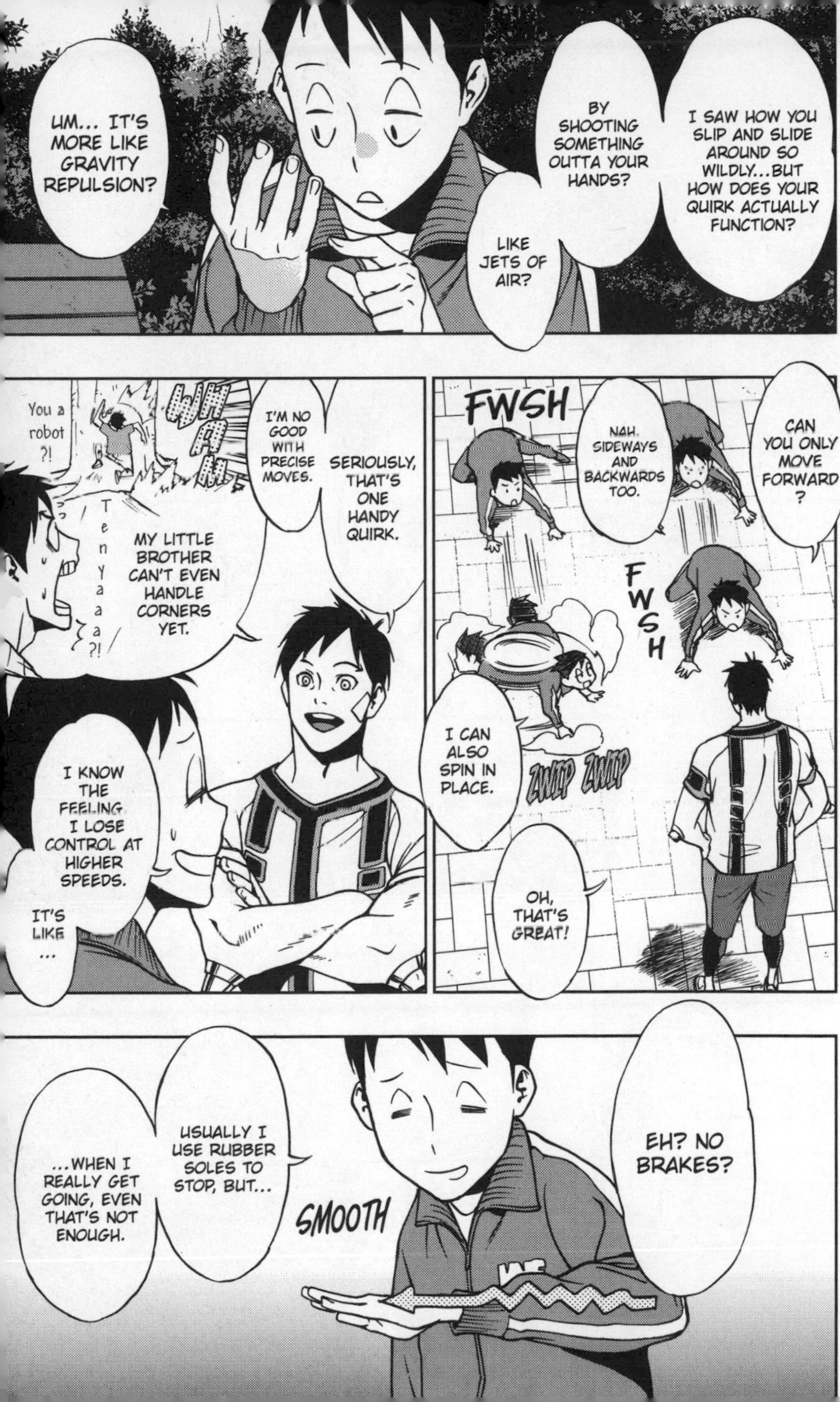
I SAW HOW YOU SLIP AND SLIDE AROUND SO WILDLY...BUT HOW DOES YOUR QUIRK ACTUALLY FUNCTION?
BY SHOOTING SOMETHING OUTTA YOUR HANDS?
LIKE JETS OF AIR?
UM... IT'S MORE LIKE GRAVITY REPULSION?
CAN YOU ONLY MOVE FORWARD?
FWSH
NAH. SIDEWAYS AND BACKWARDS TOO.
FWSH
I CAN ALSO SPIN IN PLACE.
ZWIP ZWIP
OH, THAT'S GREAT!
SERIOUSLY, THAT'S ONE HANDY QUIRK.
I'M NO GOOD WITH PRECISE MOVES.
MY LITTLE BROTHER CAN'T EVEN HANDLE CORNERS YET.
You a robot?!
Tenyaaaa?!
I KNOW THE FEELING. I LOSE CONTROL AT HIGHER SPEEDS.
IT'S LIKE...
EH? NO BRAKES?
USUALLY I USE RUBBER SOLES TO STOP, BUT...
...WHEN I REALLY GET GOING, EVEN THAT'S NOT ENOUGH.
SMOOTH

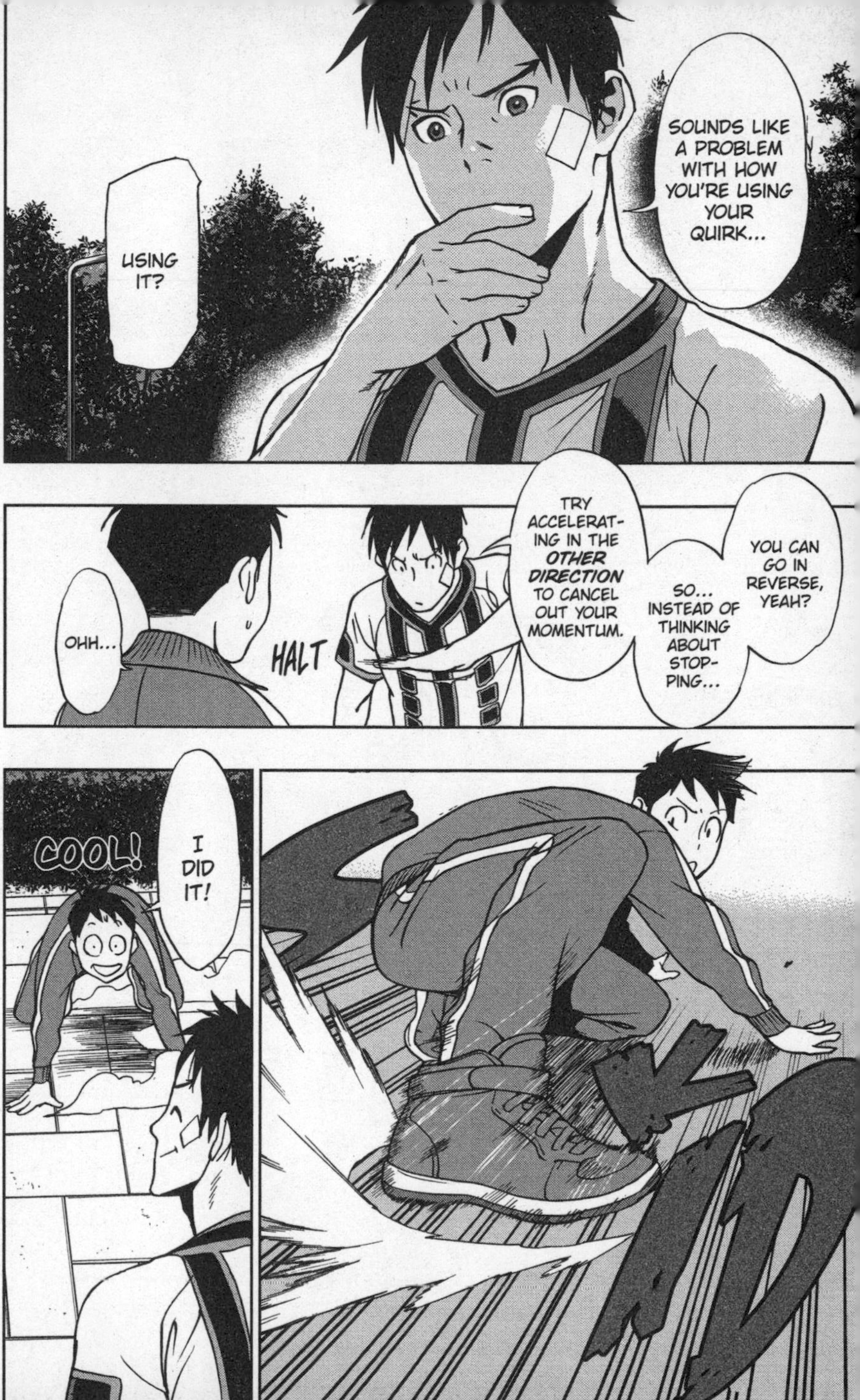
SOUNDS LIKE A PROBLEM WITH HOW YOU'RE USING YOUR QUIRK...
USING IT?
YOU CAN GO IN REVERSE, YEAH?
SO... INSTEAD OF THINKING ABOUT STOPPING...
TRY ACCELERATING IN THE *OTHER DIRECTION* TO CANCEL OUT YOUR MOMENTUM.
HALT
OHH...
SKID
I DID IT!
COOL!

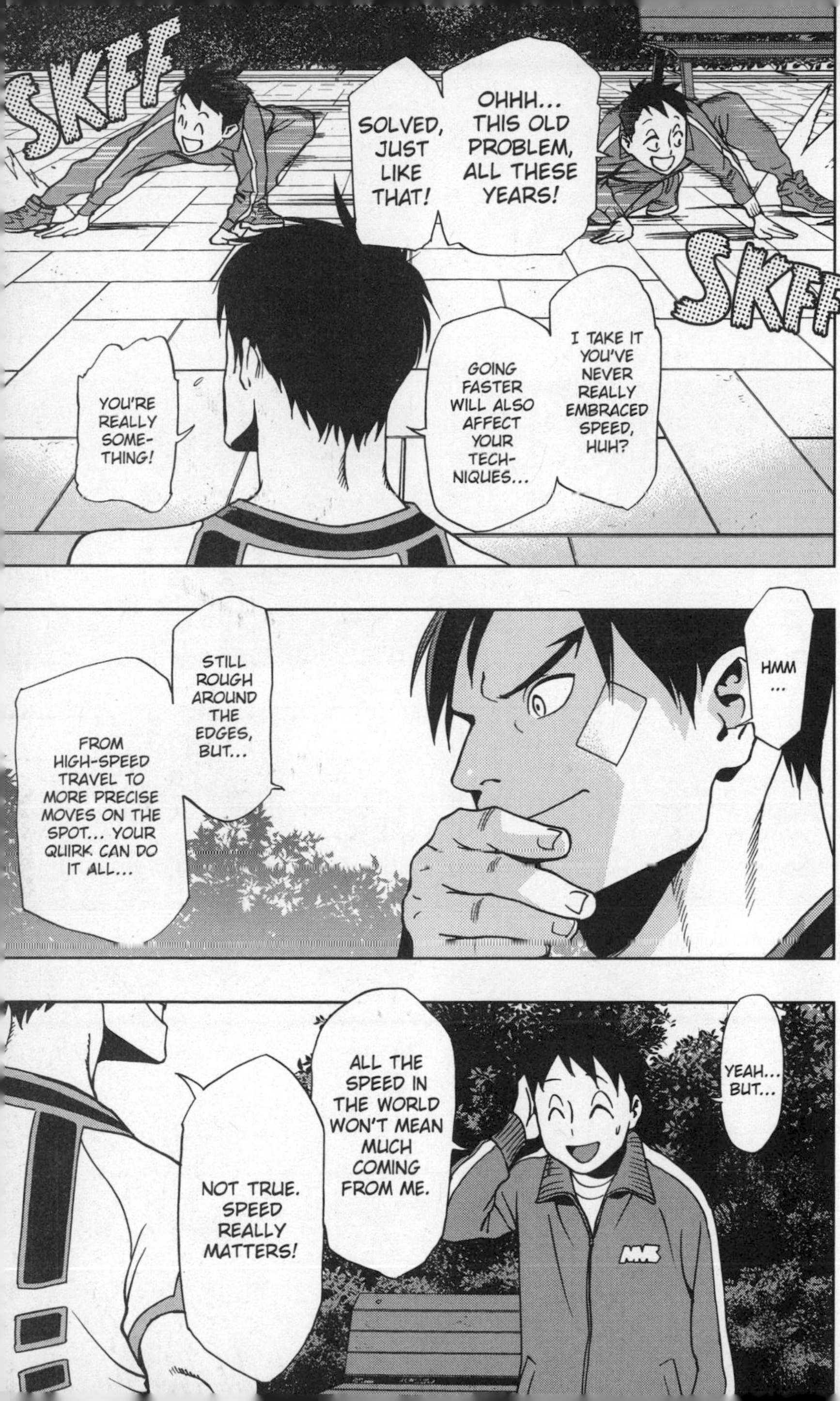
SKFF
OHHH... THIS OLD PROBLEM, ALL THESE YEARS!
SOLVED, JUST LIKE THAT!
SKFF
I TAKE IT YOU'VE NEVER REALLY EMBRACED SPEED, HUH?
GOING FASTER WILL ALSO AFFECT YOUR TECH-NIQUES...
YOU'RE REALLY SOME-THING!
HMM...
STILL ROUGH AROUND THE EDGES, BUT...
FROM HIGH-SPEED TRAVEL TO MORE PRECISE MOVES ON THE SPOT... YOUR QUIRK CAN DO IT ALL...
YEAH... BUT...
ALL THE SPEED IN THE WORLD WON'T MEAN MUCH COMING FROM ME.
NOT TRUE. SPEED REALLY MATTERS!

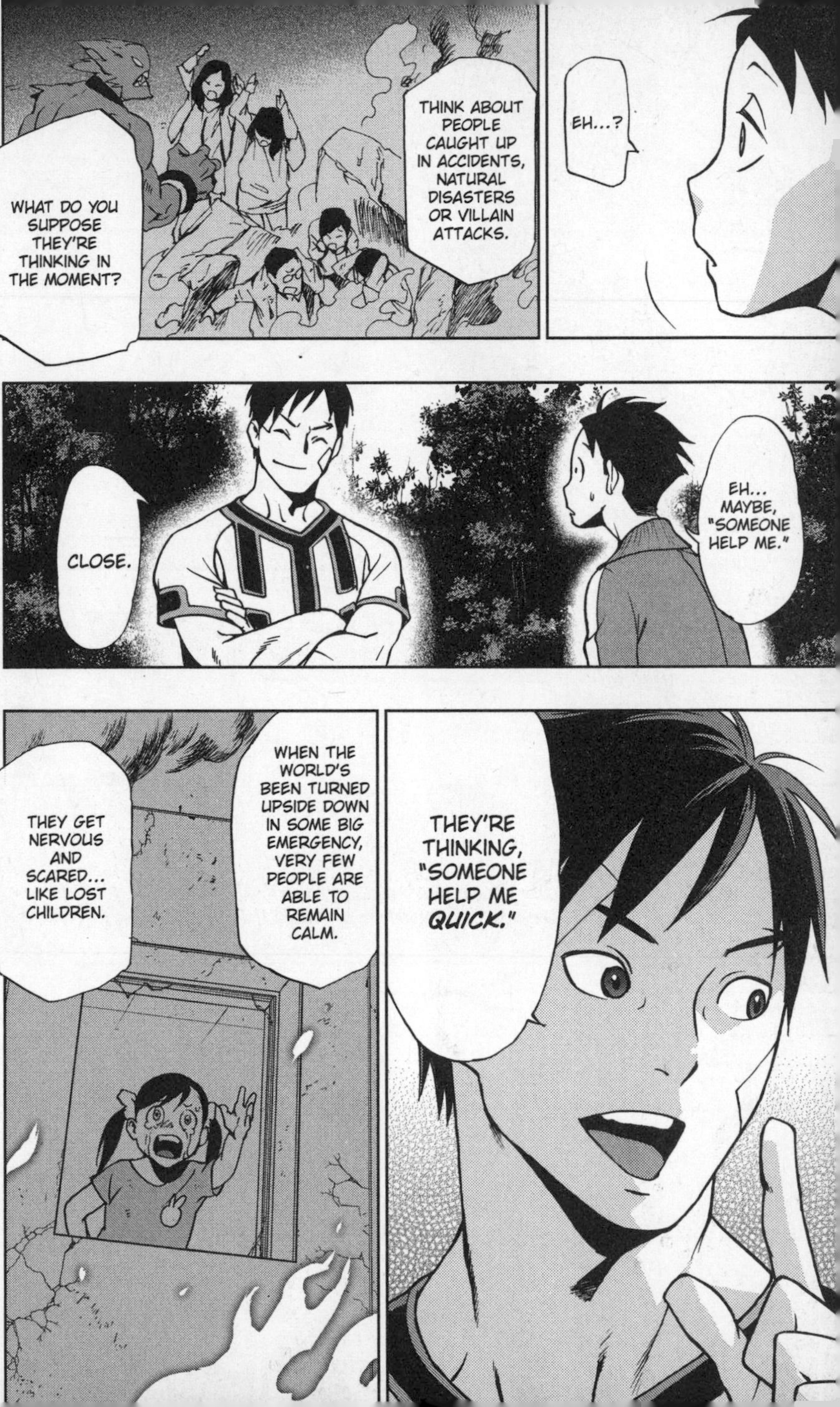
EH...?
THINK ABOUT PEOPLE CAUGHT UP IN ACCIDENTS, NATURAL DISASTERS OR VILLAIN ATTACKS.
WHAT DO YOU SUPPOSE THEY'RE THINKING IN THE MOMENT?
EH... MAYBE, "SOMEONE HELP ME."
CLOSE.
THEY'RE THINKING, "SOMEONE HELP ME *QUICK*."
WHEN THE WORLD'S BEEN TURNED UPSIDE DOWN IN SOME BIG EMERGENCY, VERY FEW PEOPLE ARE ABLE TO REMAIN CALM.
THEY GET NERVOUS AND SCARED... LIKE LOST CHILDREN.

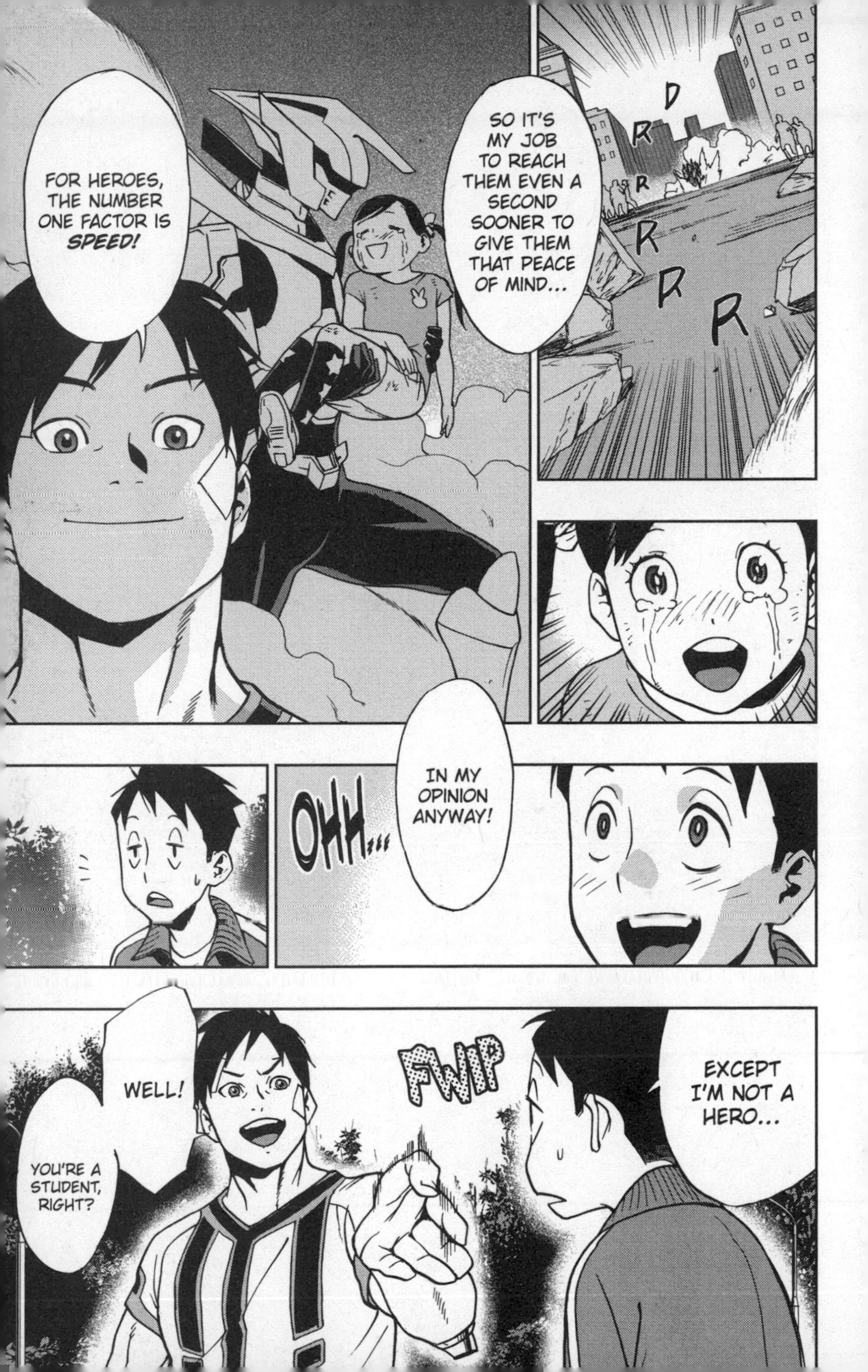
DRRRRRR
SO IT'S MY JOB TO REACH THEM EVEN A SECOND SOONER TO GIVE THEM THAT PEACE OF MIND...
FOR HEROES, THE NUMBER ONE FACTOR IS ***SPEED!***
IN MY OPINION ANYWAY!
OHH...
EXCEPT I'M NOT A HERO...
FWIP
WELL!
YOU'RE A STUDENT, RIGHT?

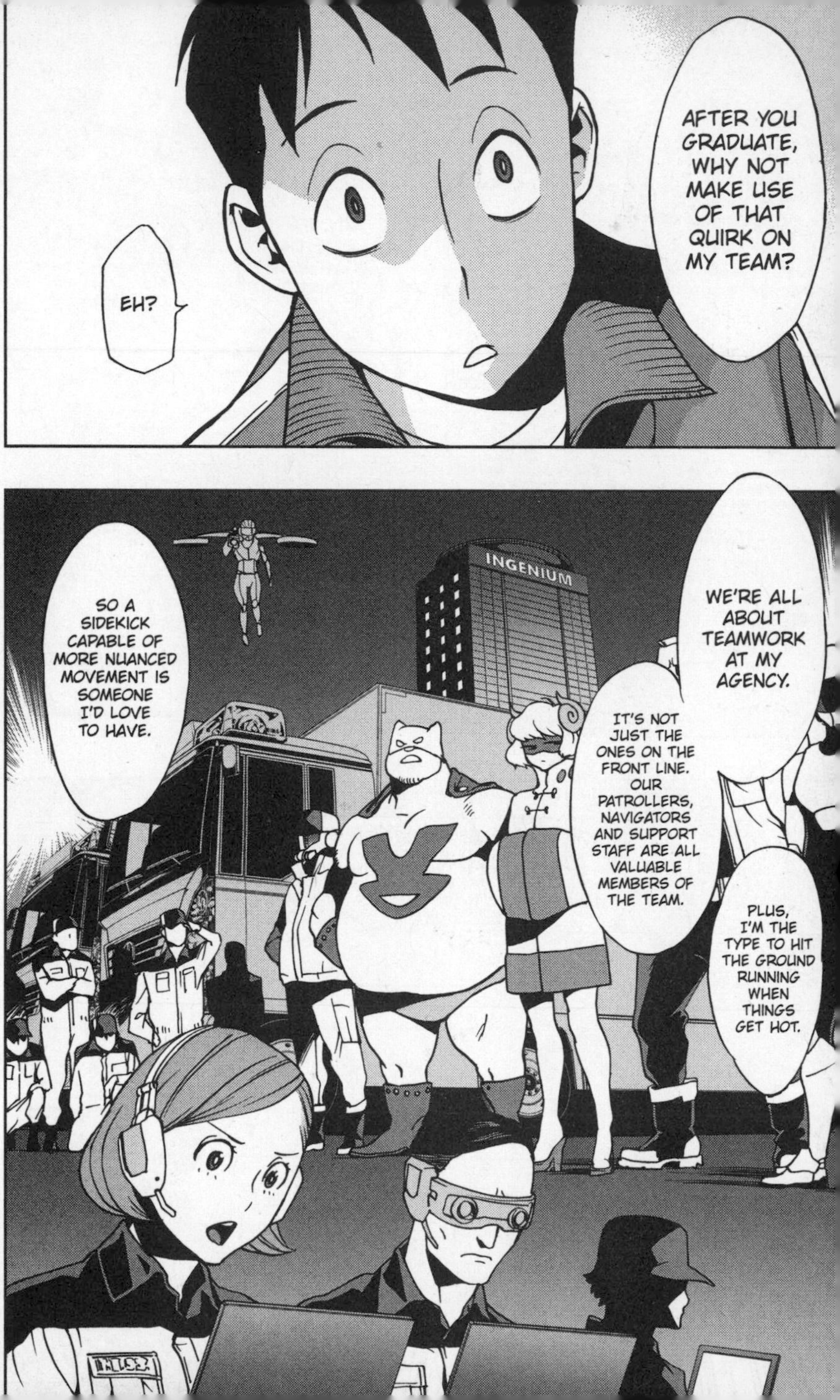
AFTER YOU GRADUATE, WHY NOT MAKE USE OF THAT QUIRK ON MY TEAM?
EH?
WE'RE ALL ABOUT TEAMWORK AT MY AGENCY.
IT'S NOT JUST THE ONES ON THE FRONT LINE. OUR PATROLLERS, NAVIGATORS AND SUPPORT STAFF ARE ALL VALUABLE MEMBERS OF THE TEAM.
PLUS, I'M THE TYPE TO HIT THE GROUND RUNNING WHEN THINGS GET HOT.
SO A SIDEKICK CAPABLE OF MORE NUANCED MOVEMENT IS SOMEONE I'D LOVE TO HAVE.
INGENIUM

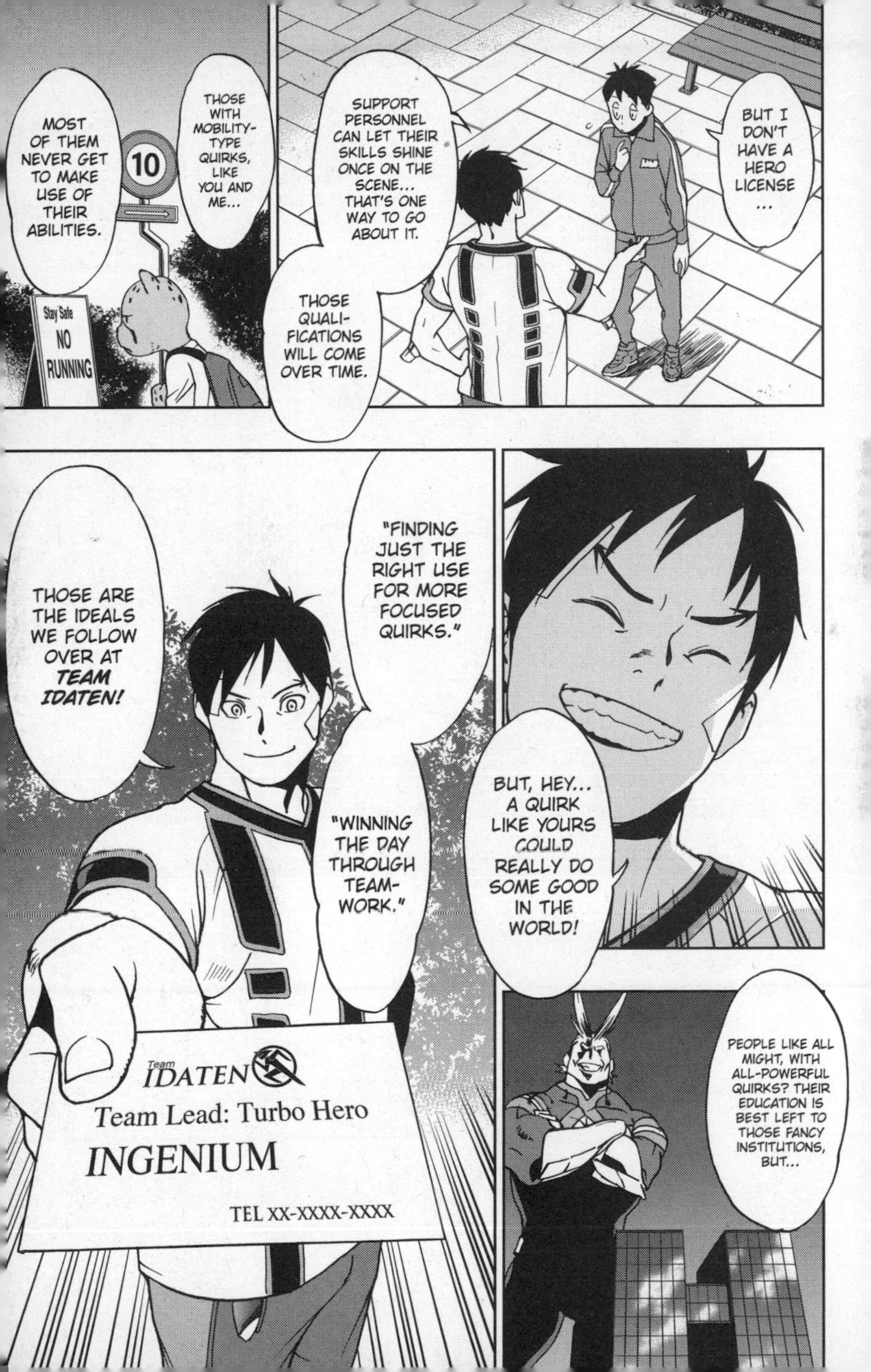

SUPPORT PERSONNEL CAN LET THEIR SKILLS SHINE ONCE ON THE SCENE... THAT'S ONE WAY TO GO ABOUT IT.
BUT I DON'T HAVE A HERO LICENSE...
THOSE QUALIFICATIONS WILL COME OVER TIME.
THOSE WITH MOBILITY-TYPE QUIRKS, LIKE YOU AND ME...
MOST OF THEM NEVER GET TO MAKE USE OF THEIR ABILITIES.
10
Stay Safe
NO RUNNING
BUT, HEY... A QUIRK LIKE YOURS COULD REALLY DO SOME GOOD IN THE WORLD!
PEOPLE LIKE ALL MIGHT, WITH ALL-POWERFUL QUIRKS? THEIR EDUCATION IS BEST LEFT TO THOSE FANCY INSTITUTIONS, BUT...
"FINDING JUST THE RIGHT USE FOR MORE FOCUSED QUIRKS."
"WINNING THE DAY THROUGH TEAM-WORK."
THOSE ARE THE IDEALS WE FOLLOW OVER AT *TEAM IDATEN!*
Team IDATEN
Team Lead: Turbo Hero
INGENIUM
TEL XX-XXXX-XXXX

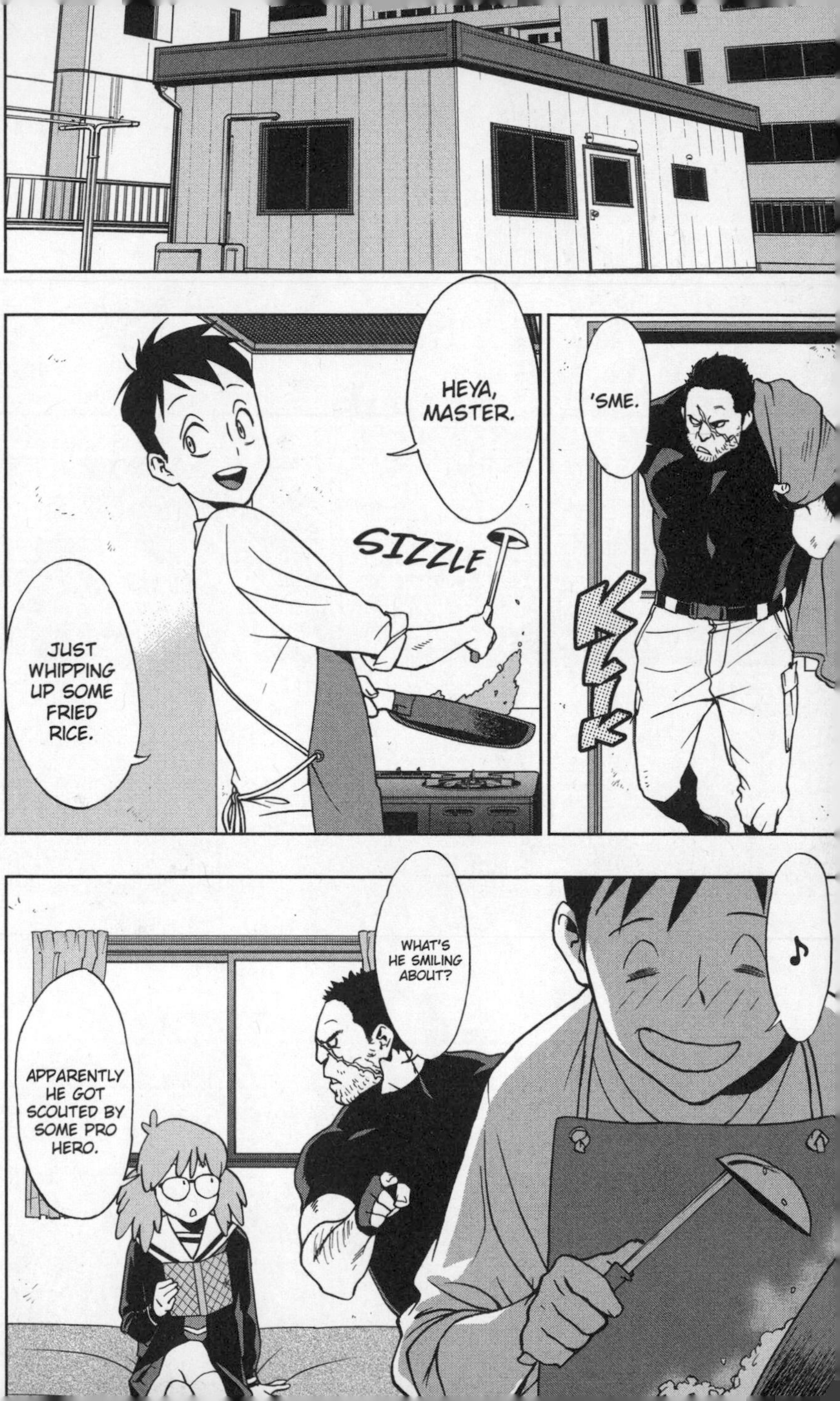
'SME.
KLIK
HEYA, MASTER.
SIZZLE
JUST WHIPPING UP SOME FRIED RICE.
♪
WHAT'S HE SMILING ABOUT?
APPARENTLY HE GOT SCOUTED BY SOME PRO HERO.

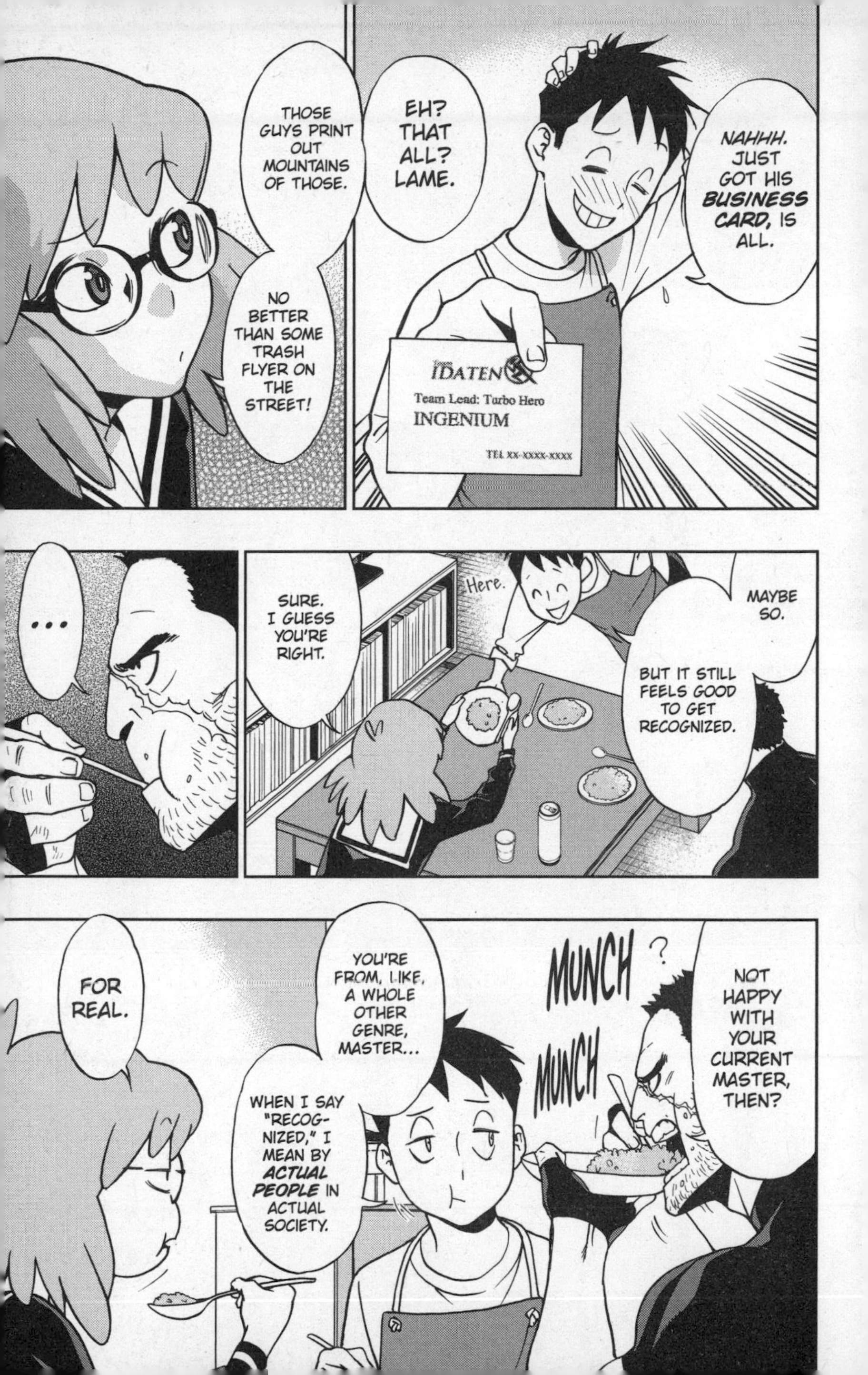
NAHHH. JUST GOT HIS BUSINESS CARD, IS ALL.
IDATEN
Team Lead: Turbo Hero
INGENIUM
TEL XX-XXXX-XXXX
EH? THAT ALL? LAME.
THOSE GUYS PRINT OUT MOUNTAINS OF THOSE.
NO BETTER THAN SOME TRASH FLYER ON THE STREET!
MAYBE SO.
BUT IT STILL FEELS GOOD TO GET RECOGNIZED.
Here.
SURE. I GUESS YOU'RE RIGHT.
...
?
NOT HAPPY WITH YOUR CURRENT MASTER, THEN?
MUNCH
MUNCH
YOU'RE FROM, LIKE, A WHOLE OTHER GENRE, MASTER...
WHEN I SAY "RECOG-NIZED," I MEAN BY ACTUAL PEOPLE IN ACTUAL SOCIETY.
FOR REAL.

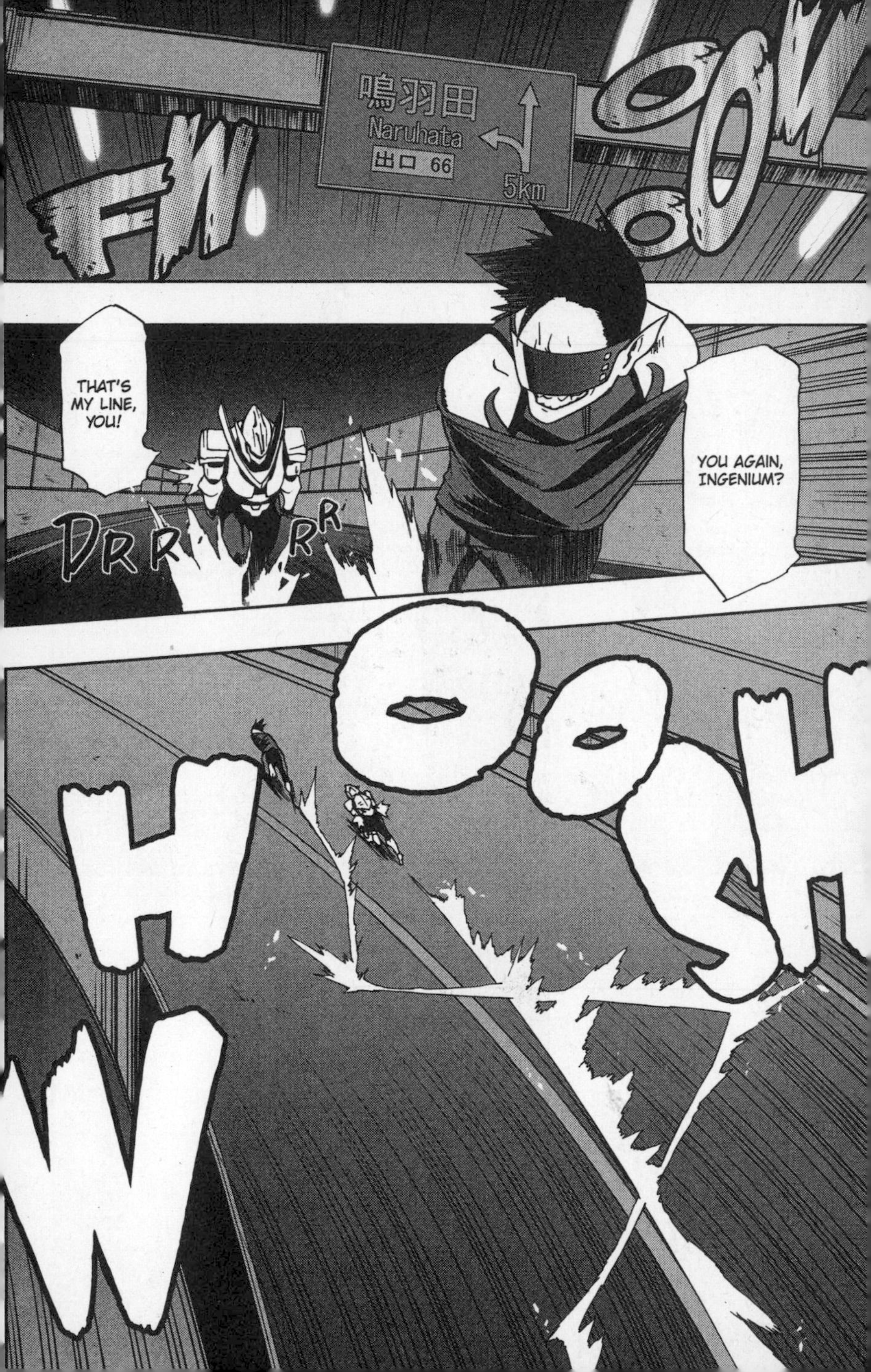

鳴羽田
Naruhata
出口 66
5km
FW
OOOM
YOU AGAIN, INGENIUM?
THAT'S MY LINE, YOU!
DRRRR
WHOOSH

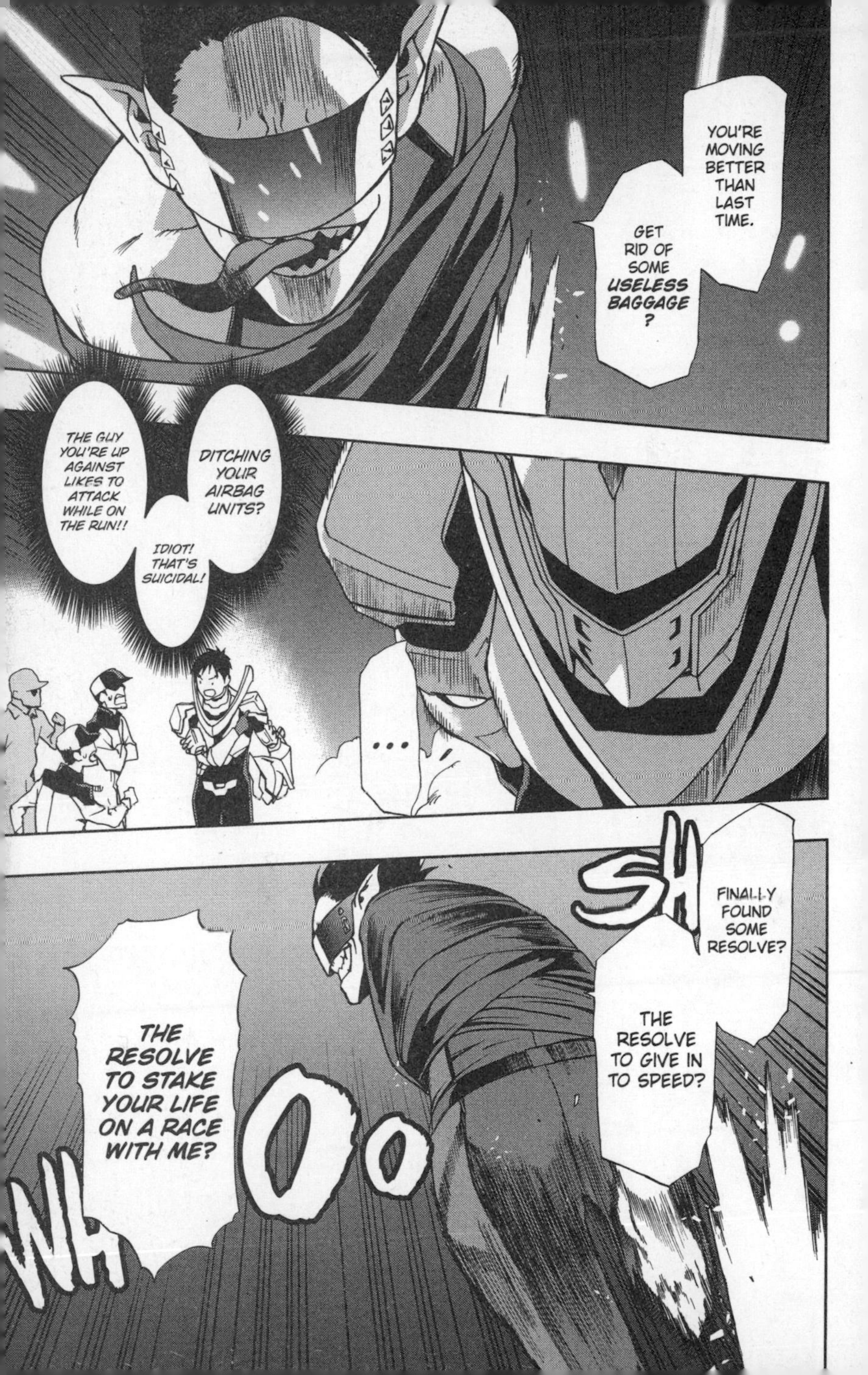
YOU'RE MOVING BETTER THAN LAST TIME.
GET RID OF SOME USELESS BAGGAGE?
DITCHING YOUR AIRBAG UNITS?
IDIOT! THAT'S SUICIDAL!
THE GUY YOU'RE UP AGAINST LIKES TO ATTACK WHILE ON THE RUN!!
...
SH
FINALLY FOUND SOME RESOLVE?
THE RESOLVE TO GIVE IN TO SPEED?
THE RESOLVE TO STAKE YOUR LIFE ON A RACE WITH ME?
WHOO

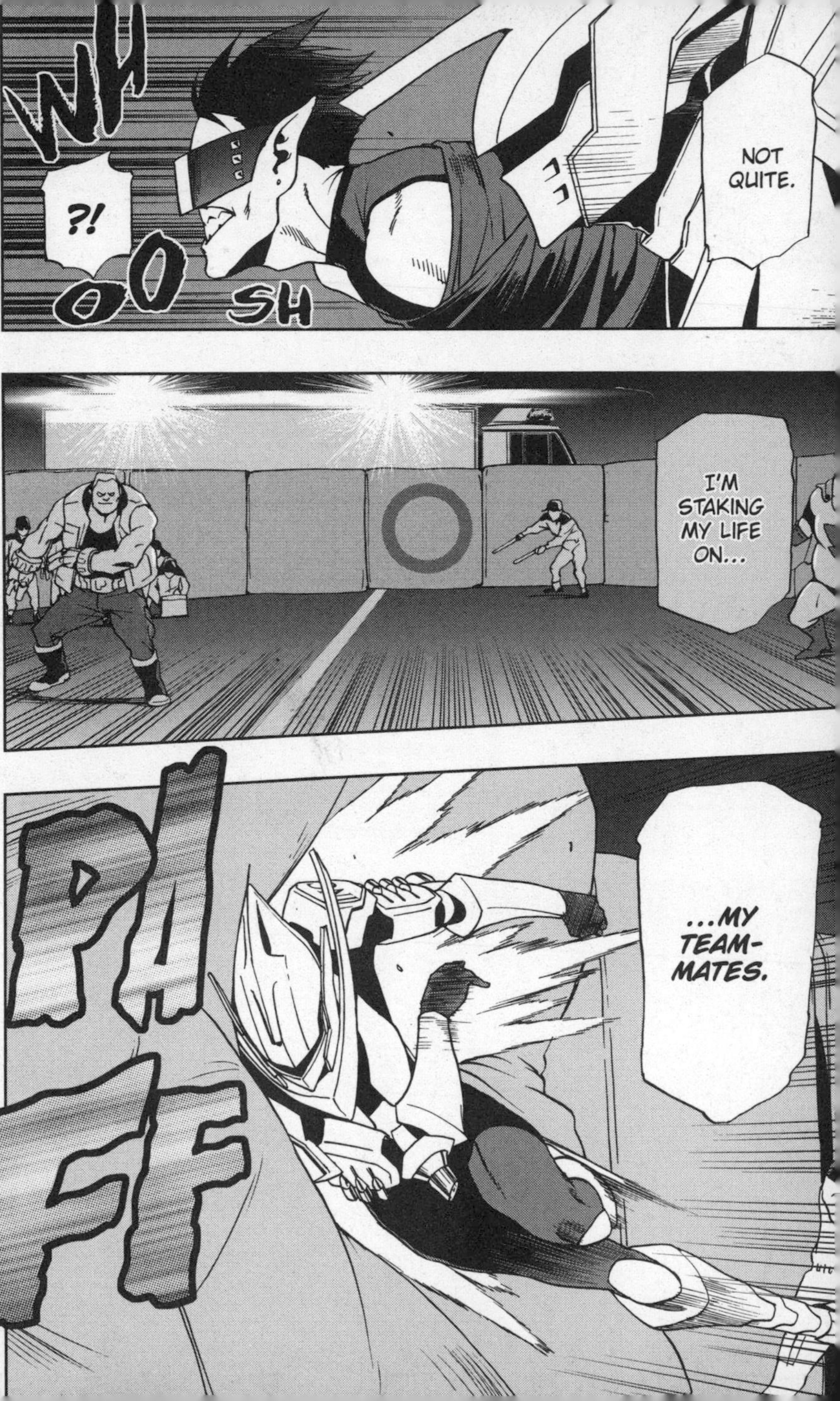
NOT QUITE.
?!
WHOOSH
I'M STAKING MY LIFE ON...
...MY TEAM-MATES.
PAFF

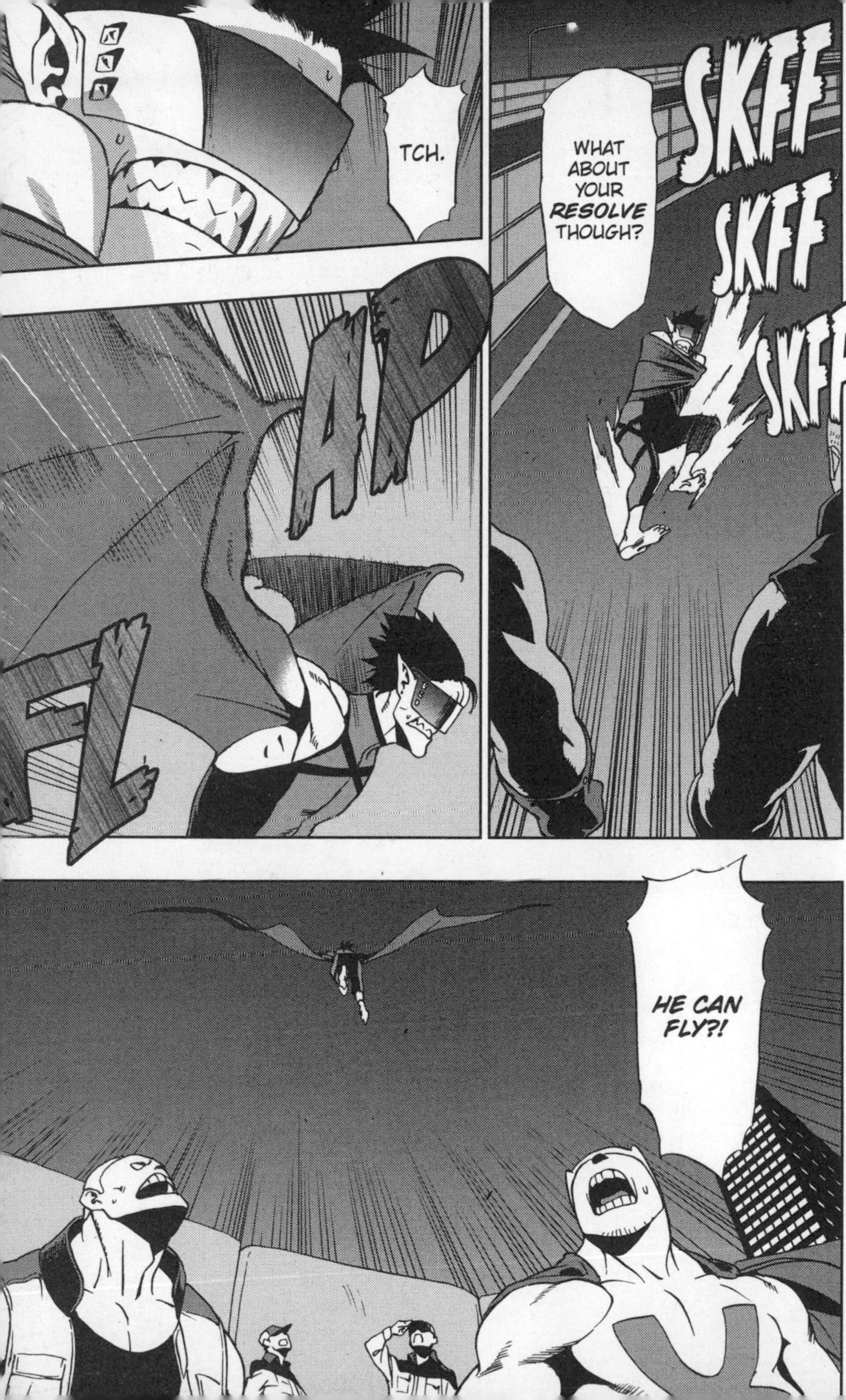
WHAT ABOUT YOUR *RESOLVE* THOUGH?
SKFF SKFF SKFF SKFF
TCH.
FLAP
HE CAN FLY?!

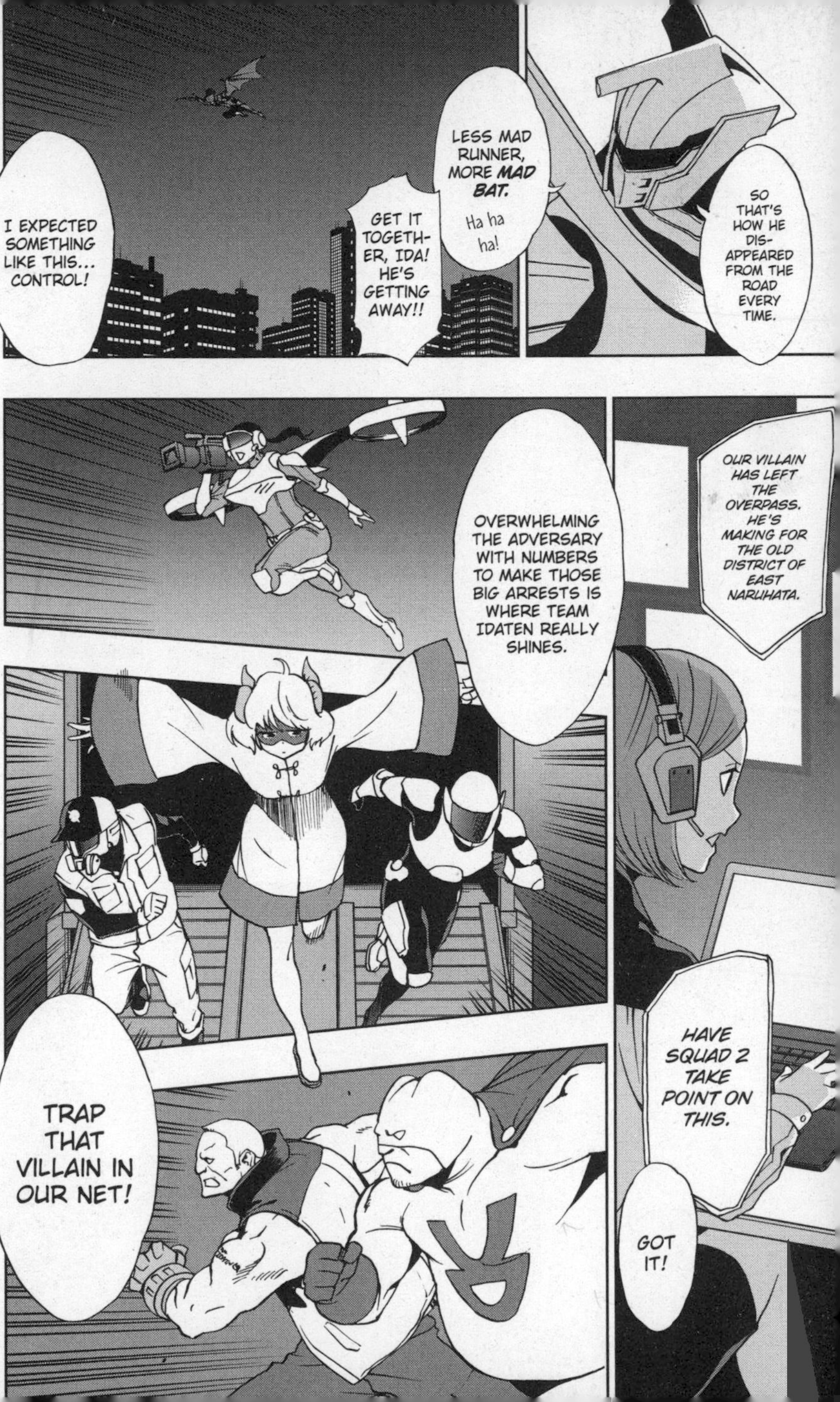
SO THAT'S HOW HE DIS-APPEARED FROM THE ROAD EVERY TIME.
LESS MAD RUNNER, MORE *MAD BAT.*
Ha ha ha!
GET IT TOGETH-ER, IDA! HE'S GETTING AWAY!!
I EXPECTED SOMETHING LIKE THIS... CONTROL!
OUR VILLAIN HAS LEFT THE OVERPASS. HE'S MAKING FOR THE OLD DISTRICT OF EAST NARUHATA.
HAVE SQUAD 2 TAKE POINT ON THIS.
GOT IT!
OVERWHELMING THE ADVERSARY WITH NUMBERS TO MAKE THOSE BIG ARRESTS IS WHERE TEAM IDATEN REALLY SHINES.
TRAP THAT VILLAIN IN OUR NET!

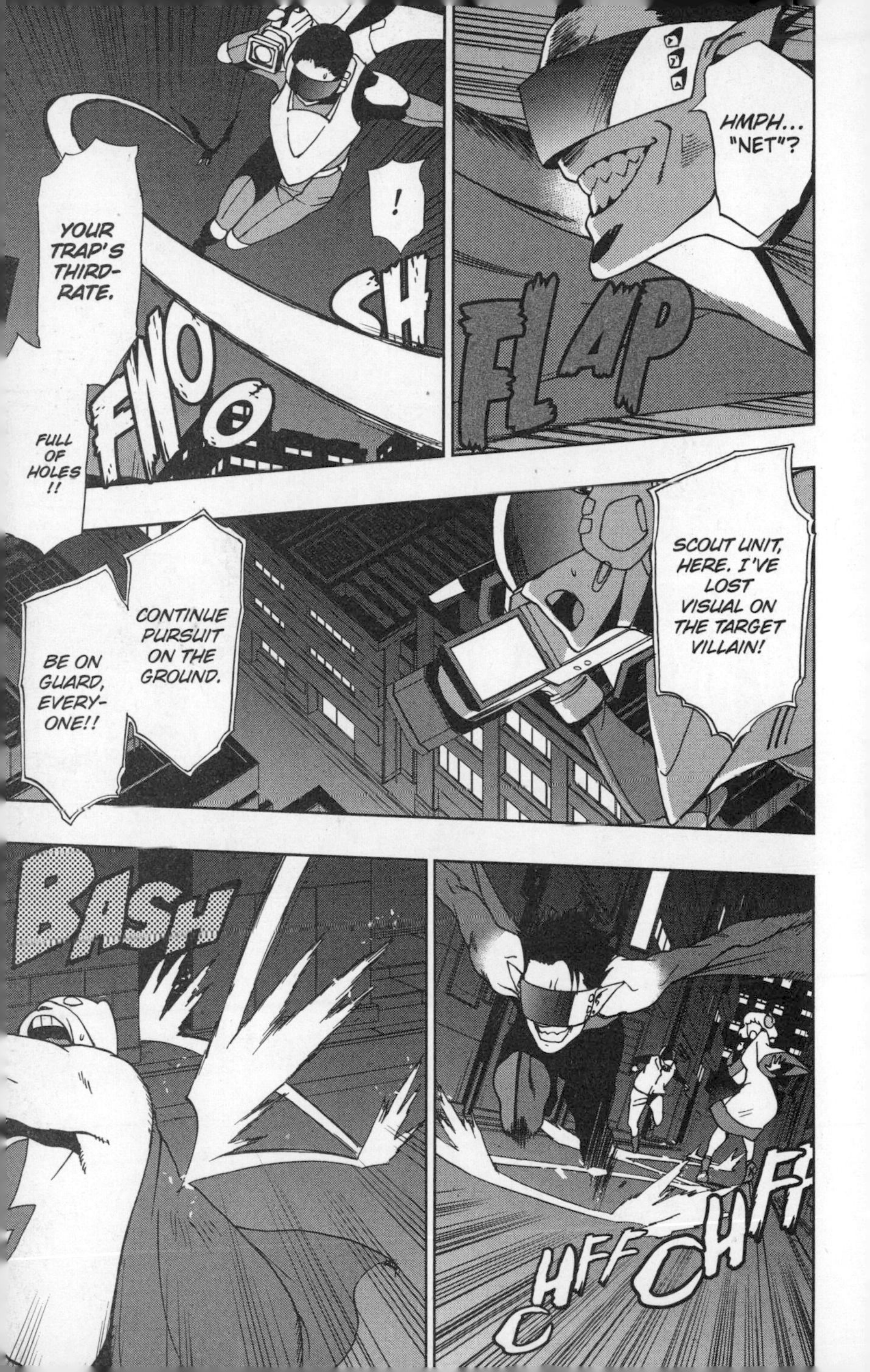
HMPH... "NET"?
FLAP
!
YOUR TRAP'S THIRD-RATE.
SH
FWO
FULL OF HOLES!!
SCOUT UNIT, HERE. I'VE LOST VISUAL ON THE TARGET VILLAIN!
CONTINUE PURSUIT ON THE GROUND.
BE ON GUARD, EVERY-ONE!!
CHFF CHFF
BASH

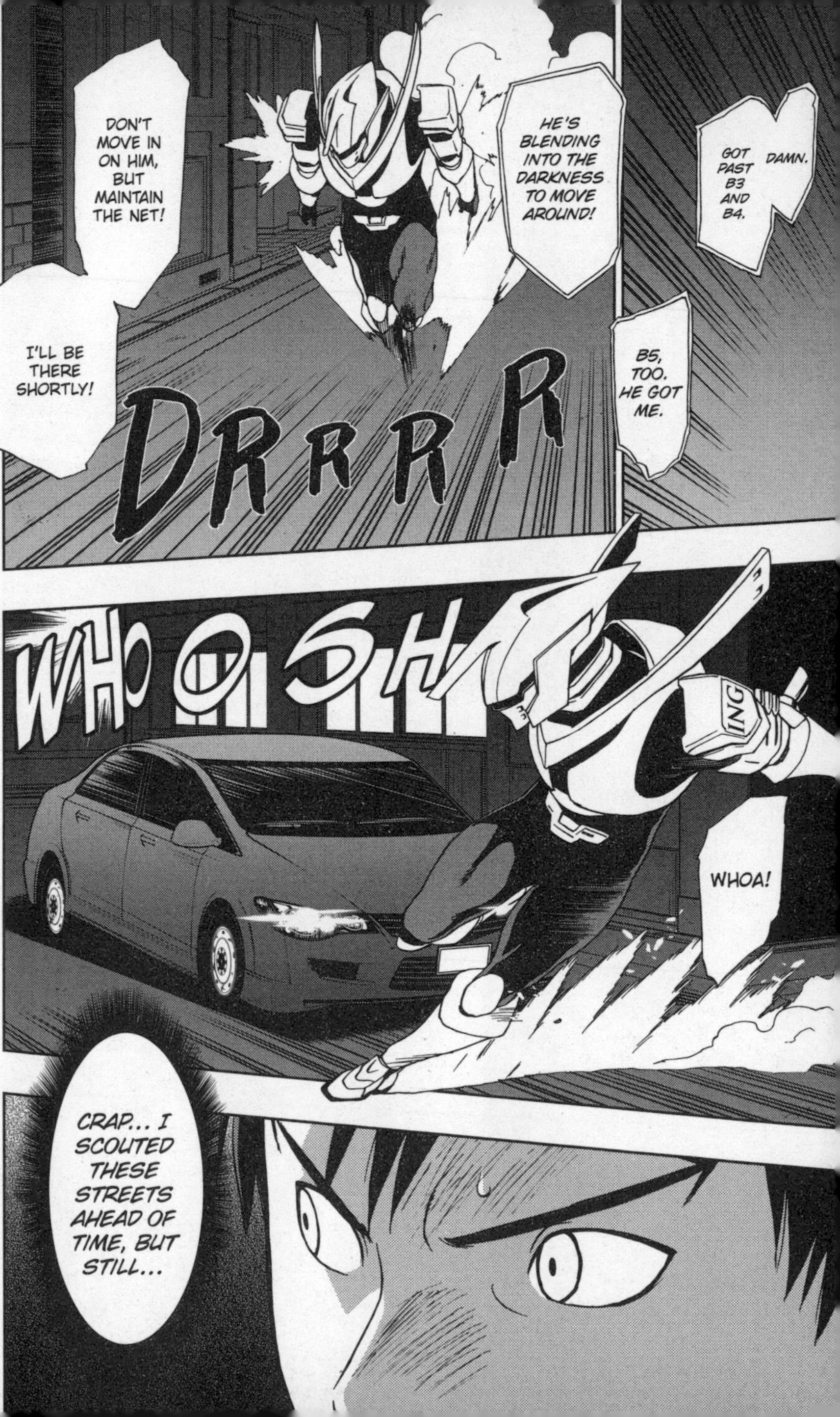
DAMN.
GOT PAST B3 AND B4.
B5, TOO. HE GOT ME.
HE'S BLENDING INTO THE DARKNESS TO MOVE AROUND!
DON'T MOVE IN ON HIM, BUT MAINTAIN THE NET!
I'LL BE THERE SHORTLY!
DRRRRR
WHOOSH
WHOA!
CRAP... I SCOUTED THESE STREETS AHEAD OF TIME, BUT STILL...

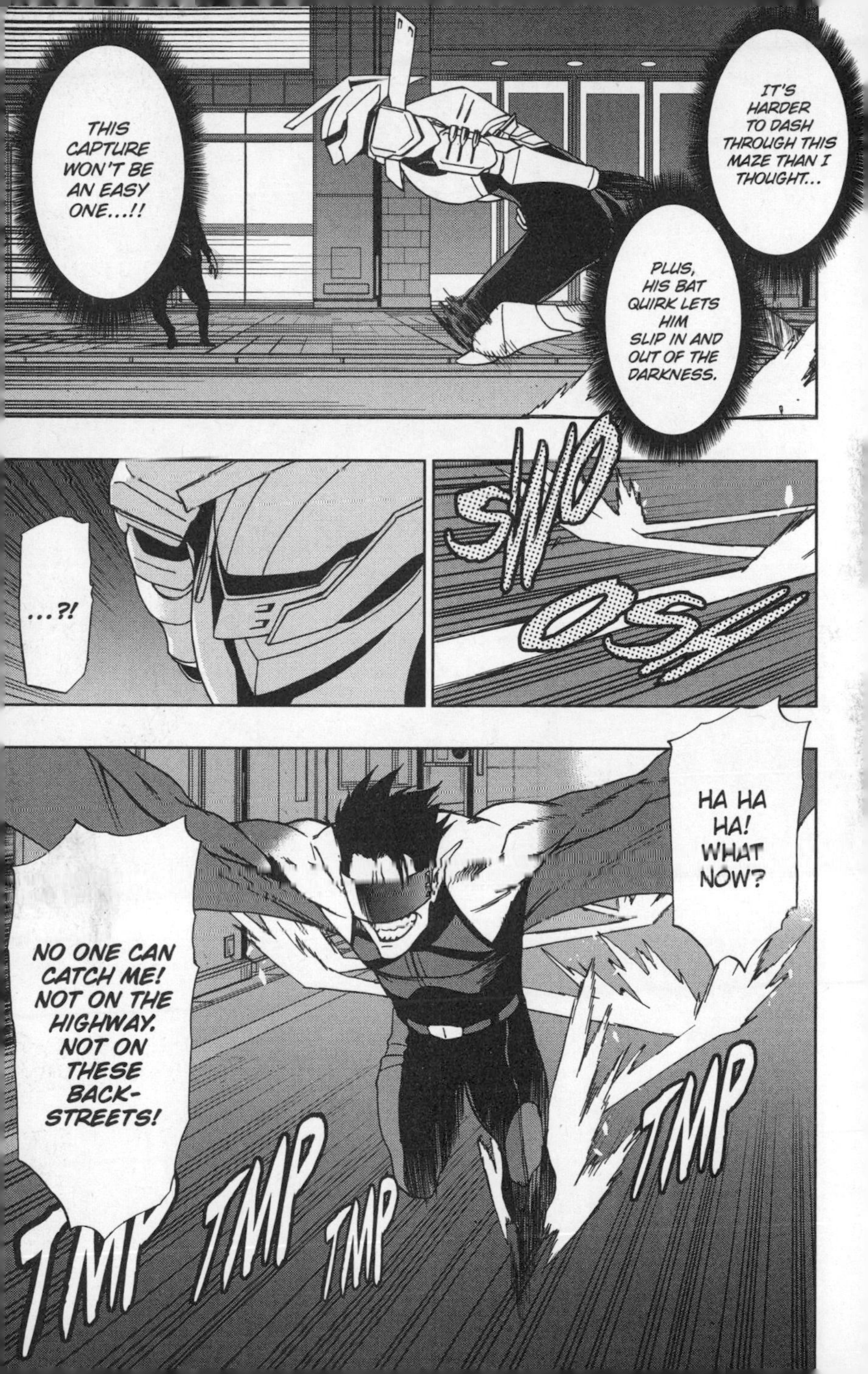
IT'S HARDER TO DASH THROUGH THIS MAZE THAN I THOUGHT...
PLUS, HIS BAT QUIRK LETS HIM SLIP IN AND OUT OF THE DARKNESS.
THIS CAPTURE WON'T BE AN EASY ONE...!!
SWOOSH
...?!
HA HA HA! WHAT NOW?
NO ONE CAN CATCH ME! NOT ON THE HIGHWAY. NOT ON THESE BACK-STREETS!
TMP
TMP
TMP
TMP

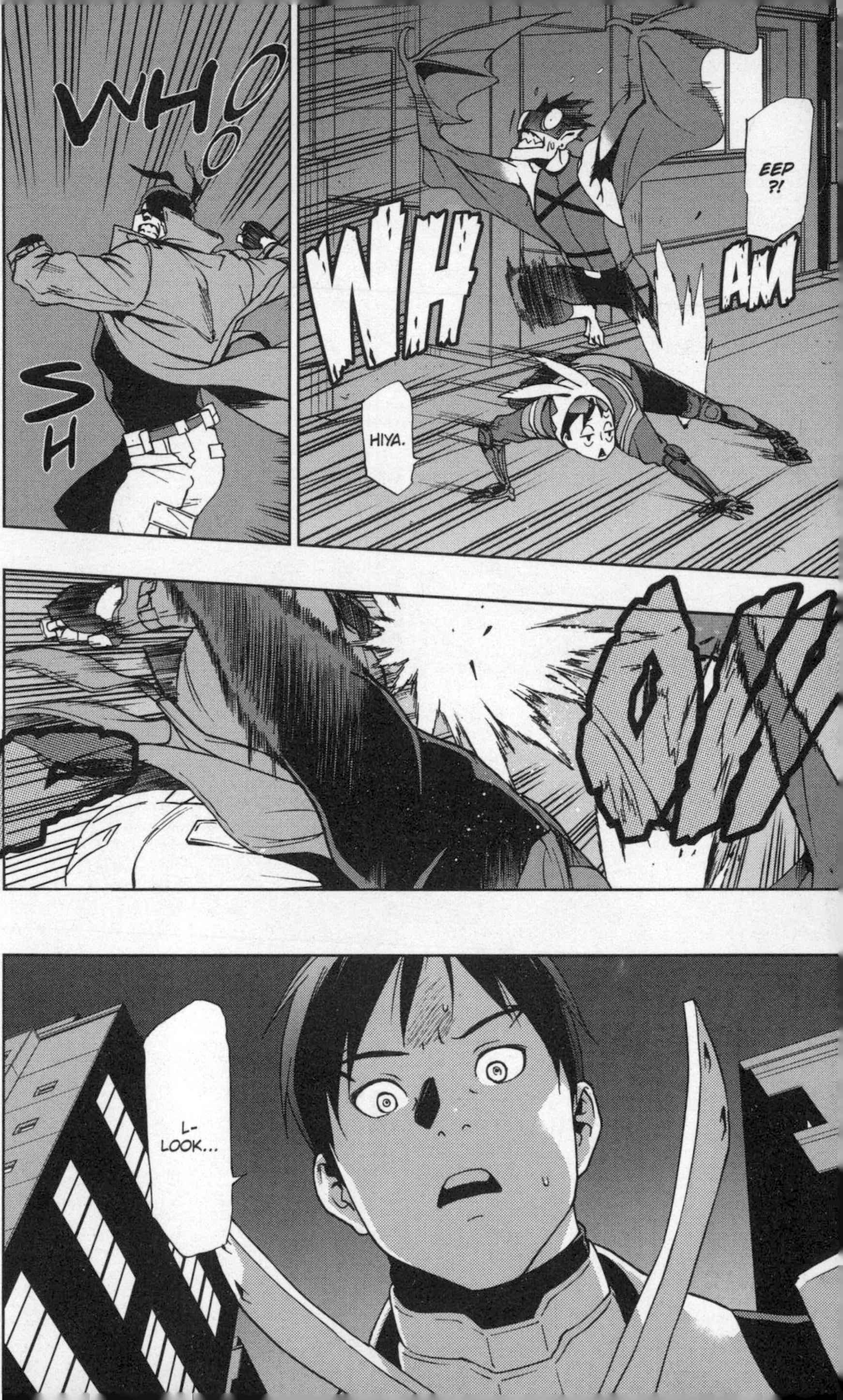
EEP ?!
WH AM
HIYA.
WHOO
SH
P OW
L- LOOK...

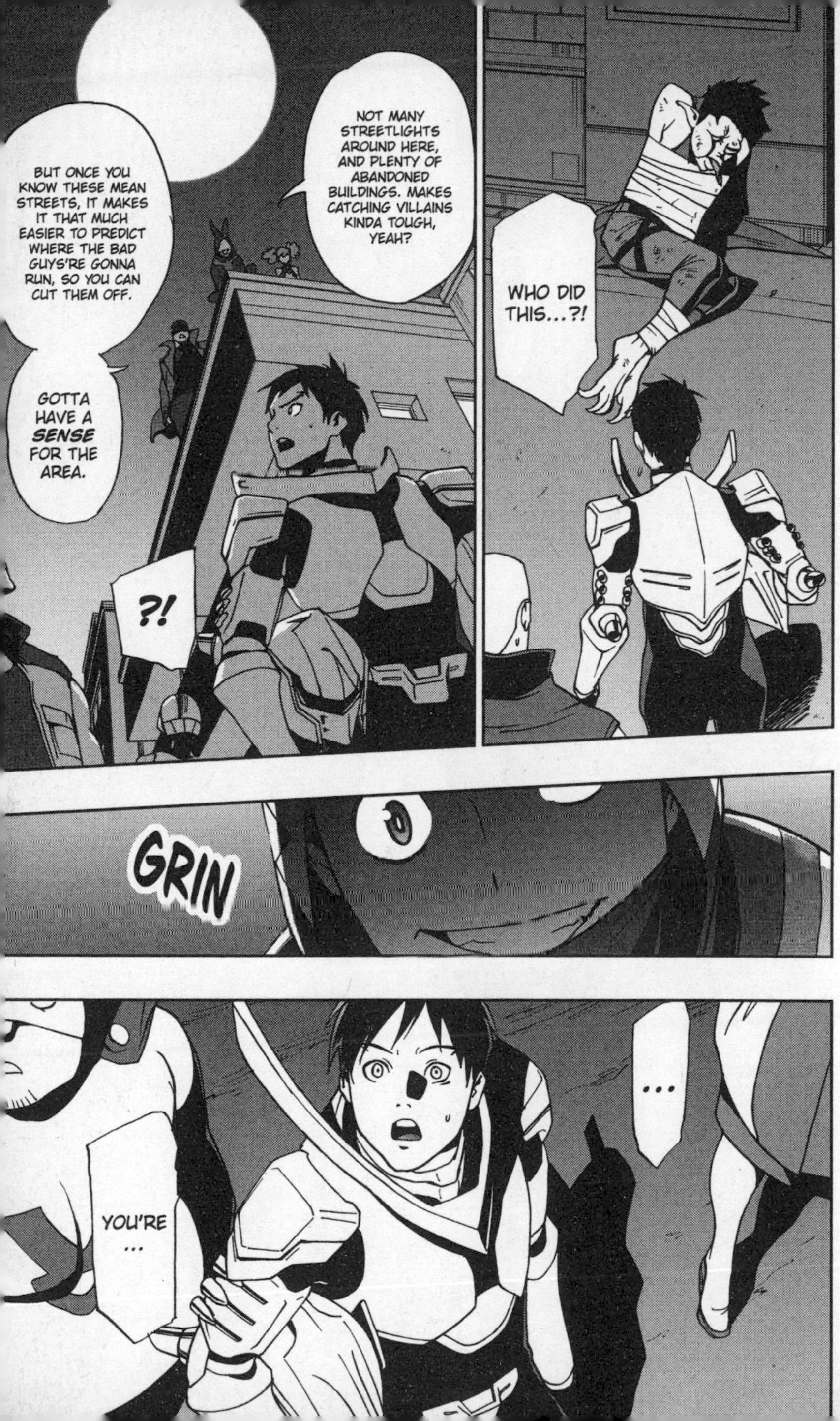
WHO DID THIS...?!
NOT MANY STREETLIGHTS AROUND HERE, AND PLENTY OF ABANDONED BUILDINGS. MAKES CATCHING VILLAINS KINDA TOUGH, YEAH?
BUT ONCE YOU KNOW THESE MEAN STREETS, IT MAKES IT THAT MUCH EASIER TO PREDICT WHERE THE BAD GUYS'RE GONNA RUN, SO YOU CAN CUT THEM OFF.
GOTTA HAVE A SENSE FOR THE AREA.
?!
GRIN
...
YOU'RE ...

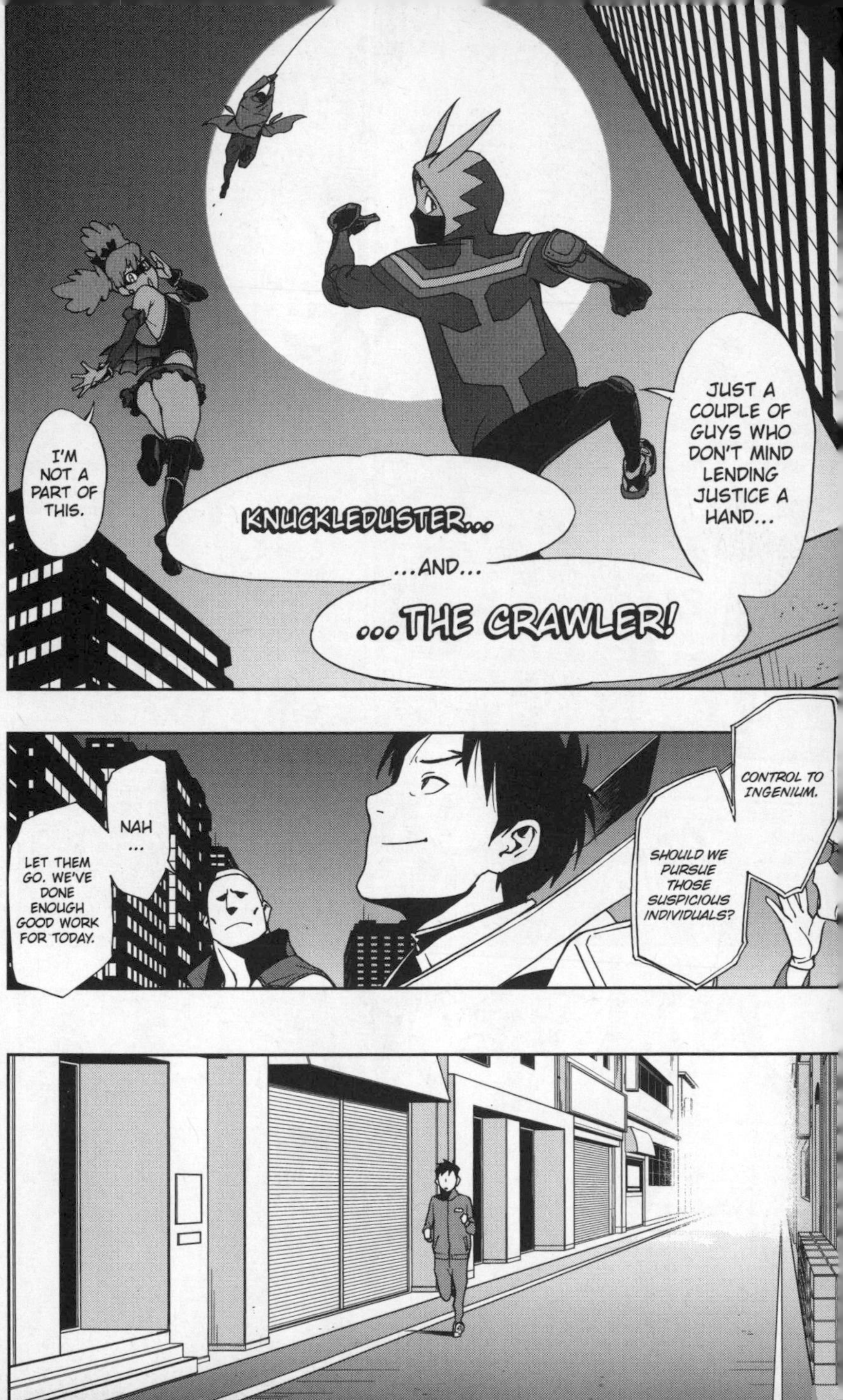
JUST A COUPLE OF GUYS WHO DON'T MIND LENDING JUSTICE A HAND...
KNUCKLEDUSTER...
...AND...
...THE CRAWLER!
I'M NOT A PART OF THIS.
CONTROL TO INGENIUM.
SHOULD WE PURSUE THOSE SUSPICIOUS INDIVIDUALS?
NAH...
LET THEM GO. WE'VE DONE ENOUGH GOOD WORK FOR TODAY.

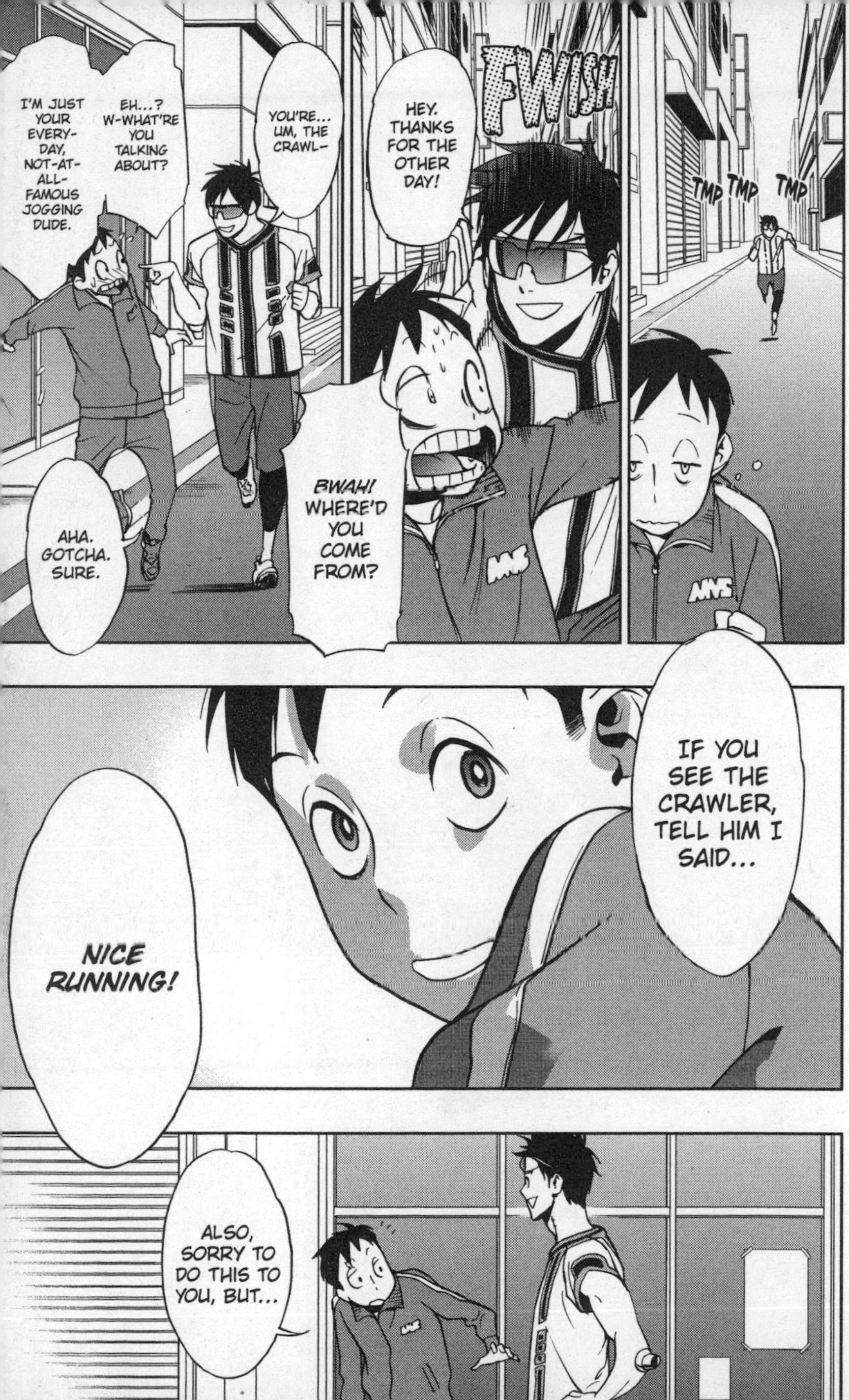

TMP TMP TMP
FWISH
HEY. THANKS FOR THE OTHER DAY!
BWAH! WHERE'D YOU COME FROM?
YOU'RE... UM, THE CRAWL-
EH...? W-WHAT'RE YOU TALKING ABOUT?
I'M JUST YOUR EVERY-DAY, NOT-AT-ALL-FAMOUS JOGGING DUDE.
AHA. GOTCHA. SURE.
IF YOU SEE THE CRAWLER, TELL HIM I SAID...
NICE RUNNING!
ALSO, SORRY TO DO THIS TO YOU, BUT...

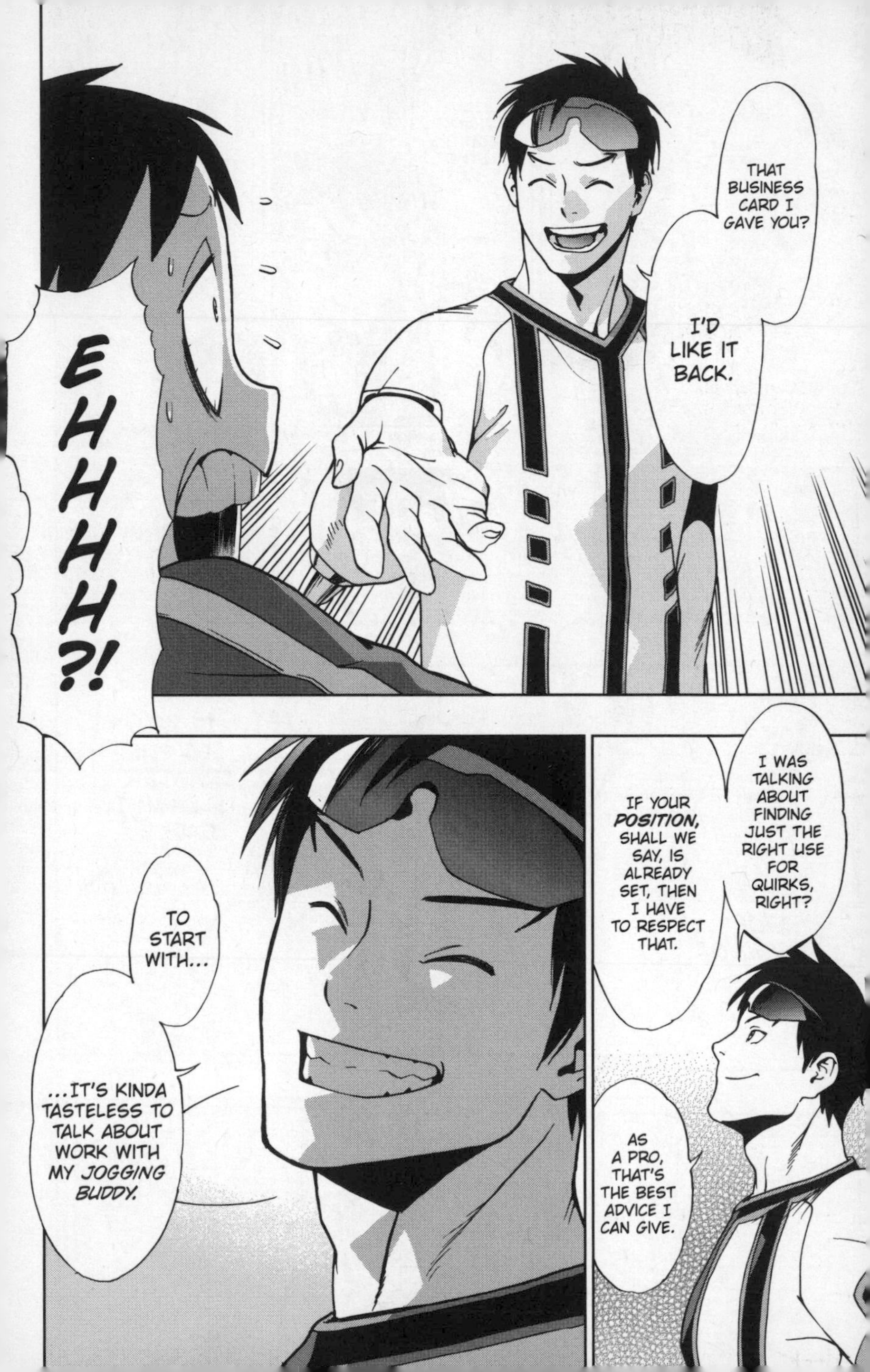
THAT BUSINESS CARD I GAVE YOU?
I'D LIKE IT BACK.
EHHHH?!
I WAS TALKING ABOUT FINDING JUST THE RIGHT USE FOR QUIRKS, RIGHT?
IF YOUR *POSITION*, SHALL WE SAY, IS ALREADY SET, THEN I HAVE TO RESPECT THAT.
AS A PRO, THAT'S THE BEST ADVICE I CAN GIVE.
TO START WITH...
...IT'S KINDA TASTELESS TO TALK ABOUT WORK WITH MY *JOGGING BUDDY.*

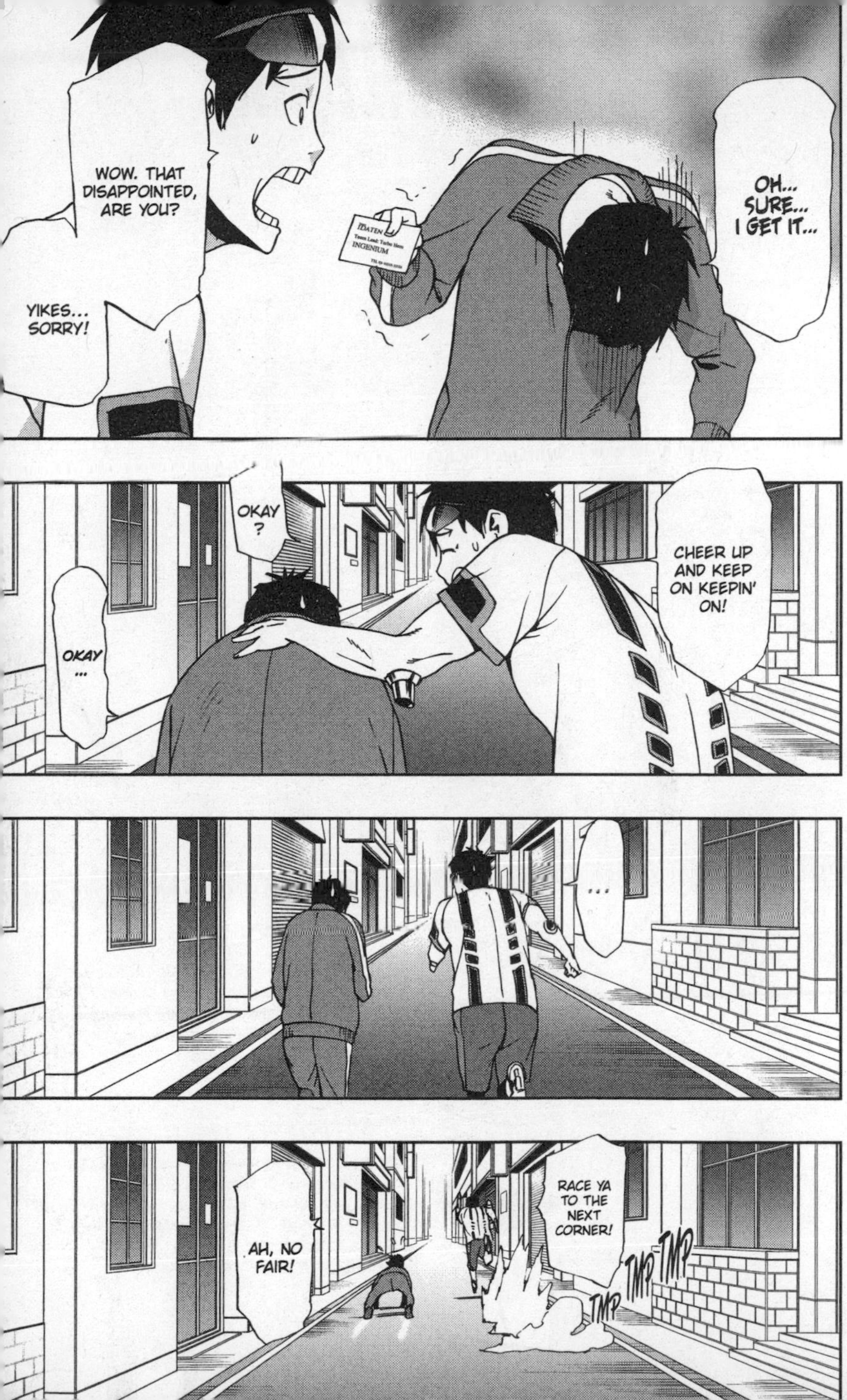
OH... SURE... I GET IT...
IDATEN
INGENIUM
WOW. THAT DISAPPOINTED, ARE YOU?
YIKES... SORRY!
CHEER UP AND KEEP ON KEEPIN' ON!
OKAY?
OKAY...
...
RACE YA TO THE NEXT CORNER!
TMP TMP TMP
AH, NO FAIR!

BAT VILLAIN

THE ROUGH DESIGN

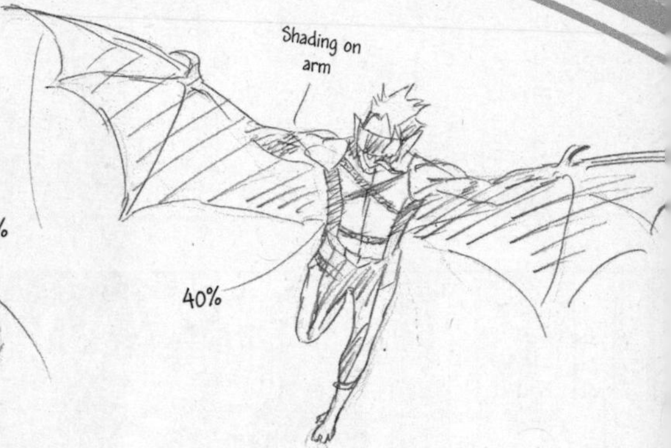
Shading on
arm
40%

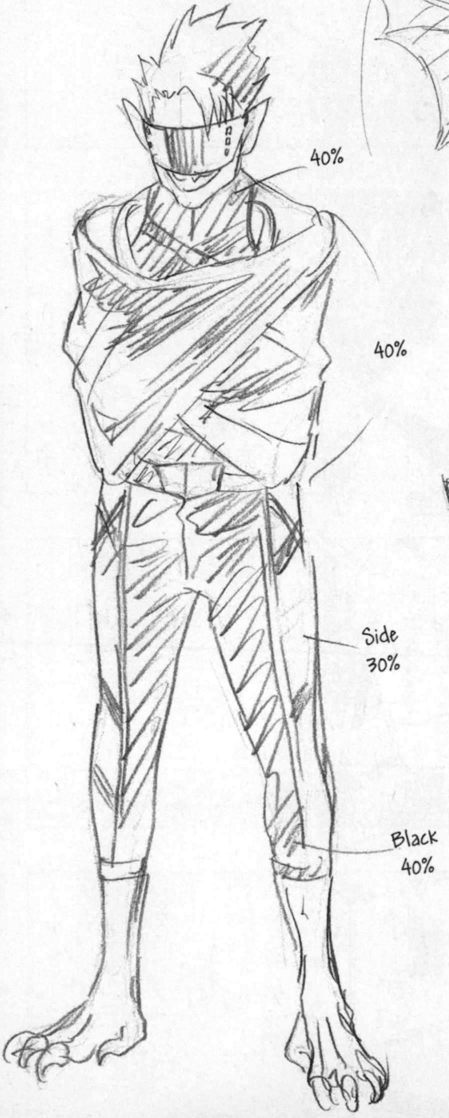
40%
40%
Side
30%
Black
40%

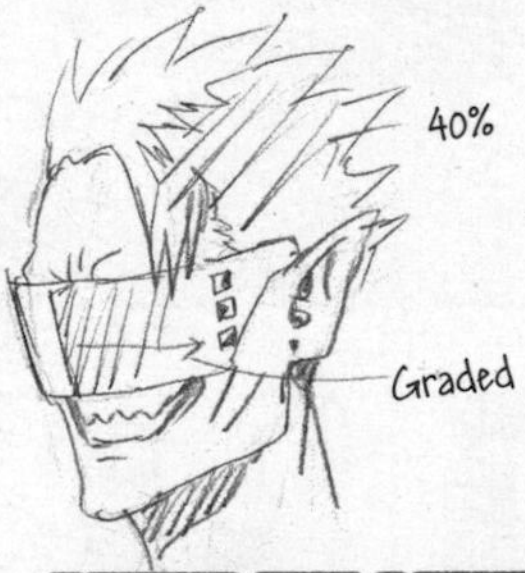
40%
Graded

BEHIND THE SCENES

What would a fight involving the Turbo Hero look like?" ➔ "Some sort of hot pursuit?" ➔ "He's got to run down and tackle a villain who's running away..." ➔ "Oh, so it's like *Eyeshield 21*!" That's the train of thought that led to this man-bat. Devil Bats!

—Furuhashi

I wavered between sticking more closely to the inspiration or getting away from that. I sort of lost track and wound up moving away from it in the end (LOL). In hindsight, I subconsciously took inspiration from [redacted] with the whole bat design...!

—Betten

★ See page 202 for more on Ingenium.

Ep. 7.5 - Appearance Matters

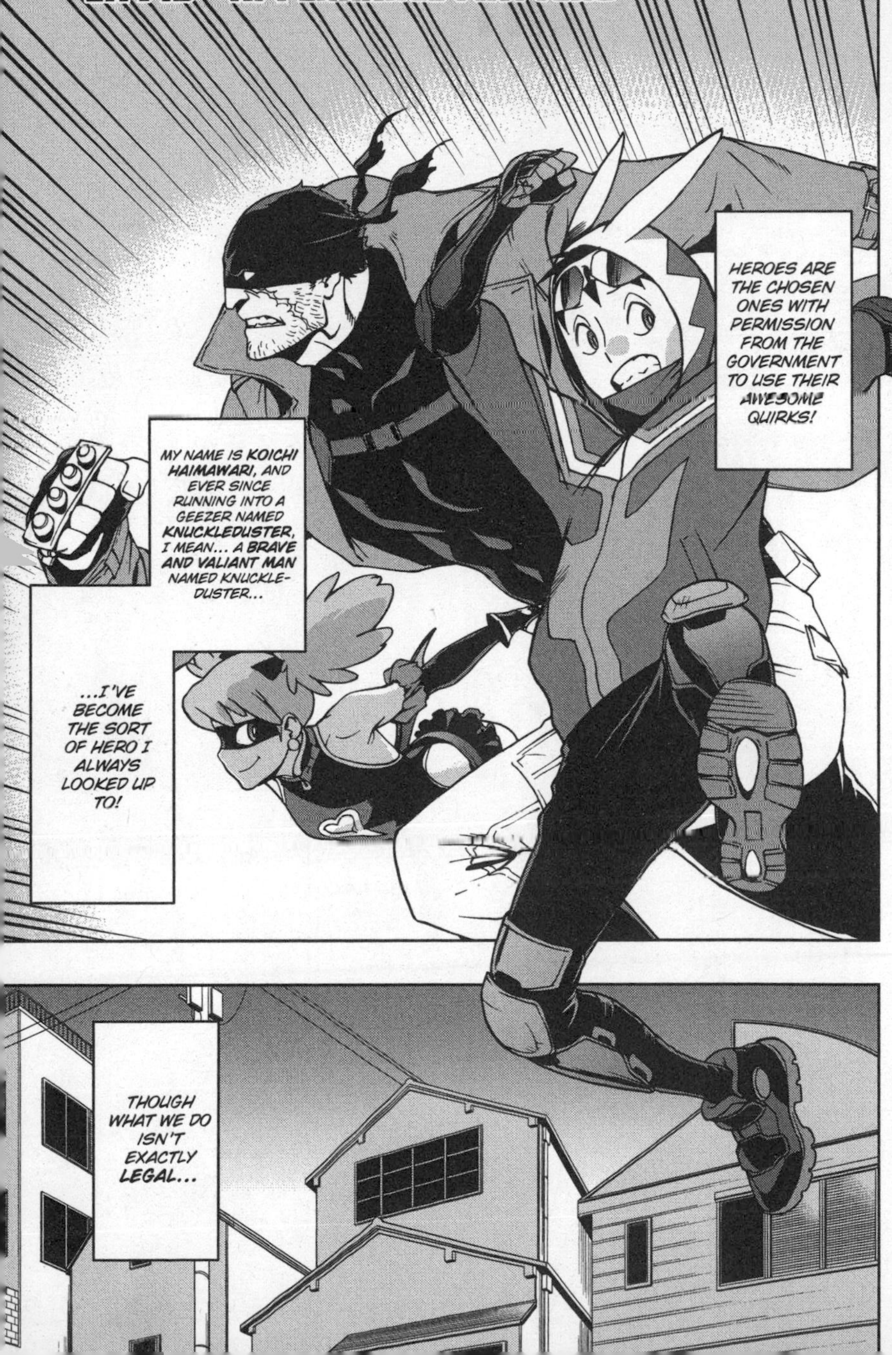
HEROES ARE THE CHOSEN ONES WITH PERMISSION FROM THE GOVERNMENT TO USE THEIR AWESOME QUIRKS!
MY NAME IS KOICHI HAIMAWARI, AND EVER SINCE RUNNING INTO A GEEZER NAMED KNUCKLEDUSTER, I MEAN... A BRAVE AND VALIANT MAN NAMED KNUCKLE-DUSTER...
...I'VE BECOME THE SORT OF HERO I ALWAYS LOOKED UP TO!
THOUGH WHAT WE DO ISN'T EXACTLY LEGAL...

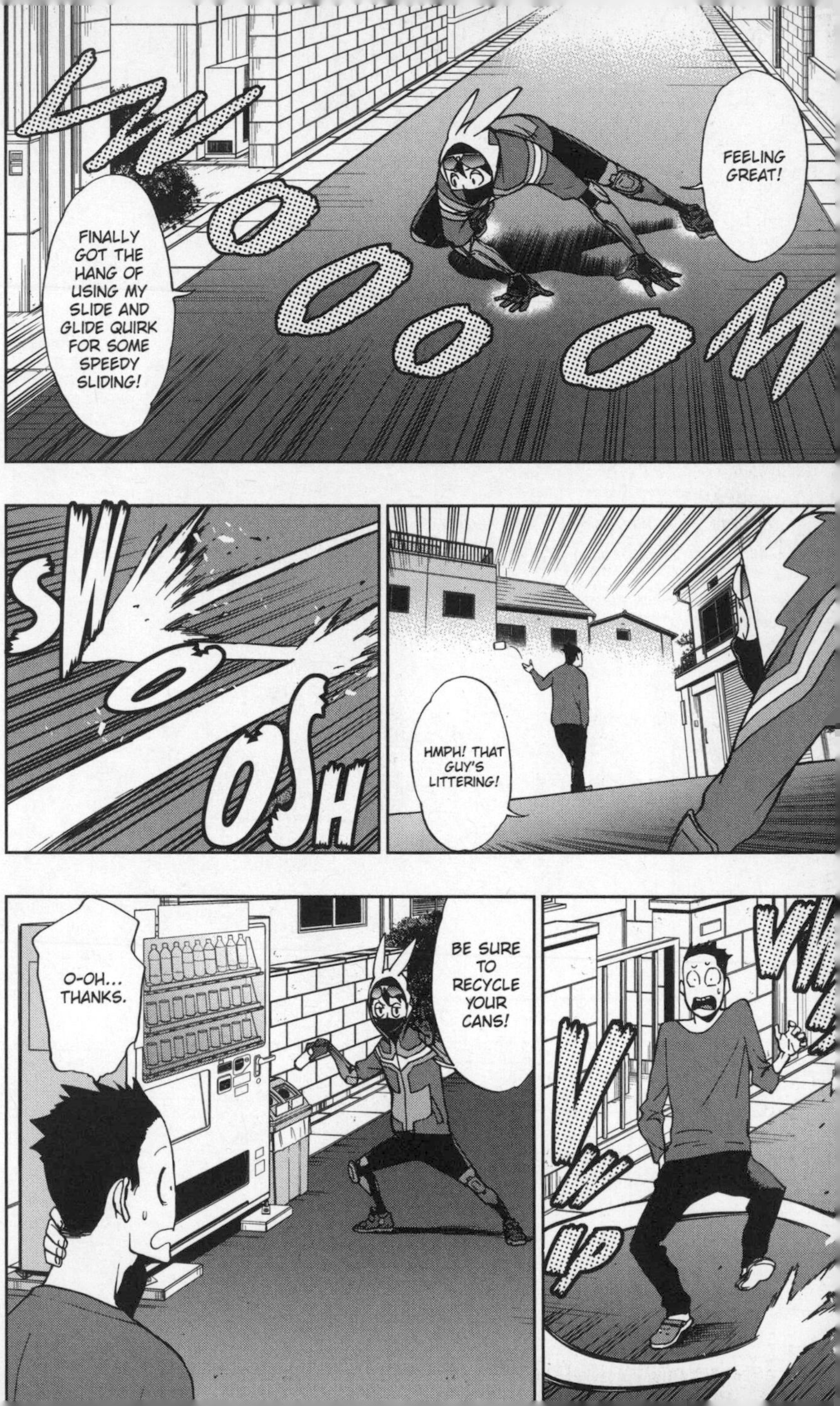
FEELING GREAT!
WHOOOOOM
FINALLY GOT THE HANG OF USING MY SLIDE AND GLIDE QUIRK FOR SOME SPEEDY SLIDING!
HMPH! THAT GUY'S LITTERING!
SWOOSH
WHIP
BE SURE TO RECYCLE YOUR CANS!
O-OH... THANKS.

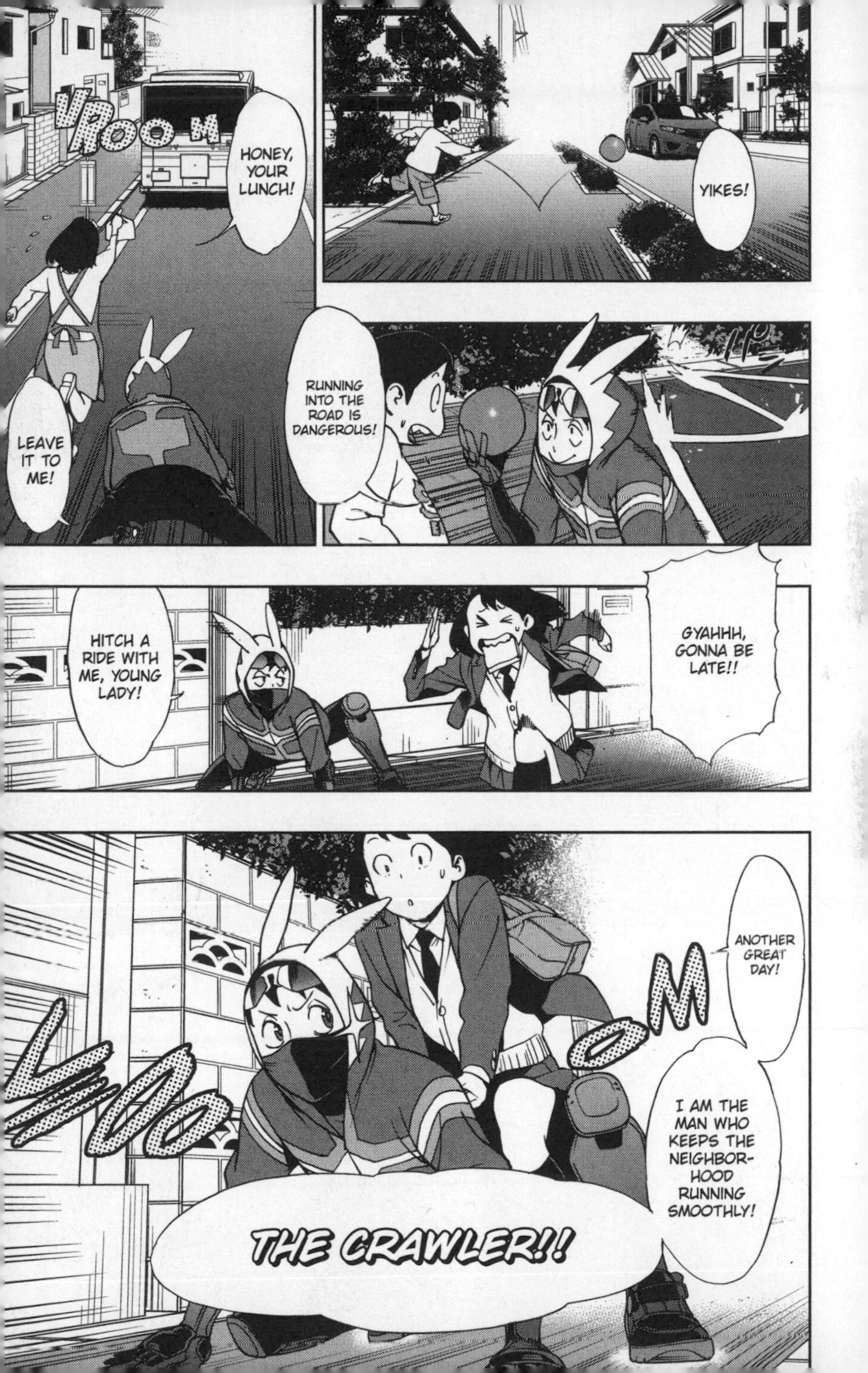
YIKES!
RUNNING INTO THE ROAD IS DANGEROUS!
VROOOM
HONEY, YOUR LUNCH!
LEAVE IT TO ME!
GYAHHH, GONNA BE LATE!!
HITCH A RIDE WITH ME, YOUNG LADY!
ANOTHER GREAT DAY!
I AM THE MAN WHO KEEPS THE NEIGHBORHOOD RUNNING SMOOTHLY!
VROOOM
THE CRAWLER!!

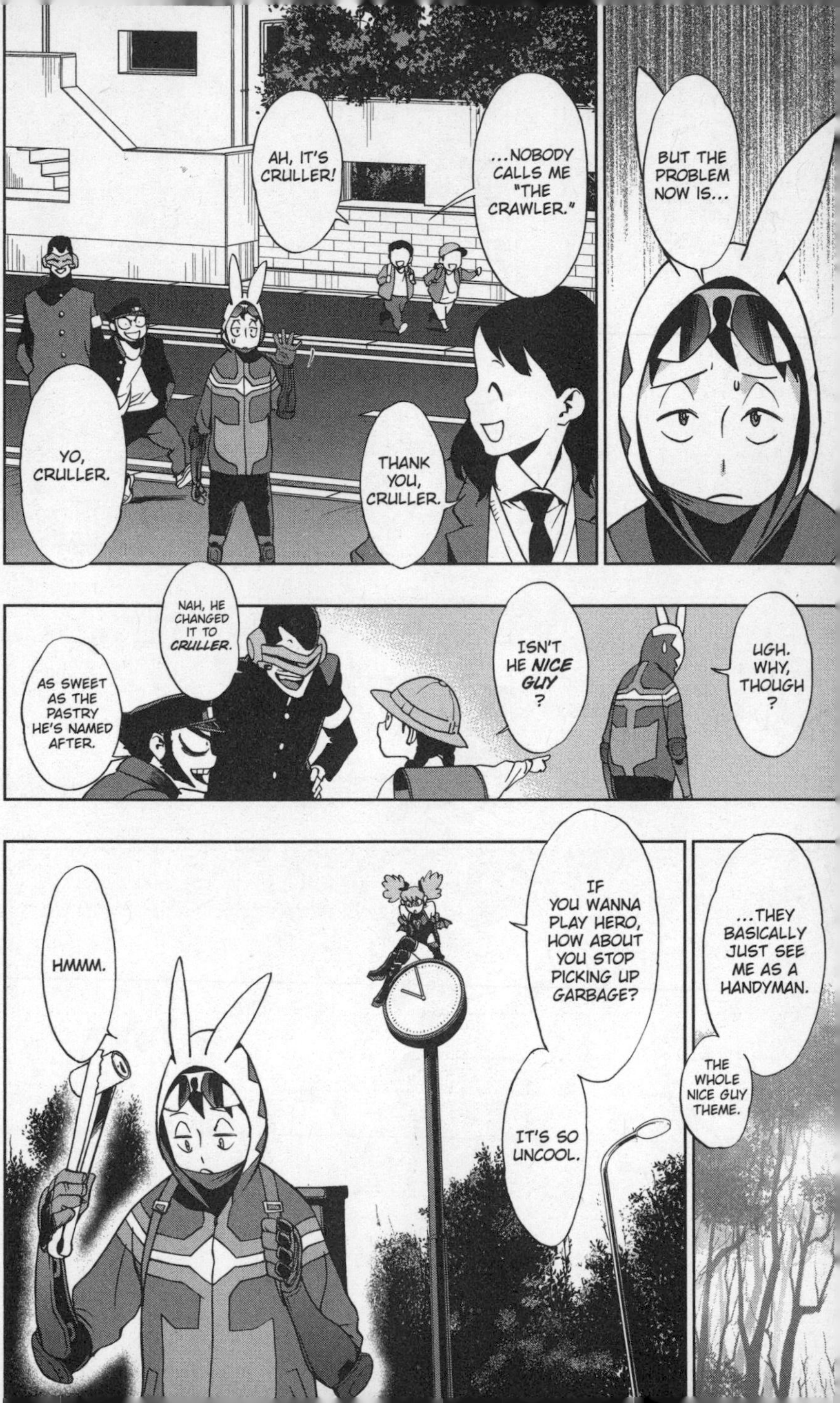
BUT THE PROBLEM NOW IS...
...NOBODY CALLS ME "THE CRAWLER."
AH, IT'S CRULLER!
THANK YOU, CRULLER.
YO, CRULLER.
UGH. WHY, THOUGH?
ISN'T HE ***NICE GUY***?
NAH, HE CHANGED IT TO ***CRULLER***.
AS SWEET AS THE PASTRY HE'S NAMED AFTER.
...THEY BASICALLY JUST SEE ME AS A HANDYMAN.
THE WHOLE NICE GUY THEME.
IF YOU WANNA PLAY HERO, HOW ABOUT YOU STOP PICKING UP GARBAGE?
IT'S SO UNCOOL.
HMMM.

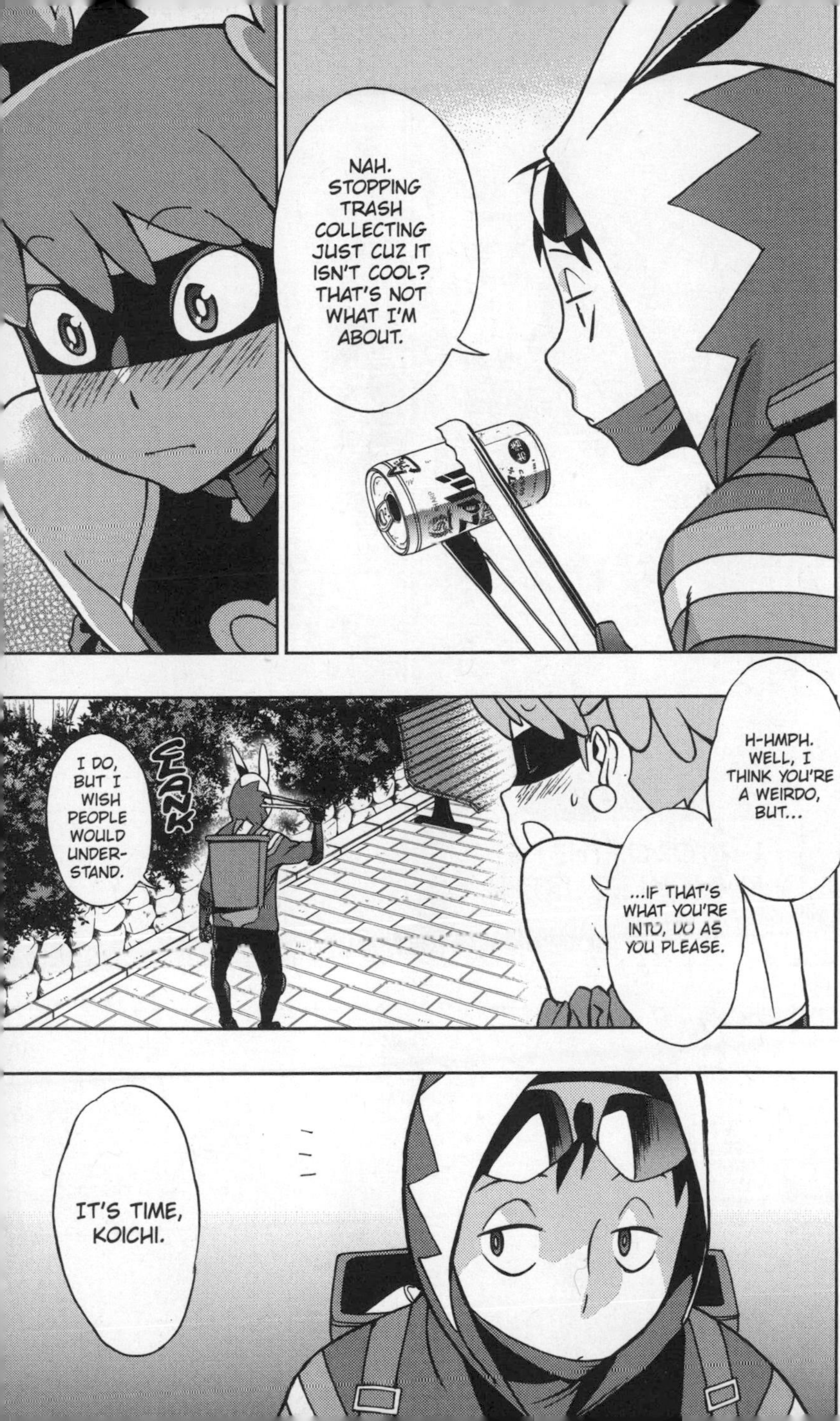
NAH. STOPPING TRASH COLLECTING JUST CUZ IT ISN'T COOL? THAT'S NOT WHAT I'M ABOUT.
H-HMPH. WELL, I THINK YOU'RE A WEIRDO, BUT...
...IF THAT'S WHAT YOU'RE INTO, DO AS YOU PLEASE.
I DO, BUT I WISH PEOPLE WOULD UNDER-STAND.
IT'S TIME, KOICHI.

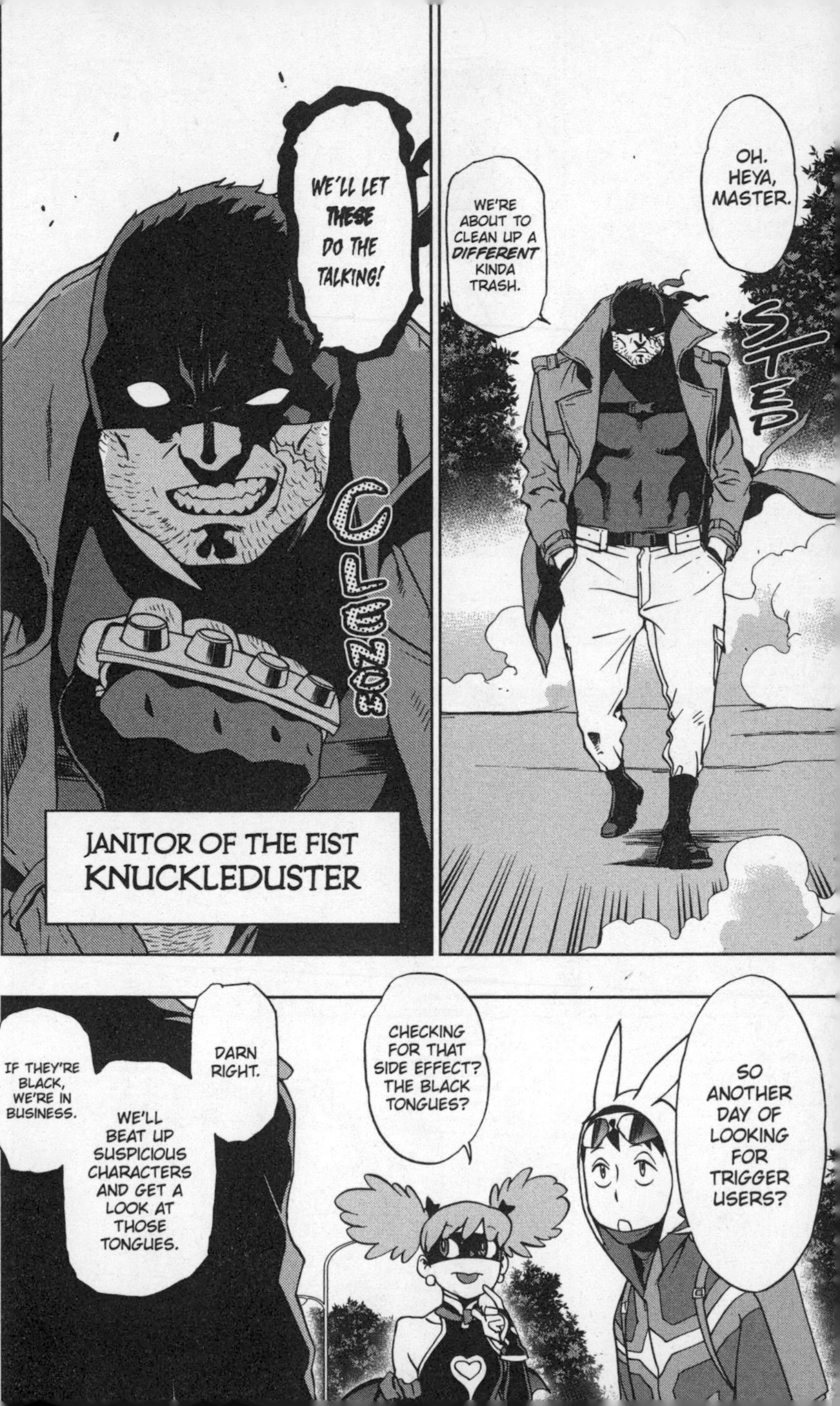
OH. HEYA, MASTER.
WE'RE ABOUT TO CLEAN UP A DIFFERENT KINDA TRASH.
STEP
WE'LL LET THESE DO THE TALKING!
CLENCH
JANITOR OF THE FIST KNUCKLEDUSTER
SO ANOTHER DAY OF LOOKING FOR TRIGGER USERS?
CHECKING FOR THAT SIDE EFFECT? THE BLACK TONGUES?
DARN RIGHT.
IF THEY'RE BLACK, WE'RE IN BUSINESS.
WE'LL BEAT UP SUSPICIOUS CHARACTERS AND GET A LOOK AT THOSE TONGUES.

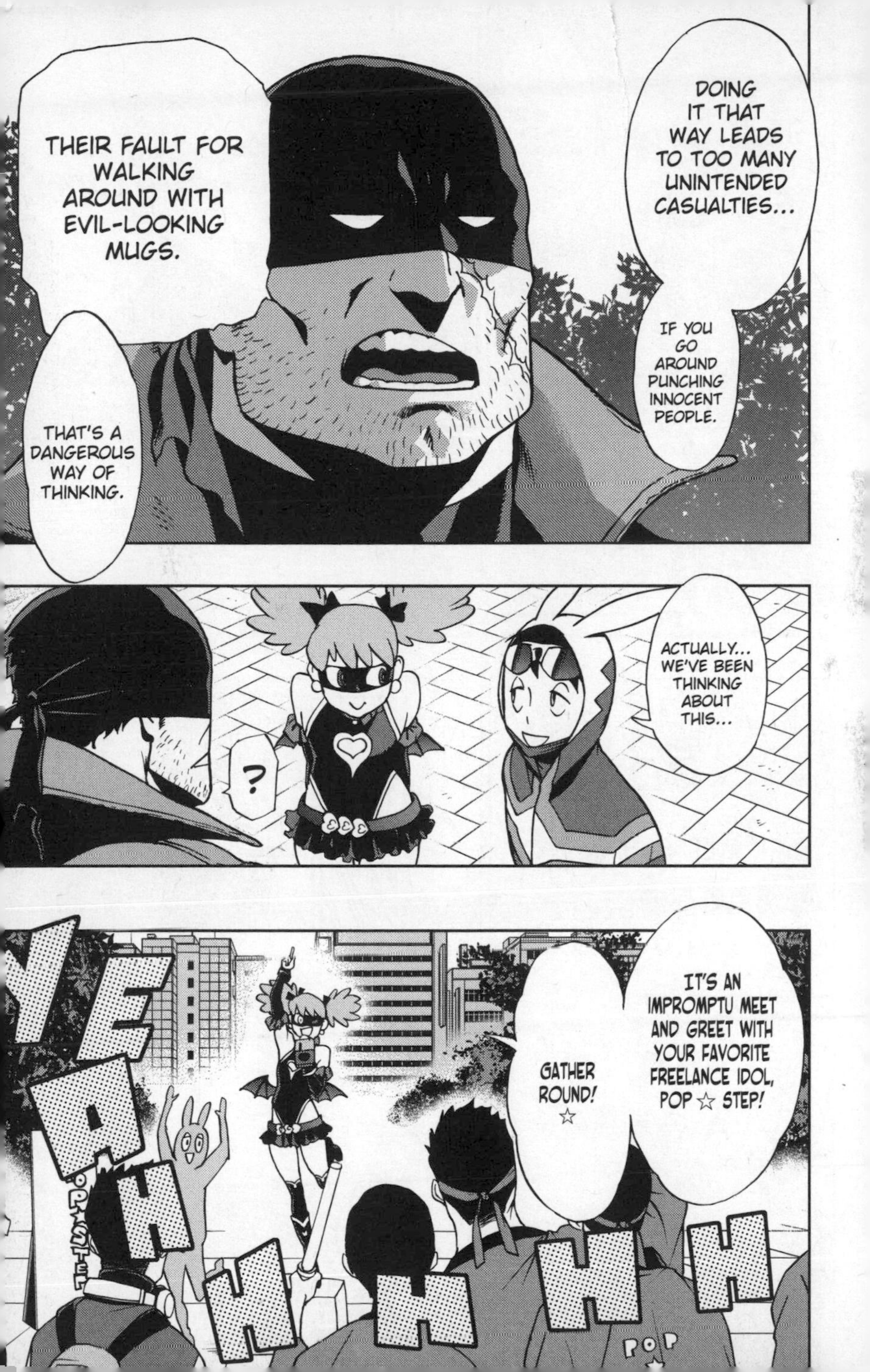
DOING IT THAT WAY LEADS TO TOO MANY UNINTENDED CASUALTIES...
IF YOU GO AROUND PUNCHING INNOCENT PEOPLE.
THEIR FAULT FOR WALKING AROUND WITH EVIL-LOOKING MUGS.
THAT'S A DANGEROUS WAY OF THINKING.
ACTUALLY... WE'VE BEEN THINKING ABOUT THIS...
?
IT'S AN IMPROMPTU MEET AND GREET WITH YOUR FAVORITE FREELANCE IDOL, POP☆STEP!
GATHER ROUND! ☆
YEAHHHHHHH
POP☆STEP
POP

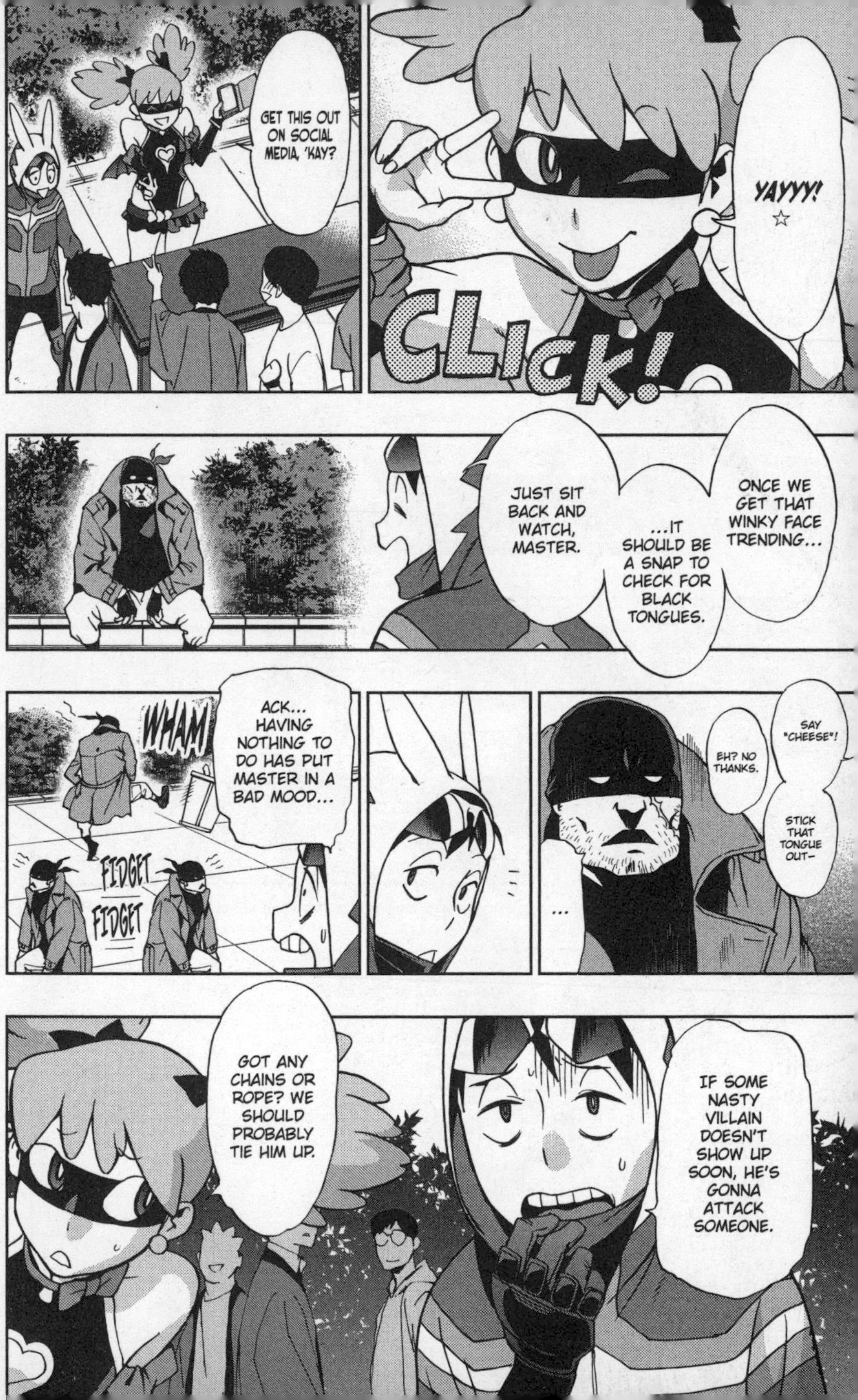
YAYYY! ☆
CLICK!
GET THIS OUT ON SOCIAL MEDIA, 'KAY?
ONCE WE GET THAT WINKY FACE TRENDING...
...IT SHOULD BE A SNAP TO CHECK FOR BLACK TONGUES.
JUST SIT BACK AND WATCH, MASTER.
SAY "CHEESE"!
EH? NO THANKS.
STICK THAT TONGUE OUT-
...
ACK... HAVING NOTHING TO DO HAS PUT MASTER IN A BAD MOOD...
WHAM
FIDGET FIDGET
IF SOME NASTY VILLAIN DOESN'T SHOW UP SOON, HE'S GONNA ATTACK SOMEONE.
GOT ANY CHAINS OR ROPE? WE SHOULD PROBABLY TIE HIM UP.

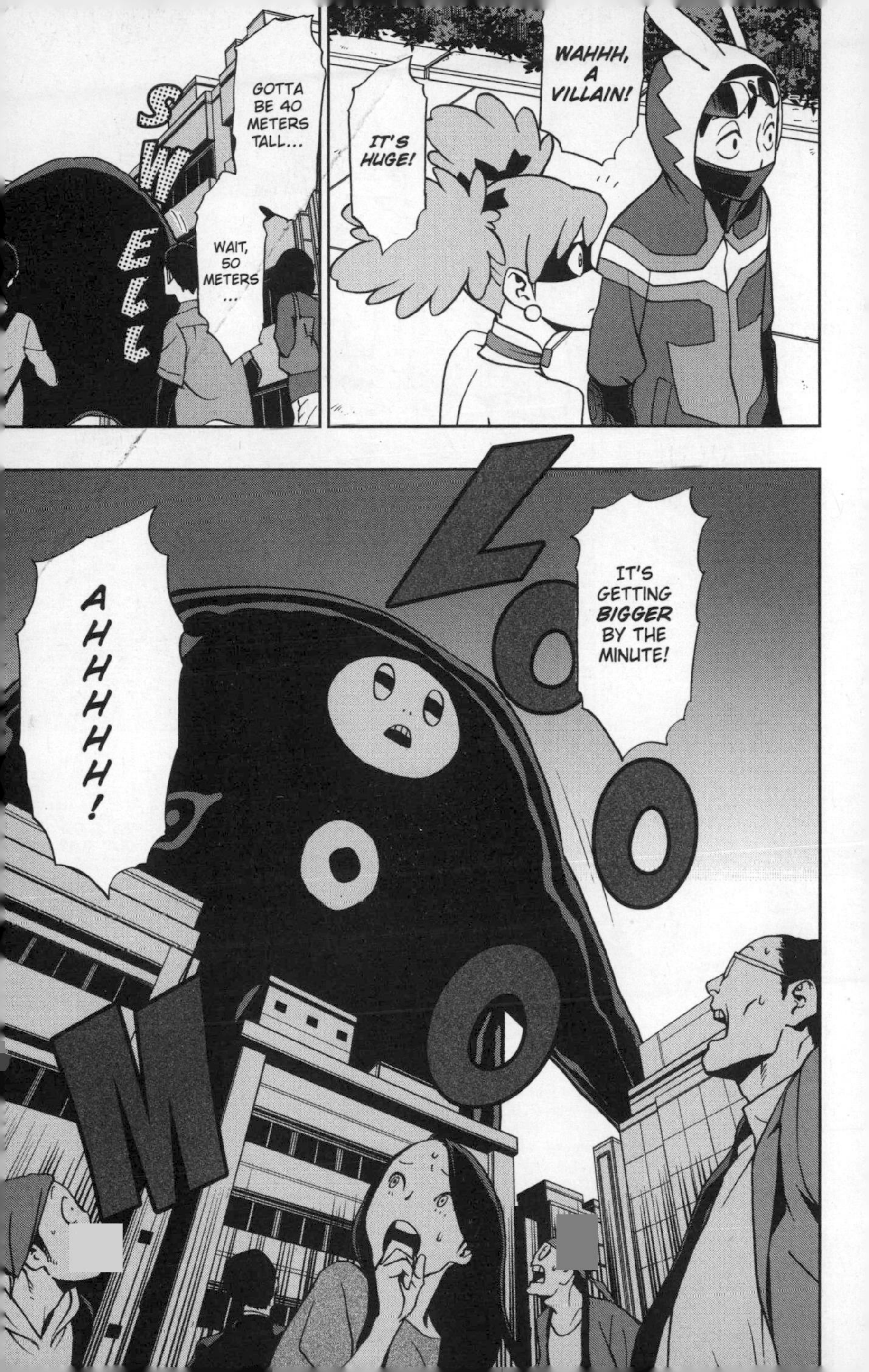
WAHHH, A VILLAIN!
IT'S HUGE!
SWELL
GOTTA BE 40 METERS TALL...
WAIT, 50 METERS ...
IT'S GETTING **BIGGER** BY THE MINUTE!
AHHHHHH!

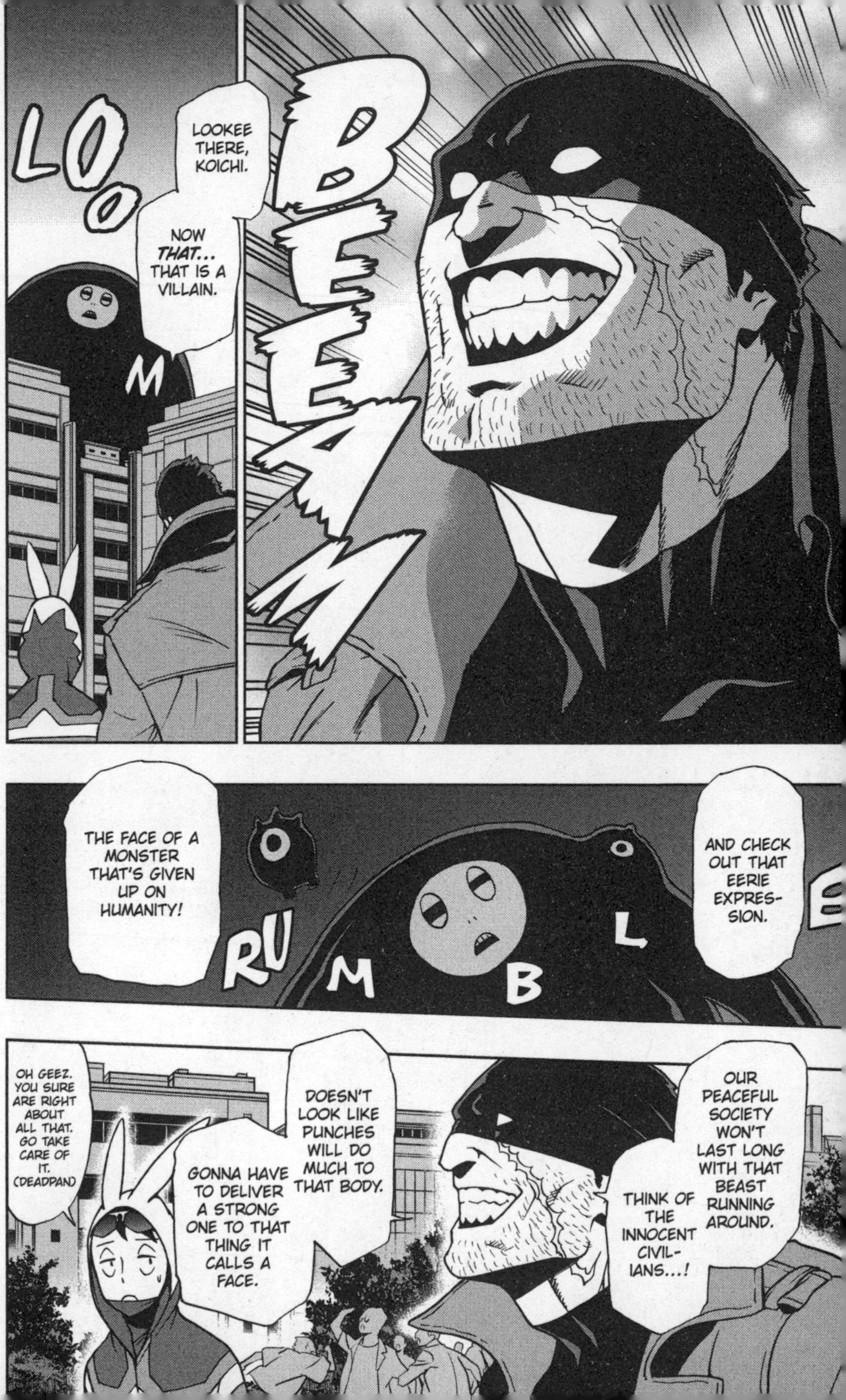
BEEAM
LOOOM
LOOKEE THERE, KOICHI.
NOW *THAT*... THAT IS A VILLAIN.
AND CHECK OUT THAT EERIE EXPRESSION.
THE FACE OF A MONSTER THAT'S GIVEN UP ON HUMANITY!
RUMBLE
OUR PEACEFUL SOCIETY WON'T LAST LONG WITH THAT BEAST RUNNING AROUND.
THINK OF THE INNOCENT CIVILIANS...!
DOESN'T LOOK LIKE PUNCHES WILL DO MUCH TO THAT BODY.
GONNA HAVE TO DELIVER A STRONG ONE TO THAT THING IT CALLS A FACE.
OH GEEZ. YOU SURE ARE RIGHT ABOUT ALL THAT. GO TAKE CARE OF IT. (DEADPAN)

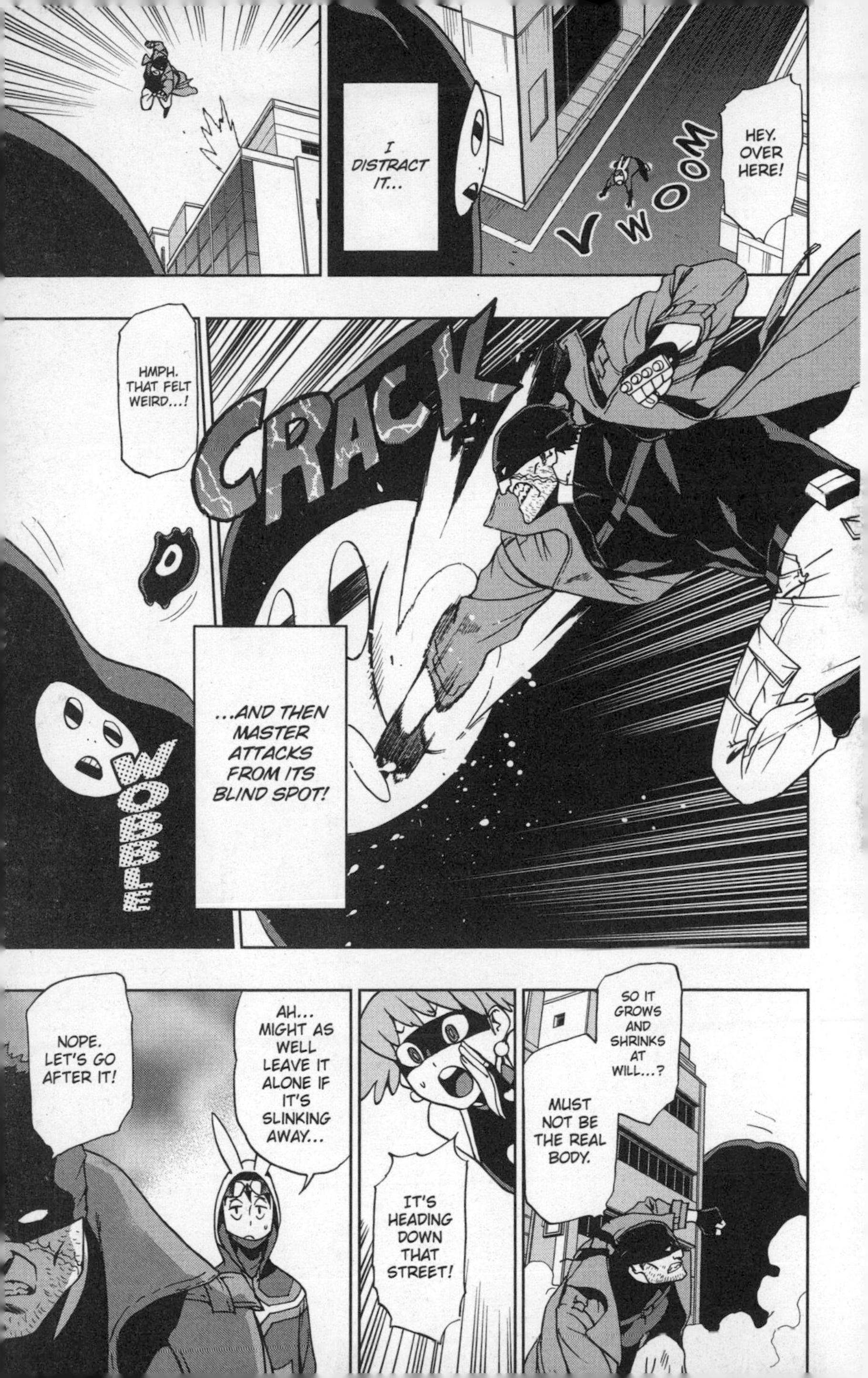
HEY. OVER HERE!
VWOOM
I DISTRACT IT...
CRACK
HMPH. THAT FELT WEIRD...!
...AND THEN MASTER ATTACKS FROM ITS BLIND SPOT!
WOBBLE
SO IT GROWS AND SHRINKS AT WILL...?
MUST NOT BE THE REAL BODY.
IT'S HEADING DOWN THAT STREET!
AH... MIGHT AS WELL LEAVE IT ALONE IF IT'S SLINKING AWAY...
NOPE. LET'S GO AFTER IT!

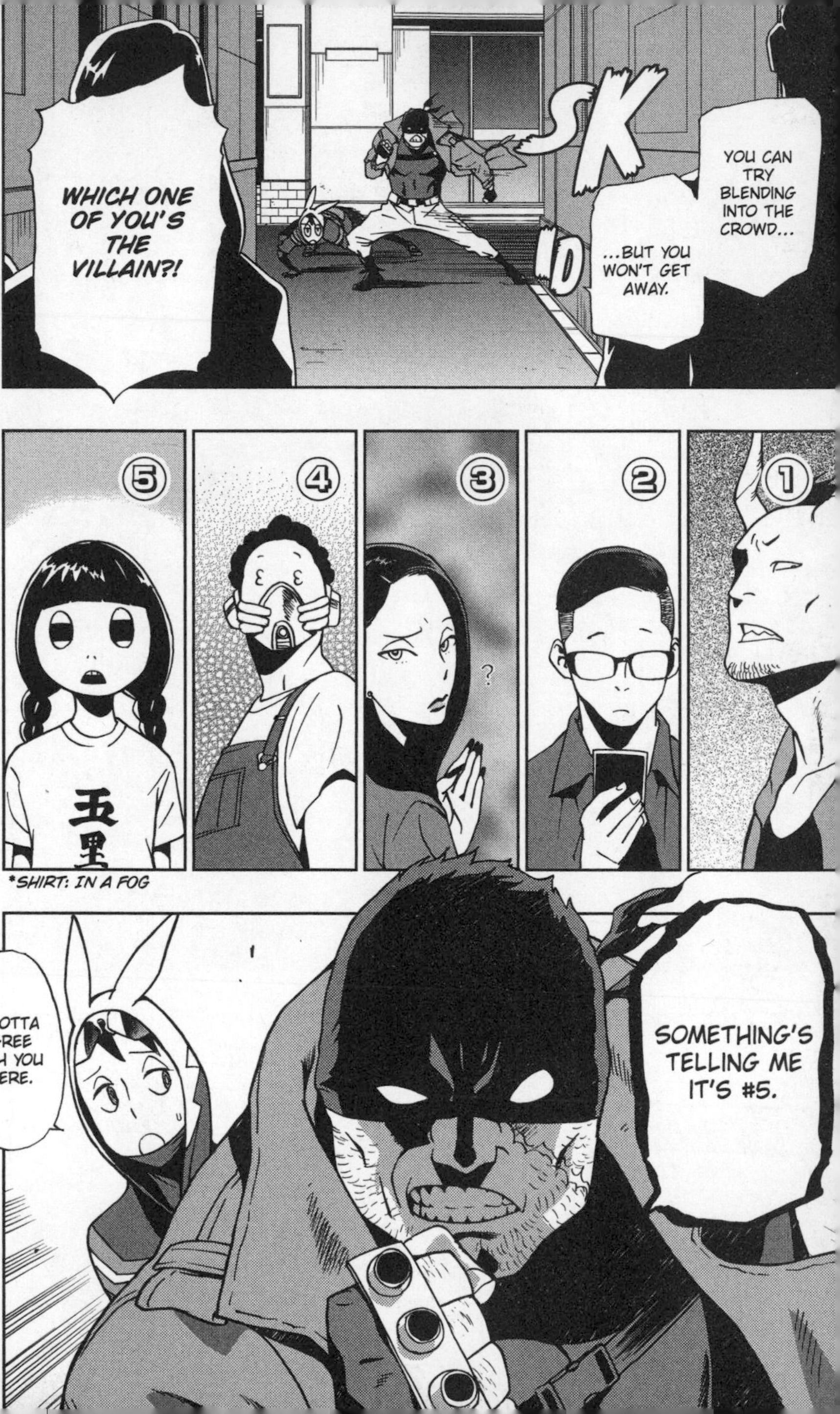
SKID
YOU CAN TRY BLENDING INTO THE CROWD...
...BUT YOU WON'T GET AWAY.
WHICH ONE OF YOU'S THE VILLAIN?!
1
2
3
?
4
5
SOMETHING'S TELLING ME IT'S #5.
I GOTTA AGREE WITH YOU THERE.
*SHIRT: IN A FOG

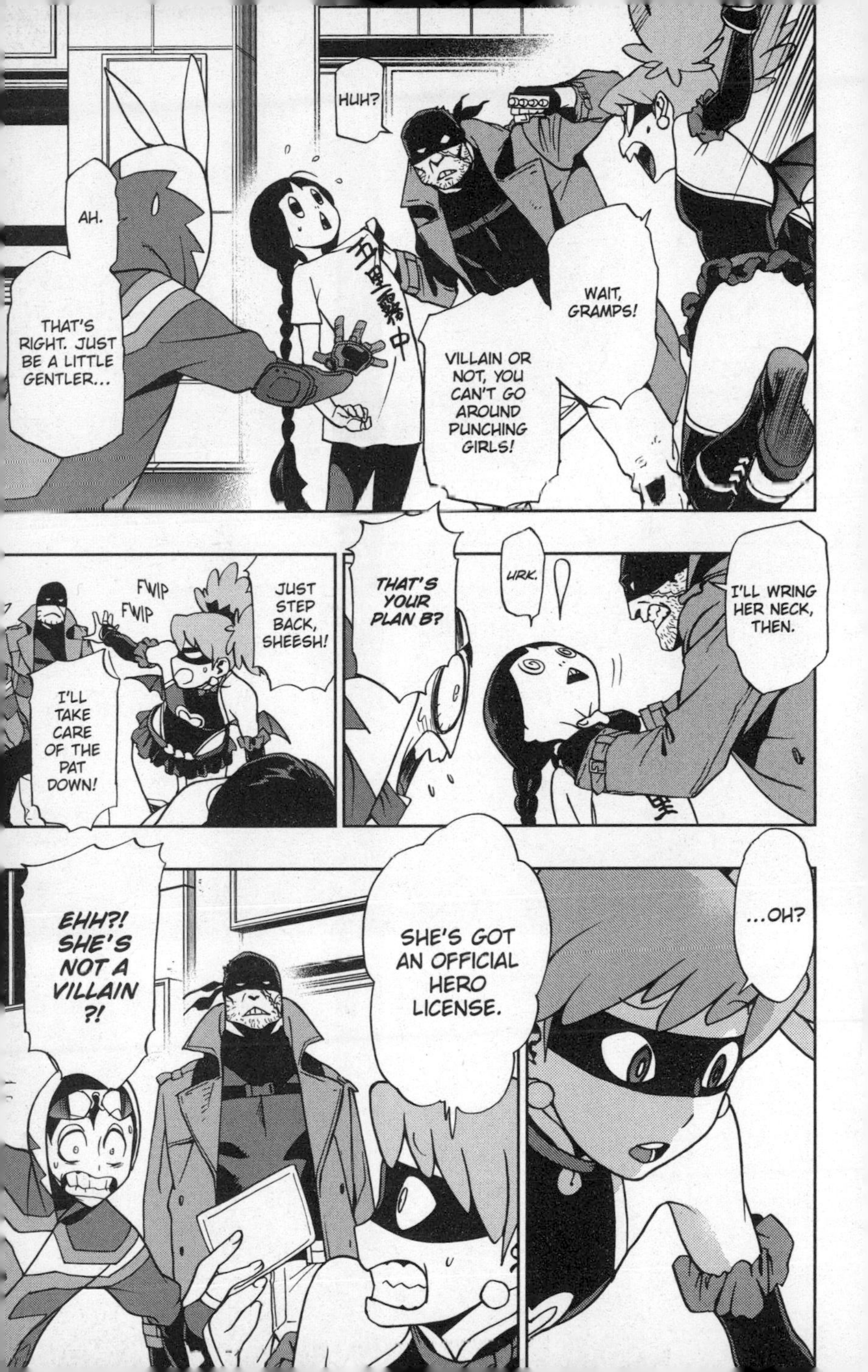
WAIT, GRAMPS!
VILLAIN OR NOT, YOU CAN'T GO AROUND PUNCHING GIRLS!
HUH?
五里霧中
AH.
THAT'S RIGHT. JUST BE A LITTLE GENTLER...
I'LL WRING HER NECK, THEN.
URK.
THAT'S YOUR PLAN B?
JUST STEP BACK, SHEESH!
FWIP
FWIP
I'LL TAKE CARE OF THE PAT DOWN!
...OH?
SHE'S GOT AN OFFICIAL HERO LICENSE.
EHH?! SHE'S NOT A VILLAIN?!

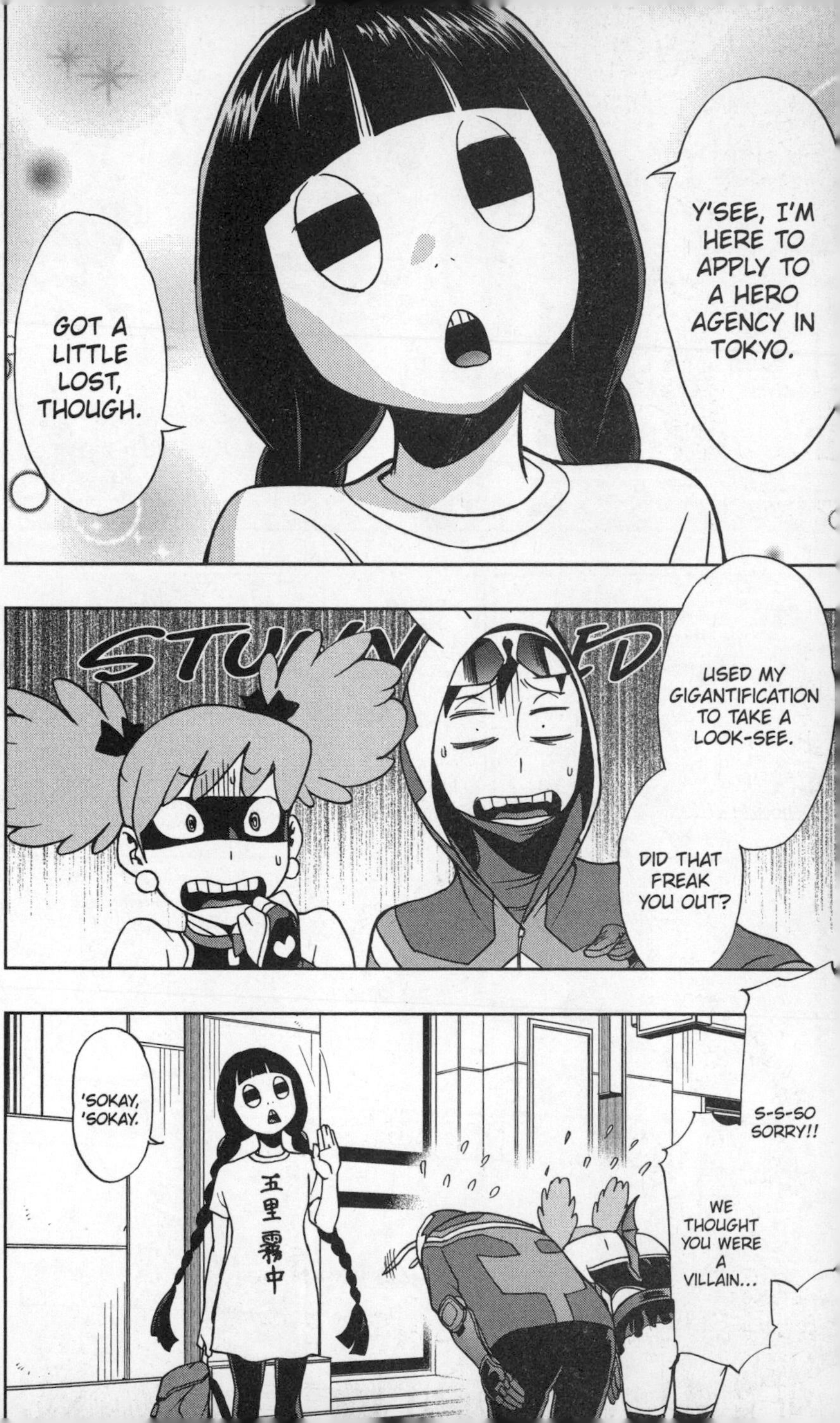
Y'SEE, I'M HERE TO APPLY TO A HERO AGENCY IN TOKYO.
GOT A LITTLE LOST, THOUGH.
USED MY GIGANTIFICATION TO TAKE A LOOK-SEE.
DID THAT FREAK YOU OUT?
S-S-SO SORRY!!
WE THOUGHT YOU WERE A VILLAIN...
'SOKAY, 'SOKAY.
五里霧中

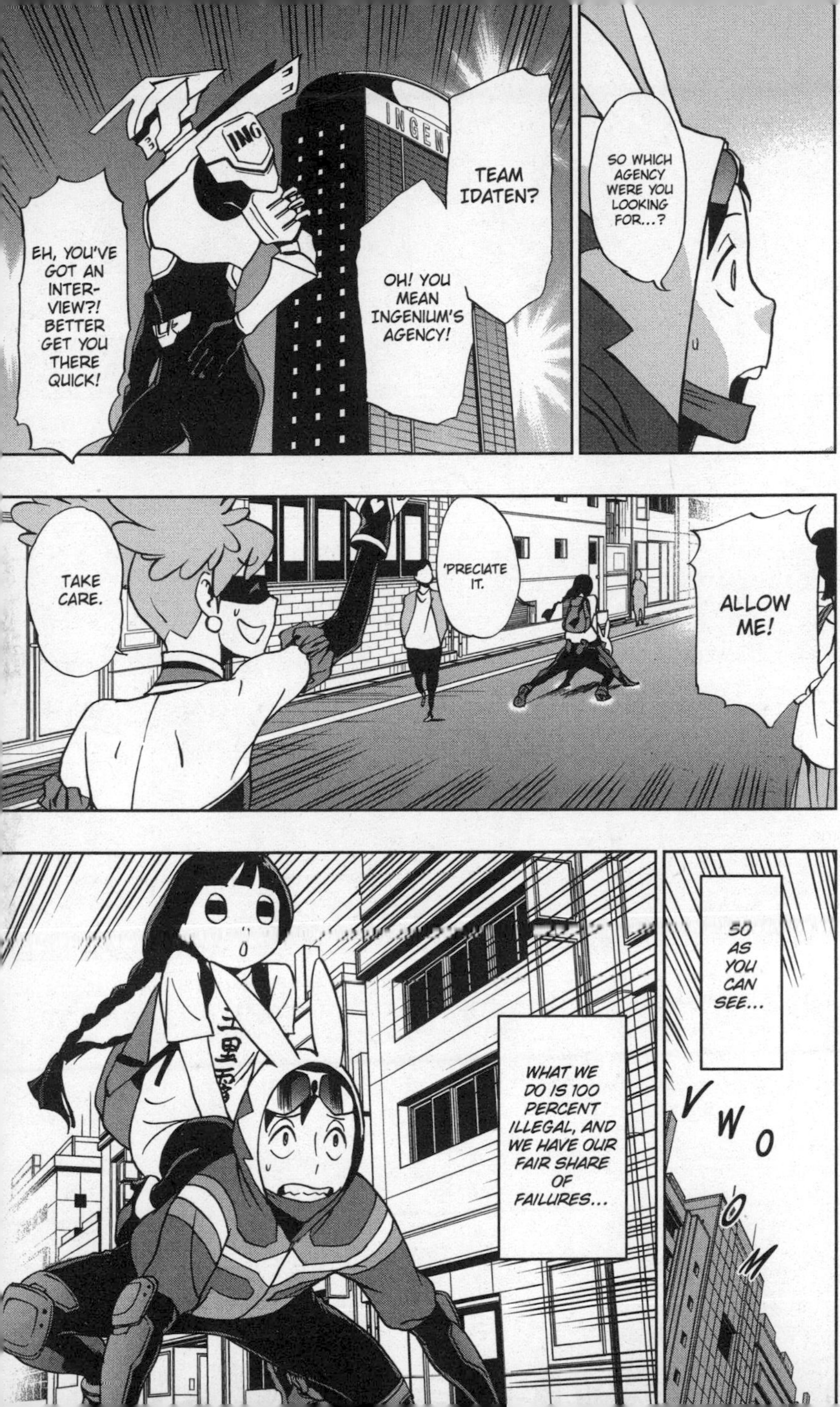
SO WHICH AGENCY WERE YOU LOOKING FOR...?
TEAM IDATEN?
OH! YOU MEAN INGENIUM'S AGENCY!
EH, YOU'VE GOT AN INTER-VIEW?! BETTER GET YOU THERE QUICK!
ALLOW ME!
'PRECIATE IT.
TAKE CARE.
SO AS YOU CAN SEE...
VWOOOM
WHAT WE DO IS 100 PERCENT ILLEGAL, AND WE HAVE OUR FAIR SHARE OF FAILURES...

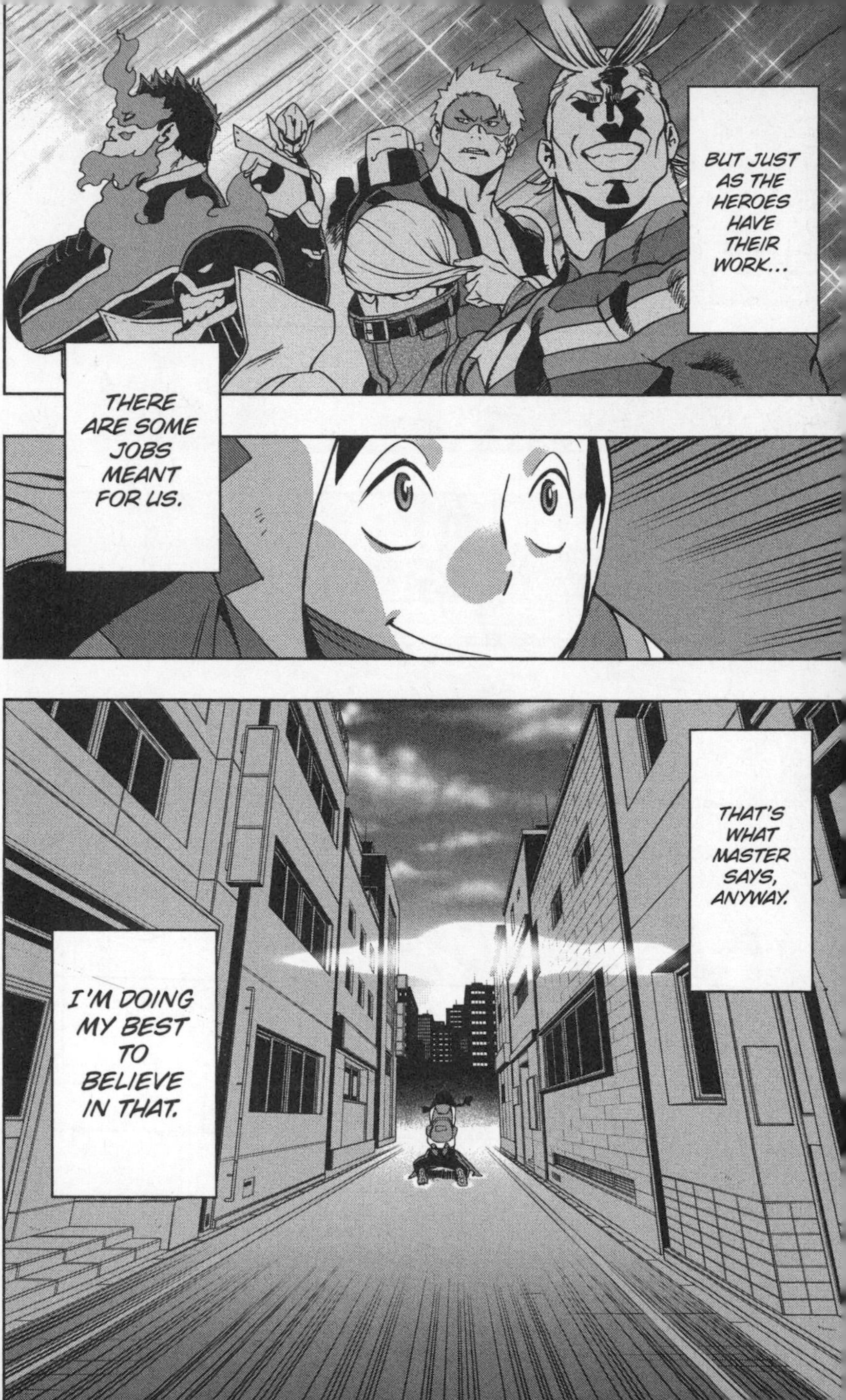
BUT JUST AS THE HEROES HAVE THEIR WORK...
THERE ARE SOME JOBS MEANT FOR US.
THAT'S WHAT MASTER SAYS, ANYWAY.
I'M DOING MY BEST TO BELIEVE IN THAT.

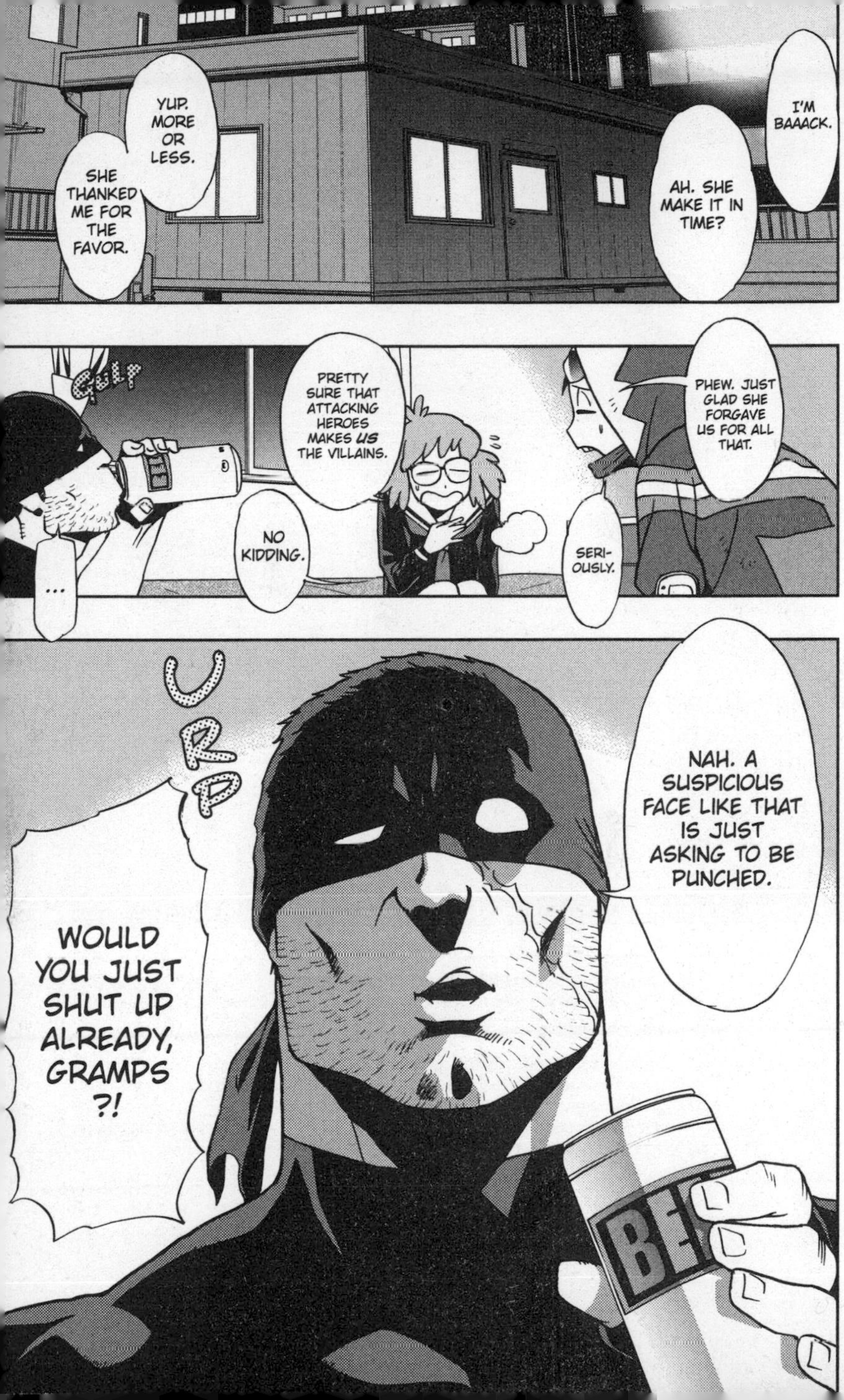
I'M BAAACK.
AH. SHE MAKE IT IN TIME?
YUP. MORE OR LESS.
SHE THANKED ME FOR THE FAVOR.
PHEW. JUST GLAD SHE FORGAVE US FOR ALL THAT.
SERIOUSLY.
PRETTY SURE THAT ATTACKING HEROES MAKES *US* THE VILLAINS.
NO KIDDING.
GULP
...
NAH. A SUSPICIOUS FACE LIKE THAT IS JUST ASKING TO BE PUNCHED.
URP
WOULD YOU JUST SHUT UP ALREADY, GRAMPS?!

BIGSHOT / ENIGMA / ONEMU SHINYA

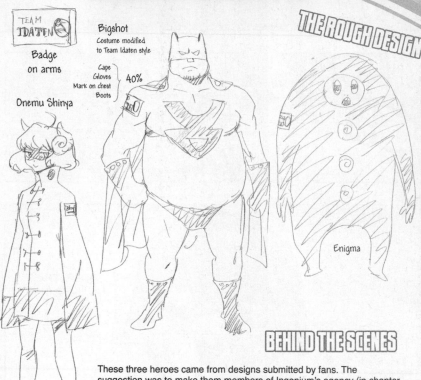

THE ROUGH DESIGN

TEAM IDATEN
Badge on arms
Bigshot
Costume modified to Team Idaten style
Cape
Gloves
Mark on chest
Boots
40%
Onemu Shinya
Enigma

BEHIND THE SCENES

These three heroes came from designs submitted by fans. The suggestion was to make them members of Ingenium's agency (in chapter 7), but Enigma's gimmick was good enough to warrant a chapter of her own, so her debut was delayed a bit.

In the original submission, Enigma's real face was charmingly different, so then the question was whether to make her look nothing like the yet-to-be-identified villain, or to have her identity be really obvious. I went with the latter option and kept the face exactly the same. I also fine-tuned her to make her easier to utilize in the story, so please forgive me...

—Furuhashi

The one I chose was Onemu Shinya. I think what drew me to her was that her design isn't the sort I'd naturally come up with on my own. I had trouble drawing her, actually. With the other two, I tried to emphasize what was already appealing about the original designs...

—Betten

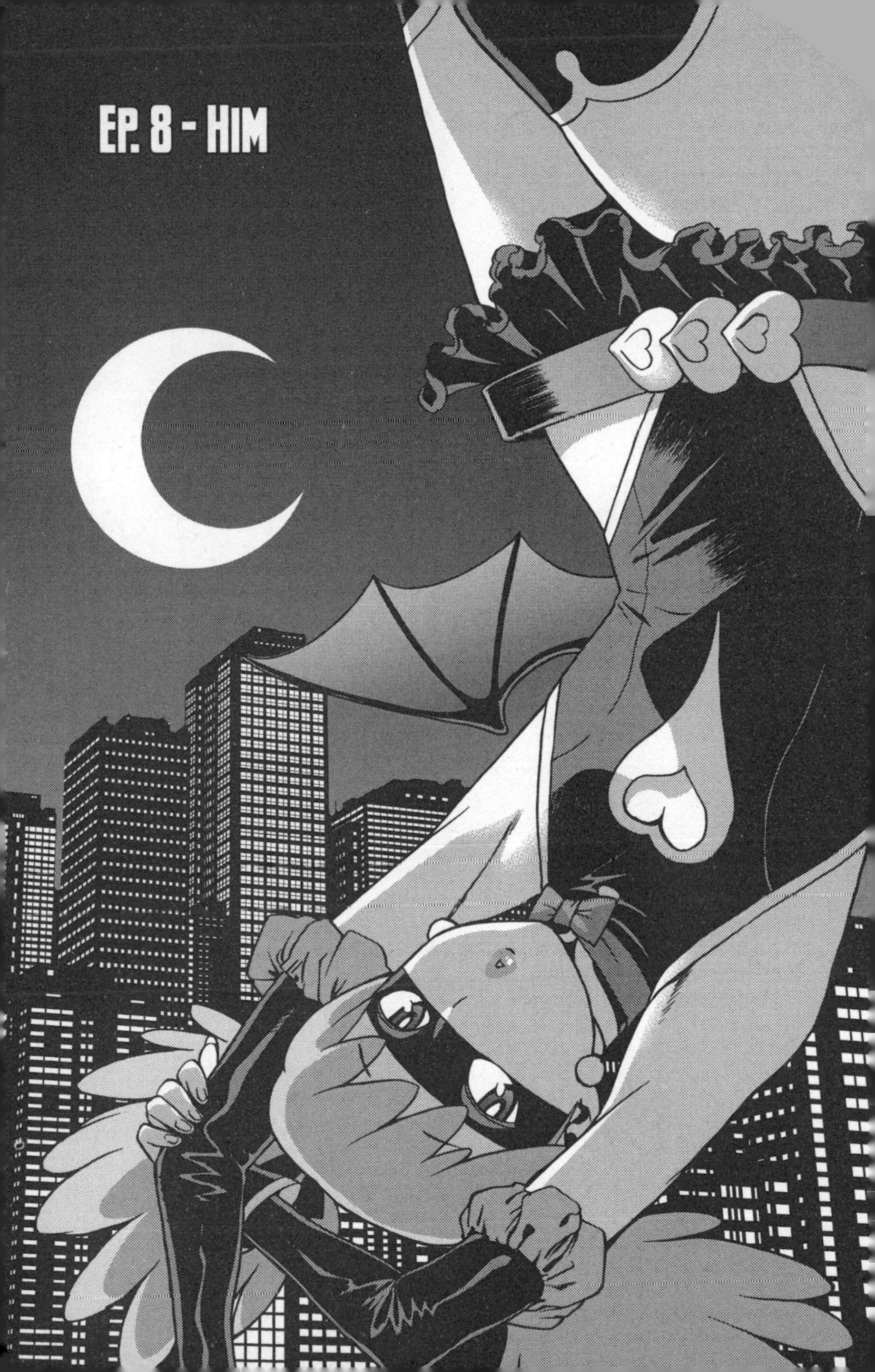
EP. 8 - HIM

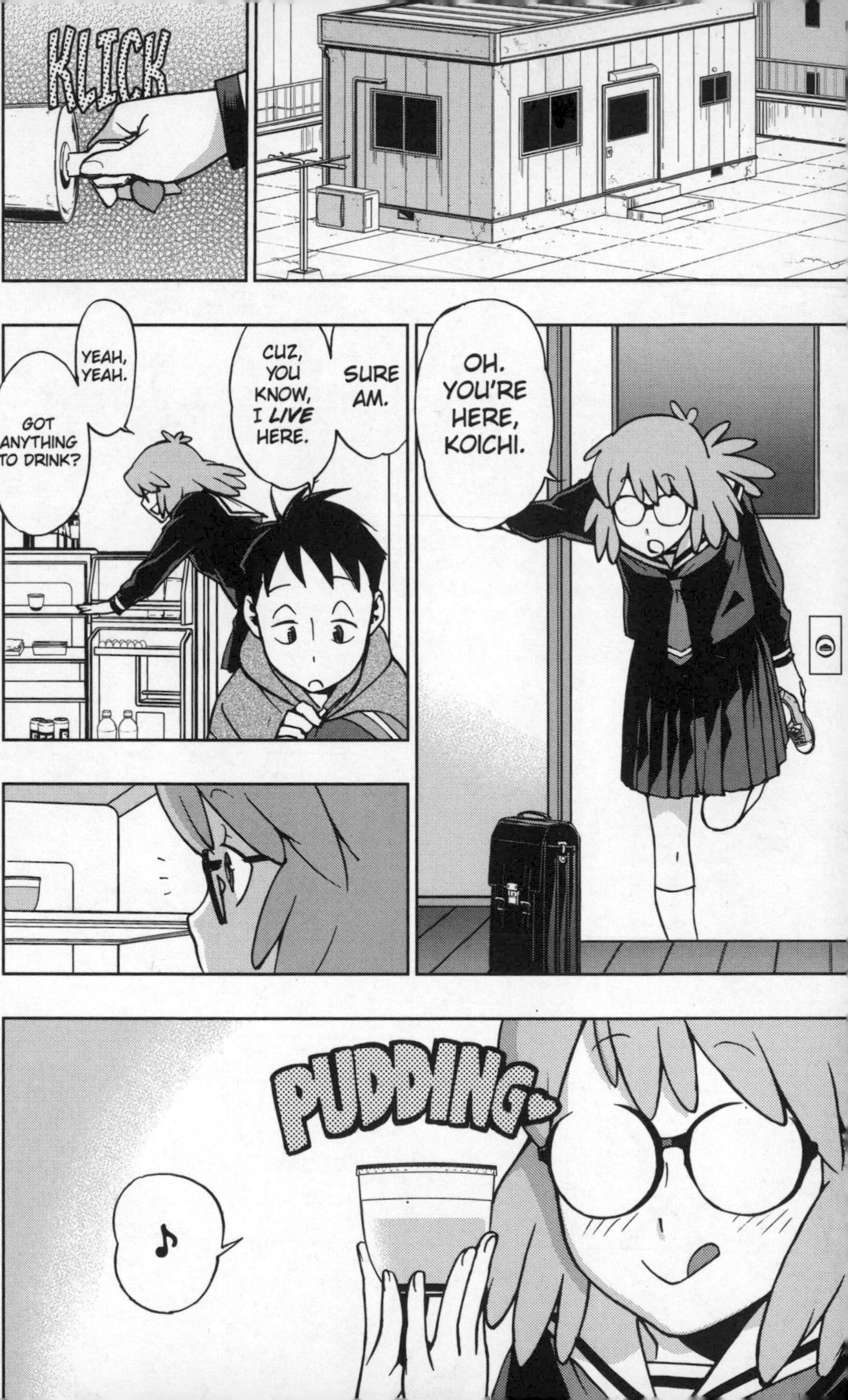
KLICK
OH. YOU'RE HERE, KOICHI.
SURE AM.
CUZ, YOU KNOW, I *LIVE* HERE.
YEAH, YEAH.
GOT ANYTHING TO DRINK?
PUDDING
♪

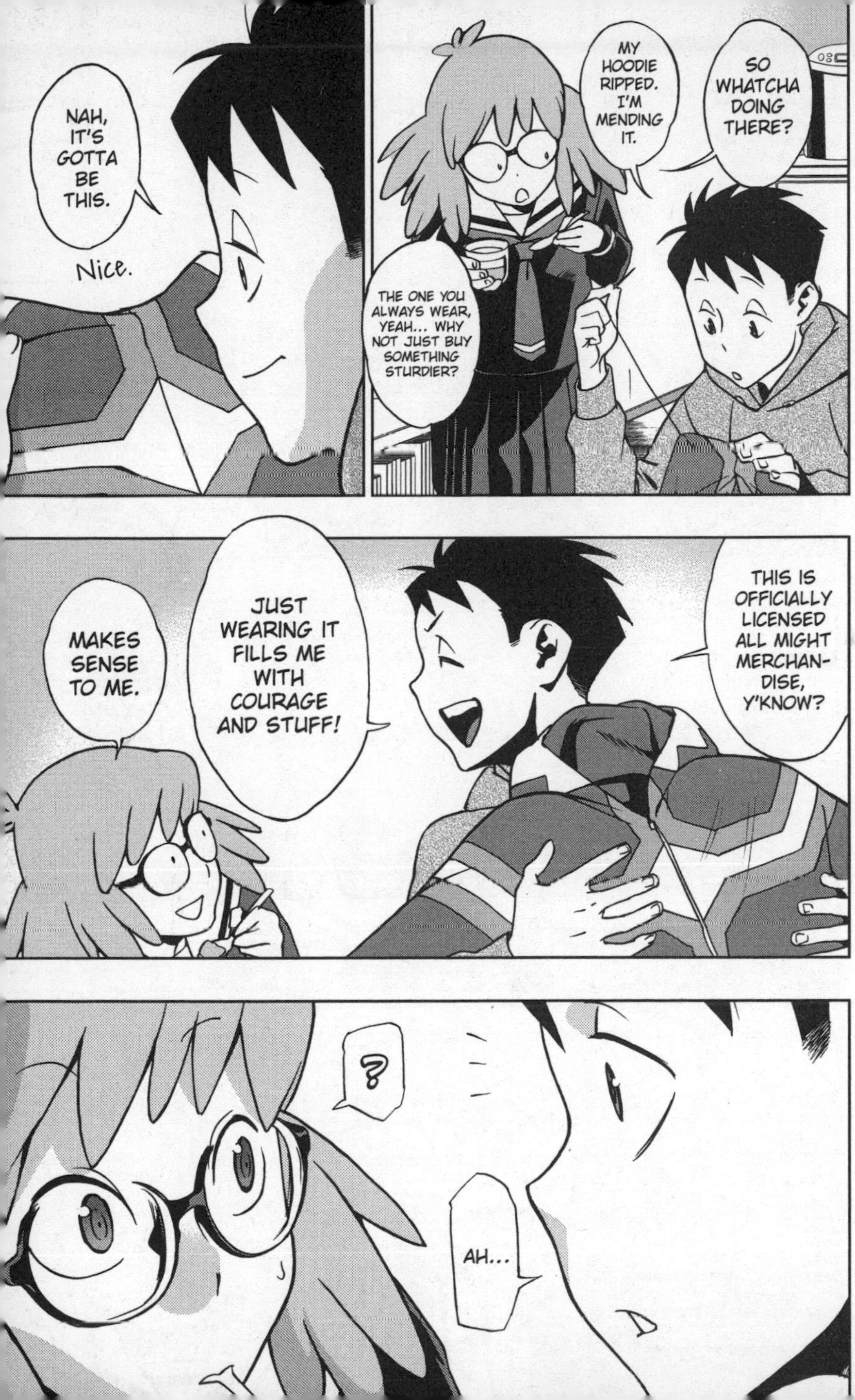
SO WHATCHA DOING THERE?
MY HOODIE RIPPED. I'M MENDING IT.
THE ONE YOU ALWAYS WEAR, YEAH... WHY NOT JUST BUY SOMETHING STURDIER?
NAH, IT'S GOTTA BE THIS.
Nice.
THIS IS OFFICIALLY LICENSED ALL MIGHT MERCHANDISE, Y'KNOW?
JUST WEARING IT FILLS ME WITH COURAGE AND STUFF!
MAKES SENSE TO ME.
?
AH...

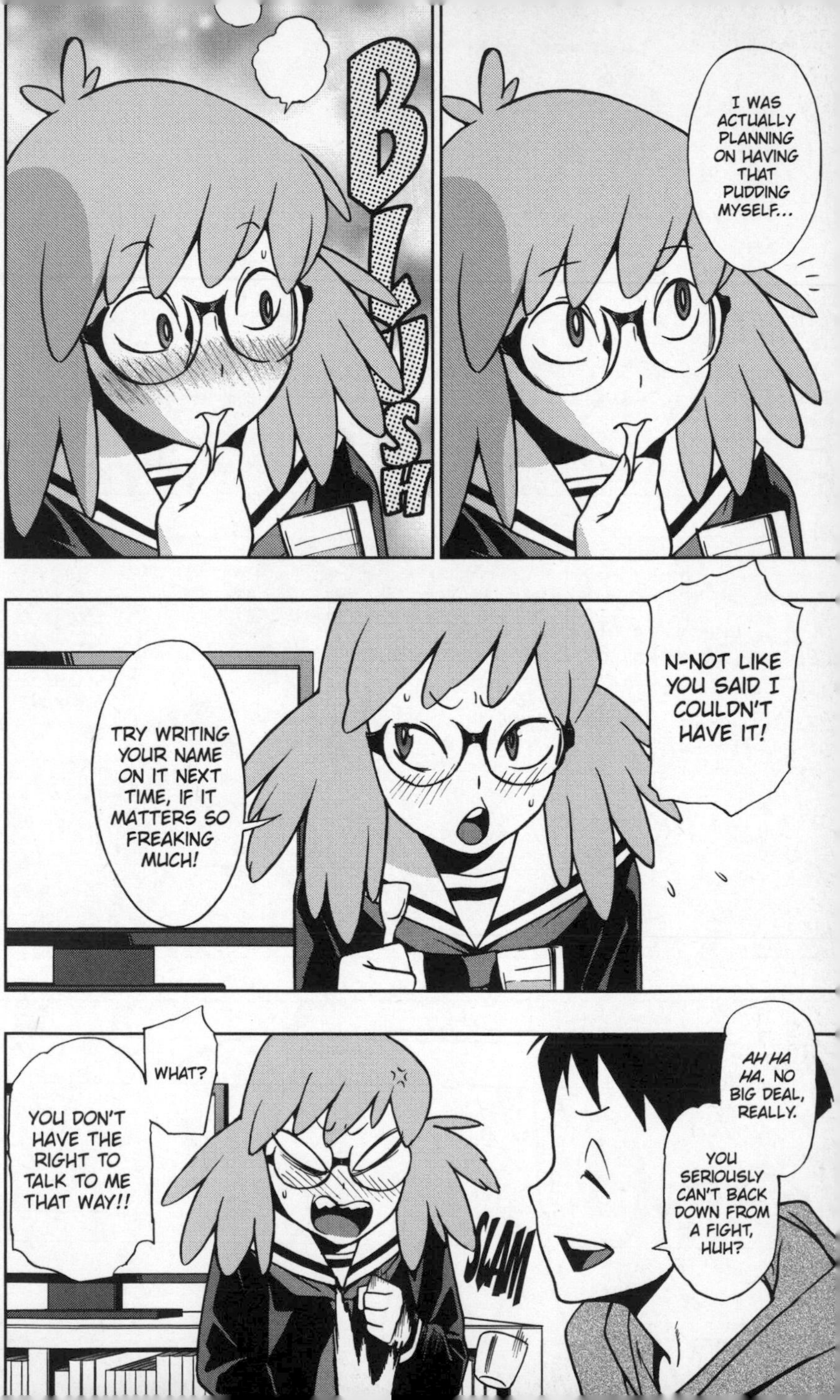
I WAS ACTUALLY PLANNING ON HAVING THAT PUDDING MYSELF...
BLUSH
N-NOT LIKE YOU SAID I COULDN'T HAVE IT!
TRY WRITING YOUR NAME ON IT NEXT TIME, IF IT MATTERS SO FREAKING MUCH!
AH HA HA. NO BIG DEAL, REALLY.
YOU SERIOUSLY CAN'T BACK DOWN FROM A FIGHT, HUH?
SLAM
WHAT?
YOU DON'T HAVE THE RIGHT TO TALK TO ME THAT WAY!!

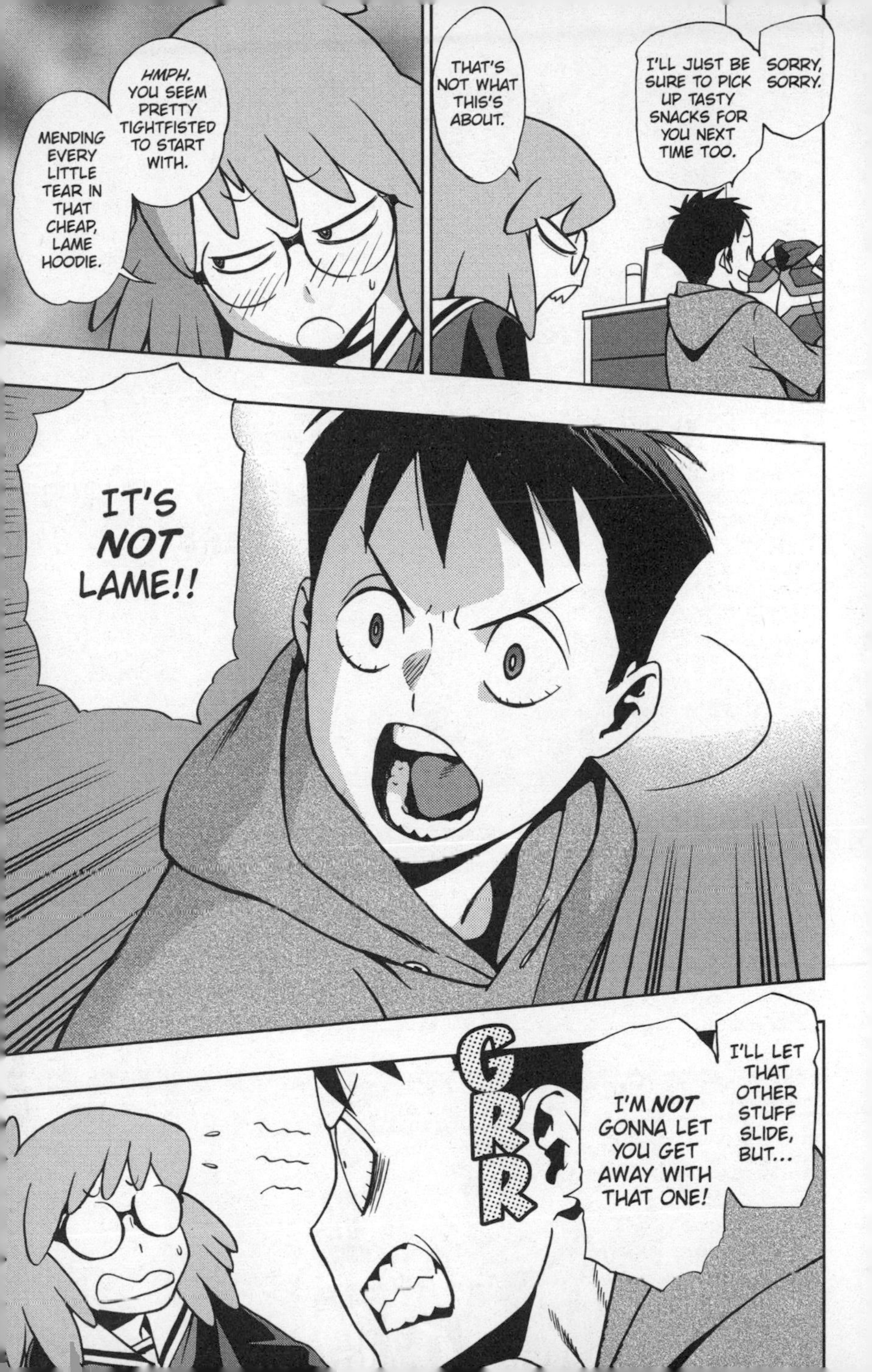
SORRY, SORRY.
I'LL JUST BE SURE TO PICK UP TASTY SNACKS FOR YOU NEXT TIME TOO.
THAT'S NOT WHAT THIS'S ABOUT.
HMPH. YOU SEEM PRETTY TIGHTFISTED TO START WITH.
MENDING EVERY LITTLE TEAR IN THAT CHEAP, LAME HOODIE.
IT'S *NOT* LAME!!
I'LL LET THAT OTHER STUFF SLIDE, BUT...
I'M *NOT* GONNA LET YOU GET AWAY WITH THAT ONE!
GRR

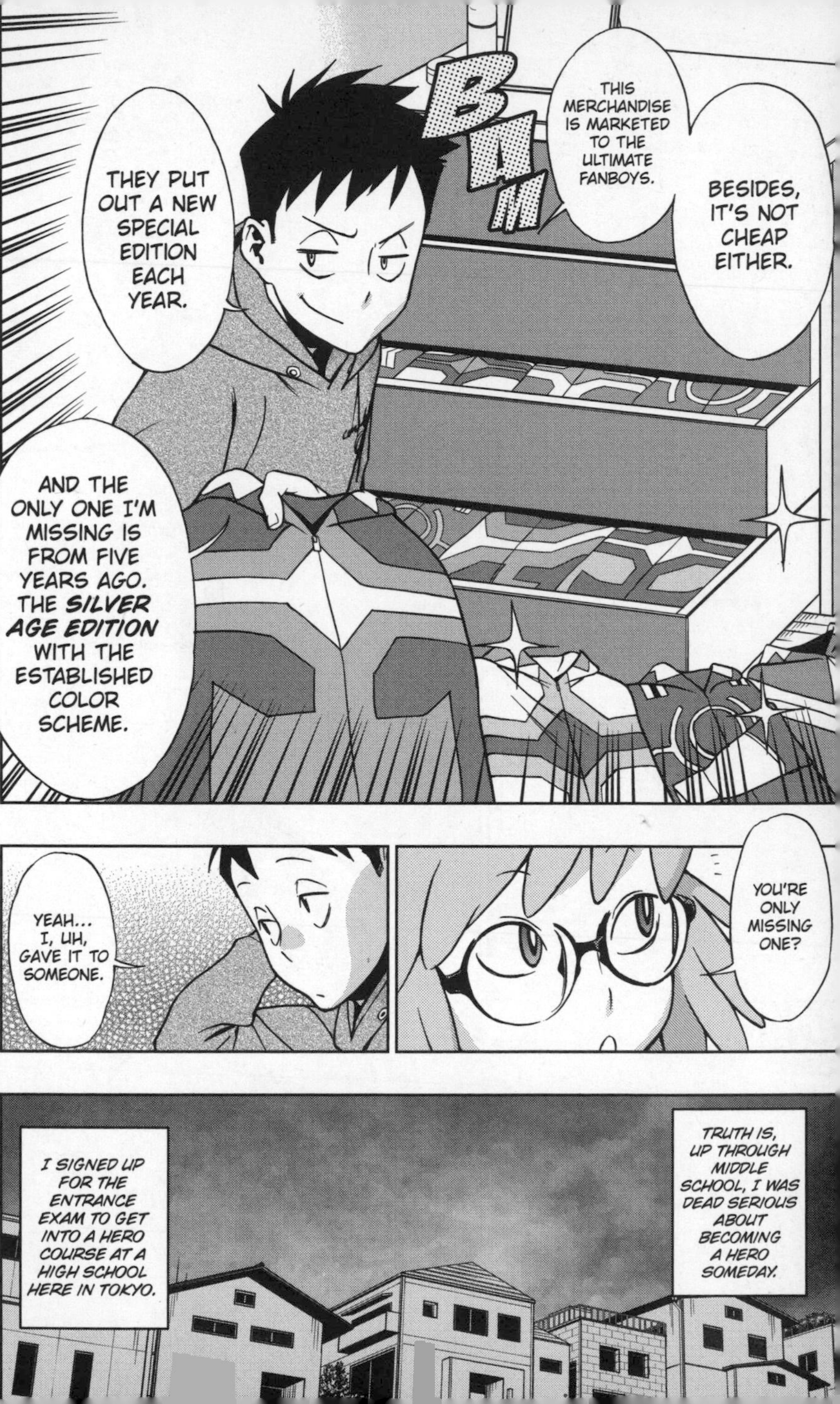
THIS MERCHANDISE IS MARKETED TO THE ULTIMATE FANBOYS.
BAM
BESIDES, IT'S NOT CHEAP EITHER.
THEY PUT OUT A NEW SPECIAL EDITION EACH YEAR.
AND THE ONLY ONE I'M MISSING IS FROM FIVE YEARS AGO. THE ***SILVER AGE EDITION*** WITH THE ESTABLISHED COLOR SCHEME.
YOU'RE ONLY MISSING ONE?
YEAH... I, UH, GAVE IT TO SOMEONE.
TRUTH IS, UP THROUGH MIDDLE SCHOOL, I WAS DEAD SERIOUS ABOUT BECOMING A HERO SOMEDAY.
I SIGNED UP FOR THE ENTRANCE EXAM TO GET INTO A HERO COURSE AT A HIGH SCHOOL HERE IN TOKYO.

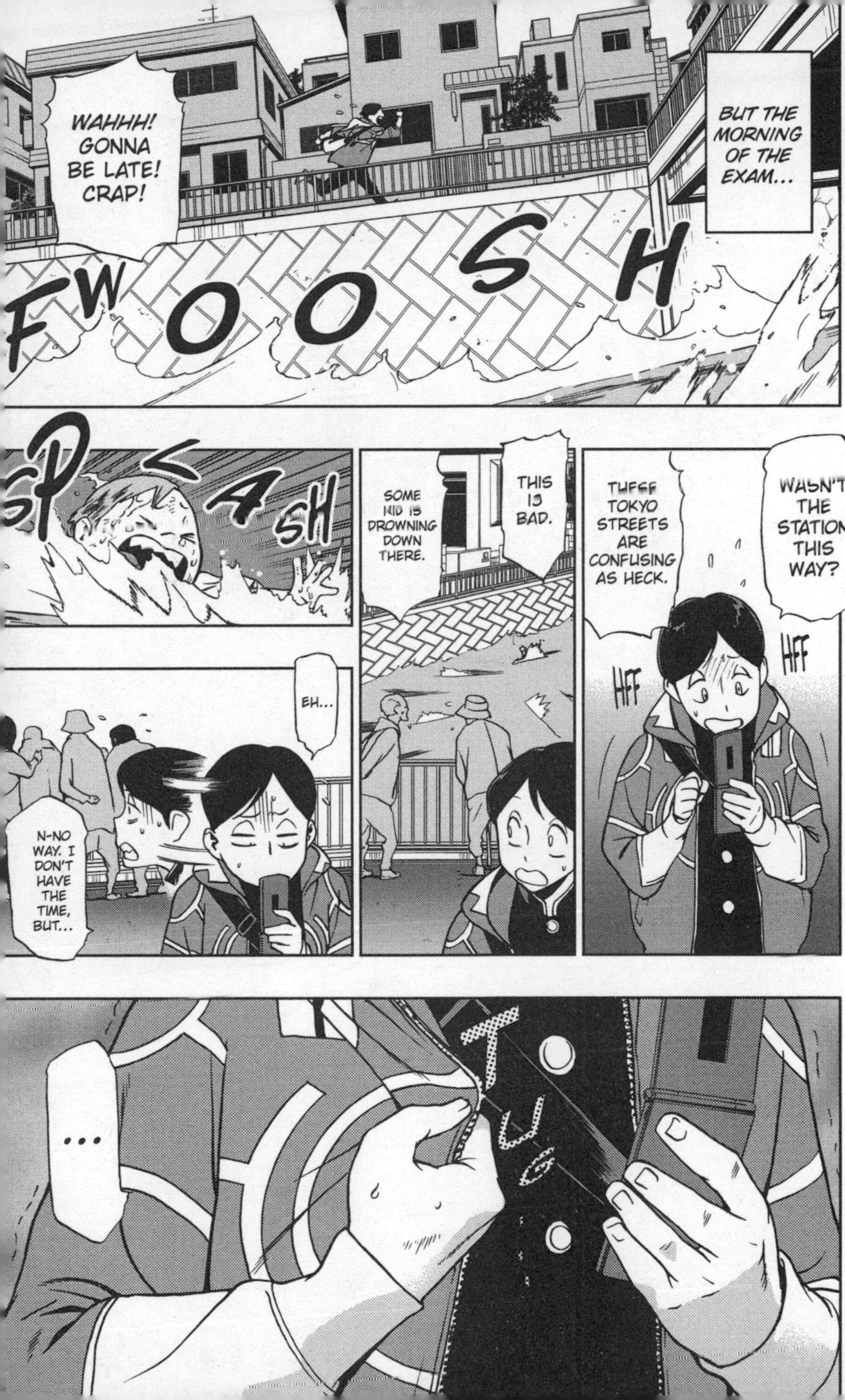
BUT THE MORNING OF THE EXAM...
WAHHH! GONNA BE LATE! CRAP!
FWOOSH
WASN'T THE STATION THIS WAY?
THESE TOKYO STREETS ARE CONFUSING AS HECK.
HFF
HFF
THIS IS BAD.
SOME KID IS DROWNING DOWN THERE.
SPLASH
EH...
N-NO WAY. I DON'T HAVE THE TIME, BUT...
TUG
...

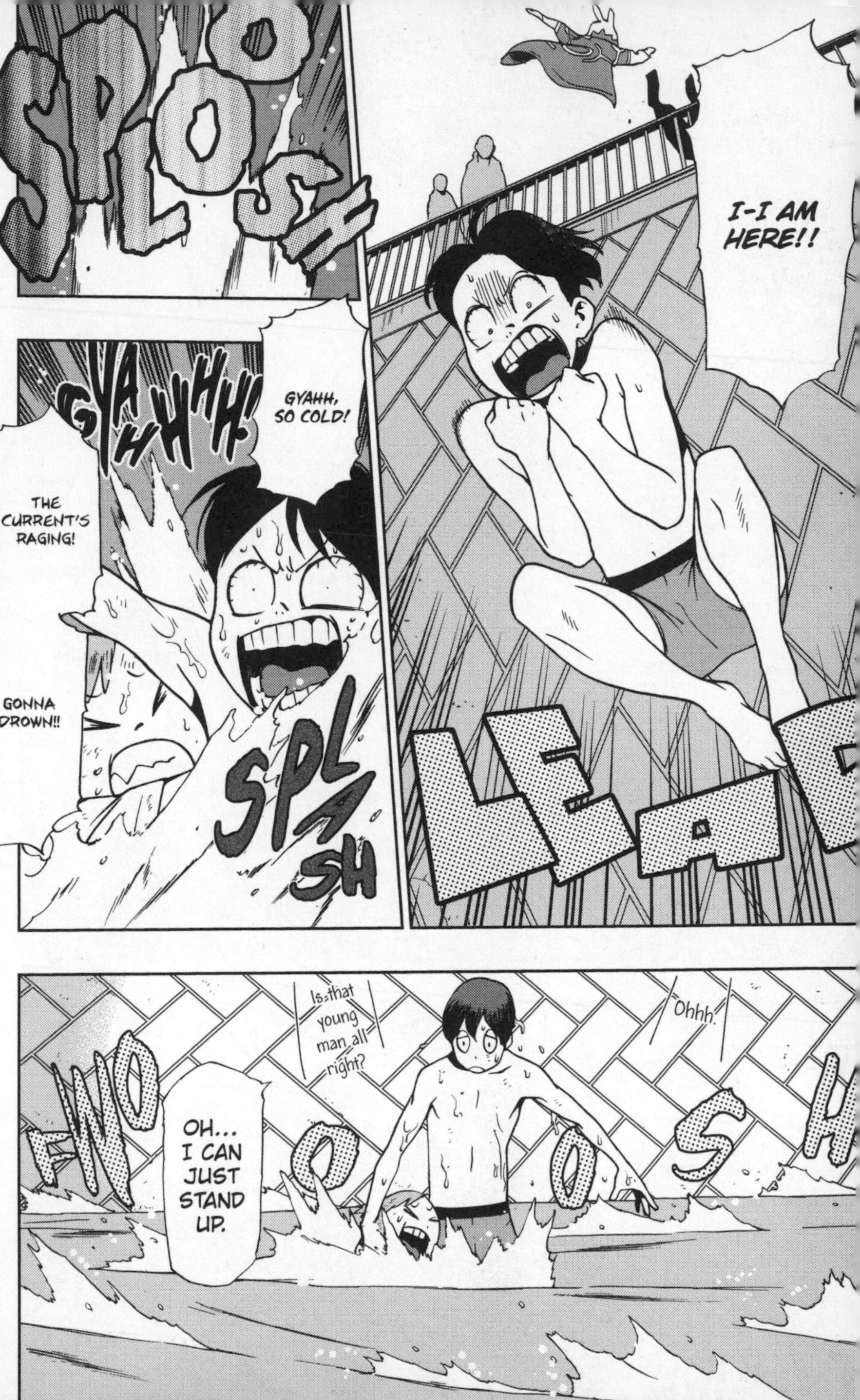
I-I AM HERE!!
LEA
SPLOOSH
GYAHHHH!
GYAHH, SO COLD!
THE CURRENT'S RAGING!
GONNA DROWN!!
SPLASH
Ohhh.
Is that young man all right?
FWOOOSH
OH... I CAN JUST STAND UP.

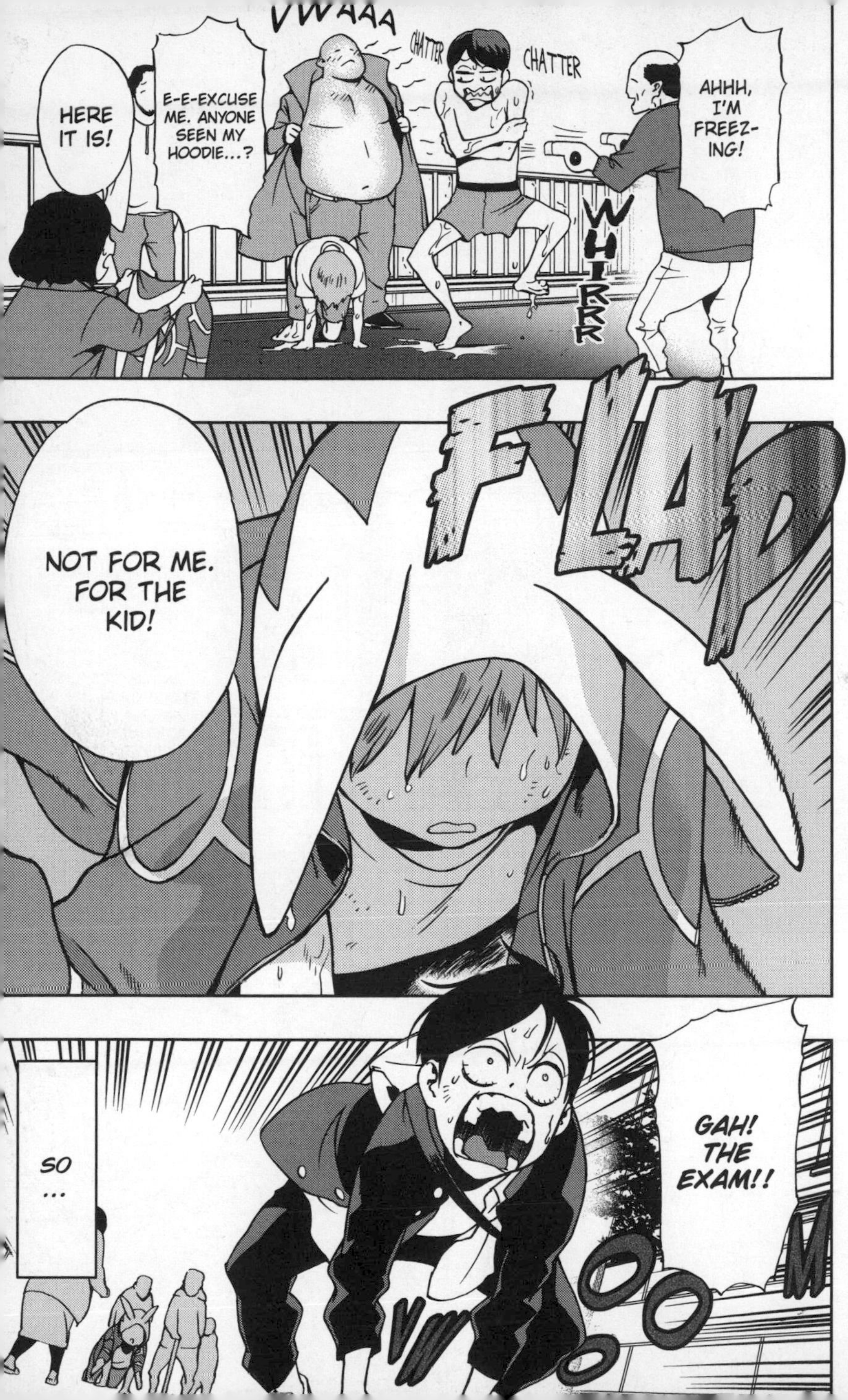
AHHH, I'M FREEZ-ING!
WHIRRR
CHATTER
CHATTER
VWAAA
E-E-EXCUSE ME. ANYONE SEEN MY HOODIE...?
HERE IT IS!
FLAP
NOT FOR ME. FOR THE KID!
GAH! THE EXAM!!
VVOOOOM
SO ...

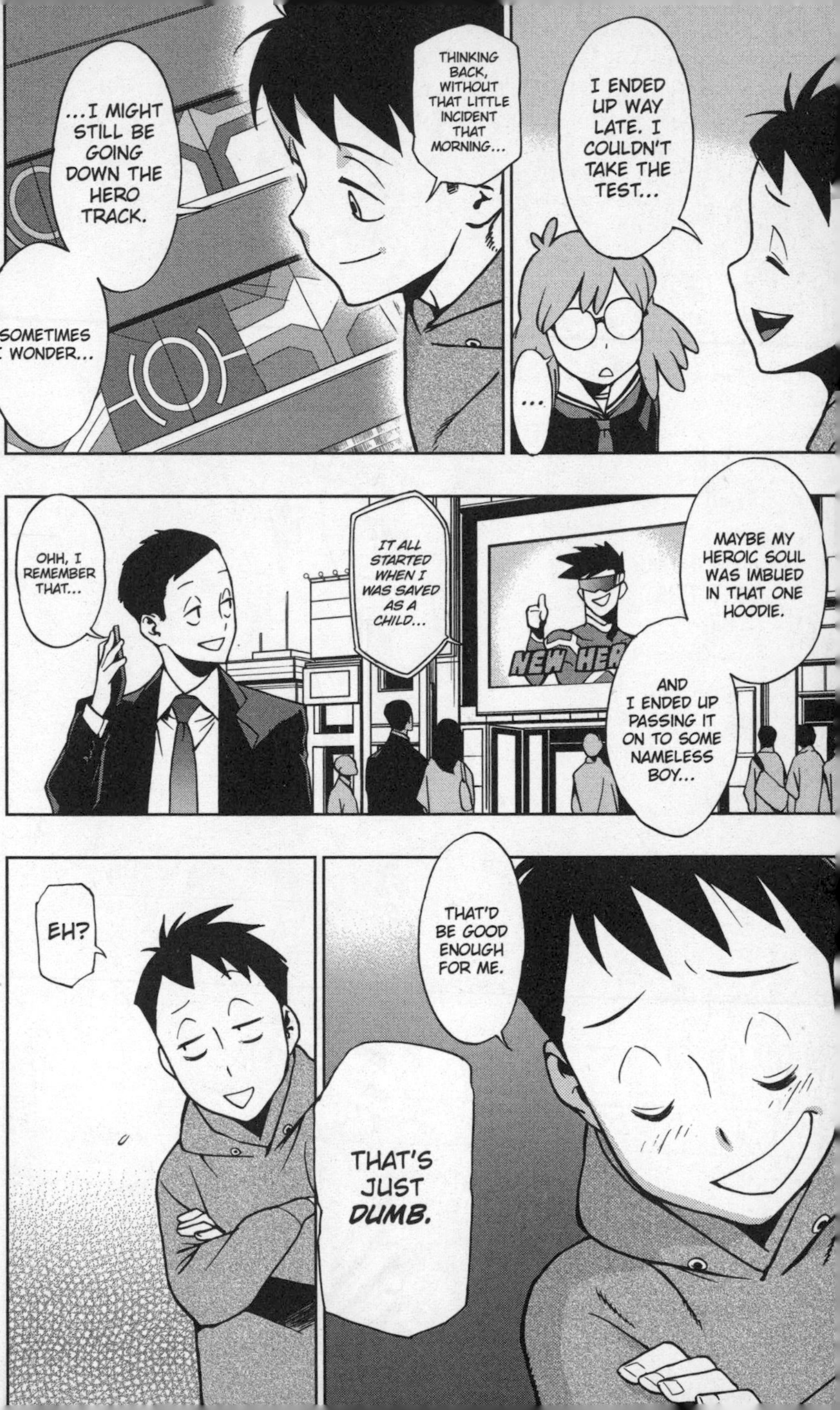
I ENDED UP WAY LATE. I COULDN'T TAKE THE TEST...
...
THINKING BACK, WITHOUT THAT LITTLE INCIDENT THAT MORNING...
...I MIGHT STILL BE GOING DOWN THE HERO TRACK.
SOMETIMES I WONDER...
MAYBE MY HEROIC SOUL WAS IMBUED IN THAT ONE HOODIE.
AND I ENDED UP PASSING IT ON TO SOME NAMELESS BOY...
NEW HER
IT ALL STARTED WHEN I WAS SAVED AS A CHILD...
OHH, I REMEMBER THAT...
THAT'D BE GOOD ENOUGH FOR ME.
THAT'S JUST **DUMB.**
EH?

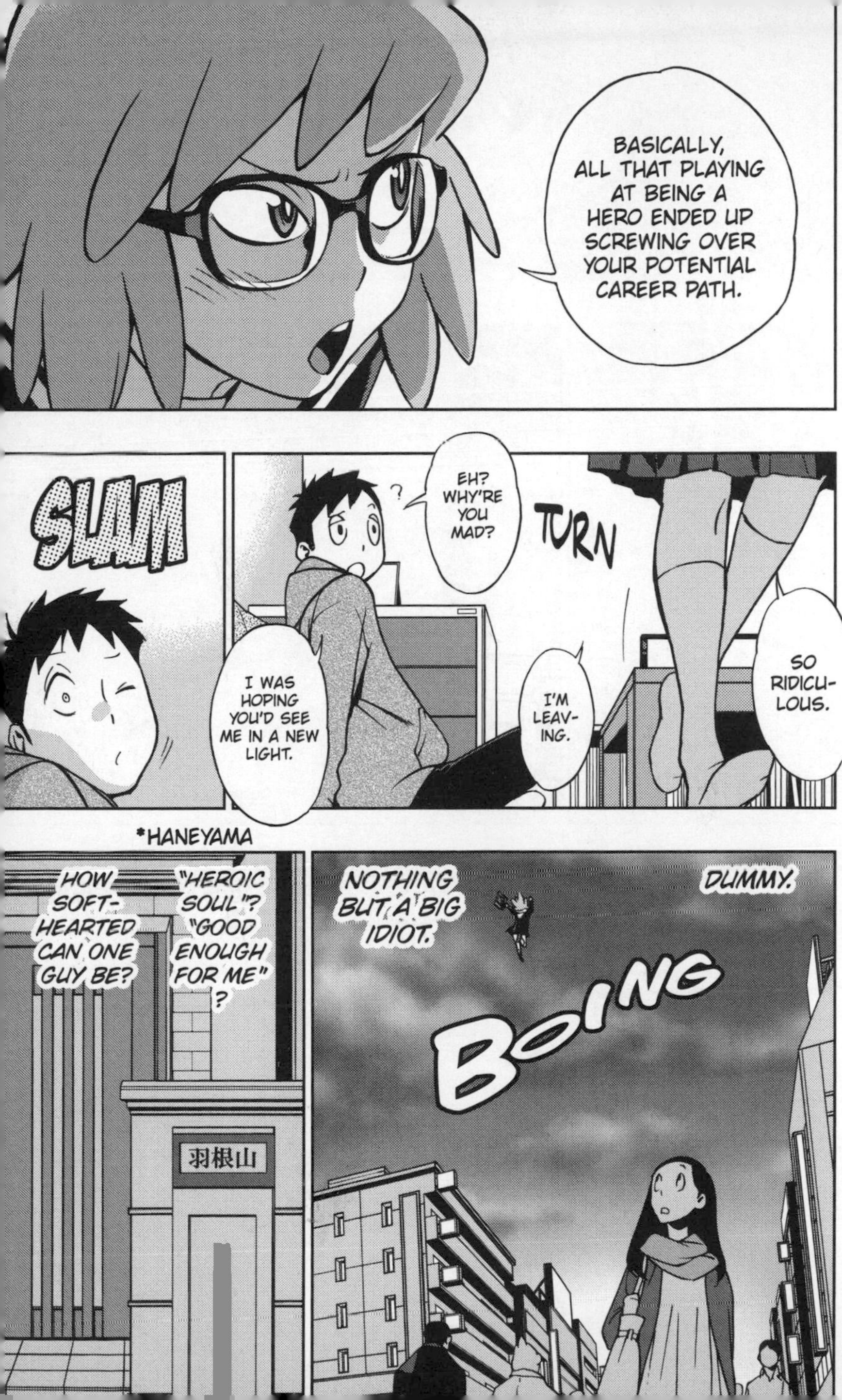
BASICALLY, ALL THAT PLAYING AT BEING A HERO ENDED UP SCREWING OVER YOUR POTENTIAL CAREER PATH.
SO RIDICULOUS.
I'M LEAVING.
TURN
EH? WHY'RE YOU MAD?
I WAS HOPING YOU'D SEE ME IN A NEW LIGHT.
SLAM
*HANEYAMA
DUMMY.
NOTHING BUT A BIG IDIOT.
BOING
"HEROIC SOUL"? "GOOD ENOUGH FOR ME"?
HOW SOFT-HEARTED CAN ONE GUY BE?
羽根山

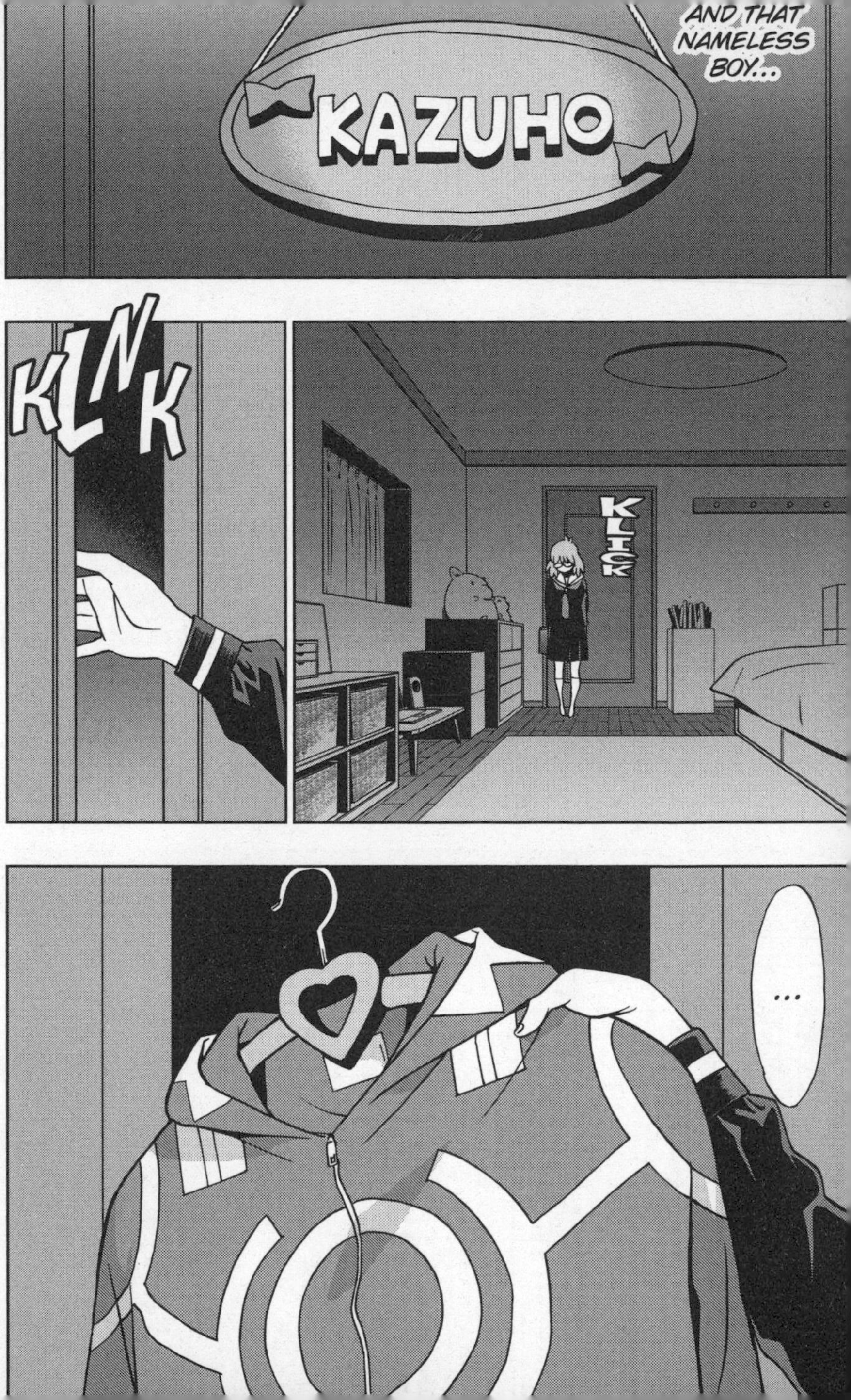
AND THAT NAMELESS BOY...
KAZUHO
KLICK
KLINK
...

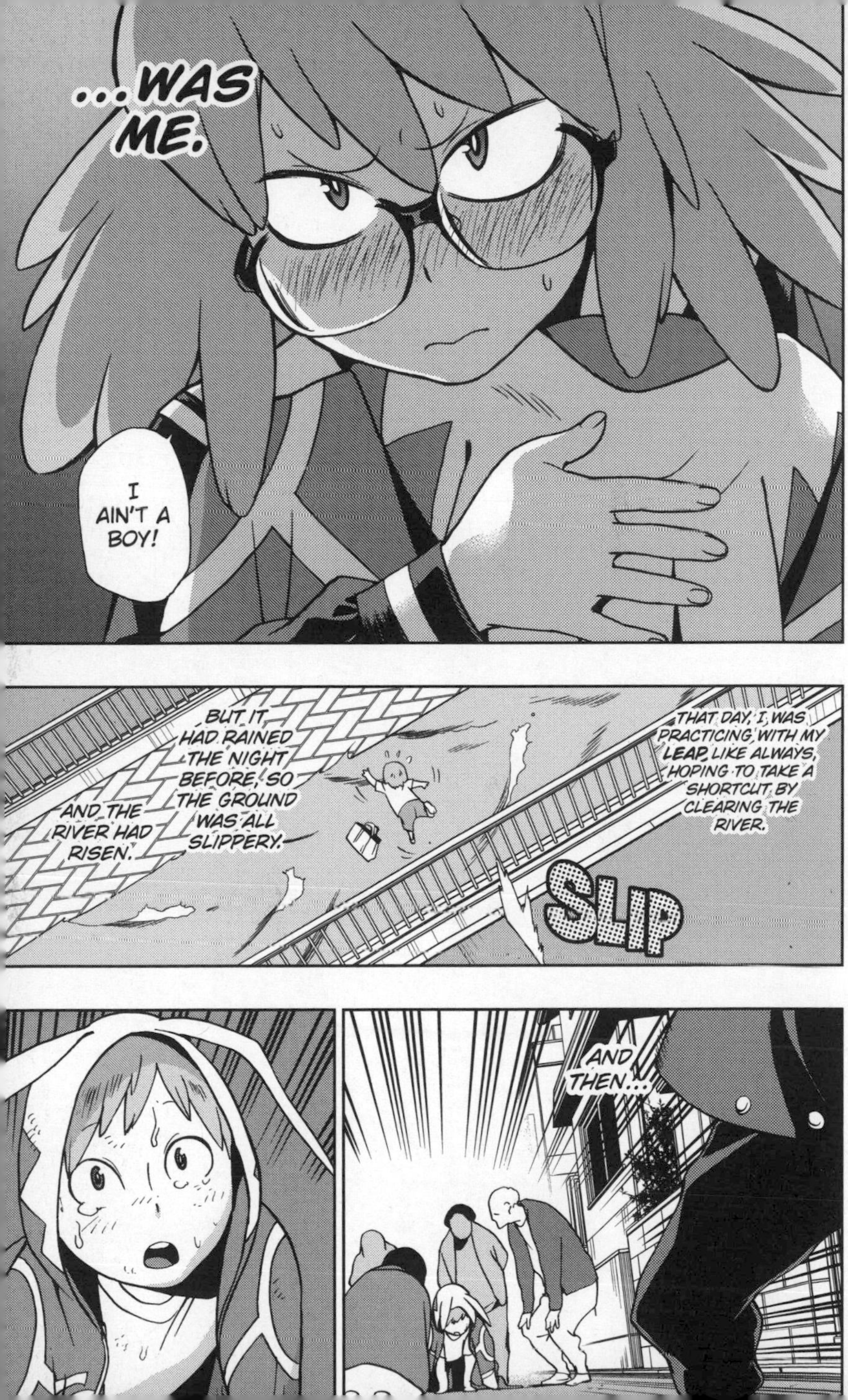
...WAS ME.
I AIN'T A BOY!
THAT DAY, I WAS PRACTICING WITH MY LEAP LIKE ALWAYS, HOPING TO TAKE A SHORTCUT BY CLEARING THE RIVER.
SLIP
BUT IT HAD RAINED THE NIGHT BEFORE, SO THE GROUND WAS ALL SLIPPERY.
AND THE RIVER HAD RISEN.
AND THEN...

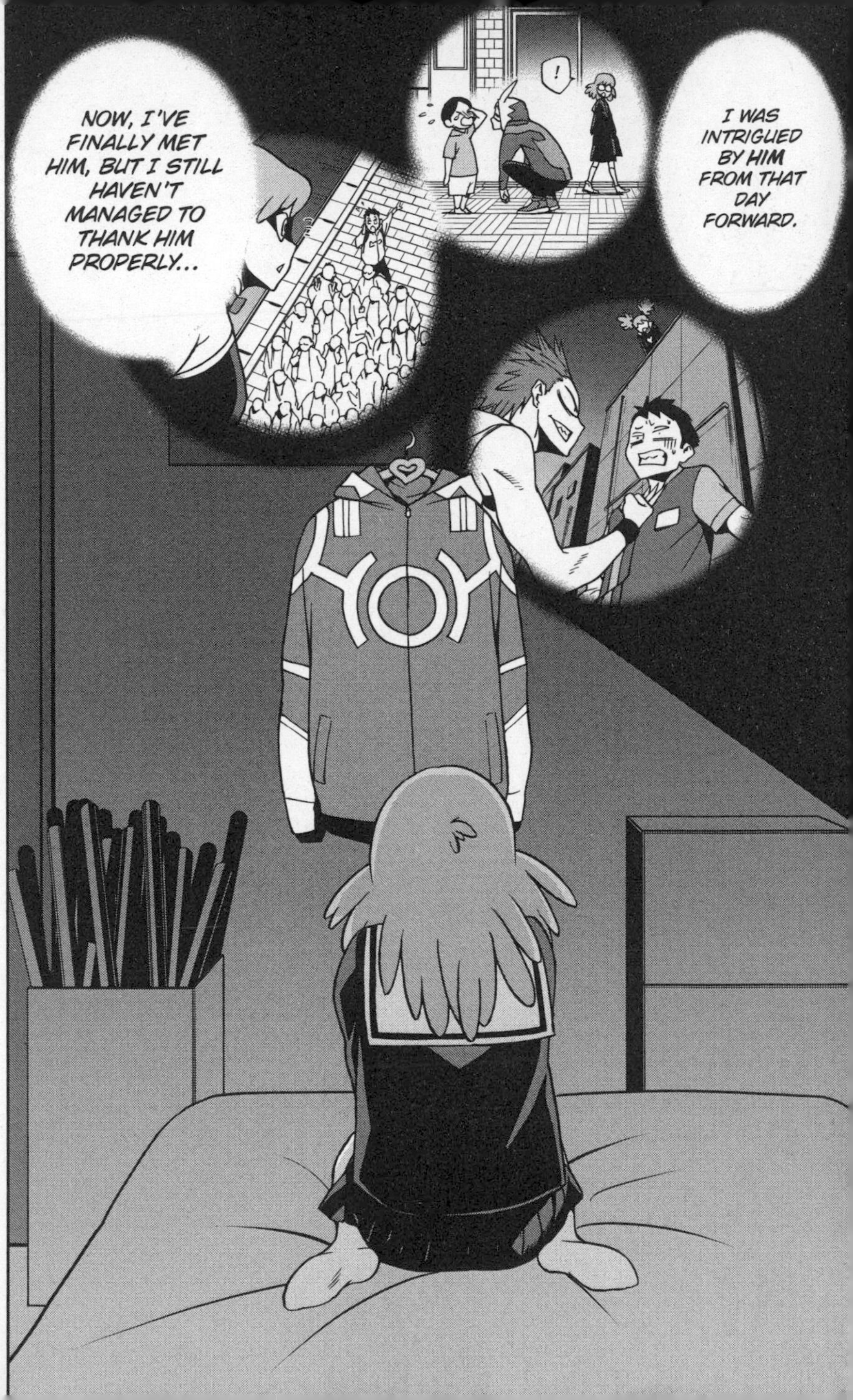
I WAS INTRIGUED BY HIM FROM THAT DAY FORWARD.
!
NOW, I'VE FINALLY MET HIM, BUT I STILL HAVEN'T MANAGED TO THANK HIM PROPERLY...

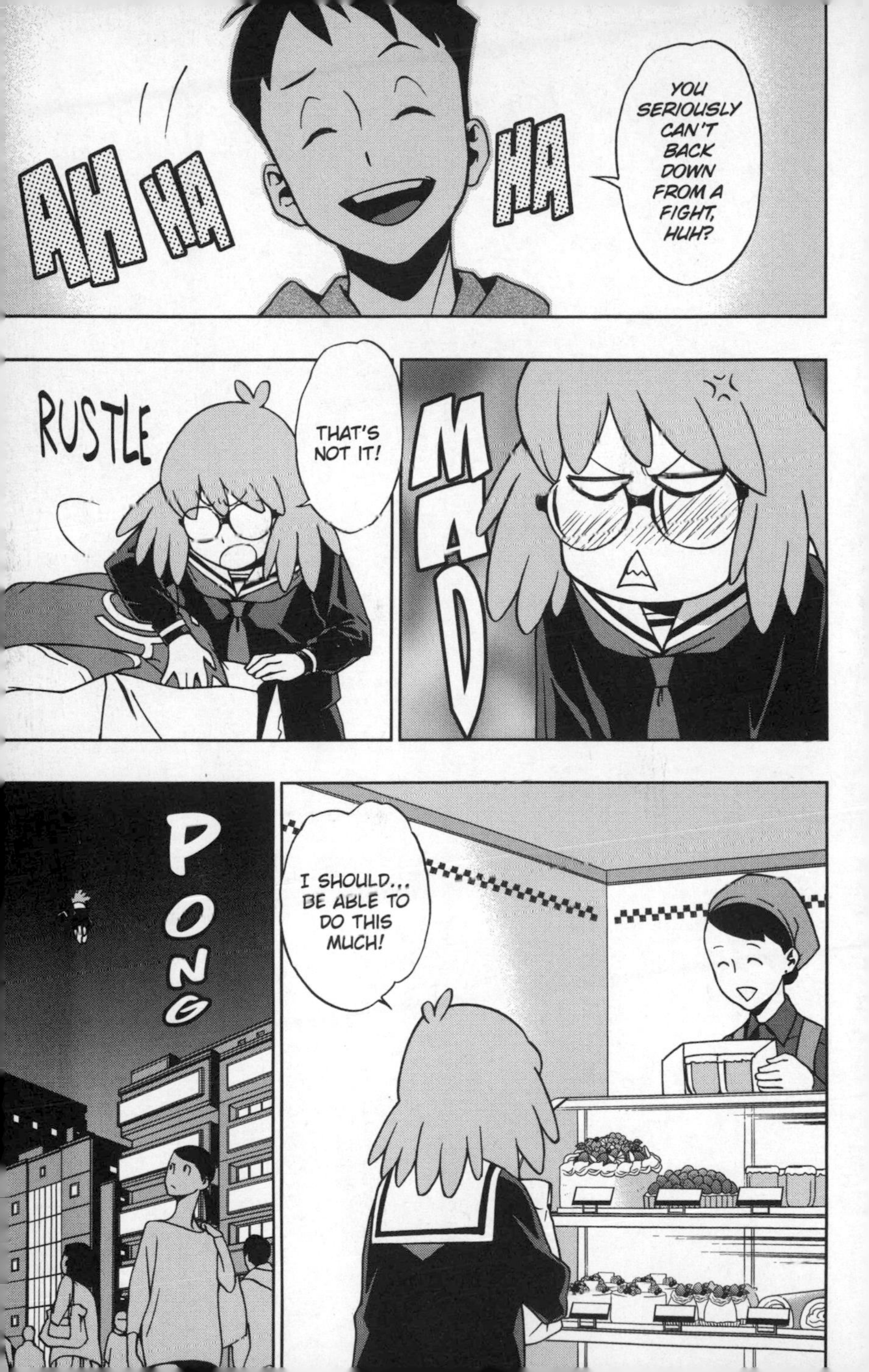
YOU SERIOUSLY CAN'T BACK DOWN FROM A FIGHT, HUH?
AH HA HA
MAD
THAT'S NOT IT!
RUSTLE
I SHOULD... BE ABLE TO DO THIS MUCH!
PONG

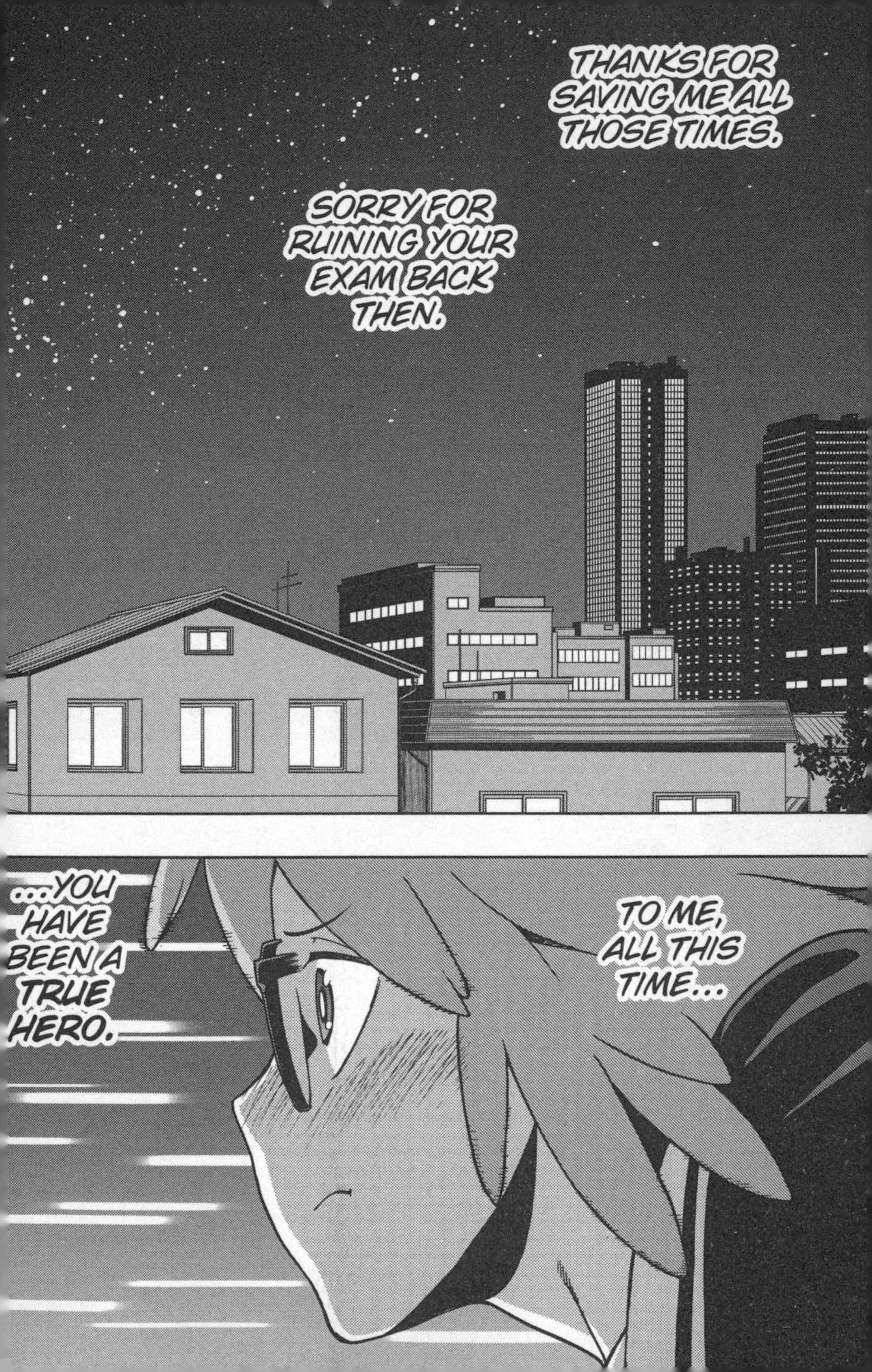
THANKS FOR SAVING ME ALL THOSE TIMES.
SORRY FOR RUINING YOUR EXAM BACK THEN.
TO ME, ALL THIS TIME...
...YOU HAVE BEEN A TRUE HERO.

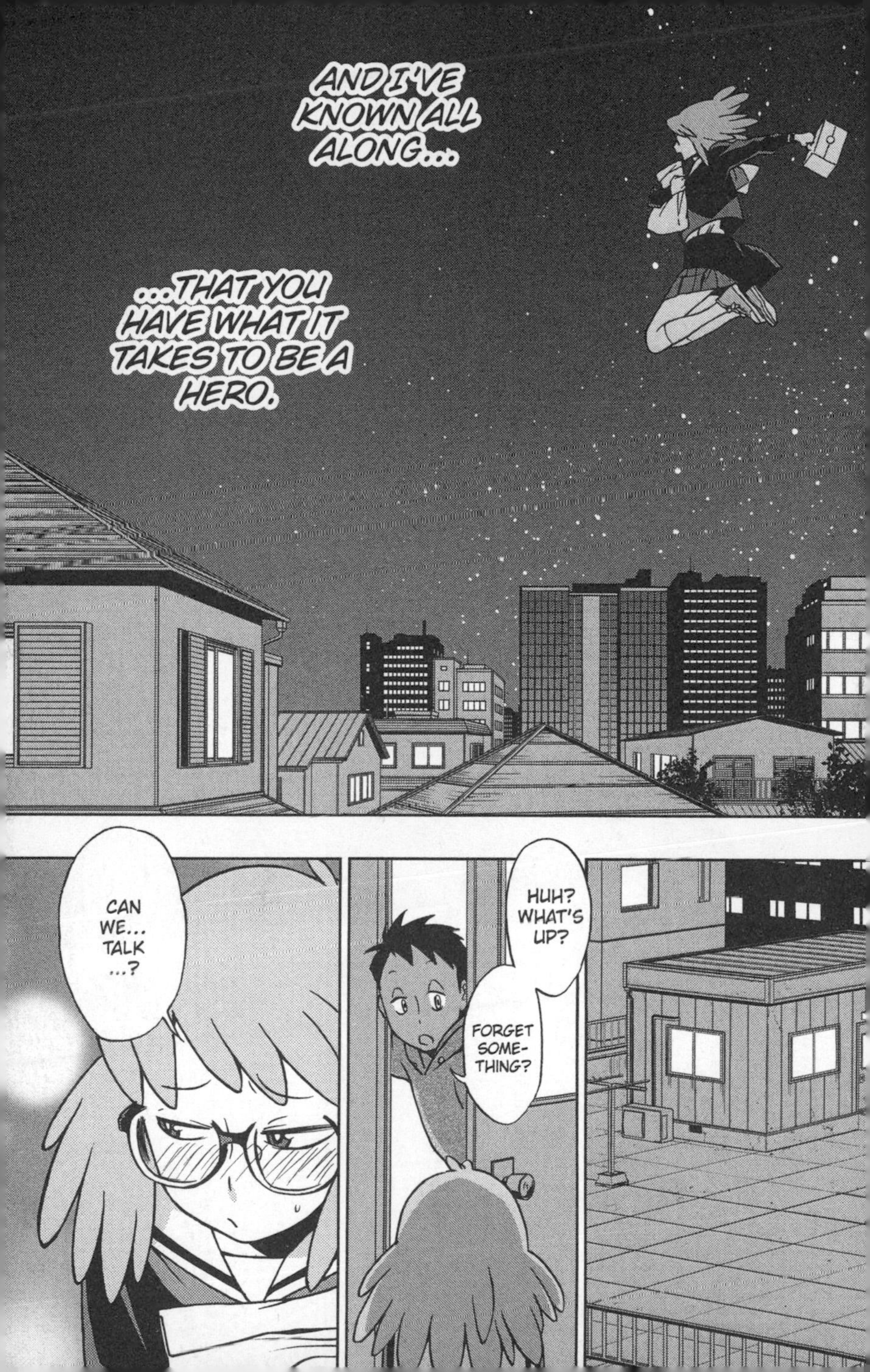
AND I'VE KNOWN ALL ALONG...
...THAT YOU HAVE WHAT IT TAKES TO BE A HERO.
HUH? WHAT'S UP?
FORGET SOME-THING?
CAN WE... TALK ...?

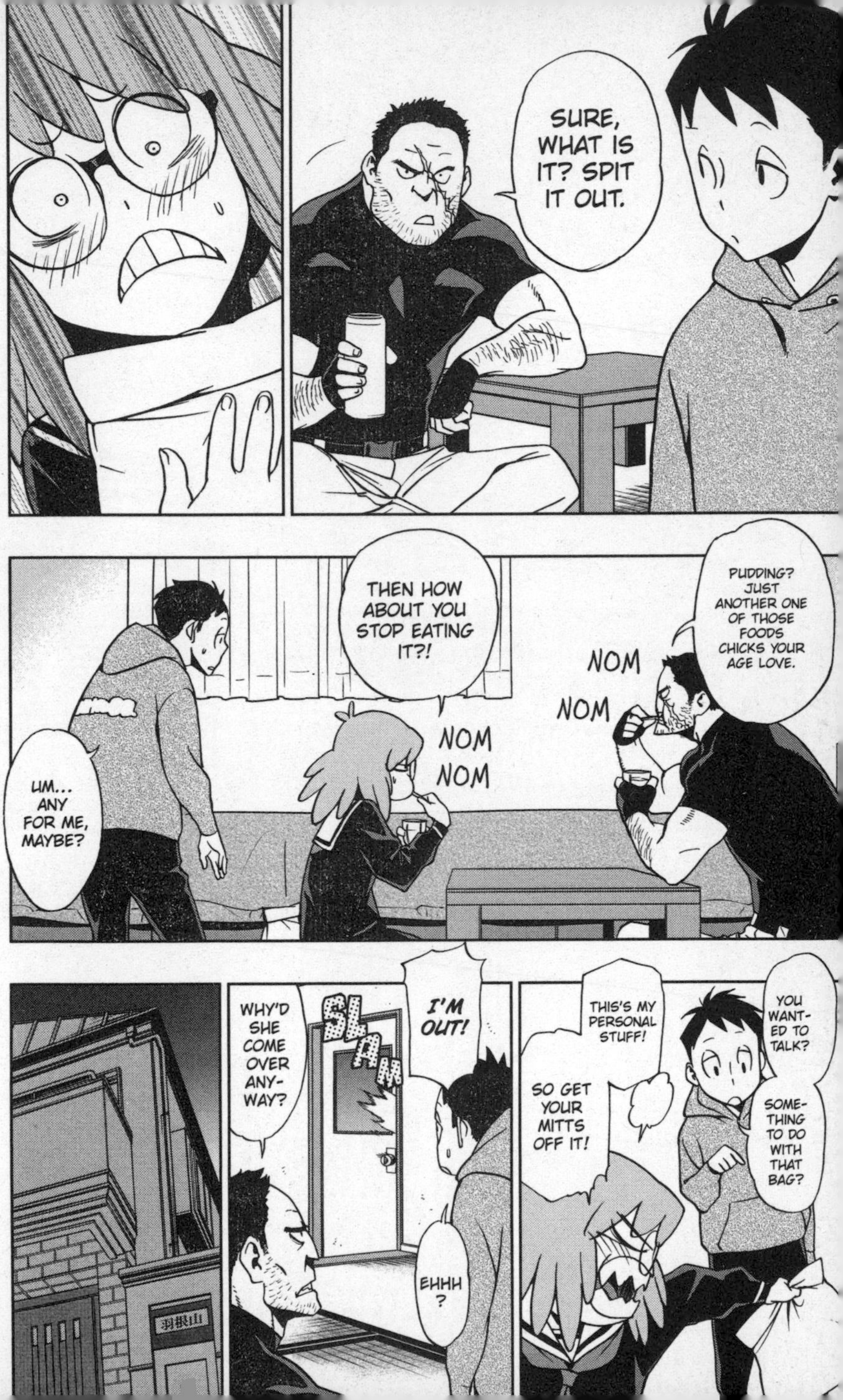
SURE, WHAT IS IT? SPIT IT OUT.
PUDDING? JUST ANOTHER ONE OF THOSE FOODS CHICKS YOUR AGE LOVE.
NOM NOM
THEN HOW ABOUT YOU STOP EATING IT?!
NOM NOM
UM... ANY FOR ME, MAYBE?
YOU WANT-ED TO TALK?
SOME-THING TO DO WITH THAT BAG?
THIS'S MY PERSONAL STUFF!
SO GET YOUR MITTS OFF IT!
I'M OUT!
SLAM
WHY'D SHE COME OVER ANY-WAY?
EHHH?
羽根山

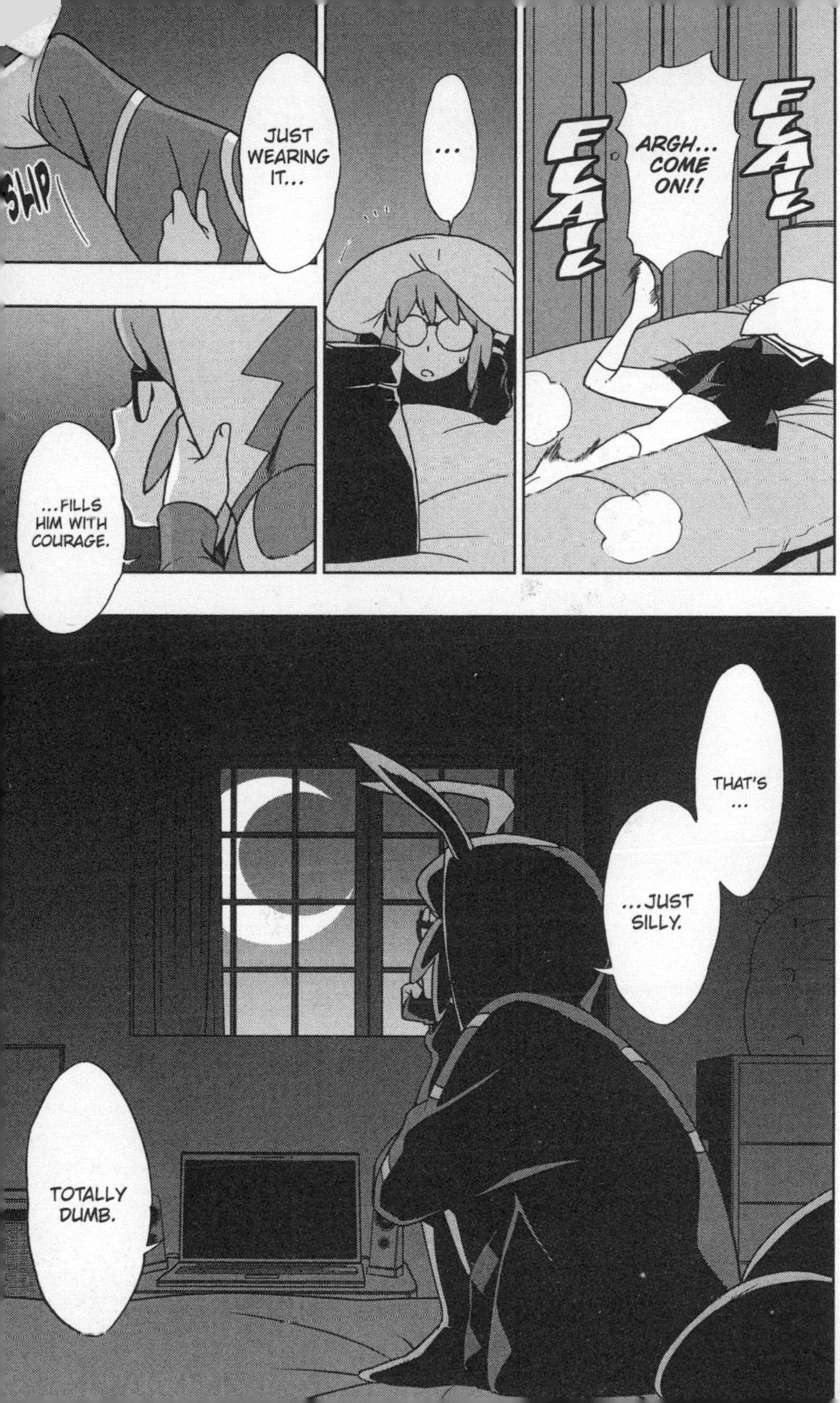
FLAIL
ARGH... COME ON!!
FLAIL
...
SLIP
JUST WEARING IT...
...FILLS HIM WITH COURAGE.
THAT'S ...
...JUST SILLY.
TOTALLY DUMB.

MIDDLE SCHOOLER KOICHI & SCHOOL UNIFORM POP

HA

THE ROUGH DESIGN

Koichi in middle school

Pop in uniform

Black sweater, collar is white

Skirt on the long side

White socks

BEHIND THE SCENES

We apparently didn't have a design for young Pop, so instead this is a two-for-one with current Pop in uniform. She and Koichi are depicted here at about the same age.

The tale of Pop and Koichi's first encounter was decided on a bit after serialization began, so if you go back and read chapters 1 and 2, you'll see that she's already head over heels for him. In this chapter, we learn that she wants to say "Thank you" someday, so that's basically her long-standing desire, going forward. Good luck!

—Furuhashi

I love Koichi's lame haircut, which looks like it was done by the neighborhood barber or even his mom. I remember dwelling on Pop's dialogue near the end of chapter 2, so seeing how it comes full circle in chapter 8 makes me say, "Well done, Furuhashi… Well done…!"

—Betten

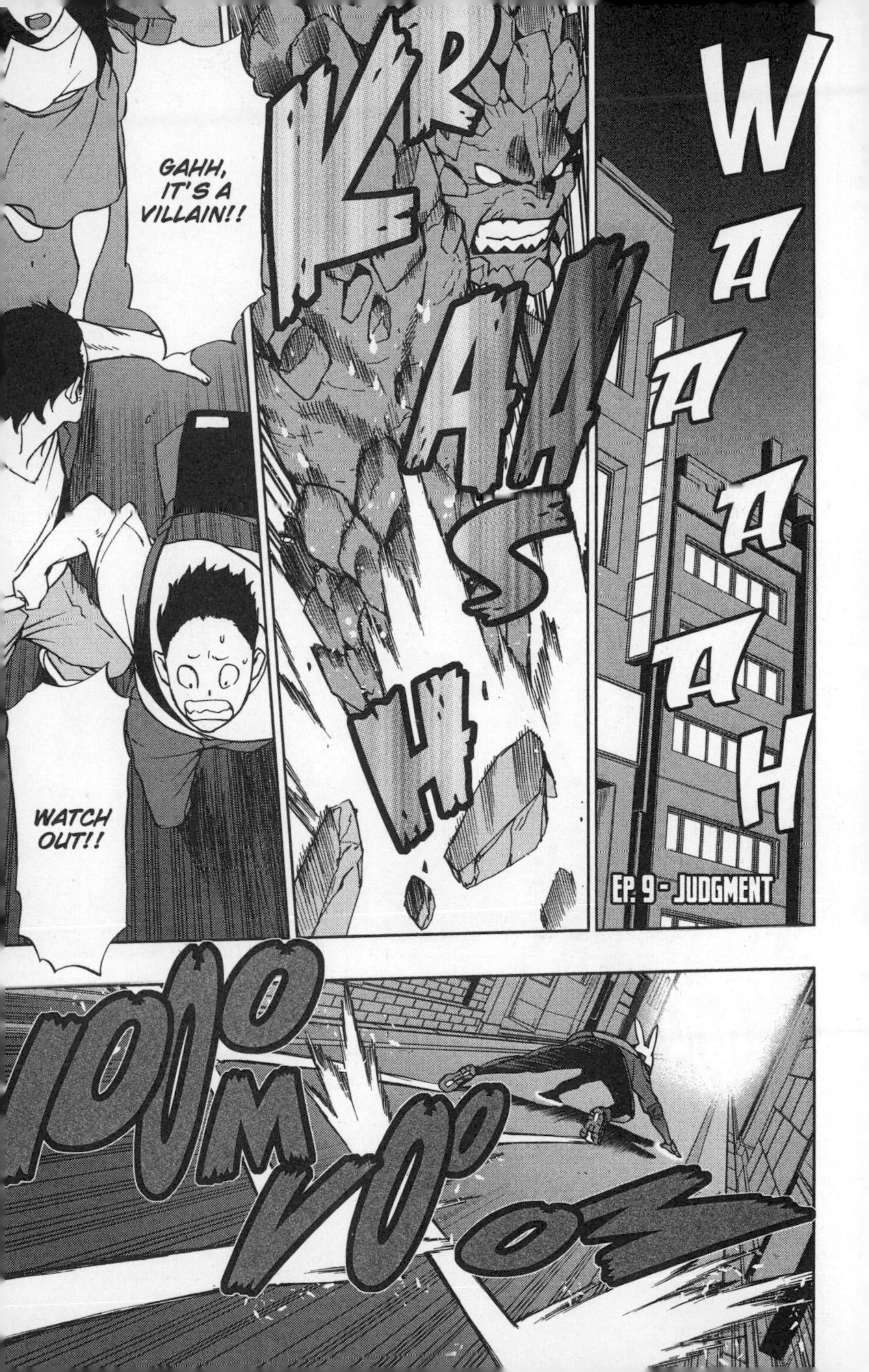
WAAAAH
EP. 9 - JUDGMENT
KRAASH
GAHH, IT'S A VILLAIN!!
WATCH OUT!!
VOOOM
VOOOM

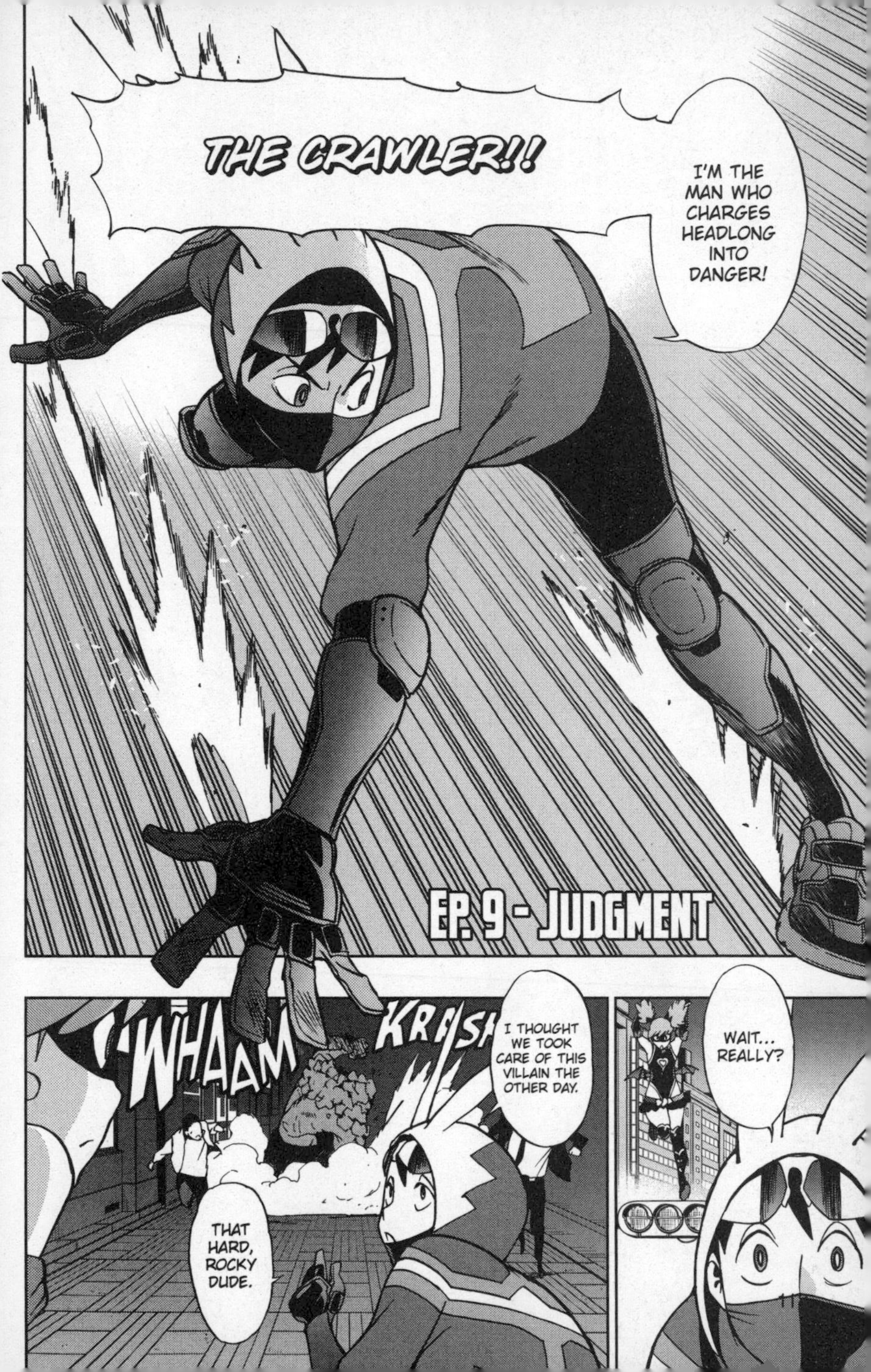
I'M THE MAN WHO CHARGES HEADLONG INTO DANGER!
THE CRAWLER!!
EP. 9 - JUDGMENT
WAIT... REALLY?
I THOUGHT WE TOOK CARE OF THIS VILLAIN THE OTHER DAY.
KRASH
WHAAM
THAT HARD, ROCKY DUDE.

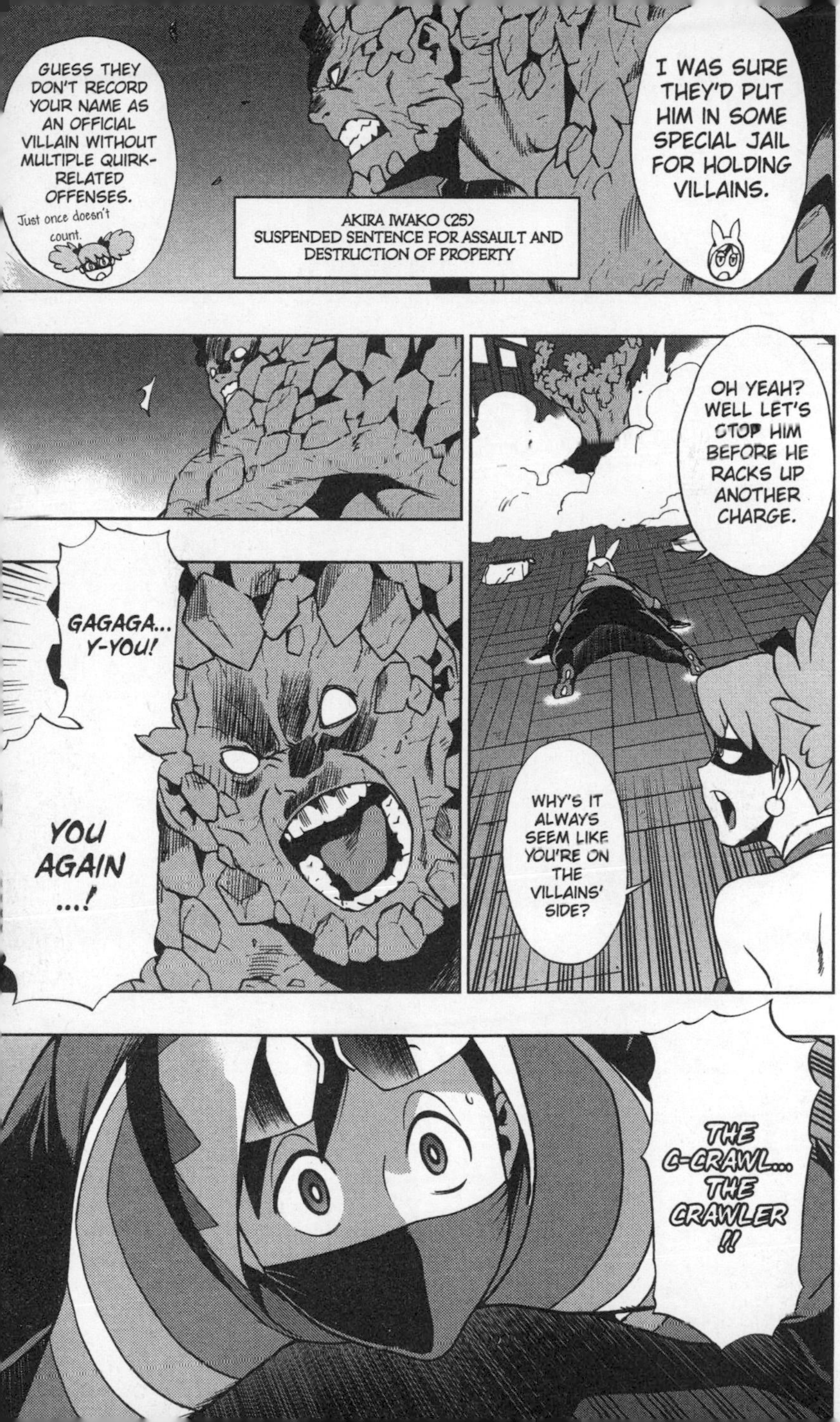
I WAS SURE THEY'D PUT HIM IN SOME SPECIAL JAIL FOR HOLDING VILLAINS.
GUESS THEY DON'T RECORD YOUR NAME AS AN OFFICIAL VILLAIN WITHOUT MULTIPLE QUIRK-RELATED OFFENSES.
Just once doesn't count.
AKIRA IWAKO (25) SUSPENDED SENTENCE FOR ASSAULT AND DESTRUCTION OF PROPERTY
OH YEAH? WELL LET'S STOP HIM BEFORE HE RACKS UP ANOTHER CHARGE.
WHY'S IT ALWAYS SEEM LIKE YOU'RE ON THE VILLAINS' SIDE?
GAGAGA... Y-YOU!
YOU AGAIN ...!
THE C-CRAWL... THE CRAWLER !!

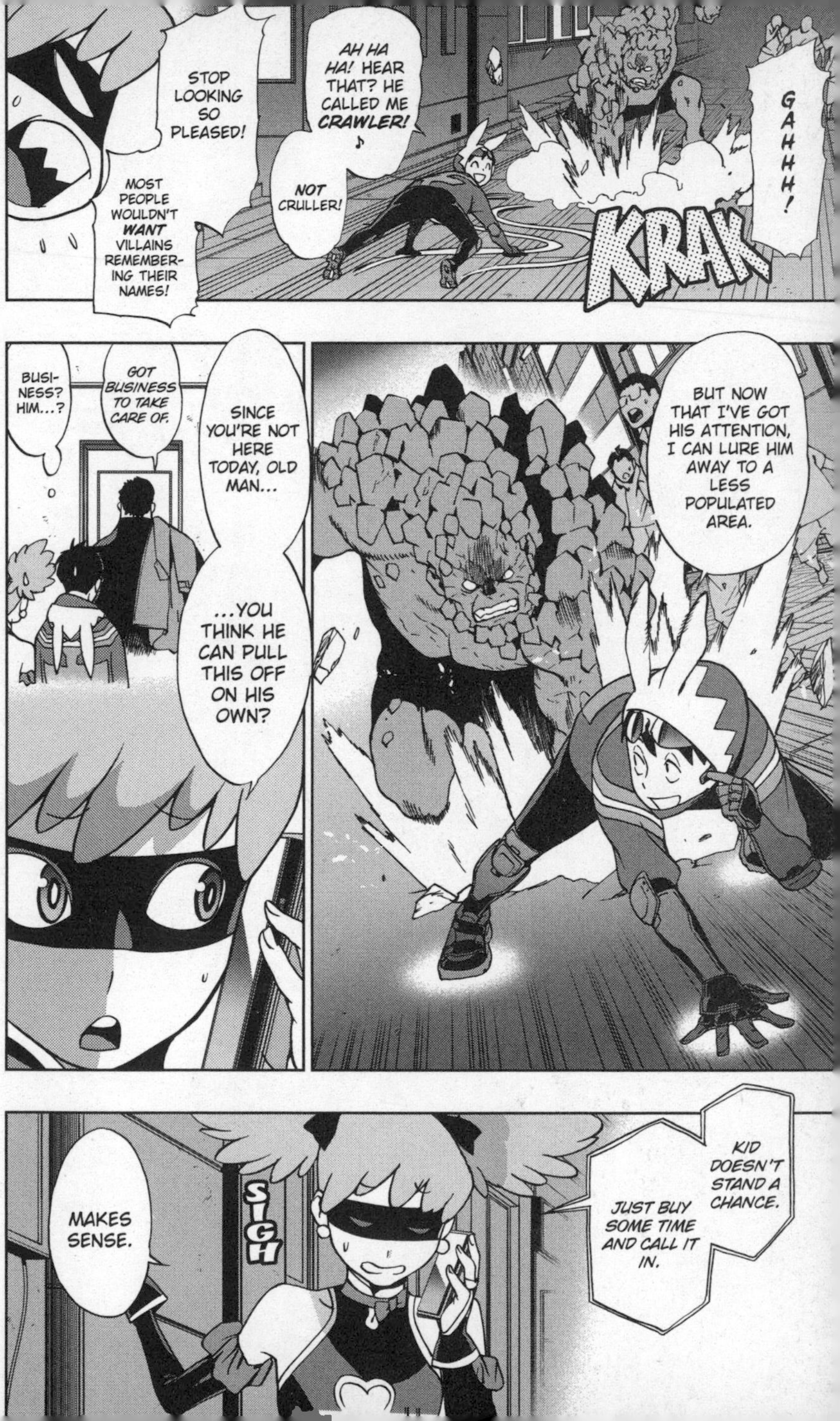
GAHHH!
KRAK
AH HA HA! HEAR THAT? HE CALLED ME CRAWLER! ♪
NOT CRULLER!
STOP LOOKING SO PLEASED!
MOST PEOPLE WOULDN'T WANT VILLAINS REMEMBERING THEIR NAMES!
BUT NOW THAT I'VE GOT HIS ATTENTION, I CAN LURE HIM AWAY TO A LESS POPULATED AREA.
SINCE YOU'RE NOT HERE TODAY, OLD MAN...
...YOU THINK HE CAN PULL THIS OFF ON HIS OWN?
GOT BUSINESS TO TAKE CARE OF.
BUSINESS? HIM...?
KID DOESN'T STAND A CHANCE.
JUST BUY SOME TIME AND CALL IT IN.
SIGH
MAKES SENSE.

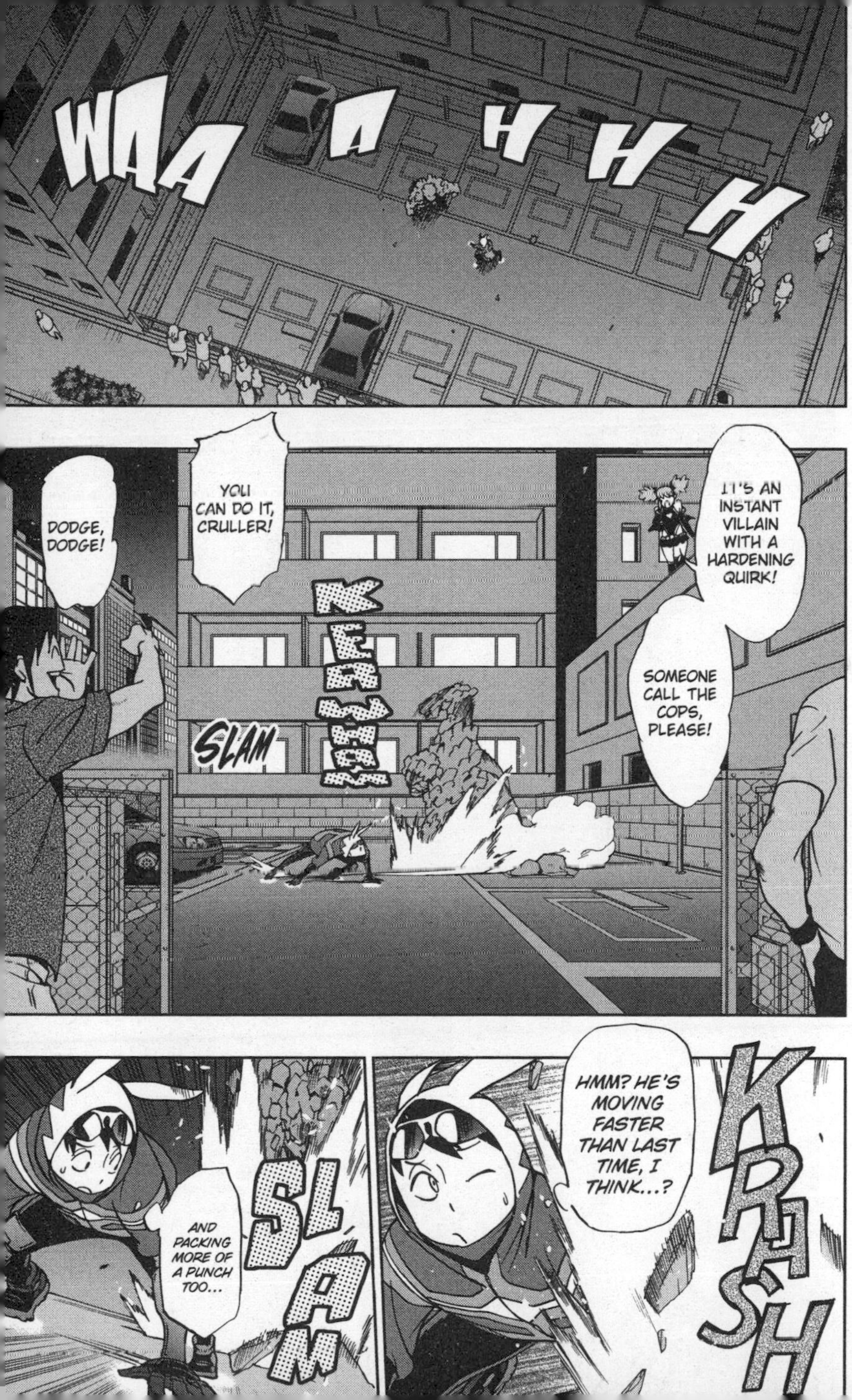
WAAAHHHH
IT'S AN INSTANT VILLAIN WITH A HARDENING QUIRK!
SOMEONE CALL THE COPS, PLEASE!
YOU CAN DO IT, CRULLER!
DODGE, DODGE!
KERWHAM
SLAM
KRASH
HMM? HE'S MOVING FASTER THAN LAST TIME, I THINK...?
SLAM
AND PACKING MORE OF A PUNCH TOO...

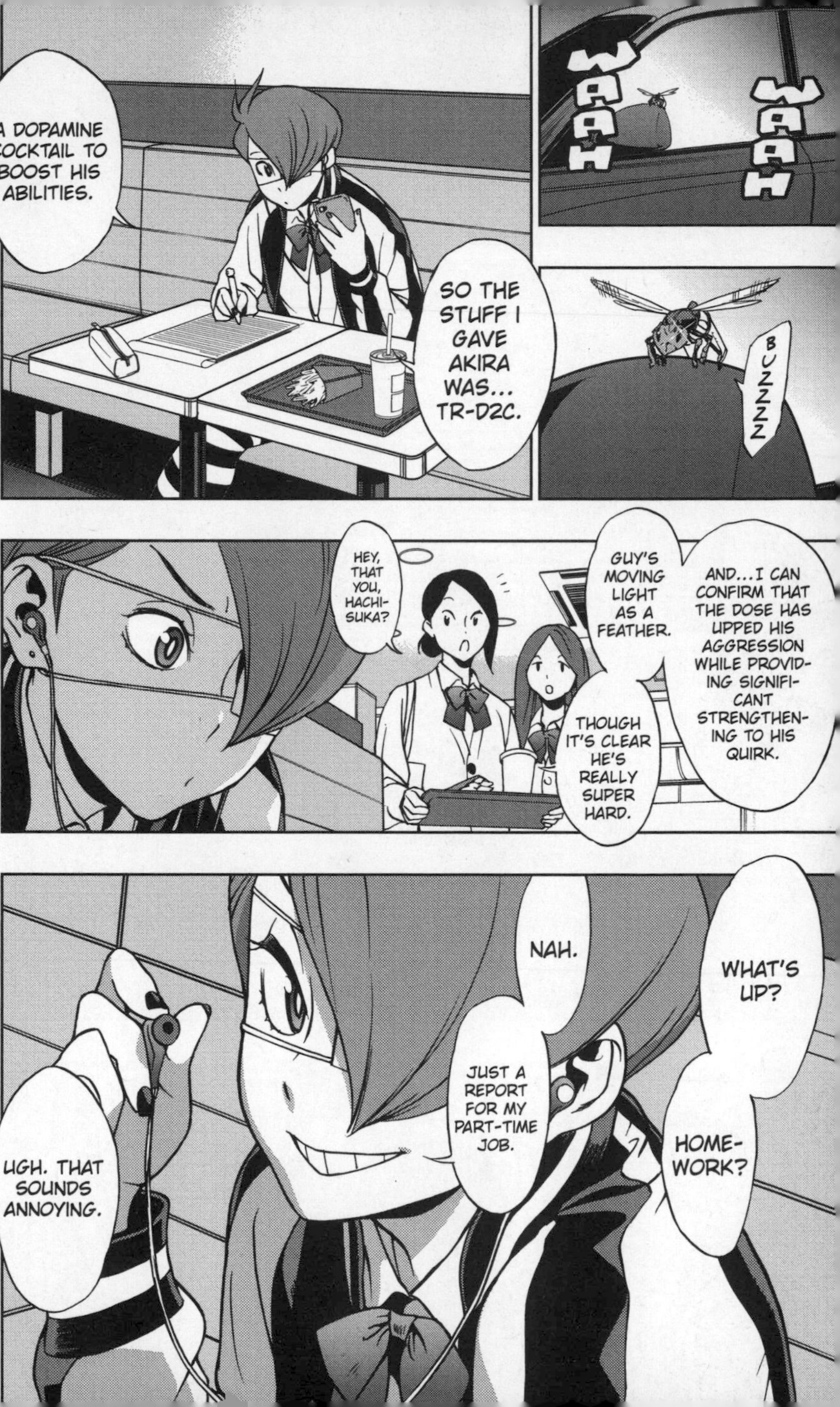
WAAAH
WAAAH
BUZZZ
SO THE STUFF I GAVE AKIRA WAS... TR-D2C.
A DOPAMINE COCKTAIL TO BOOST HIS ABILITIES.
AND...I CAN CONFIRM THAT THE DOSE HAS UPPED HIS AGGRESSION WHILE PROVIDING SIGNIFICANT STRENGTHENING TO HIS QUIRK.
GUY'S MOVING LIGHT AS A FEATHER.
THOUGH IT'S CLEAR HE'S REALLY SUPER HARD.
HEY, THAT YOU, HACHISUKA?
WHAT'S UP?
HOMEWORK?
NAH.
JUST A REPORT FOR MY PART-TIME JOB.
UGH. THAT SOUNDS ANNOYING.

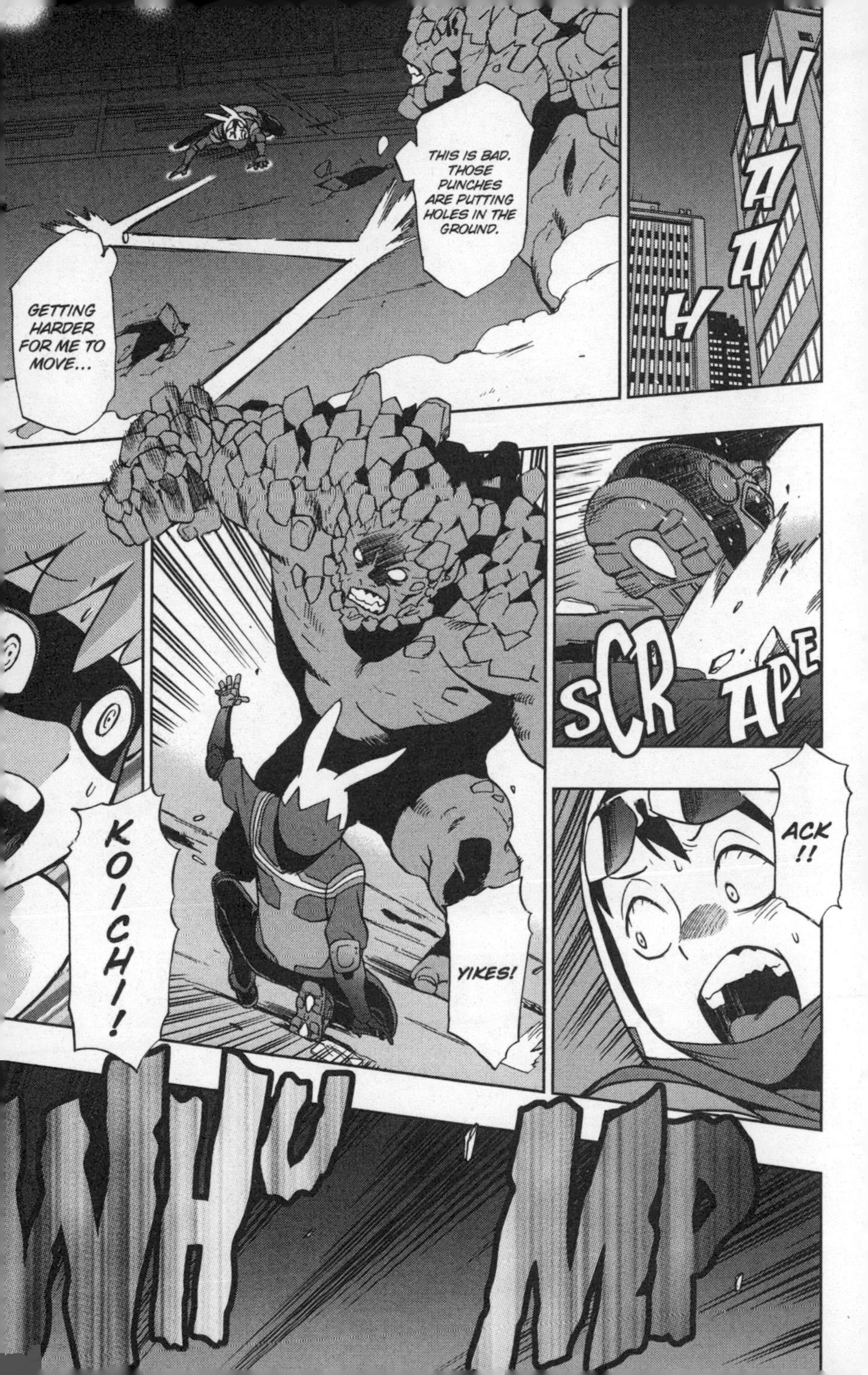
WAAH
THIS IS BAD. THOSE PUNCHES ARE PUTTING HOLES IN THE GROUND.
GETTING HARDER FOR ME TO MOVE...
SCRAPE
ACK!!
YIKES!
KOICHI!!
WHUMP

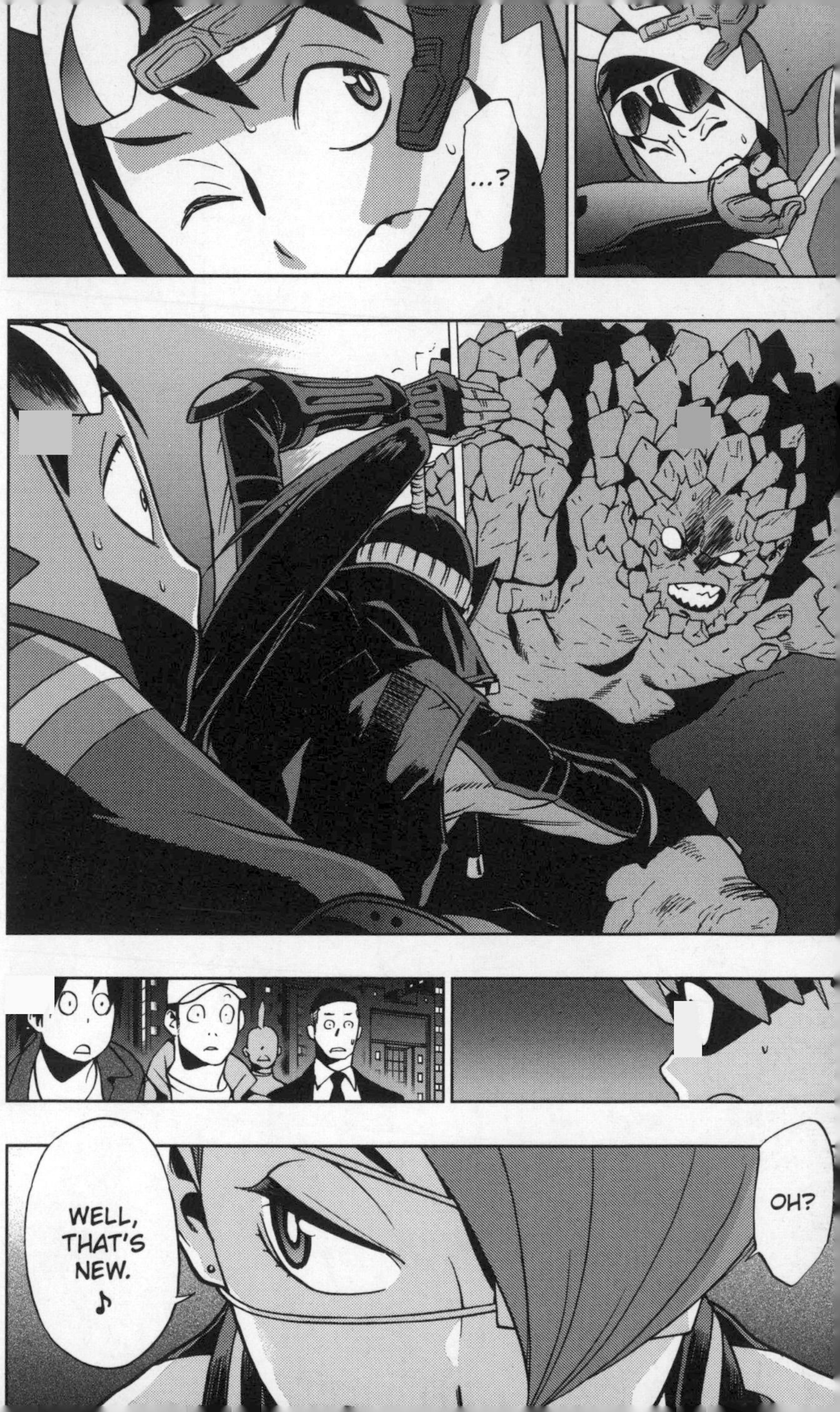
...?
OH?
WELL, THAT'S NEW. ♪

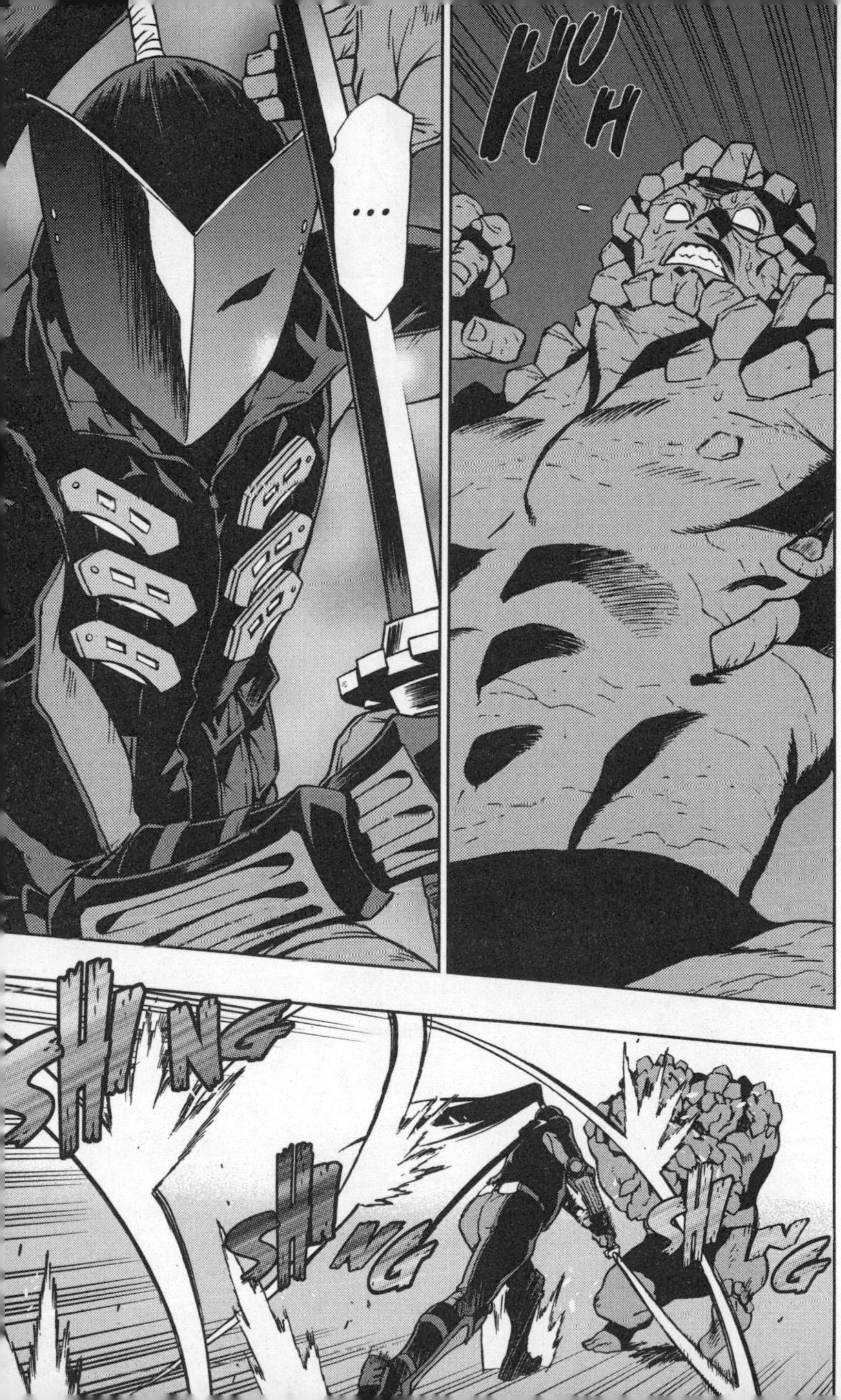
HUUH
...
SHING
SHING
SHING

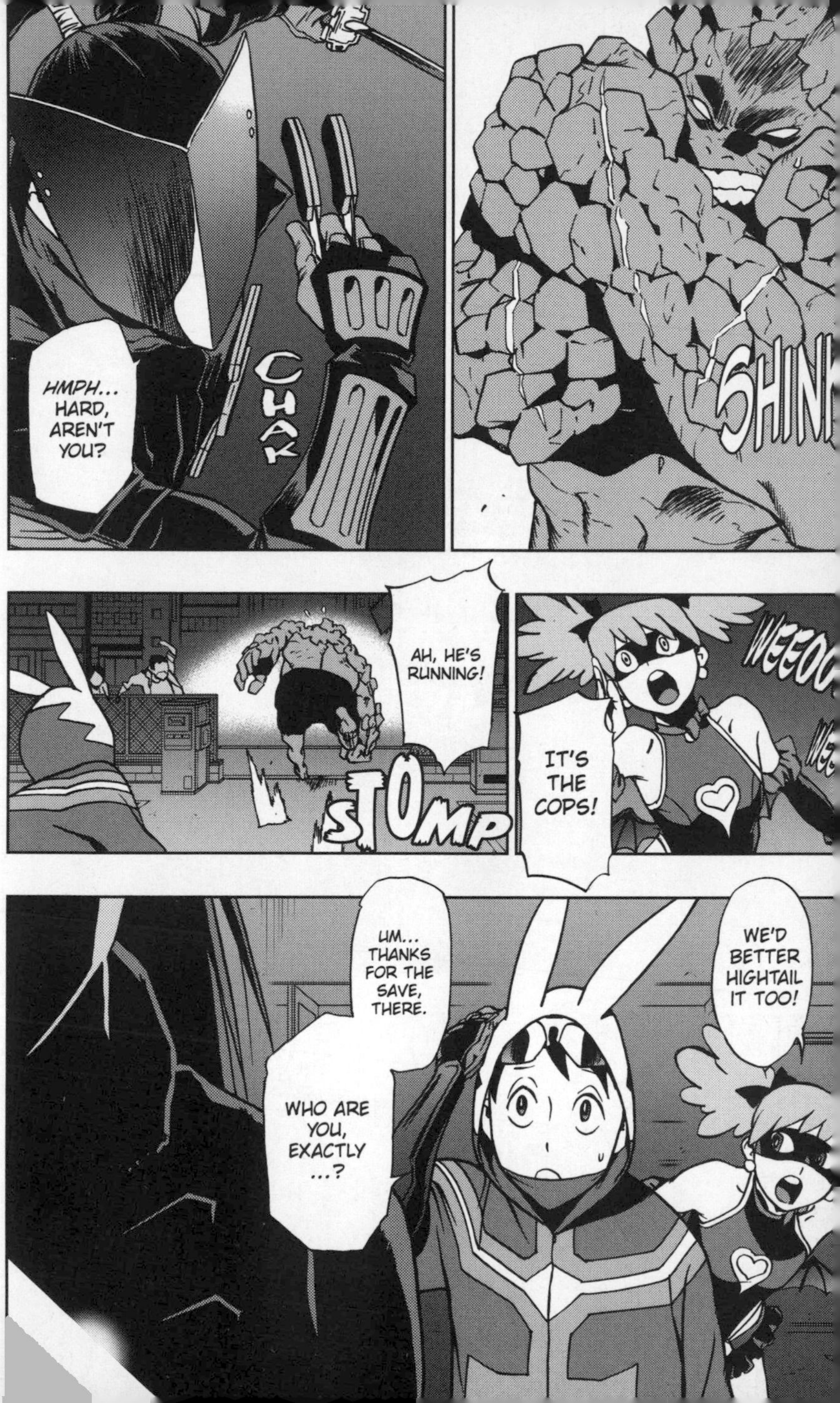
HMPH... HARD, AREN'T YOU?
CHAK
IT'S THE COPS!
AH, HE'S RUNNING!
STOMP
WE'D BETTER HIGHTAIL IT TOO!
UM... THANKS FOR THE SAVE, THERE.
WHO ARE YOU, EXACTLY ...?

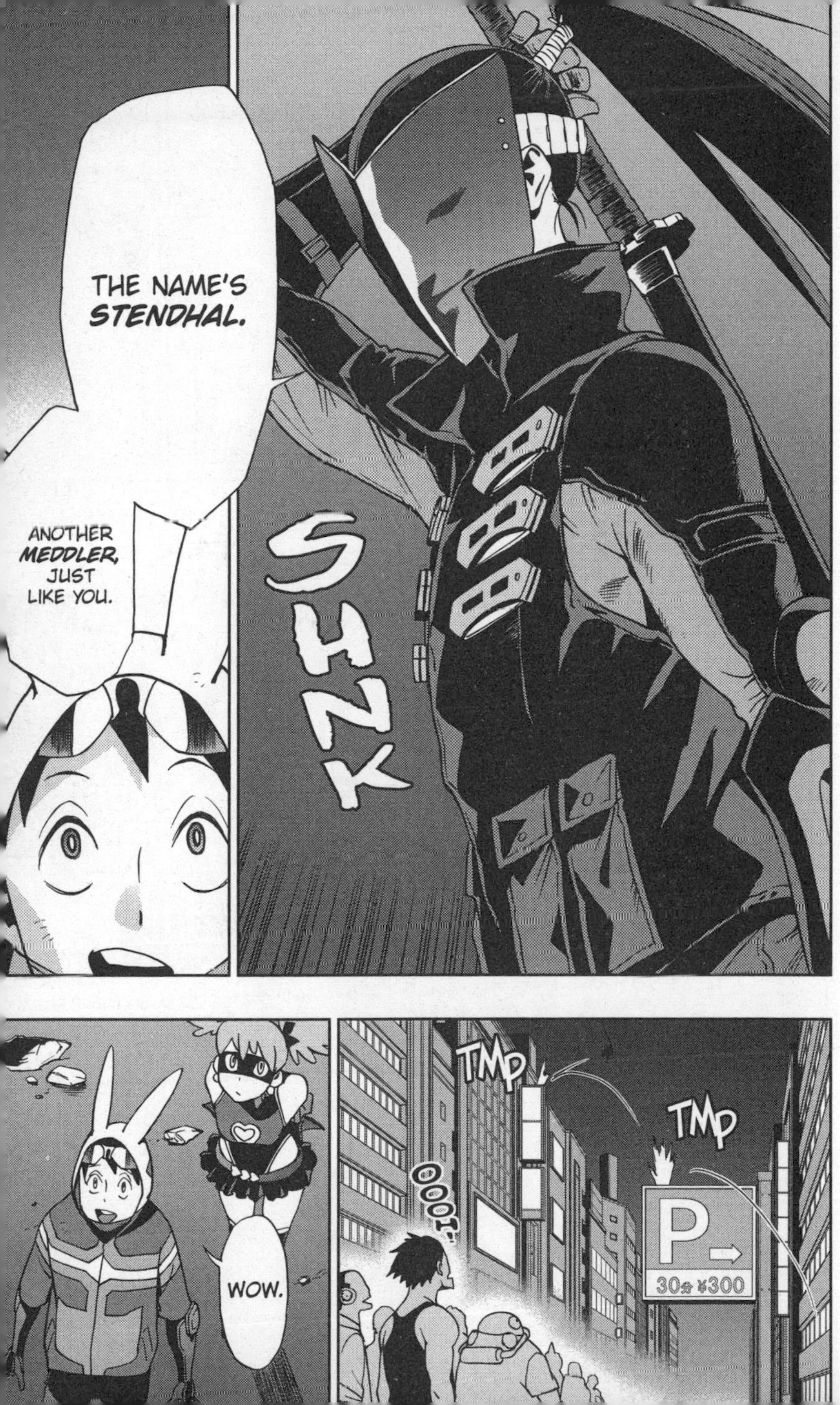
SHUNK
THE NAME'S STENDHAL.
ANOTHER MEDDLER, JUST LIKE YOU.
TMP
TMP
OOOI!
P
30分 ¥300
WOW.

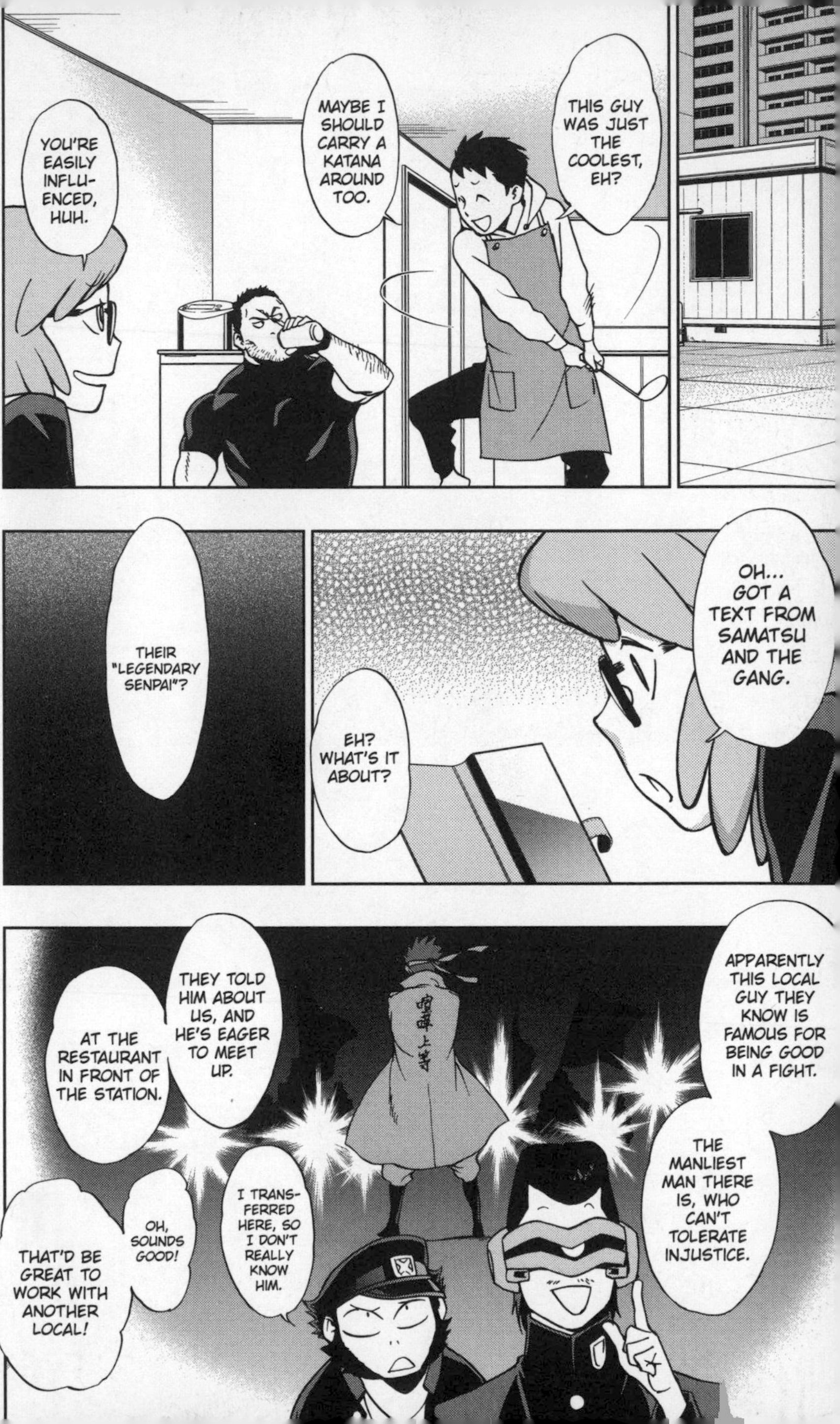
THIS GUY WAS JUST THE COOLEST, EH?
MAYBE I SHOULD CARRY A KATANA AROUND TOO.
YOU'RE EASILY INFLU-ENCED, HUH.
OH... GOT A TEXT FROM SAMATSU AND THE GANG.
EH? WHAT'S IT ABOUT?
THEIR "LEGENDARY SENPAI"?
APPARENTLY THIS LOCAL GUY THEY KNOW IS FAMOUS FOR BEING GOOD IN A FIGHT.
THE MANLIEST MAN THERE IS, WHO CAN'T TOLERATE INJUSTICE.
THEY TOLD HIM ABOUT US, AND HE'S EAGER TO MEET UP.
AT THE RESTAURANT IN FRONT OF THE STATION.
I TRANS-FERRED HERE, SO I DON'T REALLY KNOW HIM.
OH, SOUNDS GOOD!
THAT'D BE GREAT TO WORK WITH ANOTHER LOCAL!

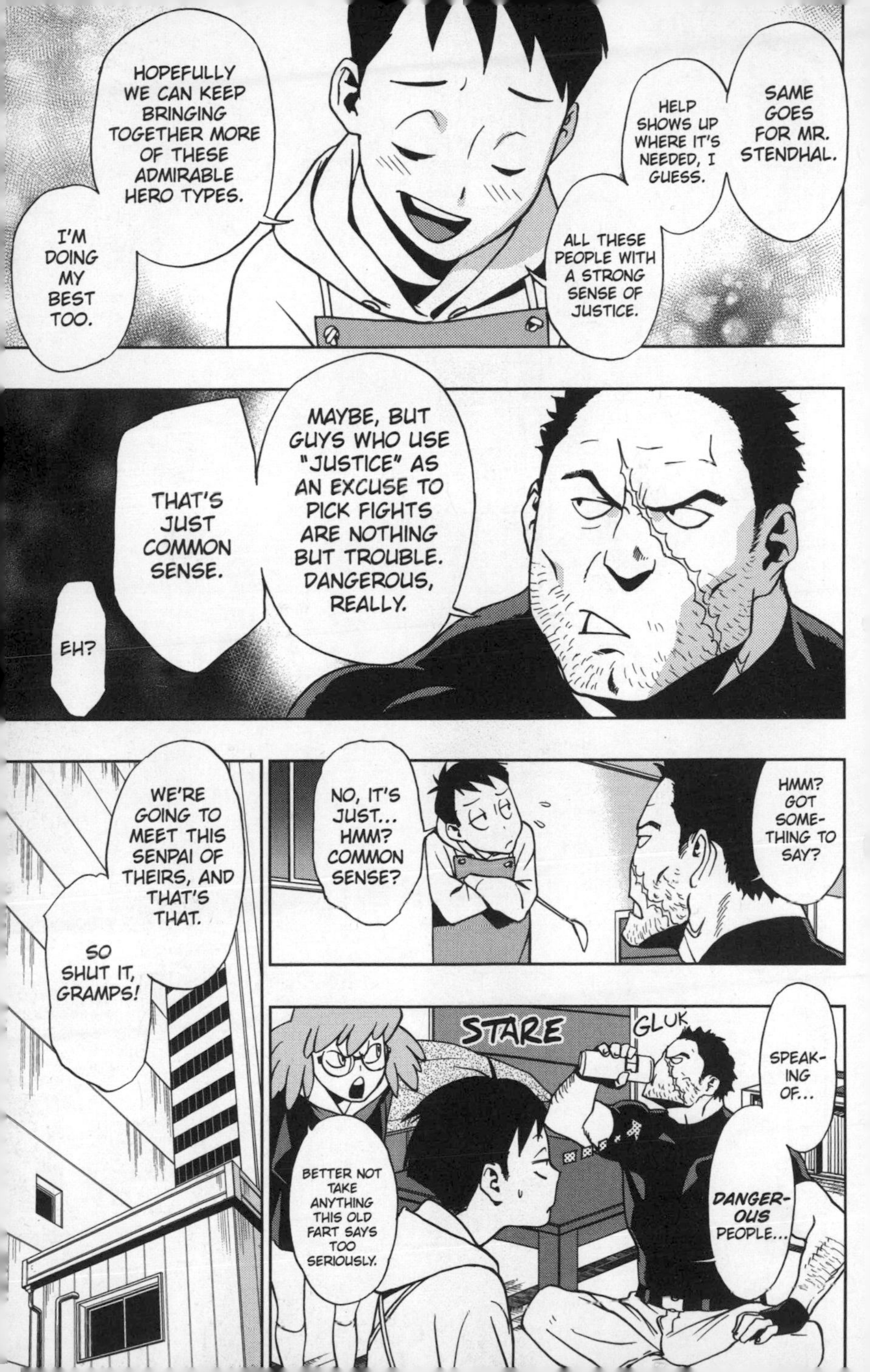
SAME GOES FOR MR. STENDHAL.
HELP SHOWS UP WHERE IT'S NEEDED, I GUESS.
ALL THESE PEOPLE WITH A STRONG SENSE OF JUSTICE.
HOPEFULLY WE CAN KEEP BRINGING TOGETHER MORE OF THESE ADMIRABLE HERO TYPES.
I'M DOING MY BEST TOO.
MAYBE, BUT GUYS WHO USE "JUSTICE" AS AN EXCUSE TO PICK FIGHTS ARE NOTHING BUT TROUBLE. DANGEROUS, REALLY.
THAT'S JUST COMMON SENSE.
EH?
HMM? GOT SOME-THING TO SAY?
NO, IT'S JUST... HMM? COMMON SENSE?
SPEAK-ING OF...
GLUK
STARE
DANGER-OUS PEOPLE...
BETTER NOT TAKE ANYTHING THIS OLD FART SAYS TOO SERIOUSLY.
WE'RE GOING TO MEET THIS SENPAI OF THEIRS, AND THAT'S THAT.
SO SHUT IT, GRAMPS!

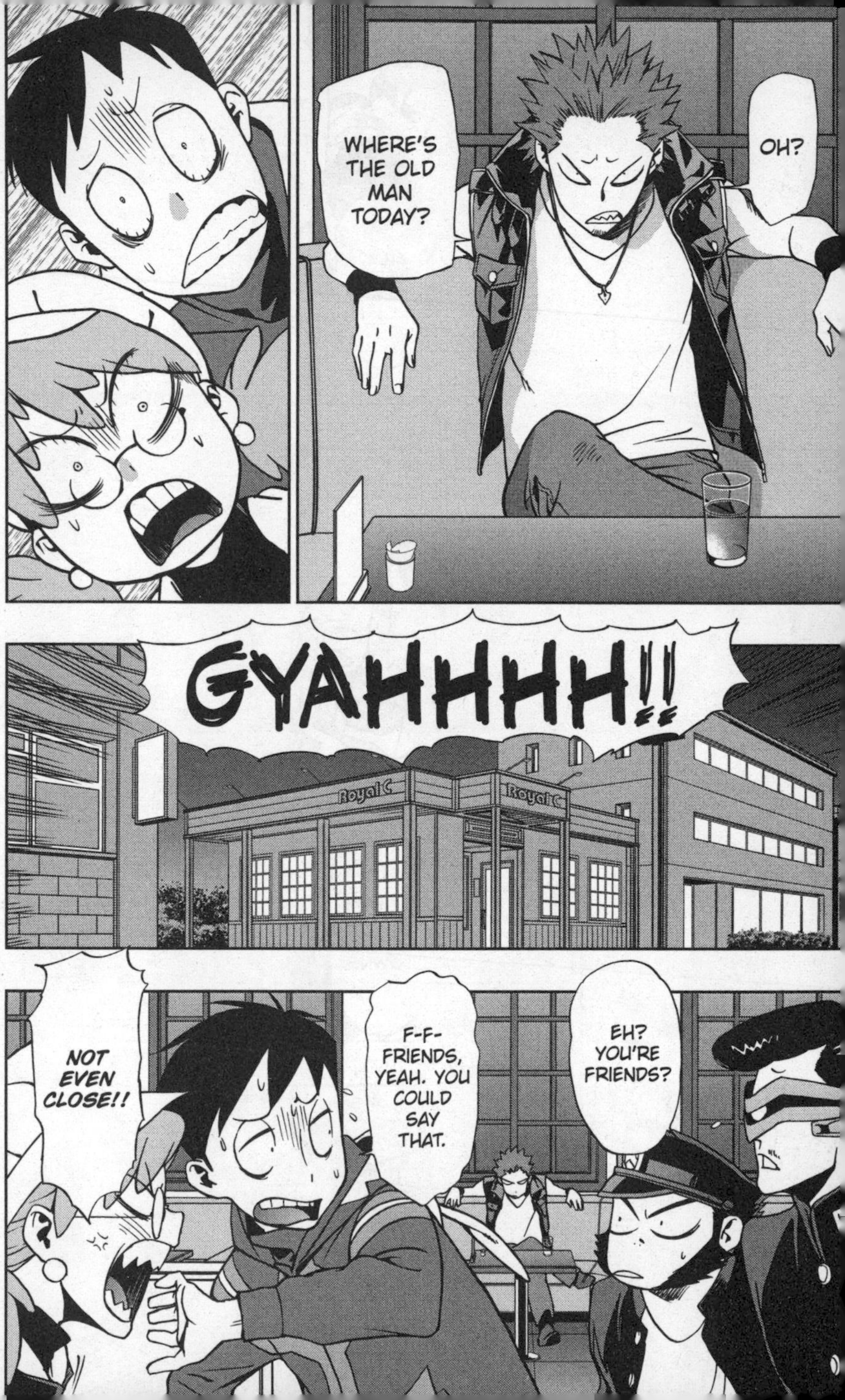
OH?
WHERE'S THE OLD MAN TODAY?
GYAHHHH!!
EH? YOU'RE FRIENDS?
F-F-FRIENDS, YEAH. YOU COULD SAY THAT.
NOT EVEN CLOSE!!

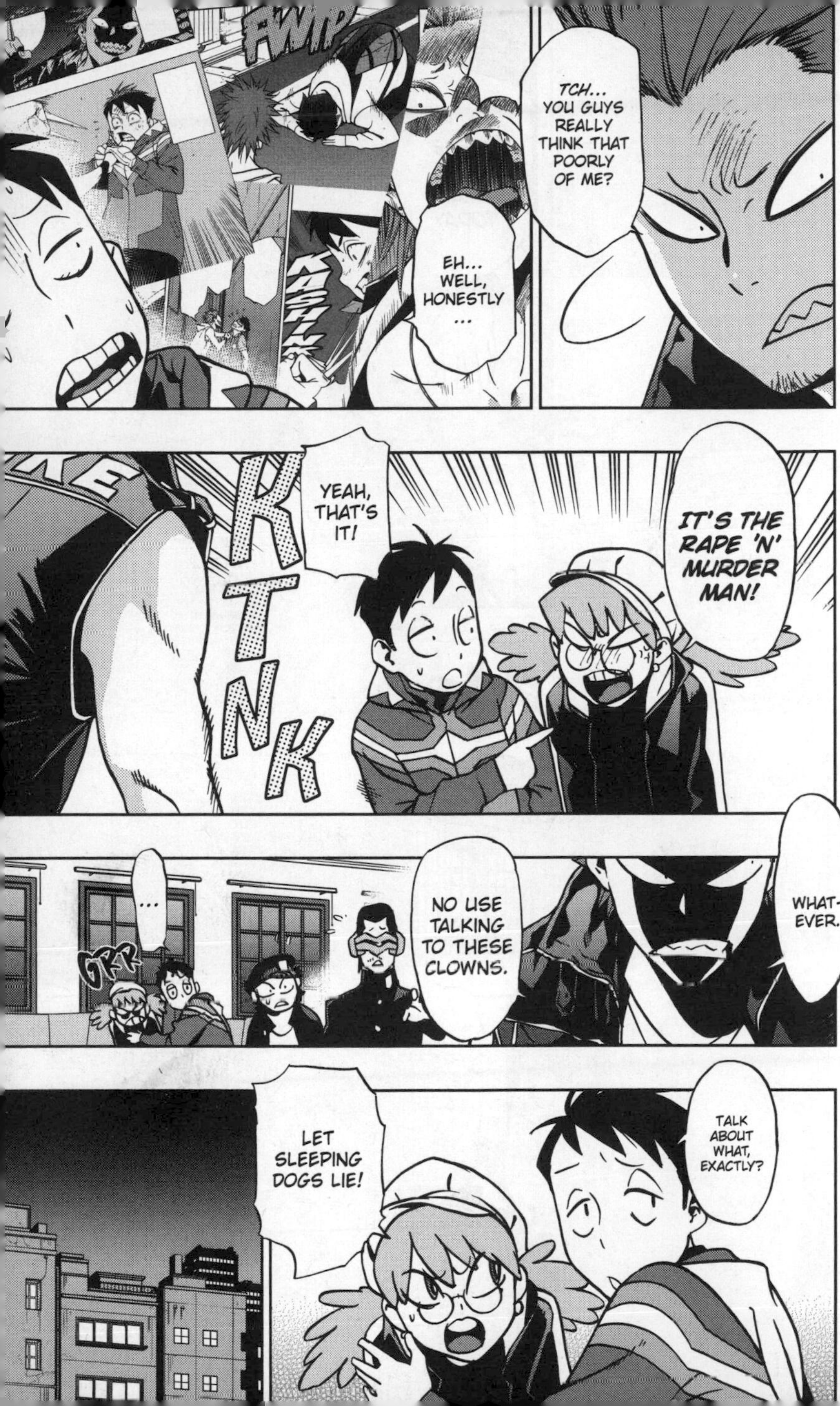
TCH... YOU GUYS REALLY THINK THAT POORLY OF ME?
FWIP
EH... WELL, HONESTLY ...
IT'S THE RAPE 'N' MURDER MAN!
YEAH, THAT'S IT!
KTNK
WHAT-EVER.
NO USE TALKING TO THESE CLOWNS.
...
GRR
TALK ABOUT WHAT, EXACTLY?
LET SLEEPING DOGS LIE!

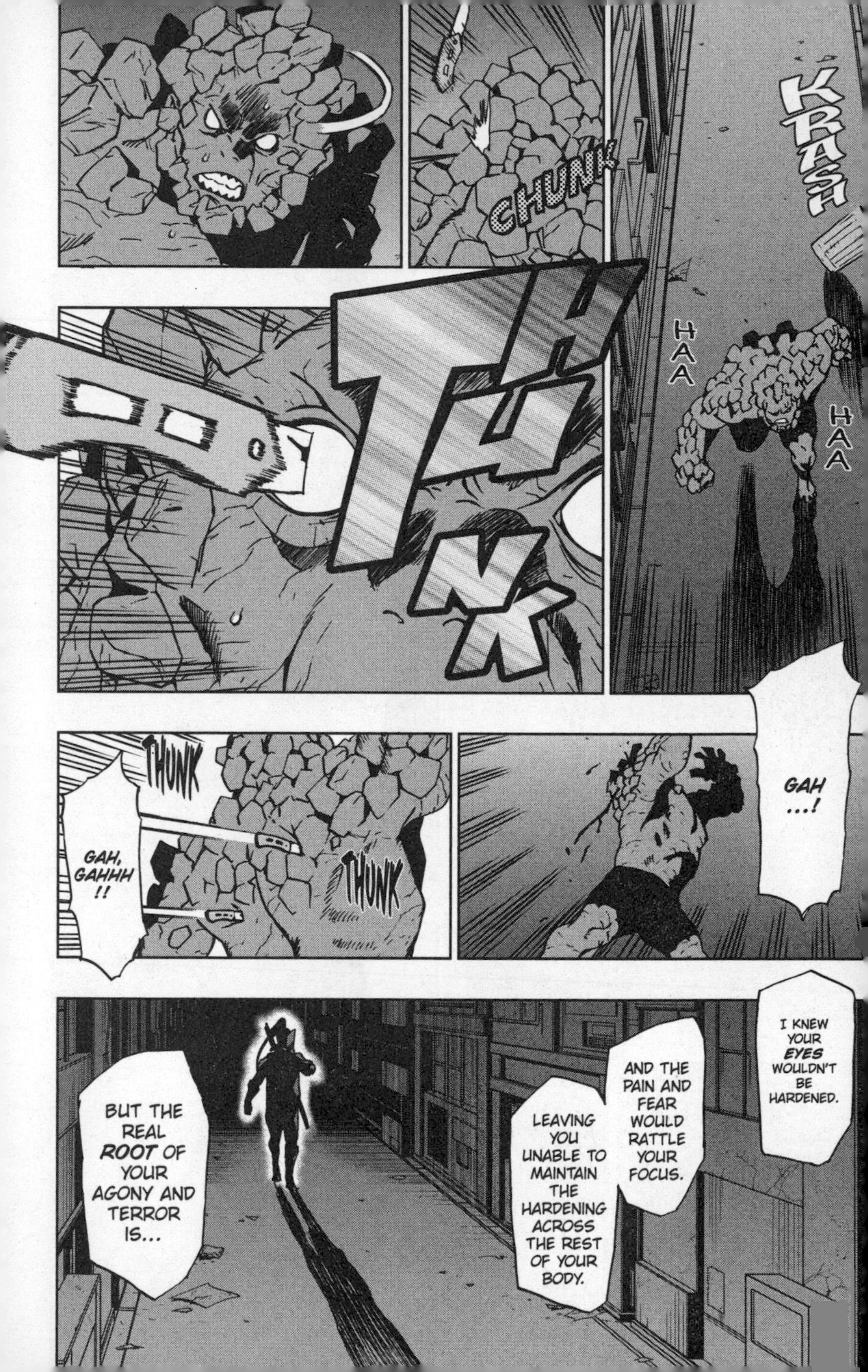
KRASH
HAA HAA
HAA HAA
CHUNK
THUNK
GAH ...!
THUNK
THUNK
GAH, GAHHH !!
I KNEW YOUR EYES WOULDN'T BE HARDENED.
AND THE PAIN AND FEAR WOULD RATTLE YOUR FOCUS.
LEAVING YOU UNABLE TO MAINTAIN THE HARDENING ACROSS THE REST OF YOUR BODY.
BUT THE REAL ROOT OF YOUR AGONY AND TERROR IS...

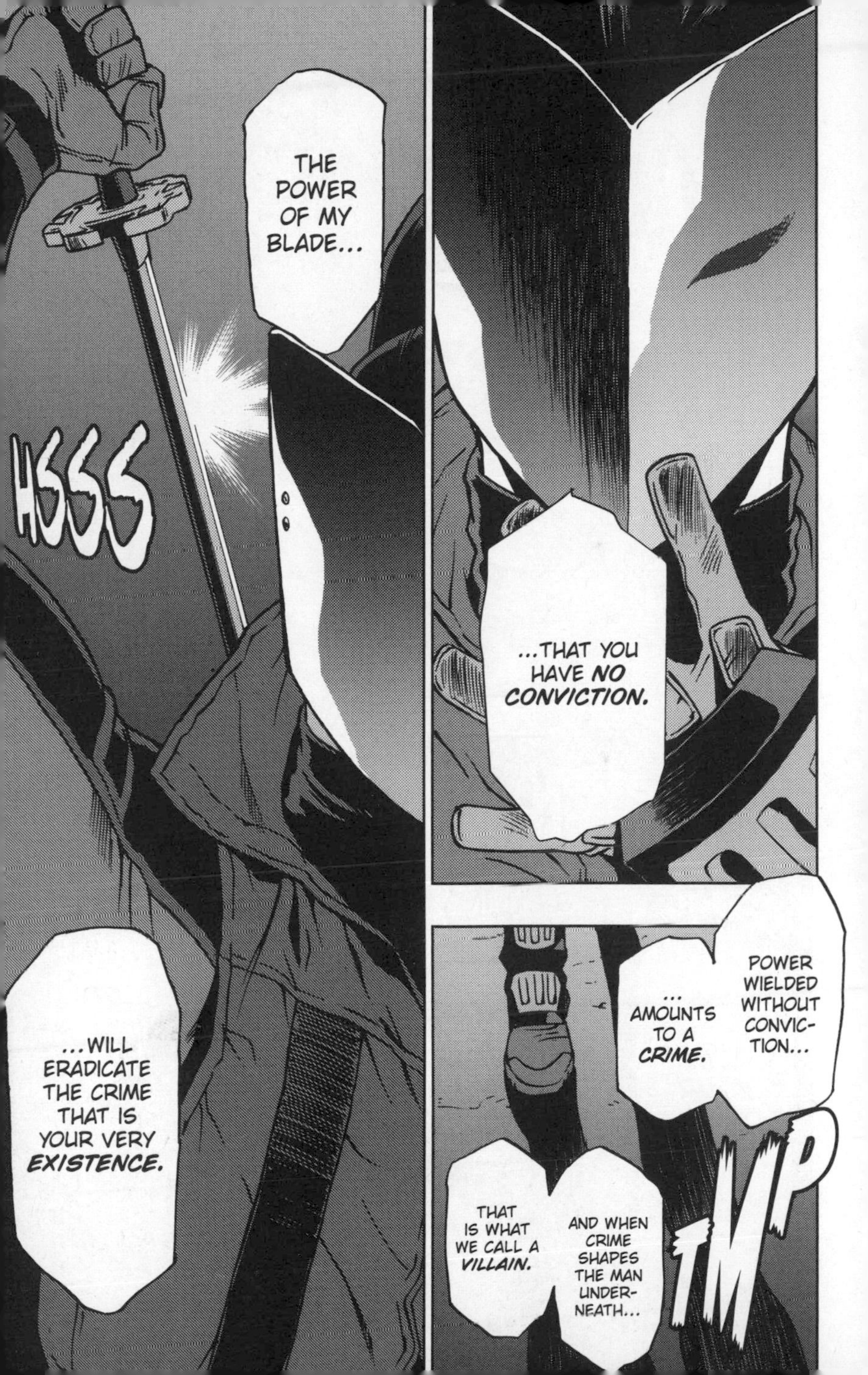
...THAT YOU HAVE NO CONVICTION.
POWER WIELDED WITHOUT CONVIC- TION...
... AMOUNTS TO A CRIME.
AND WHEN CRIME SHAPES THE MAN UNDER- NEATH...
THAT IS WHAT WE CALL A VILLAIN.
TMP
THE POWER OF MY BLADE...
HSSS
...WILL ERADICATE THE CRIME THAT IS YOUR VERY EXISTENCE.

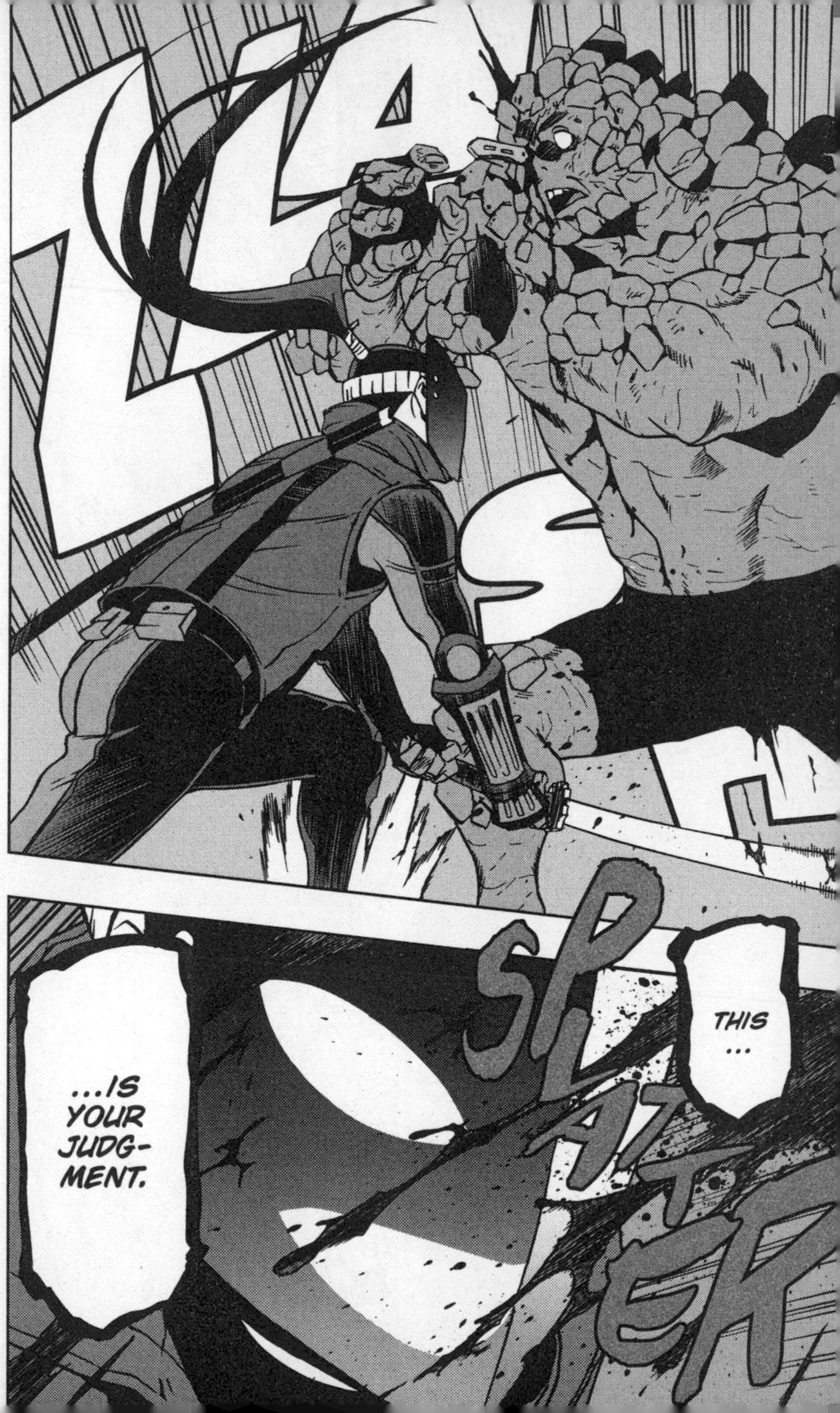
THIS ...
SPLATTER
...IS YOUR JUDGMENT.

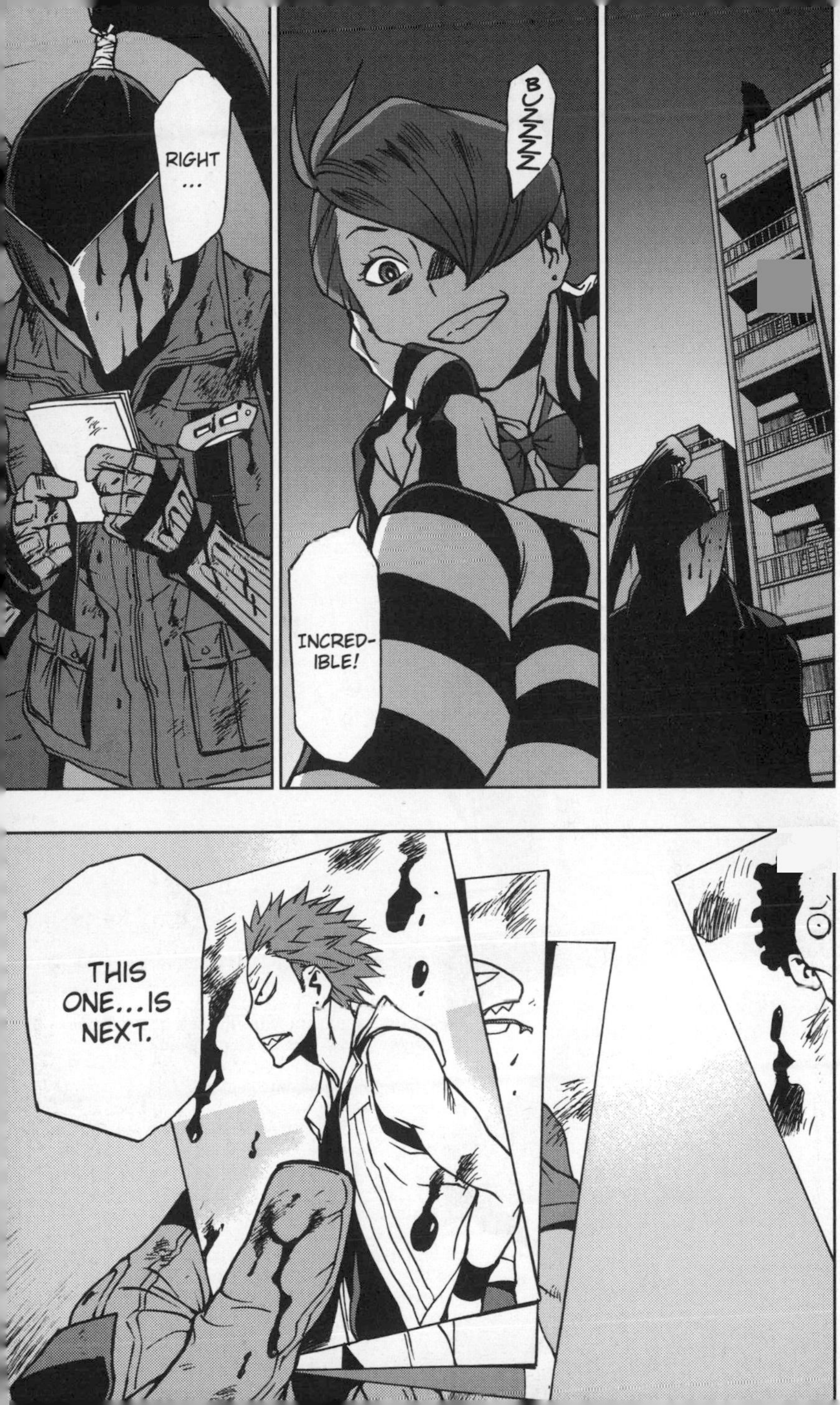
BUZZZZ
INCRED-IBLE!
RIGHT...
THIS ONE...IS NEXT.

ROCK VILLAIN/AKIRA IWAKO

THE ROUGH DESIGN

*Moves more like a beast (gorilla-like)
*More crystal protrusions

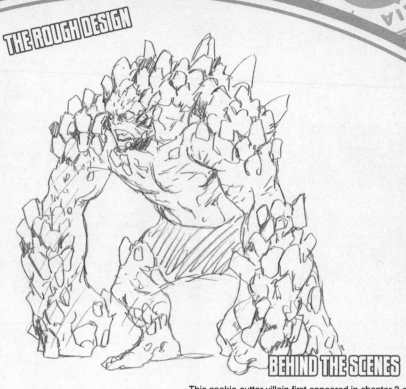

BEHIND THE SCENES

This cookie-cutter villain first appeared in chapter 3 of the last volume.

He follows the pattern of being used as a guinea pig by the "organization" before getting taken down.

That data gathered from the junkie villain in chapter 6 is what allowed for this guy's enhanced second appearance… The components of Trigger that affect the brain have been strengthened, leading to more violent mental transformations and boosted abilities.

—Furuhashi

He was already enough of a pain to draw in chapter 3, and it only got worse this time around, given his power-up and the standoff with Stendhal. A pitiable character, really.

—Betten

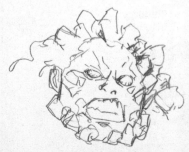

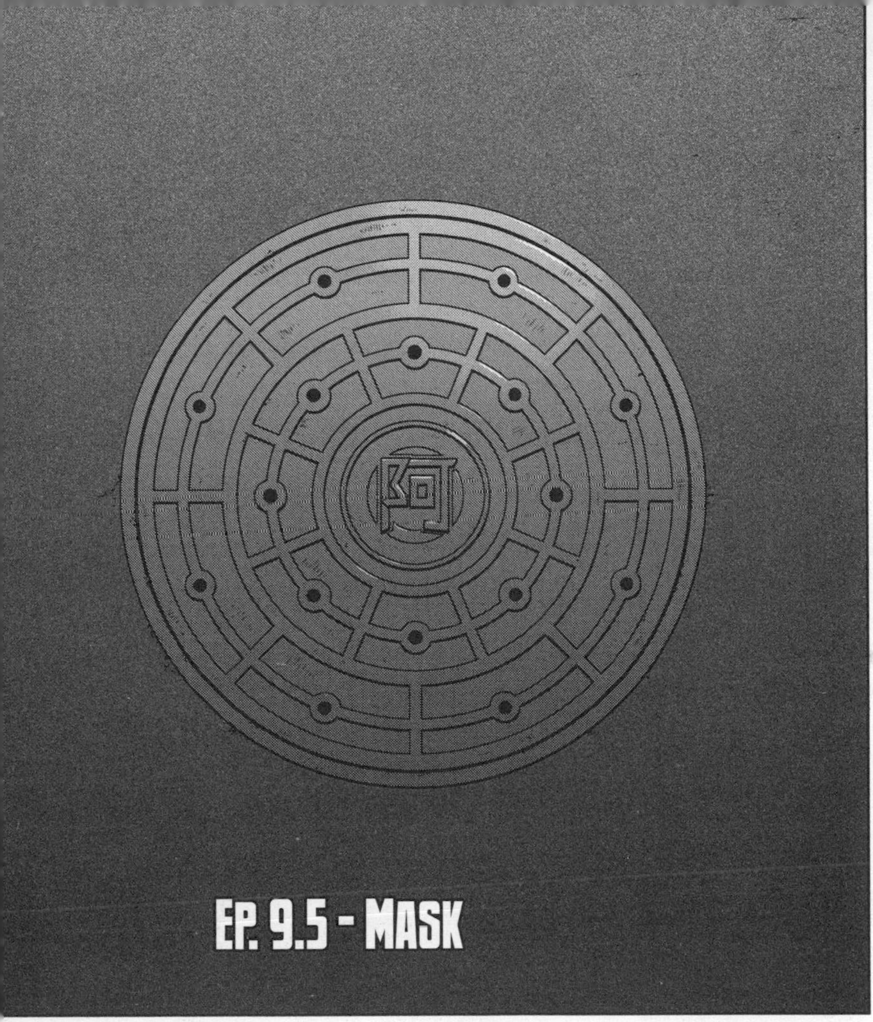
EP. 9.5 - MASK

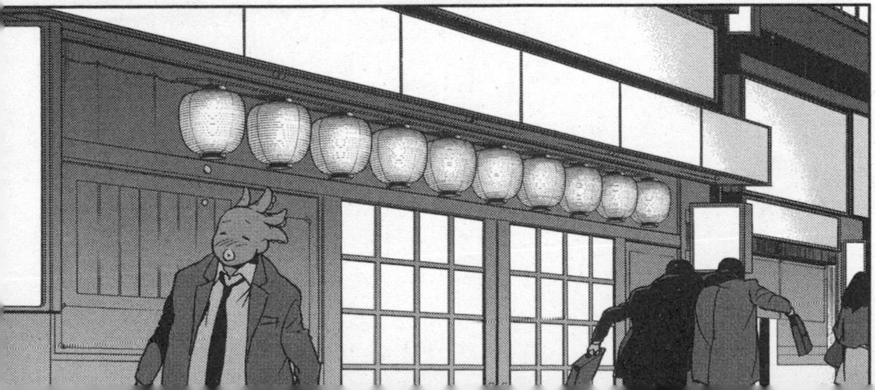

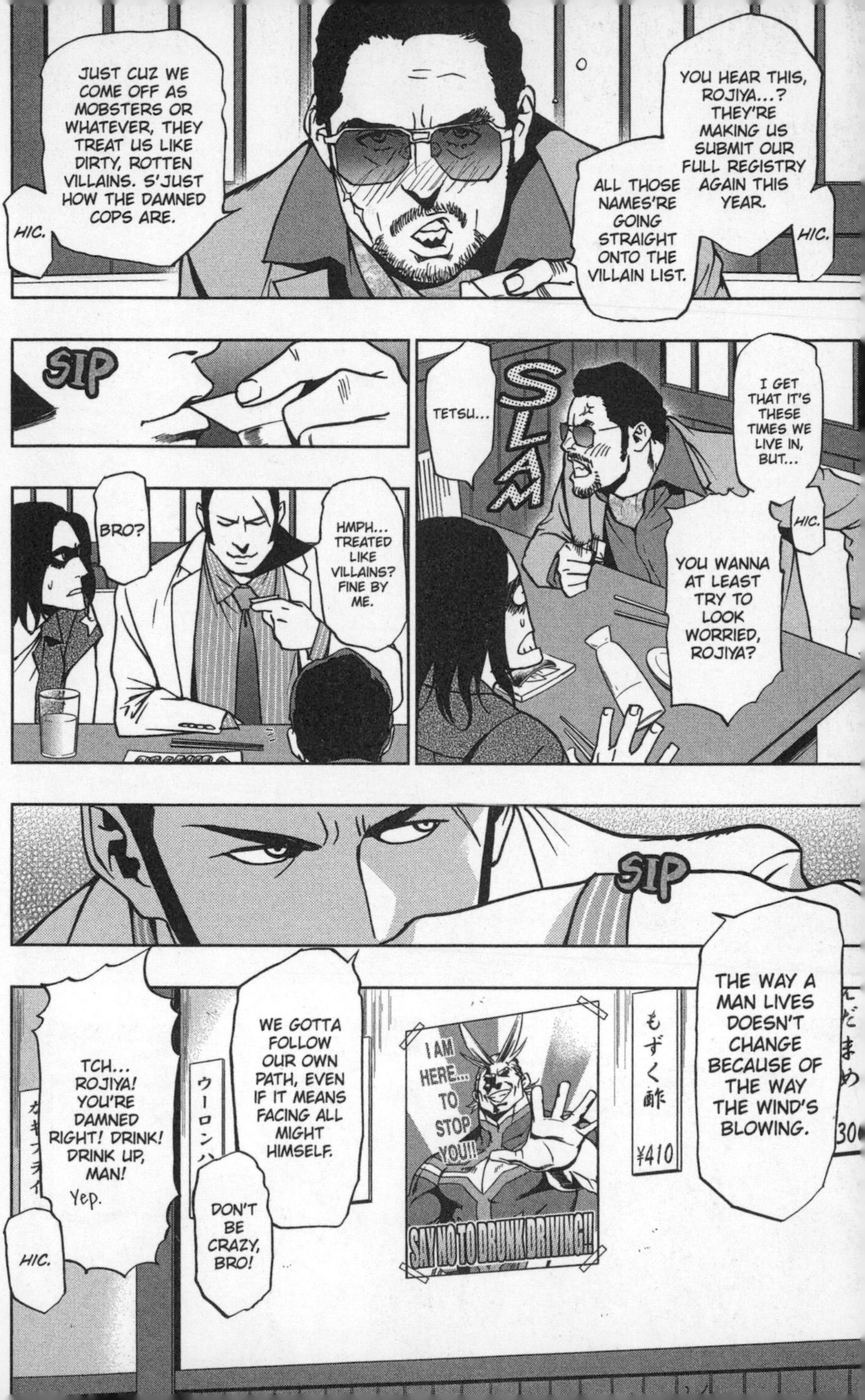
YOU HEAR THIS, ROJIYA...? THEY'RE MAKING US SUBMIT OUR FULL REGISTRY AGAIN THIS YEAR.
HIC.
ALL THOSE NAMES'RE GOING STRAIGHT ONTO THE VILLAIN LIST.
JUST CUZ WE COME OFF AS MOBSTERS OR WHATEVER, THEY TREAT US LIKE DIRTY, ROTTEN VILLAINS. S'JUST HOW THE DAMNED COPS ARE.
HIC.
I GET THAT IT'S THESE TIMES WE LIVE IN, BUT...
SLAM
TETSU...
HIC.
YOU WANNA AT LEAST TRY TO LOOK WORRIED, ROJIYA?
SIP
HMPH... TREATED LIKE VILLAINS? FINE BY ME.
BRO?
SIP
THE WAY A MAN LIVES DOESN'T CHANGE BECAUSE OF THE WAY THE WIND'S BLOWING.
もずく酢
¥410
I AM HERE... TO STOP YOU!!
SAY NO TO DRUNK DRIVING!!
WE GOTTA FOLLOW OUR OWN PATH, EVEN IF IT MEANS FACING ALL MIGHT HIMSELF.
DON'T BE CRAZY, BRO!
ウーロンハ
TCH... ROJIYA! YOU'RE DAMNED RIGHT! DRINK! DRINK UP, MAN!
Yep.
HIC.

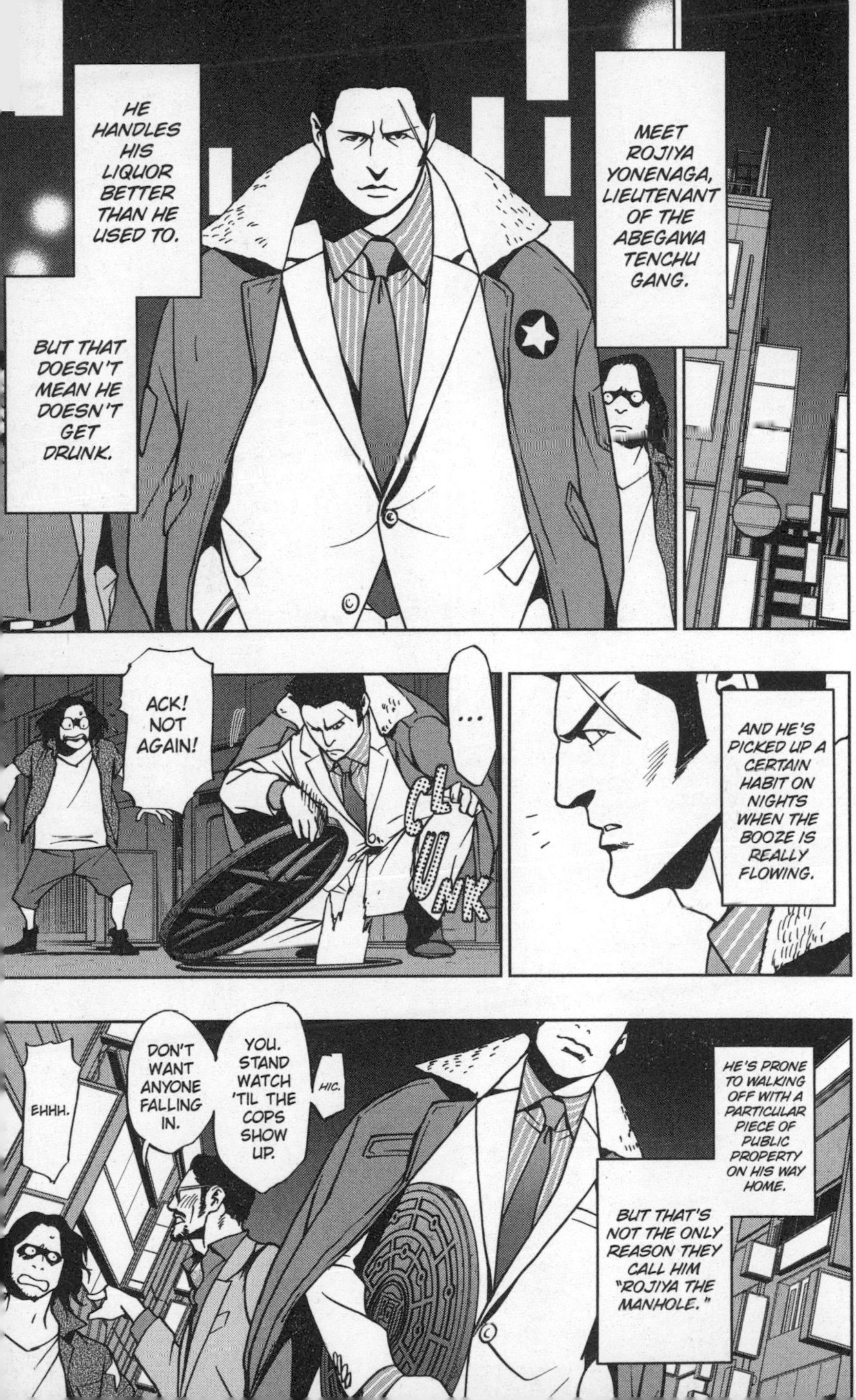
MEET ROJIYA YONENAGA, LIEUTENANT OF THE ABEGAWA TENCHU GANG.
HE HANDLES HIS LIQUOR BETTER THAN HE USED TO.
BUT THAT DOESN'T MEAN HE DOESN'T GET DRUNK.
AND HE'S PICKED UP A CERTAIN HABIT ON NIGHTS WHEN THE BOOZE IS REALLY FLOWING.
...
CLUNK
ACK! NOT AGAIN!
HE'S PRONE TO WALKING OFF WITH A PARTICULAR PIECE OF PUBLIC PROPERTY ON HIS WAY HOME.
BUT THAT'S NOT THE ONLY REASON THEY CALL HIM "ROJIYA THE MANHOLE."
HIC.
YOU. STAND WATCH 'TIL THE COPS SHOW UP.
DON'T WANT ANYONE FALLING IN.
EHHH.

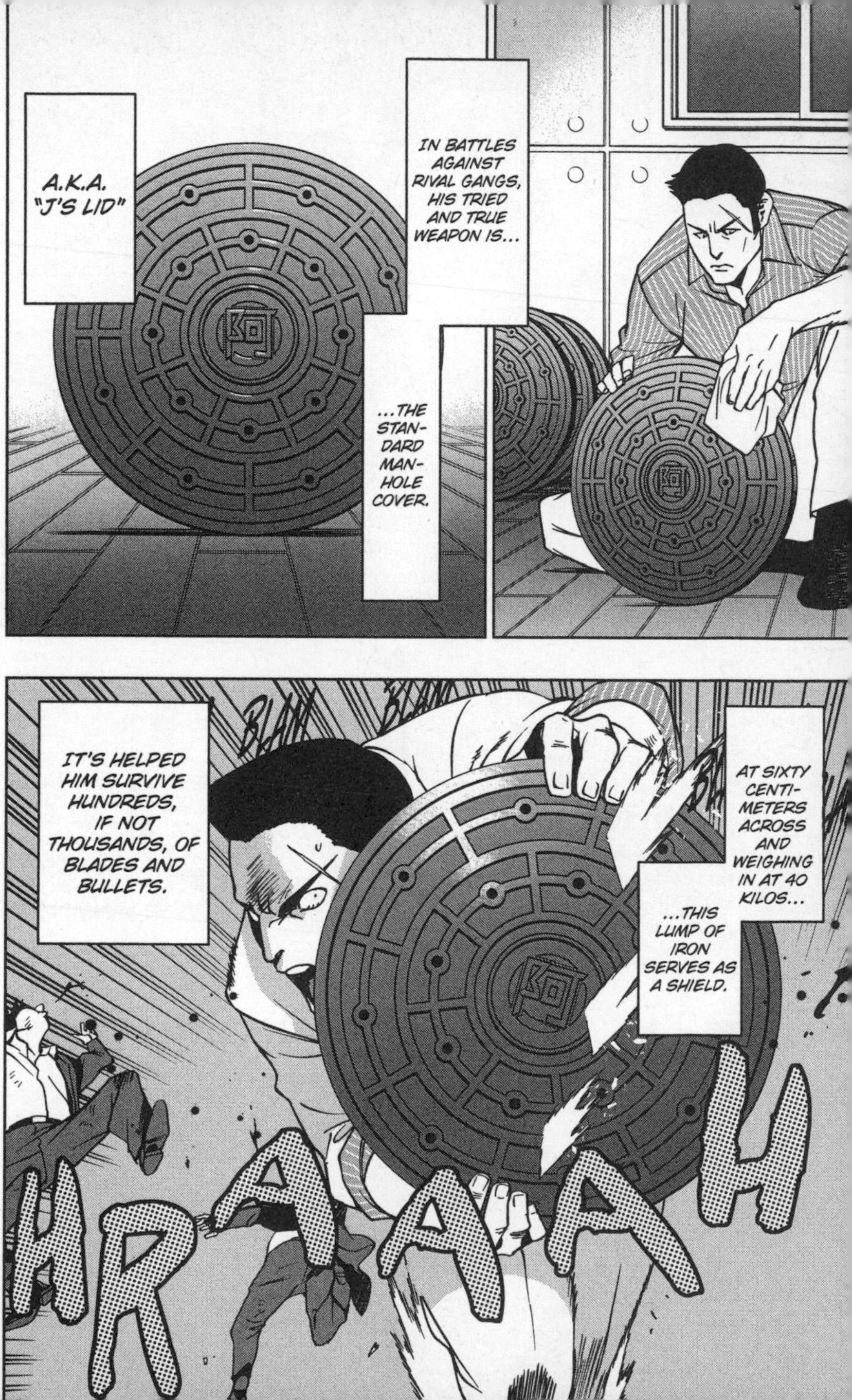
IN BATTLES AGAINST RIVAL GANGS, HIS TRIED AND TRUE WEAPON IS...
...THE STAN-DARD MAN-HOLE COVER.
A.K.A. "J'S LID"
AT SIXTY CENTI-METERS ACROSS AND WEIGHING IN AT 40 KILOS...
...THIS LUMP OF IRON SERVES AS A SHIELD.
IT'S HELPED HIM SURVIVE HUNDREDS, IF NOT THOUSANDS, OF BLADES AND BULLETS.
HRAAAH

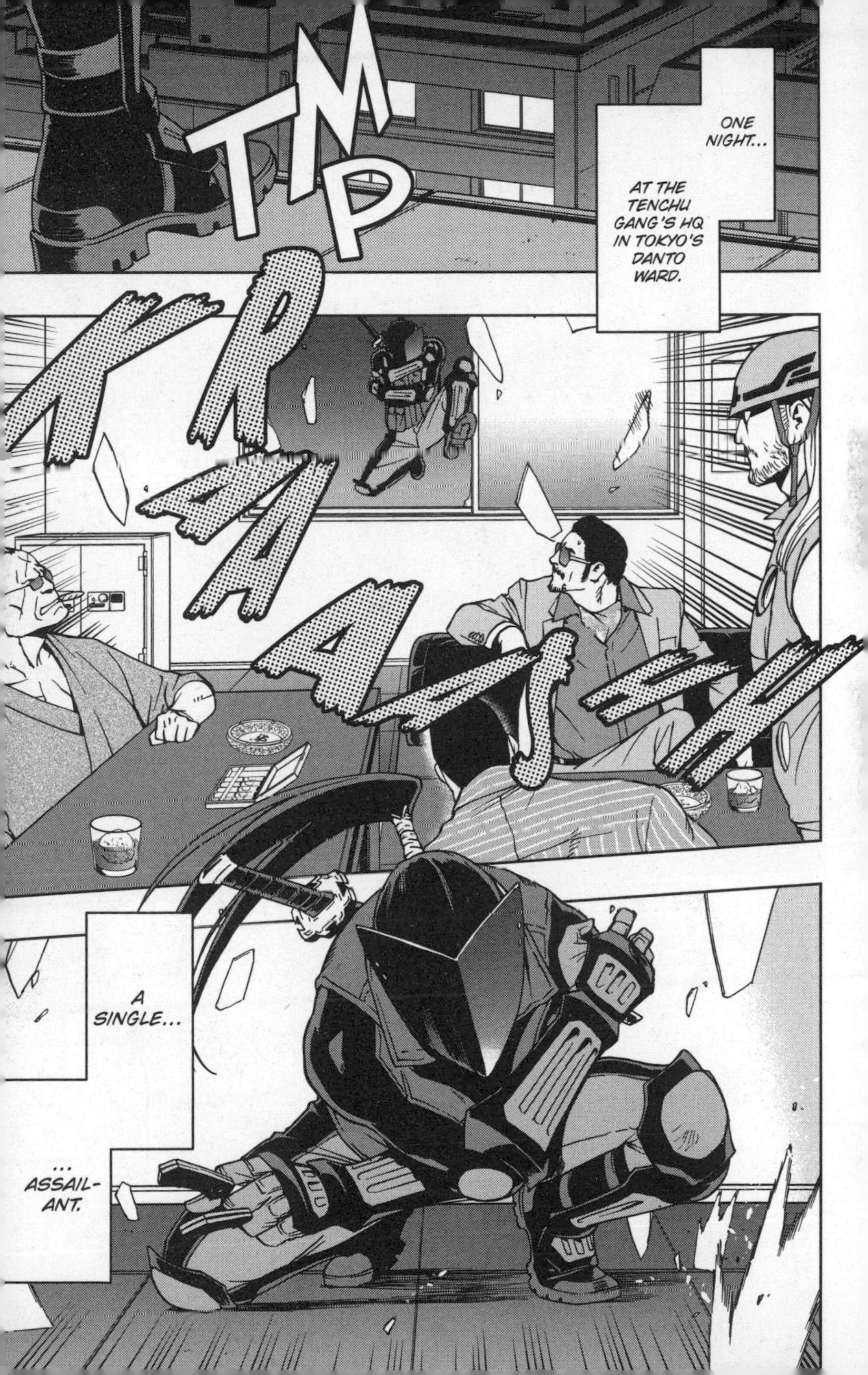
ONE NIGHT...
AT THE TENCHU GANG'S HQ IN TOKYO'S DANTO WARD.
TMP
KRAAASHH
A SINGLE...
...ASSAIL-ANT.

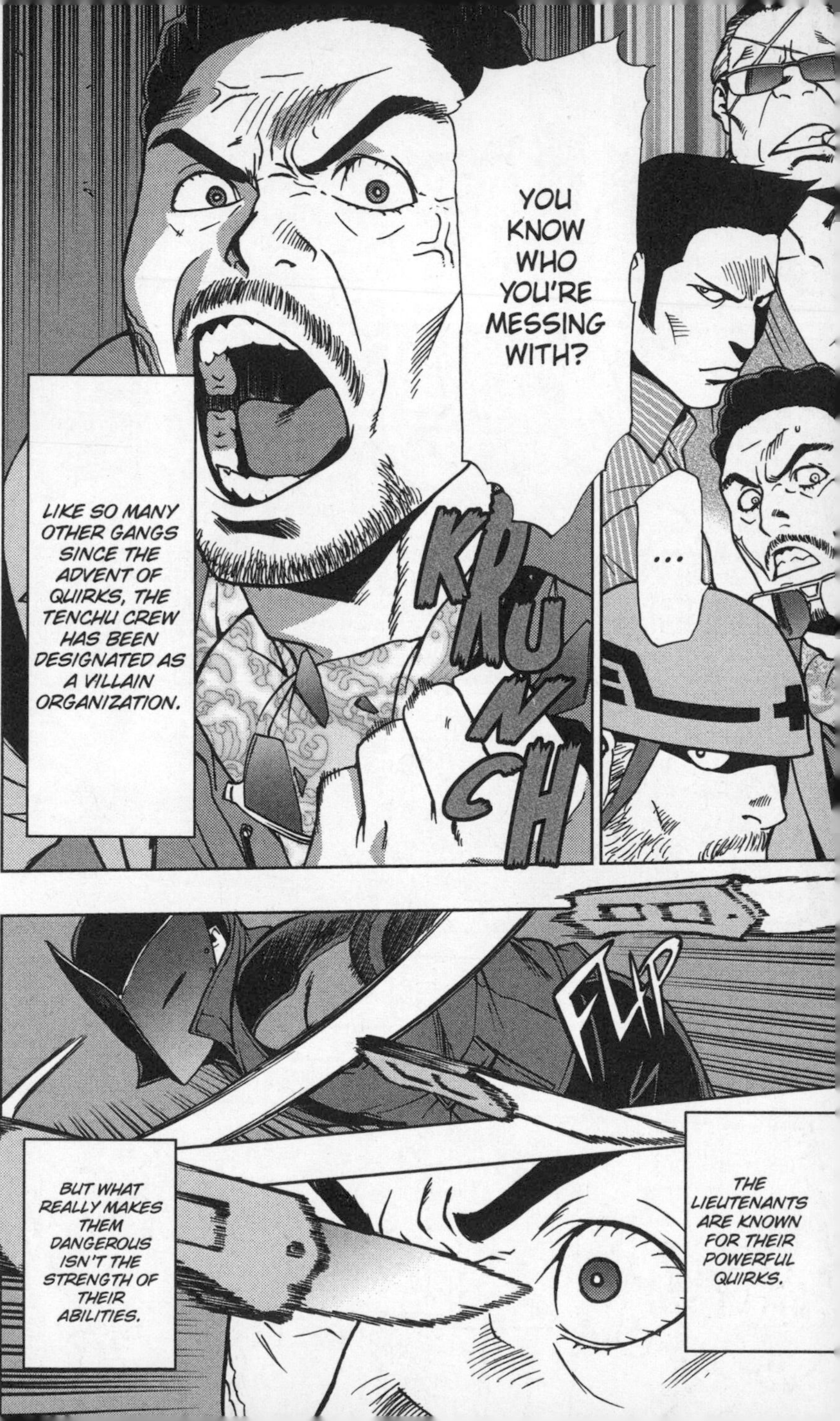
...
YOU KNOW WHO YOU'RE MESSING WITH?
KRUNCH
LIKE SO MANY OTHER GANGS SINCE THE ADVENT OF QUIRKS, THE TENCHU CREW HAS BEEN DESIGNATED AS A VILLAIN ORGANIZATION.
FLIP
THE LIEUTENANTS ARE KNOWN FOR THEIR POWERFUL QUIRKS.
BUT WHAT REALLY MAKES THEM DANGEROUS ISN'T THE STRENGTH OF THEIR ABILITIES.

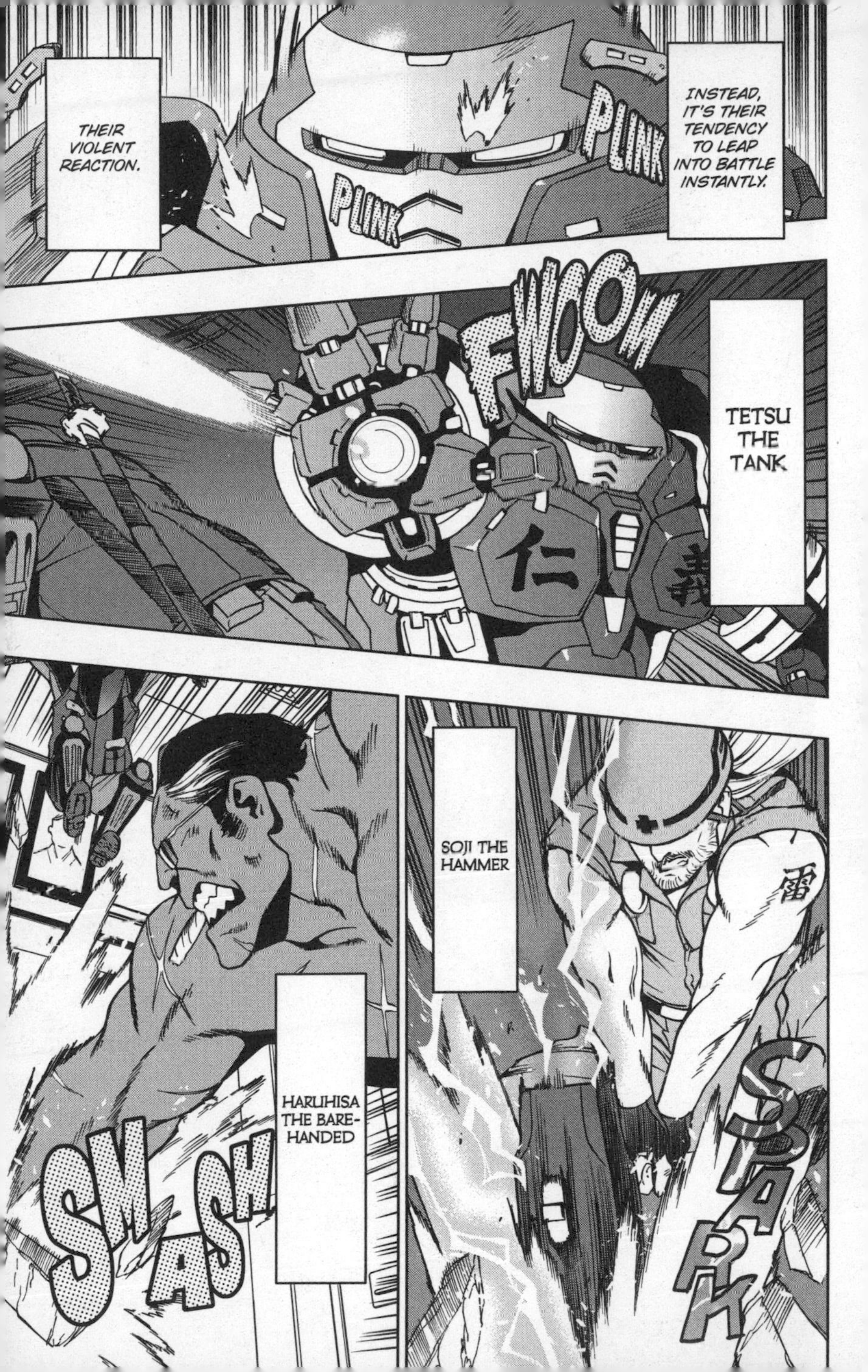
INSTEAD, IT'S THEIR TENDENCY TO LEAP INTO BATTLE INSTANTLY.
PLINK
PLINK
THEIR VIOLENT REACTION.
FWOOM
TETSU THE TANK
SOJI THE HAMMER
SPARK
HARUHISA THE BARE-HANDED
SMASH

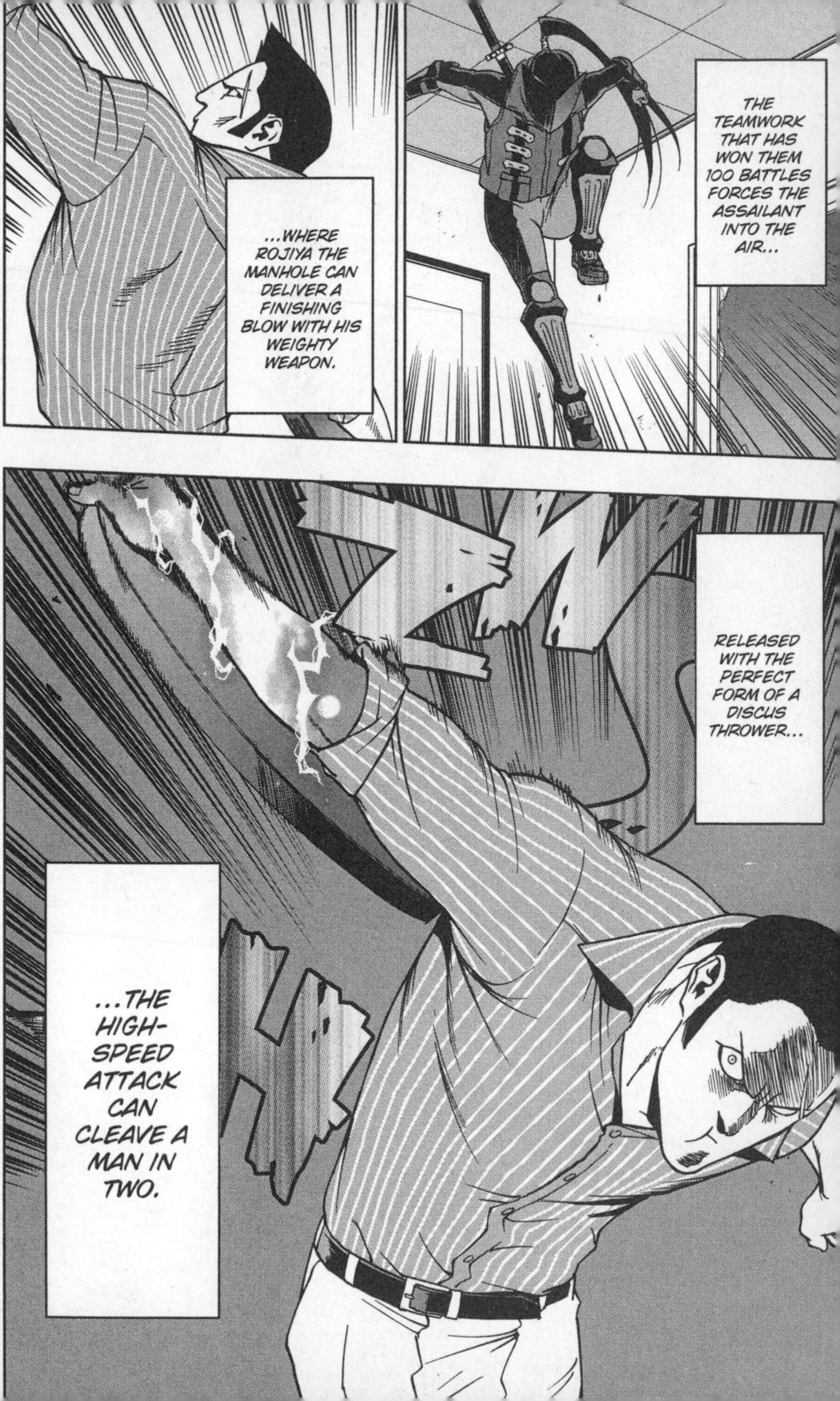
THE TEAMWORK THAT HAS WON THEM 100 BATTLES FORCES THE ASSAILANT INTO THE AIR...
...WHERE ROJIYA THE MANHOLE CAN DELIVER A FINISHING BLOW WITH HIS WEIGHTY WEAPON.
RELEASED WITH THE PERFECT FORM OF A DISCUS THROWER...
...THE HIGH-SPEED ATTACK CAN CLEAVE A MAN IN TWO.

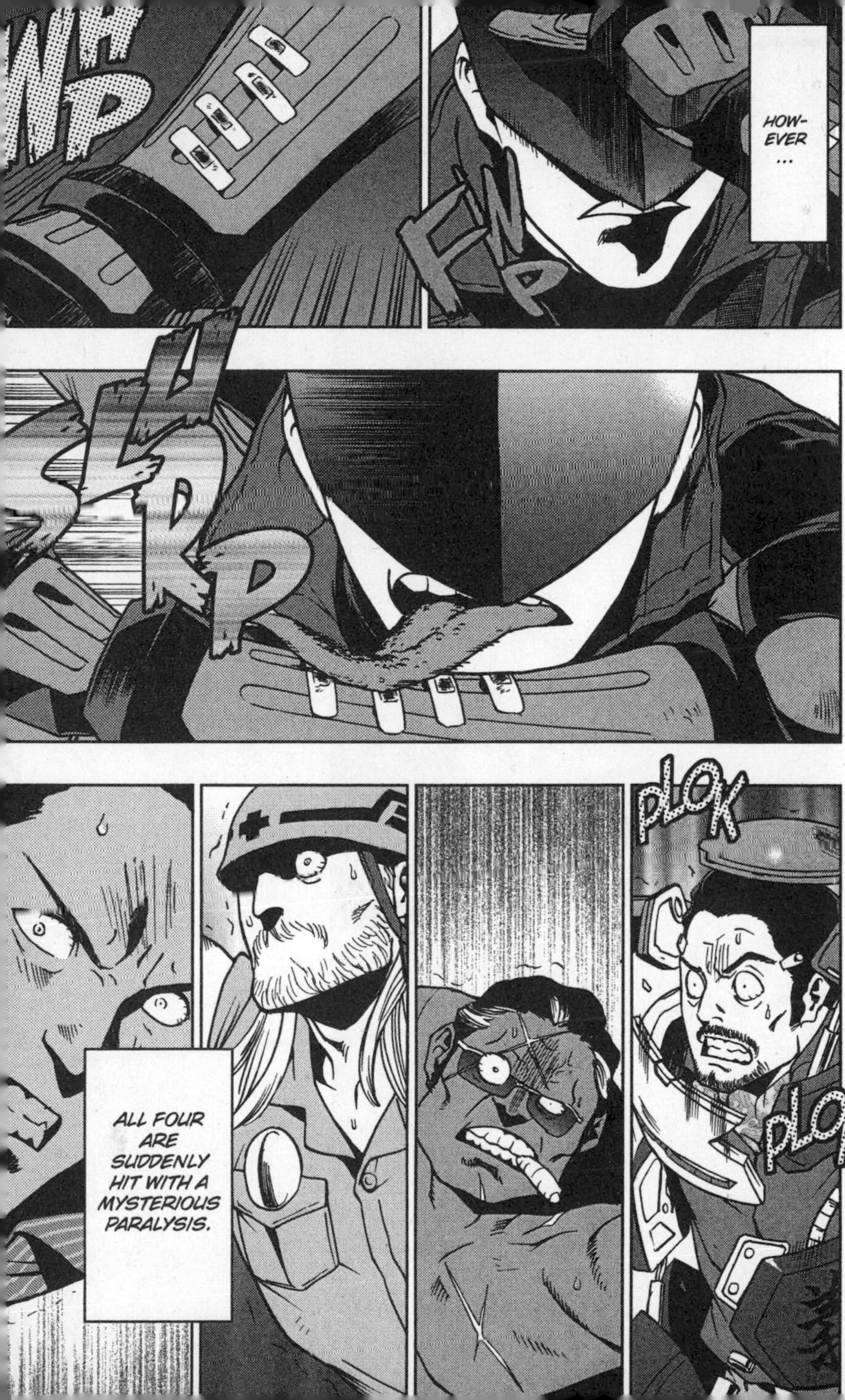
HOW-EVER...
PLOK
PLOK
ALL FOUR ARE SUDDENLY HIT WITH A MYSTERIOUS PARALYSIS.

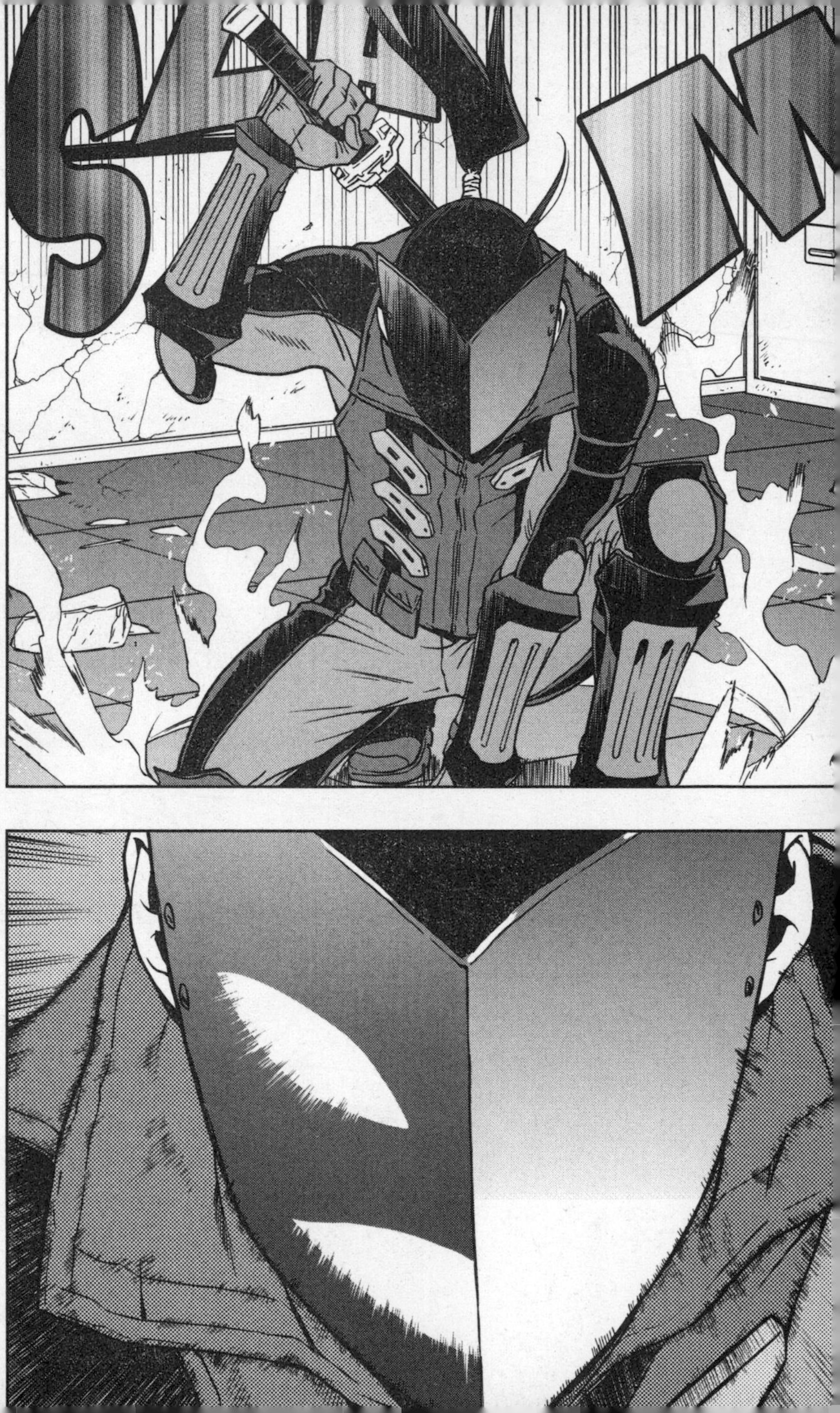

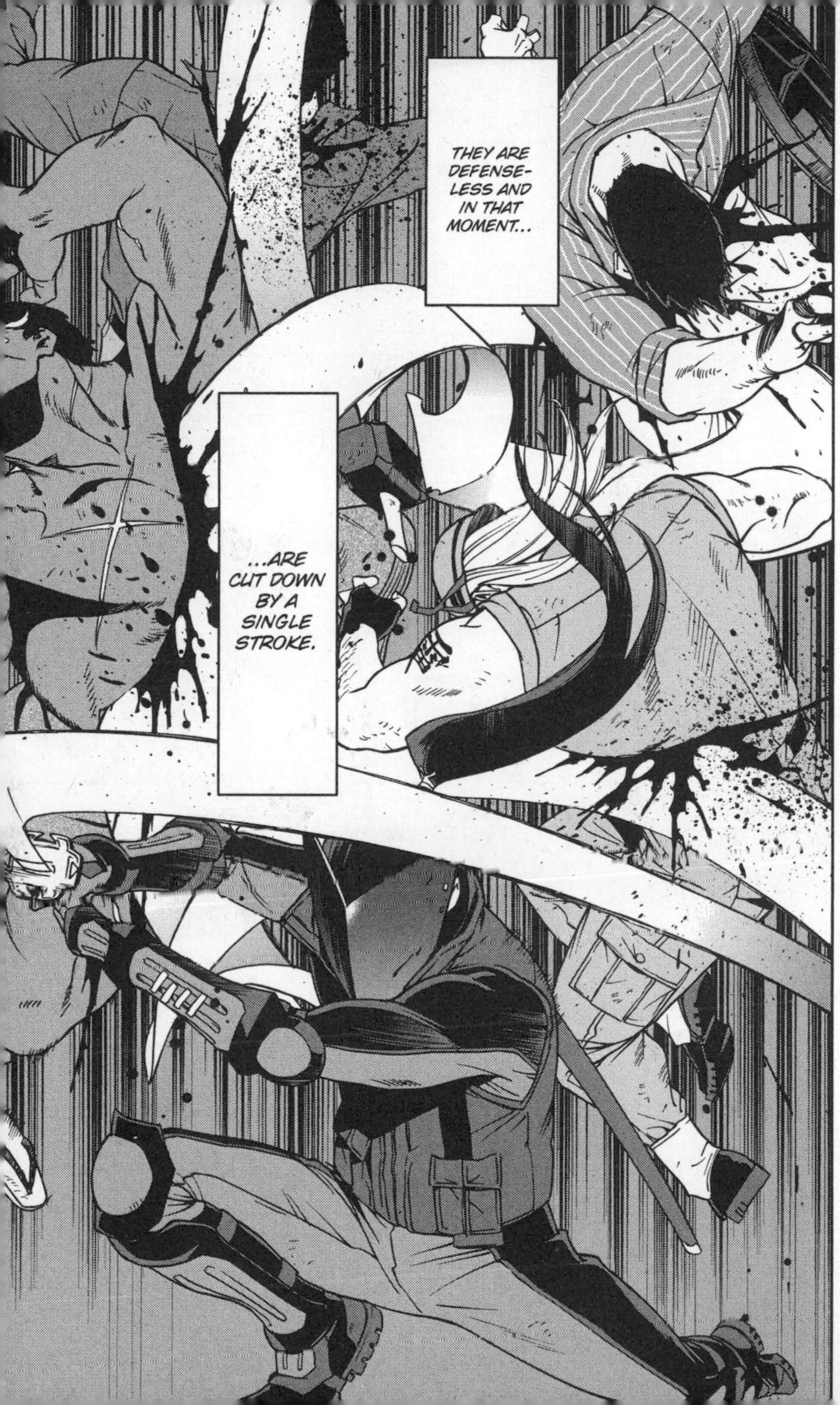
THEY ARE DEFENSE-LESS AND IN THAT MOMENT...
...ARE CUT DOWN BY A SINGLE STROKE.

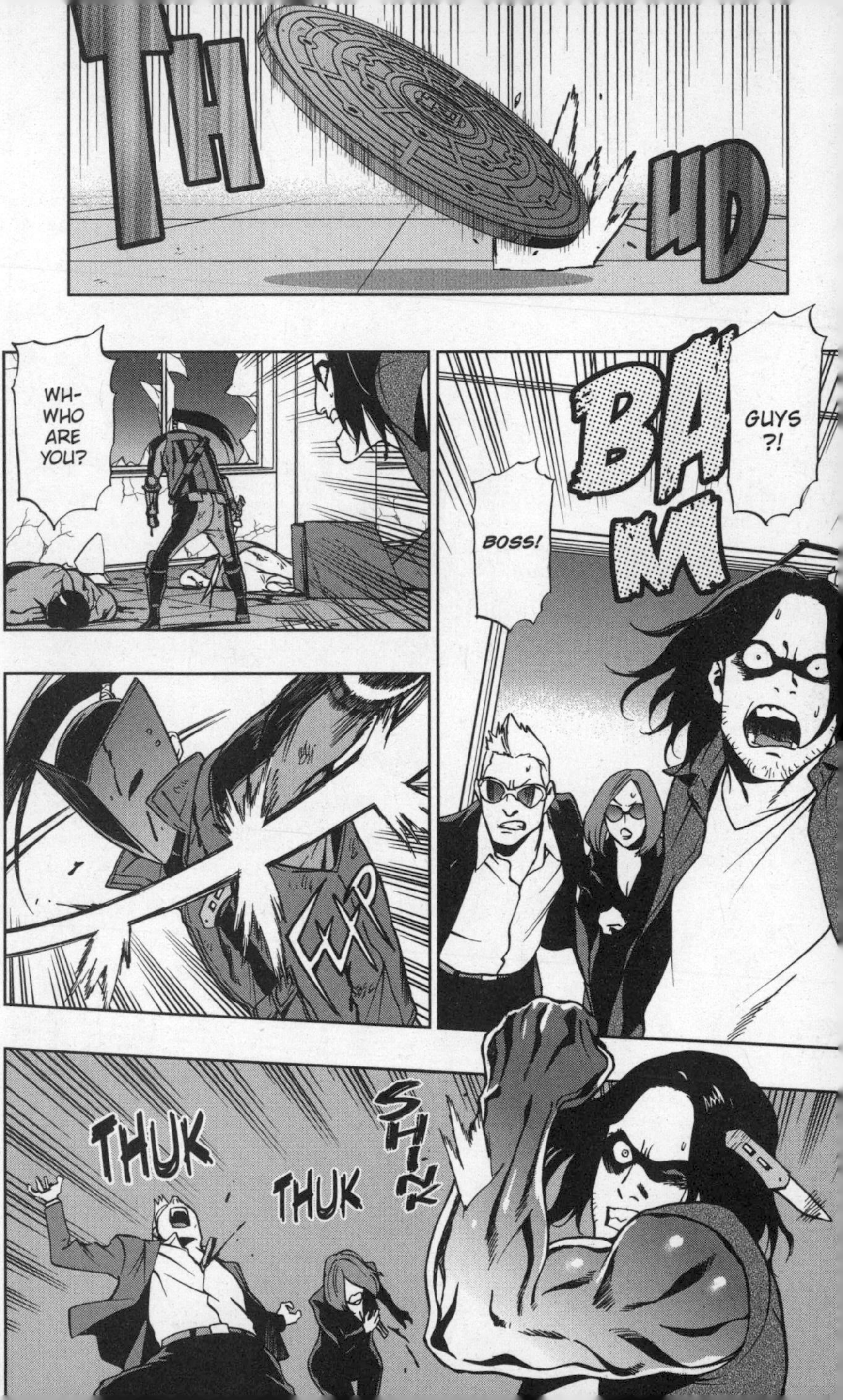
THUD
BAM
GUYS ?!
BOSS!
WH- WHO ARE YOU?
SHINK
THUK
THUK

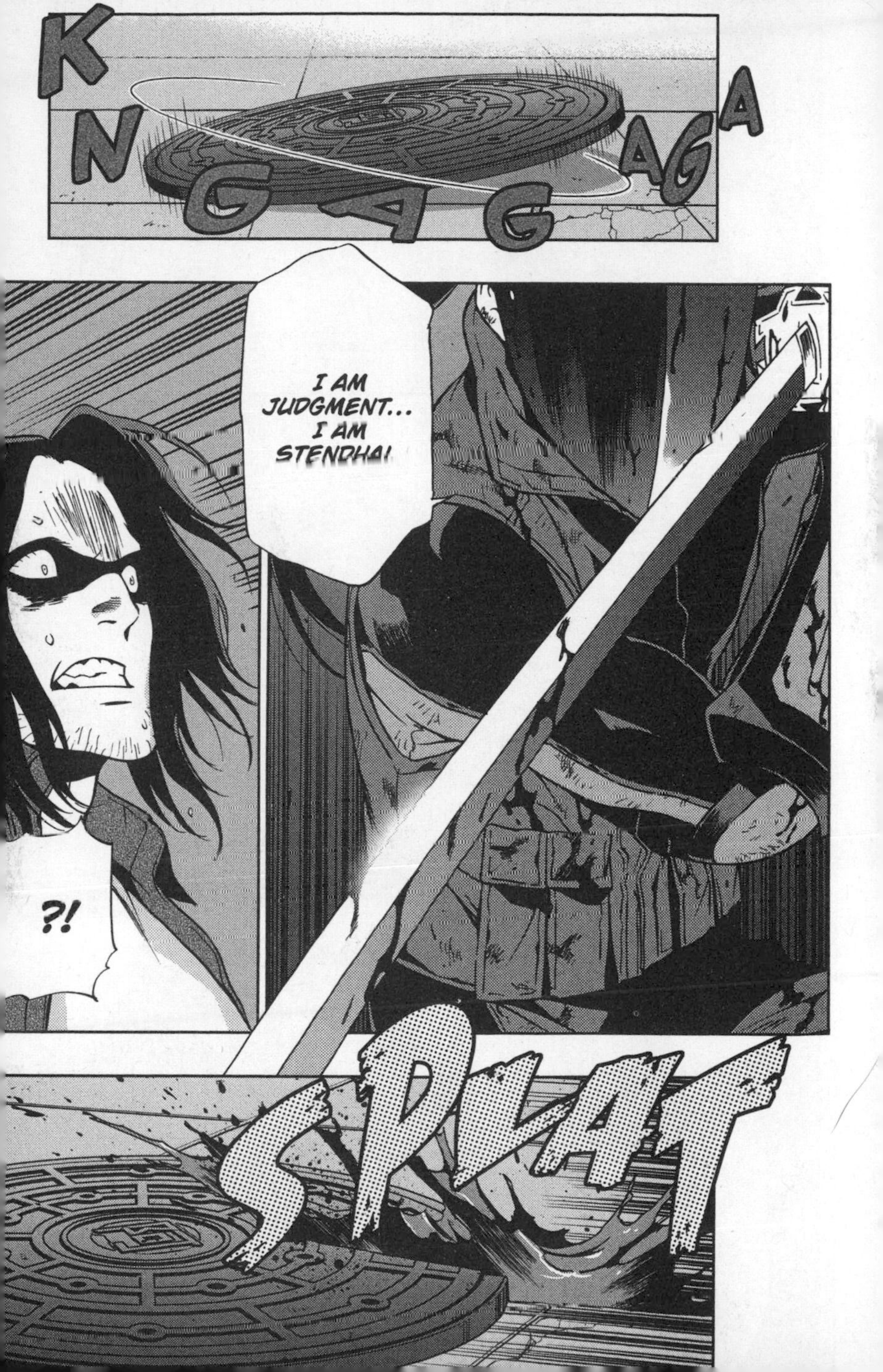
KNGAGAGA
I AM JUDGMENT... I AM STENDHAL
?!
SPLAT

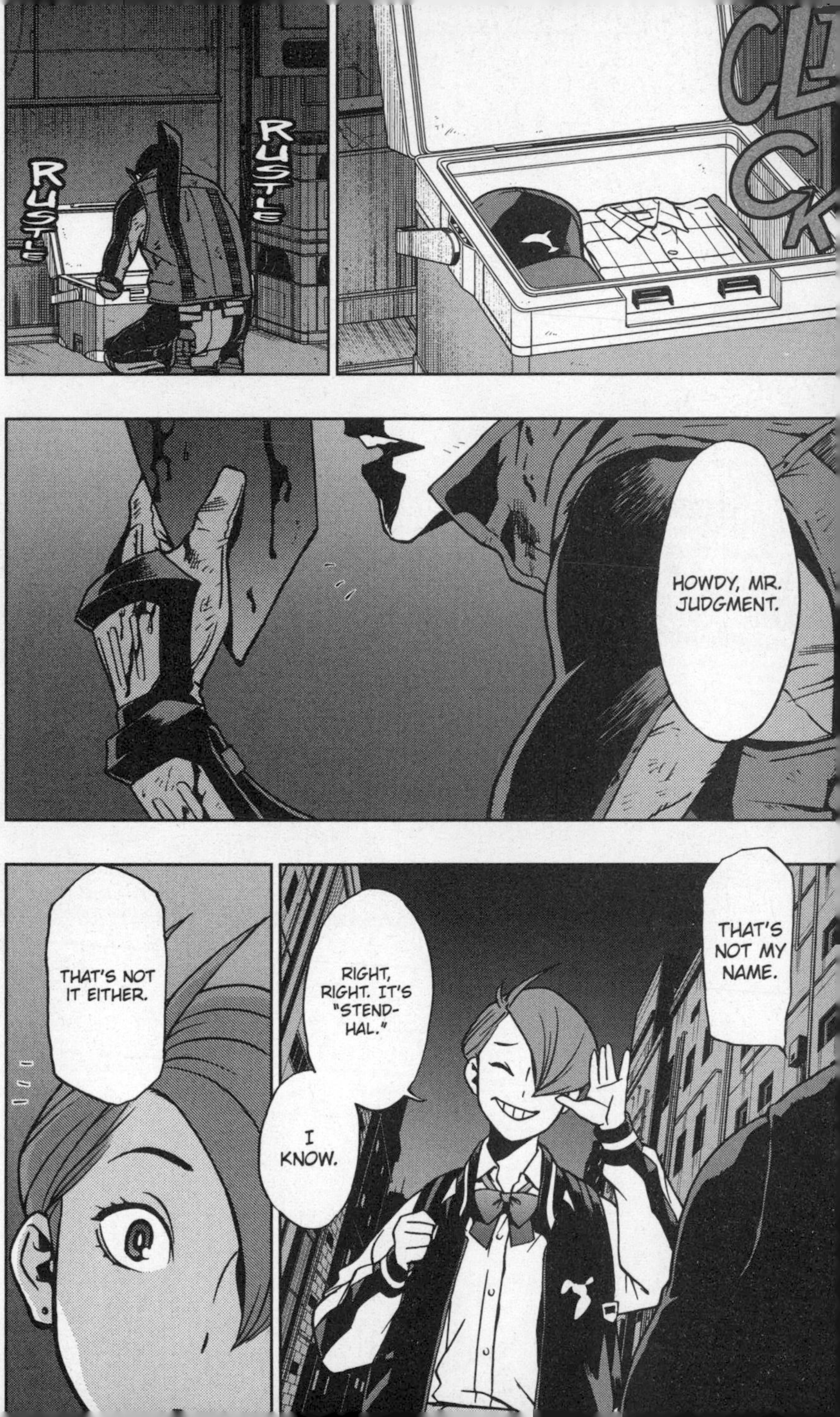
CLICK
RUSTLE
RUSTLE
HOWDY, MR. JUDGMENT.
THAT'S NOT MY NAME.
RIGHT, RIGHT. IT'S "STENDHAL."
I KNOW.
THAT'S NOT IT EITHER.

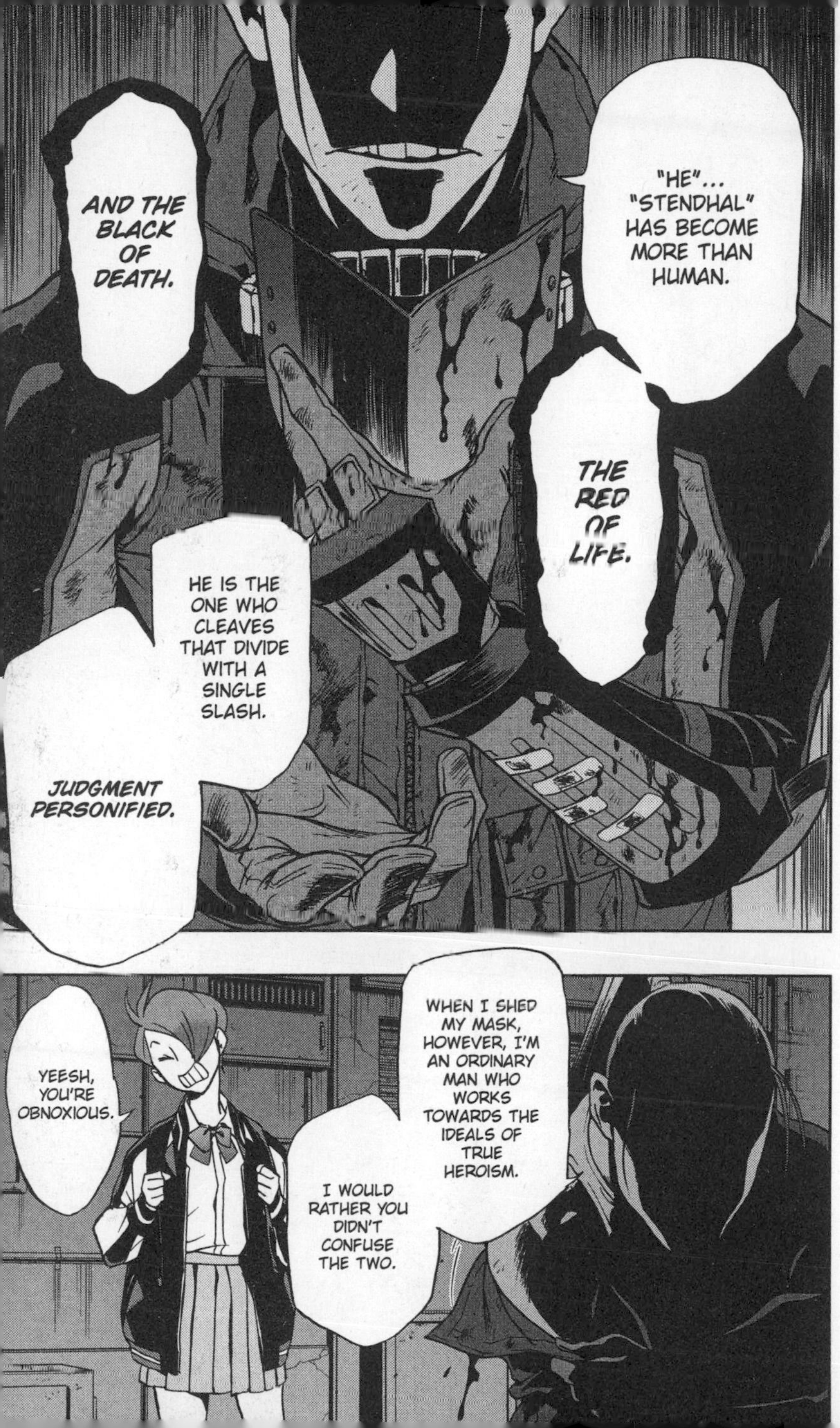
"HE"... "STENDHAL" HAS BECOME MORE THAN HUMAN.
THE RED OF LIFE.
AND THE BLACK OF DEATH.
HE IS THE ONE WHO CLEAVES THAT DIVIDE WITH A SINGLE SLASH.
JUDGMENT PERSONIFIED.
WHEN I SHED MY MASK, HOWEVER, I'M AN ORDINARY MAN WHO WORKS TOWARDS THE IDEALS OF TRUE HEROISM.
I WOULD RATHER YOU DIDN'T CONFUSE THE TWO.
YEESH, YOU'RE OBNOXIOUS.

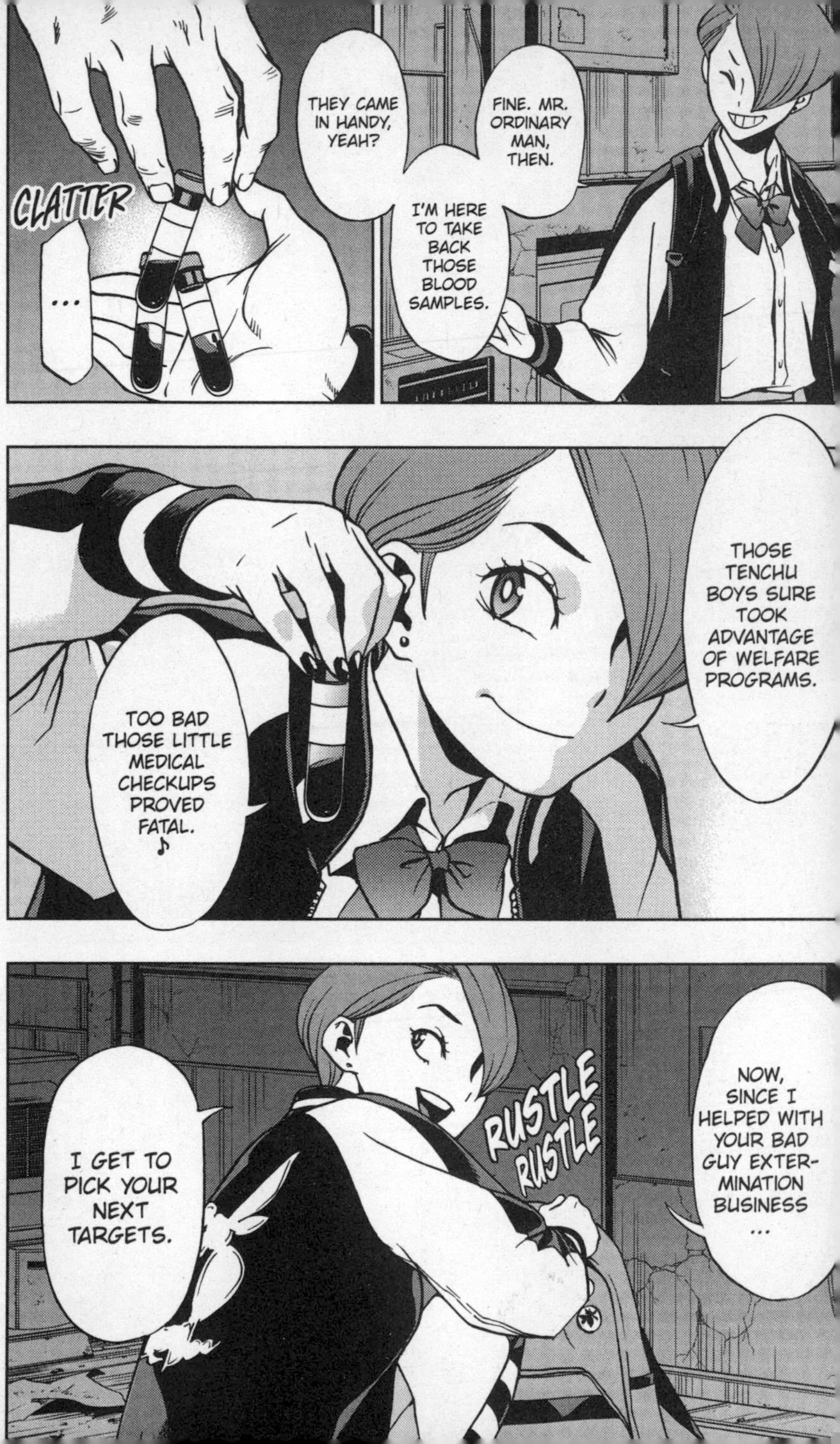
FINE. MR. ORDINARY MAN, THEN.
I'M HERE TO TAKE BACK THOSE BLOOD SAMPLES.
THEY CAME IN HANDY, YEAH?
CLATTER
...
THOSE TENCHU BOYS SURE TOOK ADVANTAGE OF WELFARE PROGRAMS.
TOO BAD THOSE LITTLE MEDICAL CHECKUPS PROVED FATAL. ♪
NOW, SINCE I HELPED WITH YOUR BAD GUY EXTER-MINATION BUSINESS ...
RUSTLE RUSTLE
I GET TO PICK YOUR NEXT TARGETS.

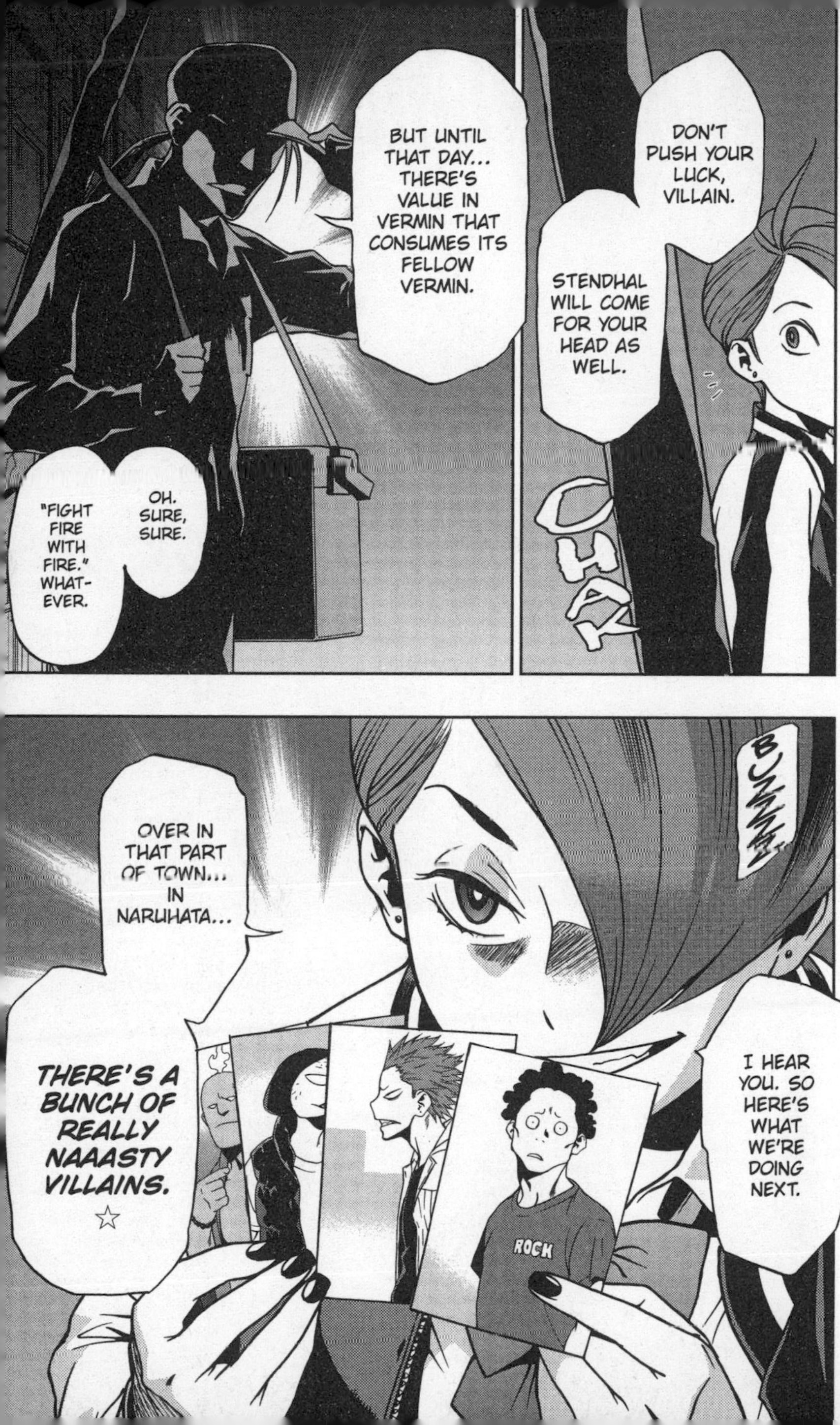
DON'T PUSH YOUR LUCK, VILLAIN.
STENDHAL WILL COME FOR YOUR HEAD AS WELL.
CHAK
BUT UNTIL THAT DAY... THERE'S VALUE IN VERMIN THAT CONSUMES ITS FELLOW VERMIN.
OH. SURE, SURE.
"FIGHT FIRE WITH FIRE." WHAT-EVER.
BUZZZZZ
I HEAR YOU. SO HERE'S WHAT WE'RE DOING NEXT.
OVER IN THAT PART OF TOWN... IN NARUHATA...
THERE'S A BUNCH OF REALLY NAAASTY VILLAINS. ☆
ROCK

KUIN HACHISUKA

HA

THE ROUGH DESIGN

Pin badges

Pin designs

REAL NAME: UNKNOWN

BIRTHDAY: UNKNOWN

HEIGHT: 162 CM

FAVORITE THING: HONEY TOAST

QUIRK: QUEEN BEE

BEHIND THE SCENES

Basically, the villain lieutenant character. She's not a straightforward fighter—the goal was to show that she's a threat through her personality and demeanor. On the visual side, I told Betten, "Make her a modern-day girl!" (I've got no sense for that myself, so I just lobbed that one at him. (-_-;))

As a result, we've got a troublemaker who's cute and competent, but also sort of apathetic. Still, she's handy for advancing the villainous plot little by little. You can count on her for that.

—Furuhashi

She was wearing something like a hoodie in the rough storyboards Furuhashi sent me, but I changed it to a varsity jacket so as not to overlap too much with Koichi. She's the easiest in this series for me to draw, since she totally matches my style. Before I knew it, I'd started drawing Hachisuka in Yokosuka jackets… I scare myself sometimes!

—Betten

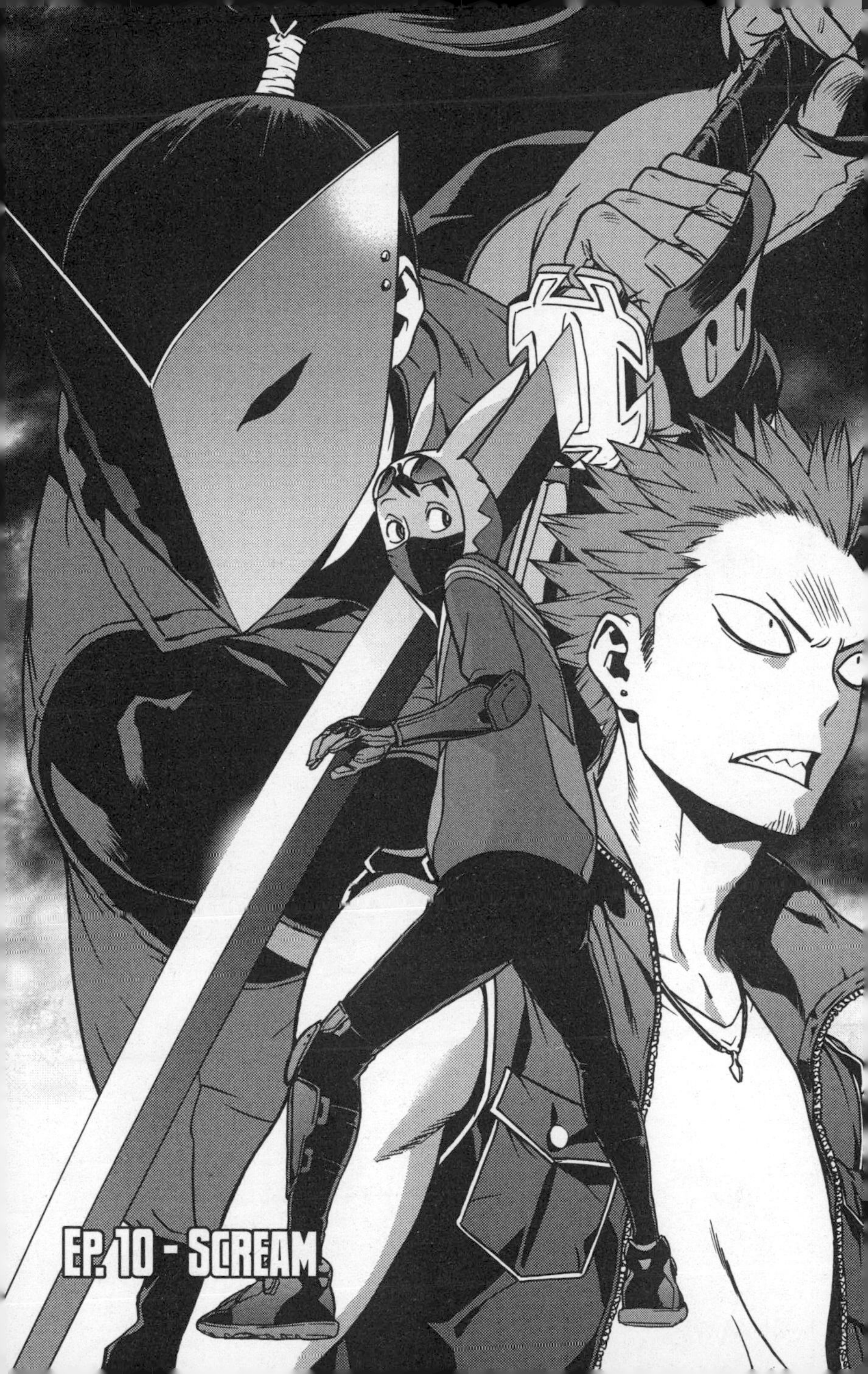
EP. 10 - SCREAM

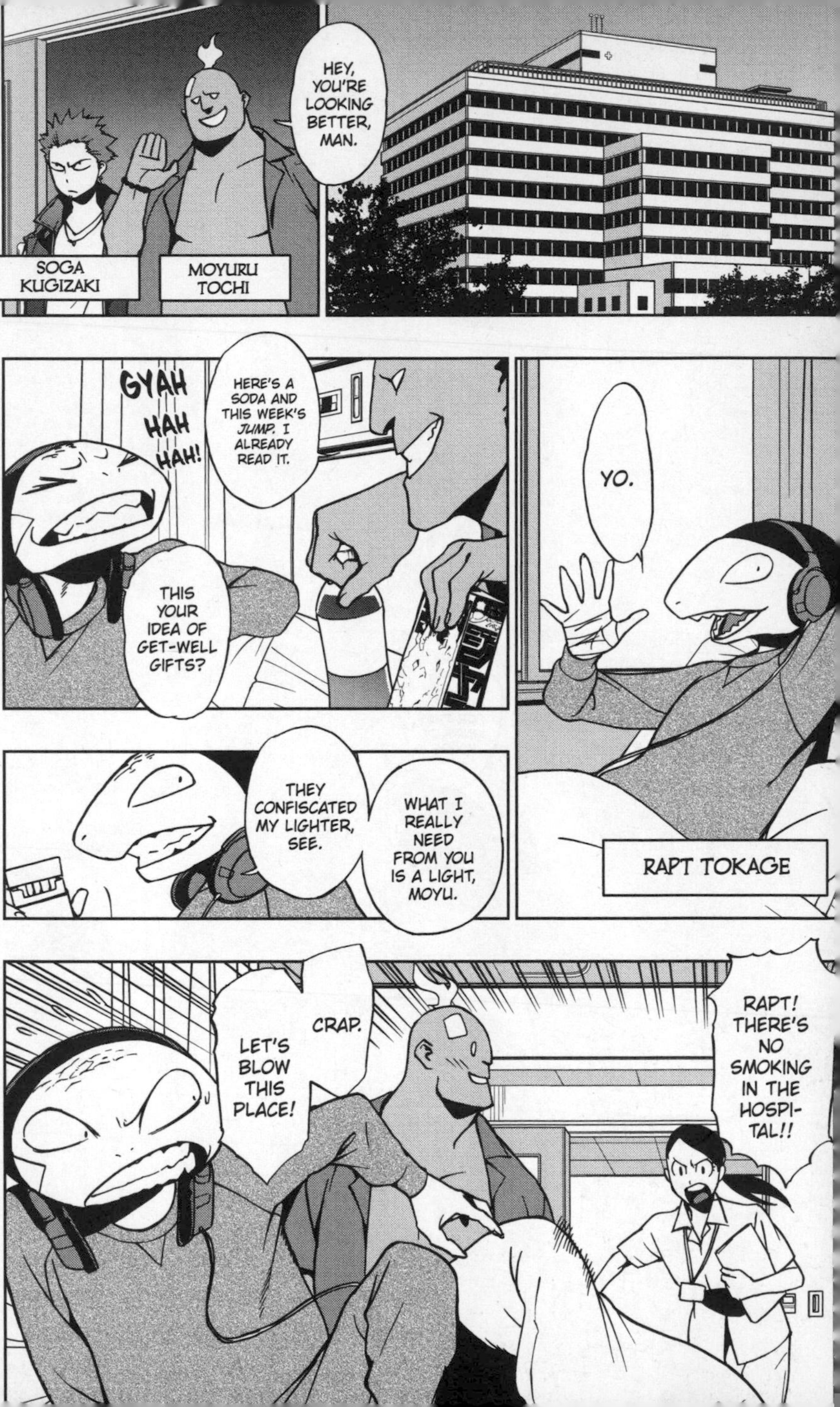
HEY, YOU'RE LOOKING BETTER, MAN.
MOYURU TOCHI
SOGA KUGIZAKI
YO.
RAPT TOKAGE
HERE'S A SODA AND THIS WEEK'S *JUMP*. I ALREADY READ IT.
GYAH HAH HAH!
THIS YOUR IDEA OF GET-WELL GIFTS?
WHAT I REALLY NEED FROM YOU IS A LIGHT, MOYU.
THEY CONFISCATED MY LIGHTER, SEE.
RAPT! THERE'S NO SMOKING IN THE HOSPI-TAL!!
CRAP.
LET'S BLOW THIS PLACE!

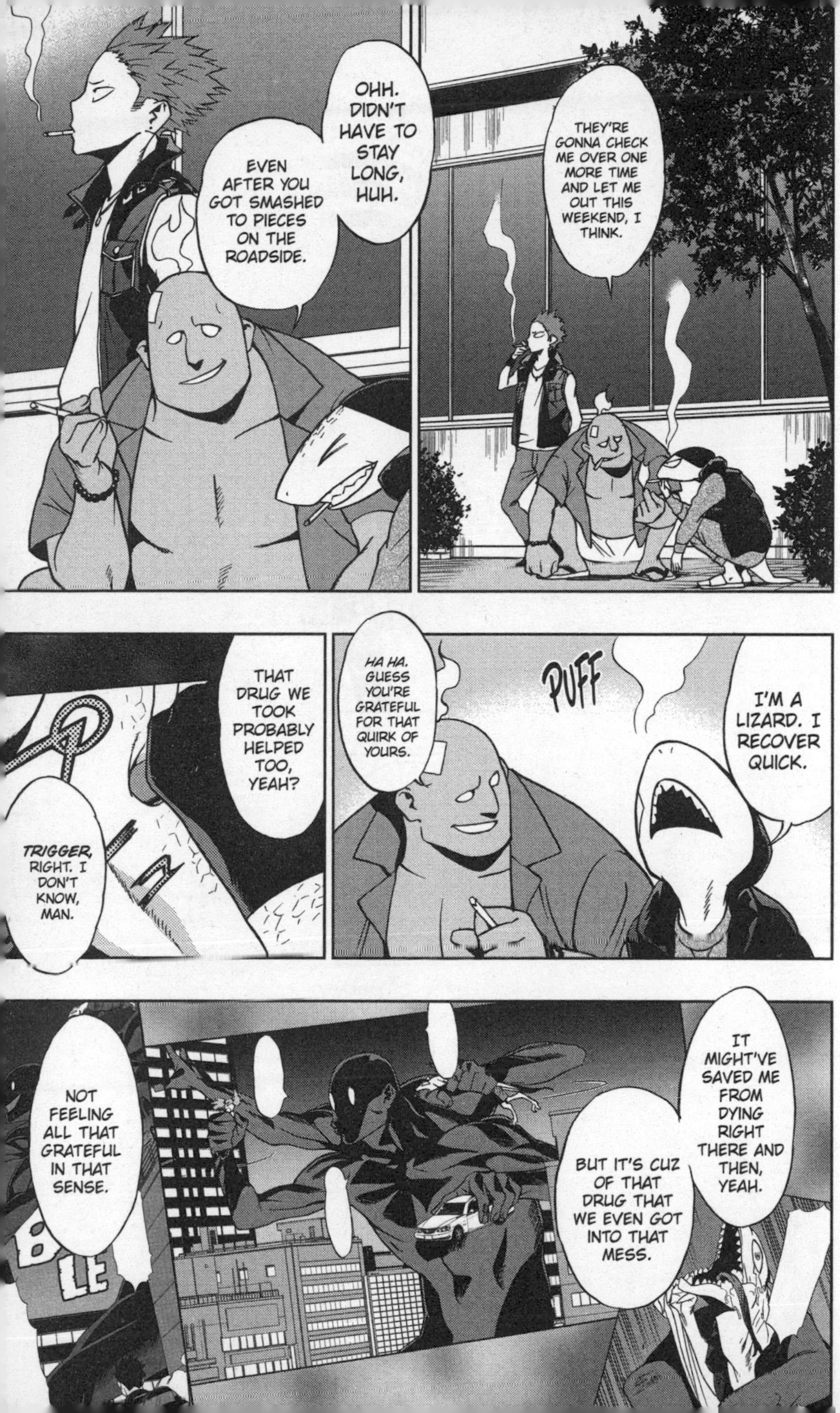
THEY'RE GONNA CHECK ME OVER ONE MORE TIME AND LET ME OUT THIS WEEKEND, I THINK.
OHH. DIDN'T HAVE TO STAY LONG, HUH.
EVEN AFTER YOU GOT SMASHED TO PIECES ON THE ROADSIDE.
PUFF
I'M A LIZARD. I RECOVER QUICK.
HA HA. GUESS YOU'RE GRATEFUL FOR THAT QUIRK OF YOURS.
THAT DRUG WE TOOK PROBABLY HELPED TOO, YEAH?
TRIGGER, RIGHT. I DON'T KNOW, MAN.
IT MIGHT'VE SAVED ME FROM DYING RIGHT THERE AND THEN, YEAH.
BUT IT'S CUZ OF THAT DRUG THAT WE EVEN GOT INTO THAT MESS.
NOT FEELING ALL THAT GRATEFUL IN THAT SENSE.

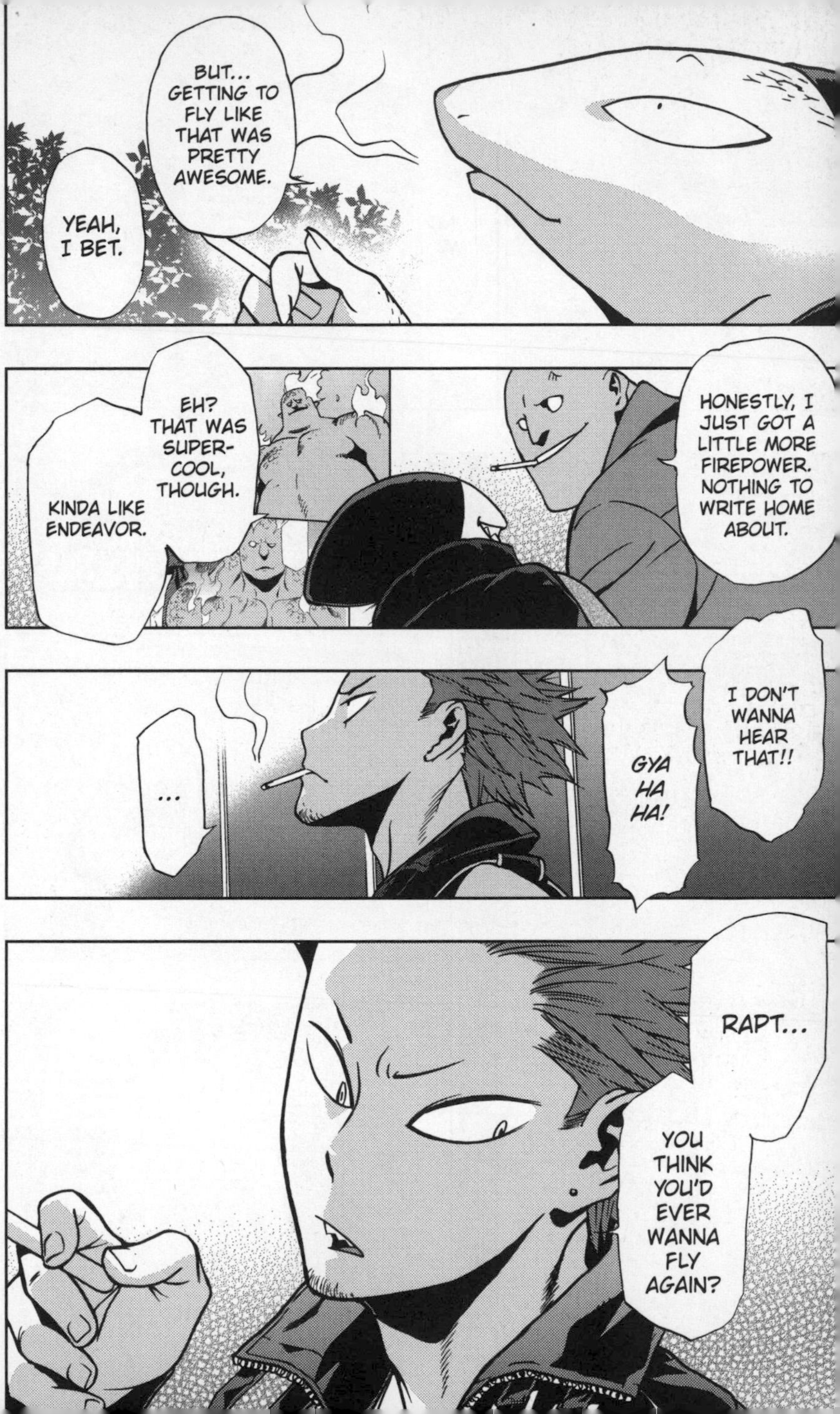
BUT... GETTING TO FLY LIKE THAT WAS PRETTY AWESOME.
YEAH, I BET.
HONESTLY, I JUST GOT A LITTLE MORE FIREPOWER. NOTHING TO WRITE HOME ABOUT.
EH? THAT WAS SUPER-COOL, THOUGH.
KINDA LIKE ENDEAVOR.
I DON'T WANNA HEAR THAT!!
GYA HA HA!
...
RAPT...
YOU THINK YOU'D EVER WANNA FLY AGAIN?

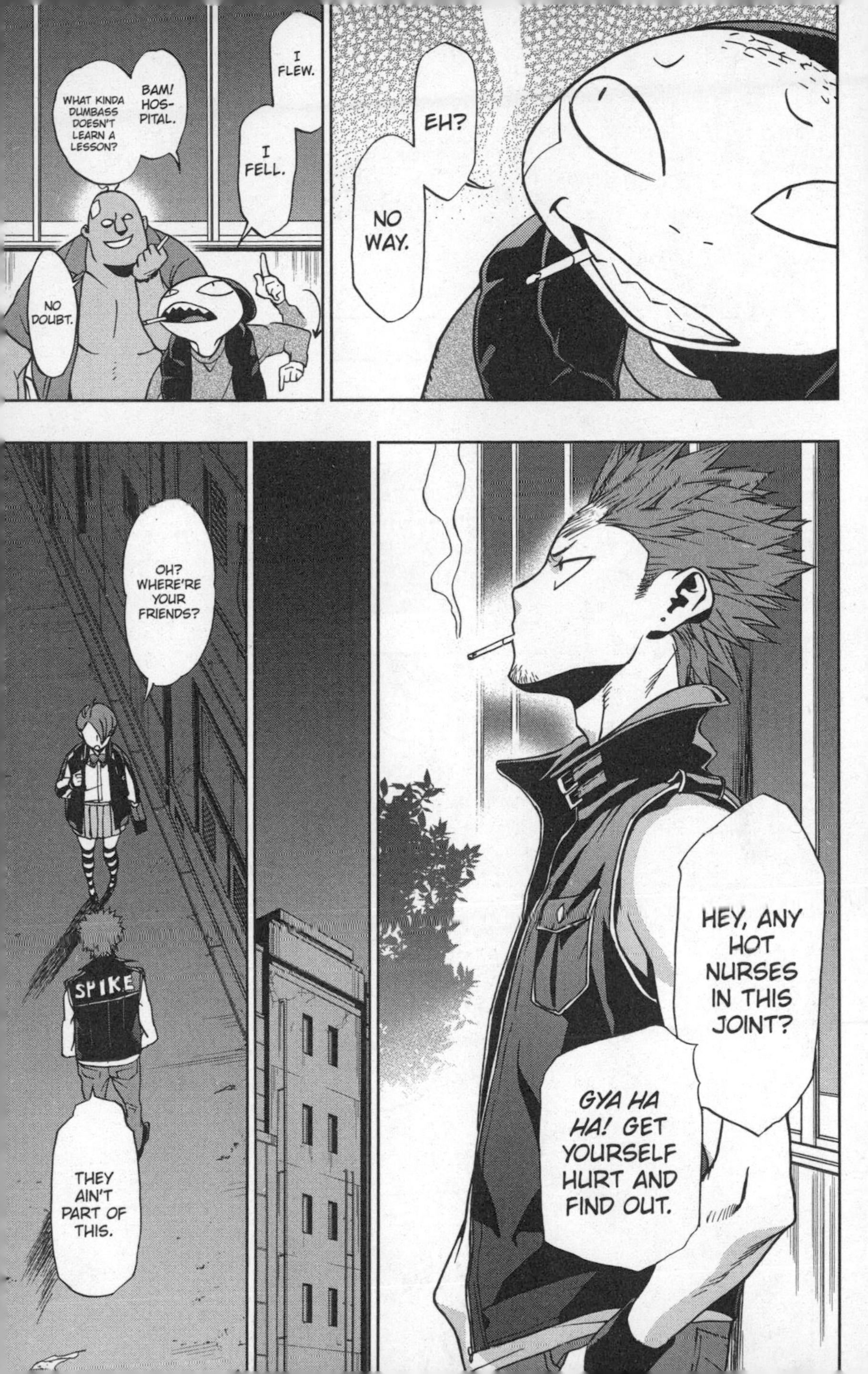
EH?
NO WAY.
I FLEW.
I FELL.
BAM! HOS-PITAL.
WHAT KINDA DUMBASS DOESN'T LEARN A LESSON?
NO DOUBT.
HEY, ANY HOT NURSES IN THIS JOINT?
GYA HA HA! GET YOURSELF HURT AND FIND OUT.
OH? WHERE'RE YOUR FRIENDS?
SPIKE
THEY AIN'T PART OF THIS.

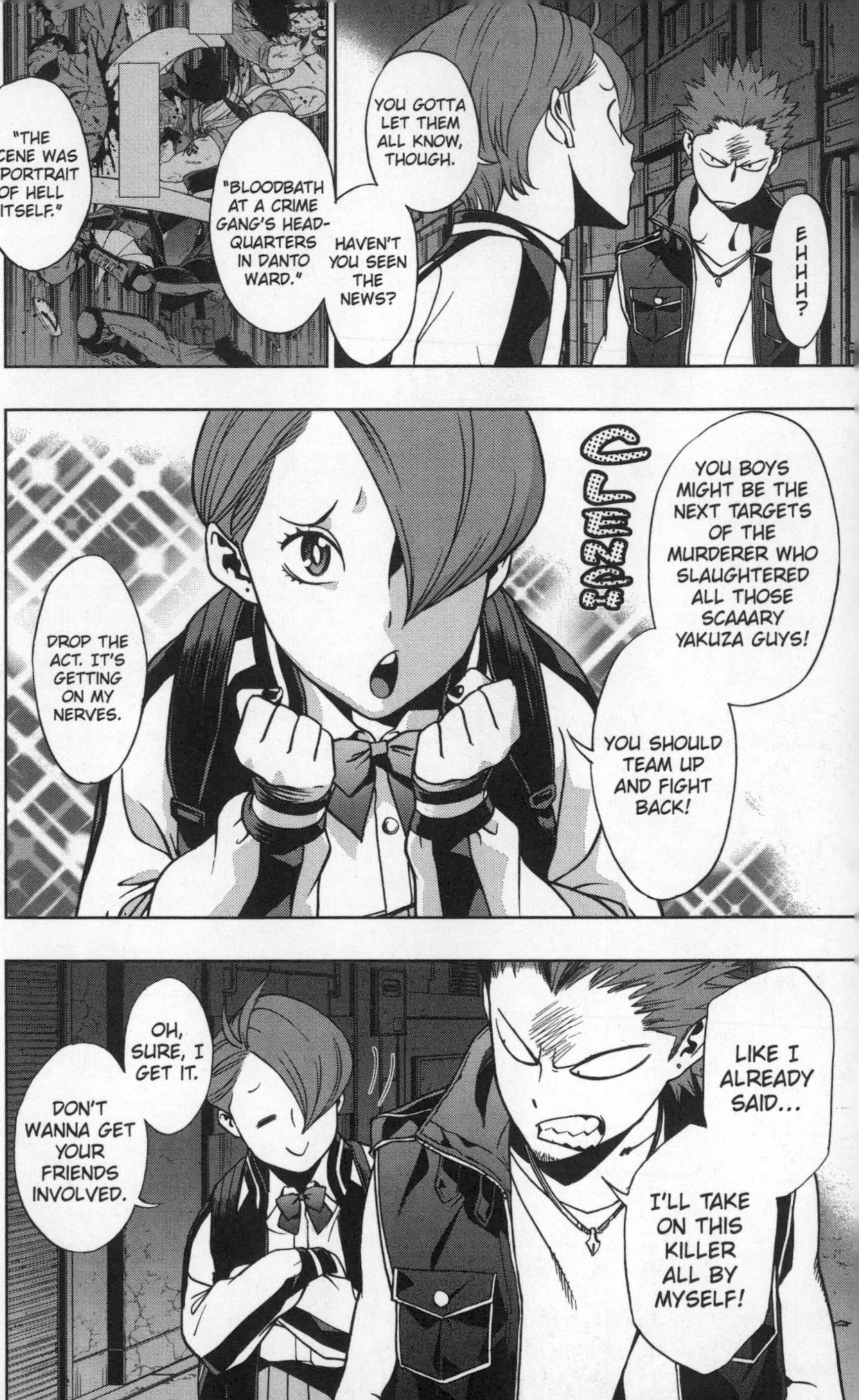
EHHHH?
YOU GOTTA LET THEM ALL KNOW, THOUGH.
HAVEN'T YOU SEEN THE NEWS?
"BLOODBATH AT A CRIME GANG'S HEAD-QUARTERS IN DANTO WARD."
"THE SCENE WAS A PORTRAIT OF HELL ITSELF."
YOU BOYS MIGHT BE THE NEXT TARGETS OF THE MURDERER WHO SLAUGHTERED ALL THOSE SCAAARY YAKUZA GUYS!
CLENCH
YOU SHOULD TEAM UP AND FIGHT BACK!
DROP THE ACT. IT'S GETTING ON MY NERVES.
LIKE I ALREADY SAID...
I'LL TAKE ON THIS KILLER ALL BY MYSELF!
OH, SURE, I GET IT.
DON'T WANNA GET YOUR FRIENDS INVOLVED.

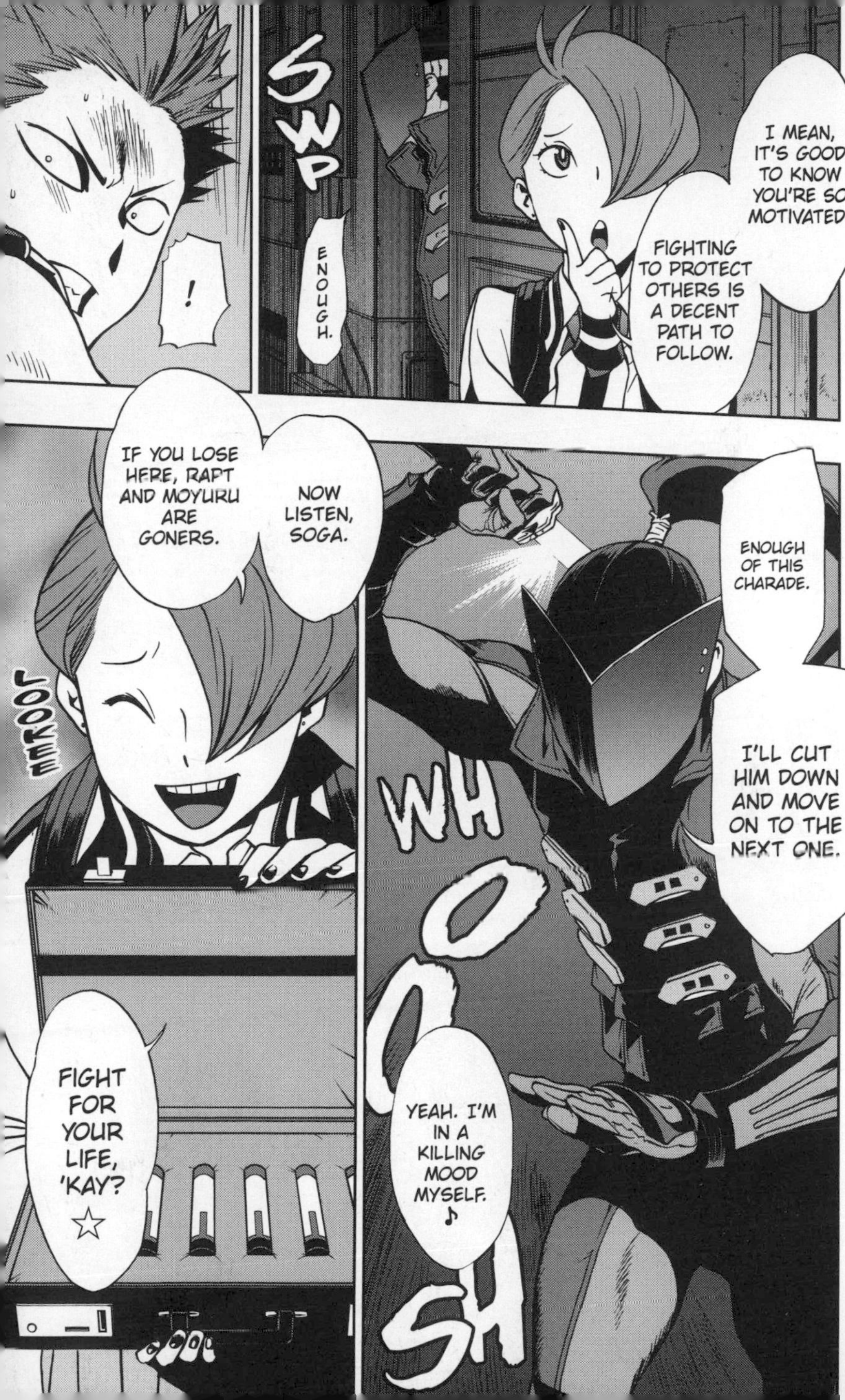
I MEAN, IT'S GOOD TO KNOW YOU'RE SO MOTIVATED.
FIGHTING TO PROTECT OTHERS IS A DECENT PATH TO FOLLOW.
SWP
ENOUGH.
!
ENOUGH OF THIS CHARADE.
I'LL CUT HIM DOWN AND MOVE ON TO THE NEXT ONE.
WHOOSH
YEAH. I'M IN A KILLING MOOD MYSELF. ♪
NOW LISTEN, SOGA.
IF YOU LOSE HERE, RAPT AND MOYURU ARE GONERS.
JOOKEE
FIGHT FOR YOUR LIFE, 'KAY? ☆

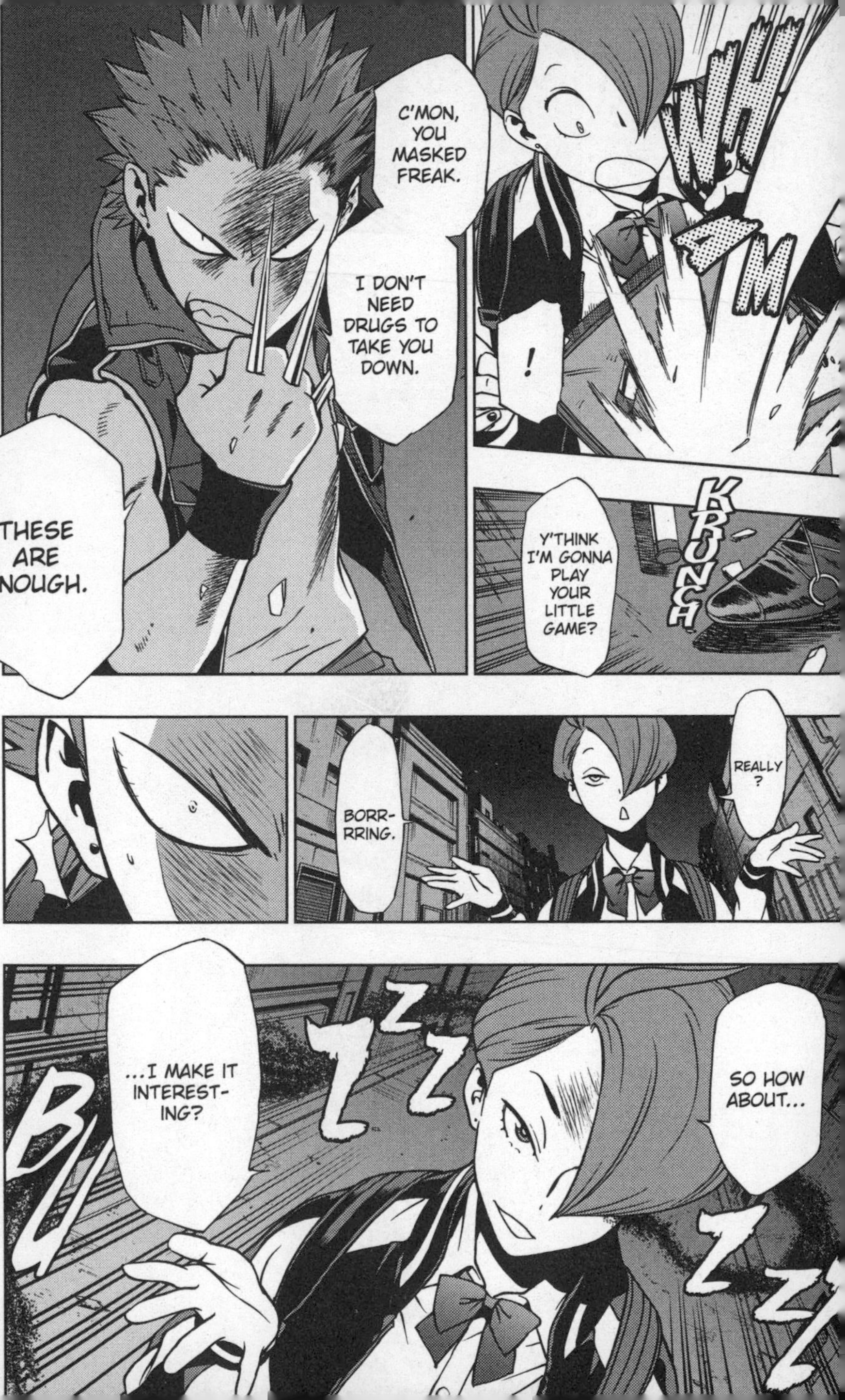
WHAM
!
KRUNCH
Y'THINK I'M GONNA PLAY YOUR LITTLE GAME?
C'MON, YOU MASKED FREAK.
I DON'T NEED DRUGS TO TAKE YOU DOWN.
THESE ARE ENOUGH.
REALLY?
BORRRRING.
SO HOW ABOUT...
...I MAKE IT INTERESTING?
ZZZ
BU
ZZZ

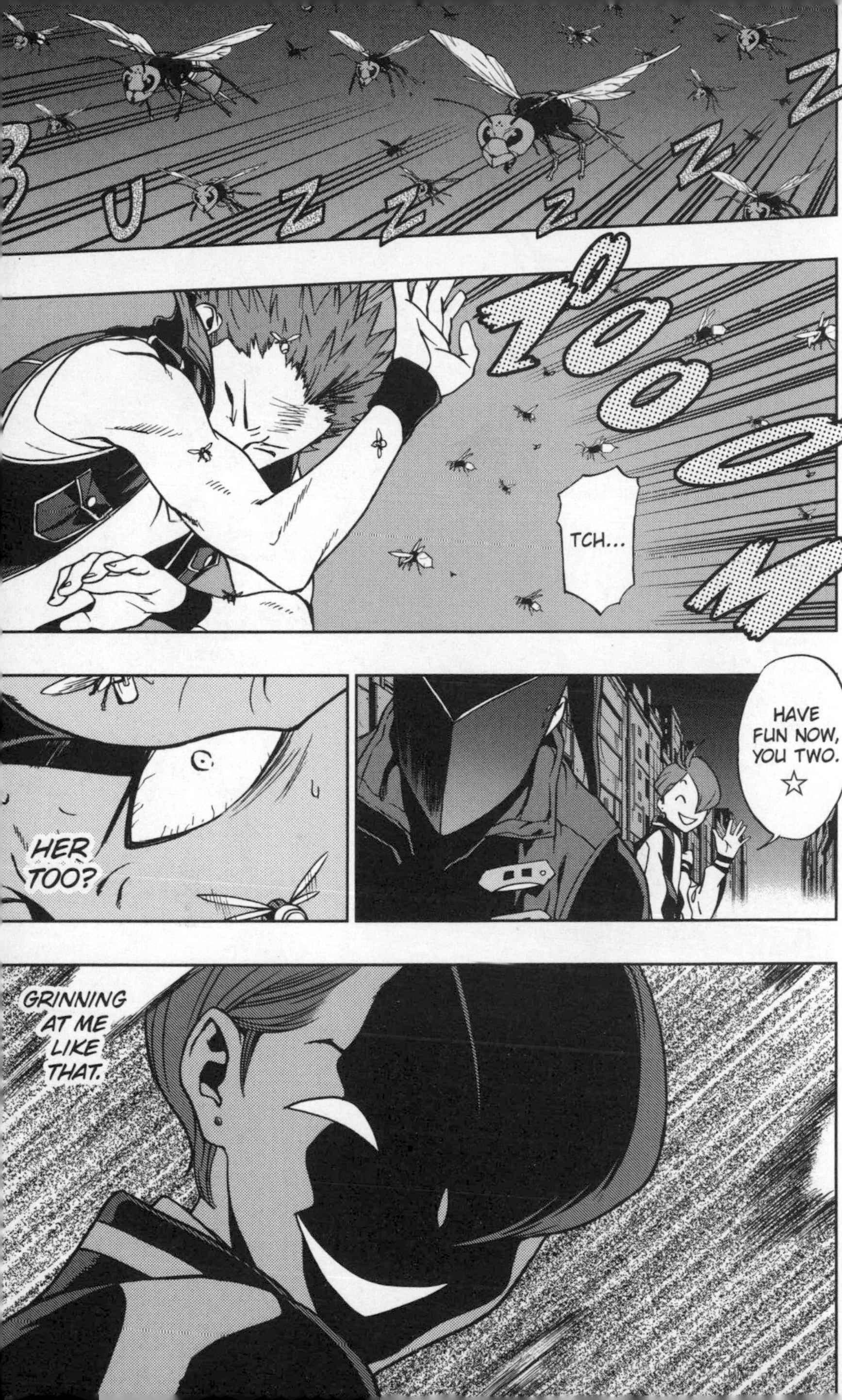
BUZZZZZZZ
TOOOOM
TCH...
HAVE FUN NOW, YOU TWO. ☆
HER TOO?
GRINNING AT ME LIKE THAT.

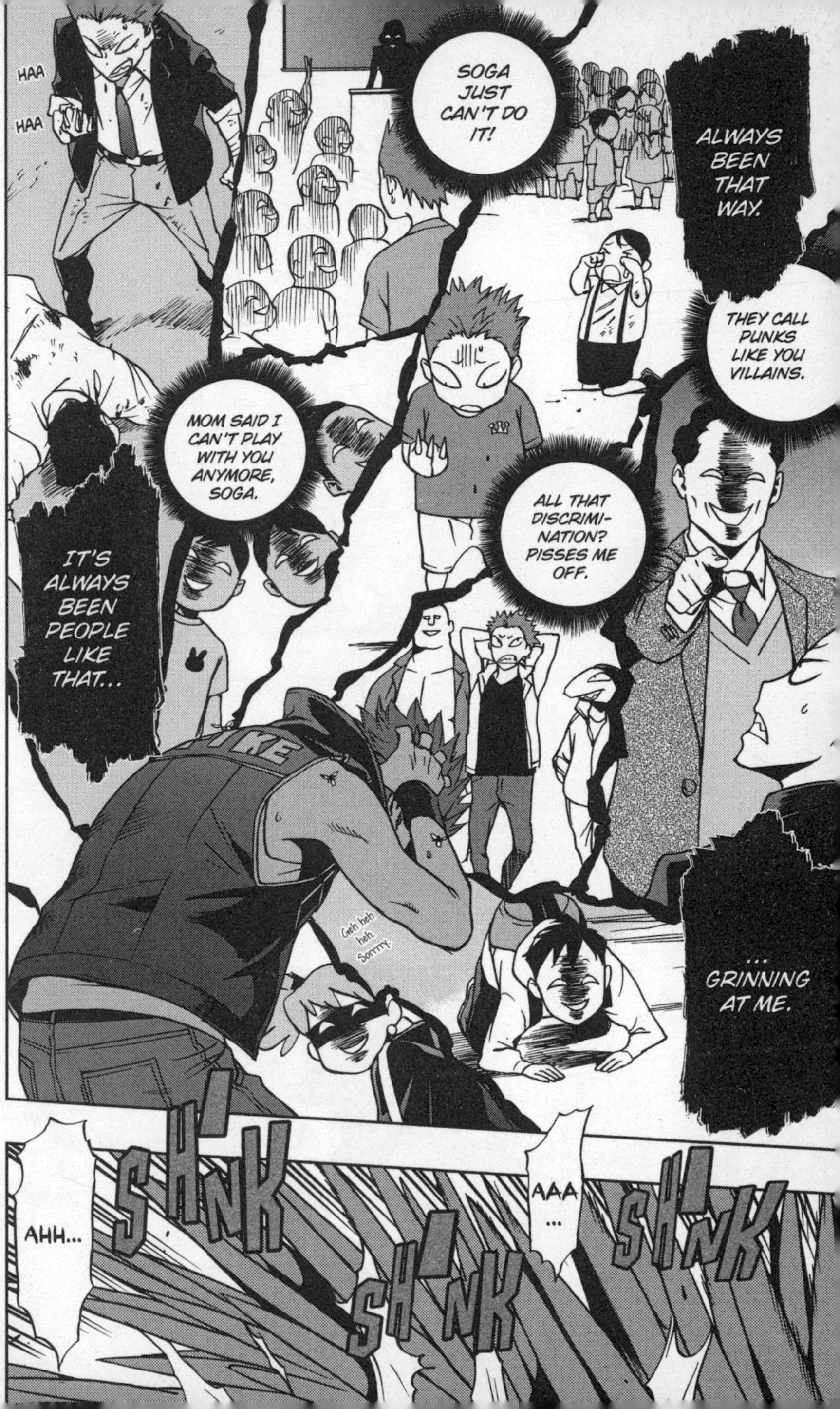
ALWAYS BEEN THAT WAY.
SOGA JUST CAN'T DO IT!
HAA
HAA
THEY CALL PUNKS LIKE YOU VILLAINS.
ALL THAT DISCRIMINATION? PISSES ME OFF.
MOM SAID I CAN'T PLAY WITH YOU ANYMORE, SOGA.
IT'S ALWAYS BEEN PEOPLE LIKE THAT...
... GRINNING AT ME.
Geh heh heh. Sorrrry.
SH'NK
AAA ...
SH'NK
SH'NK
AHH...

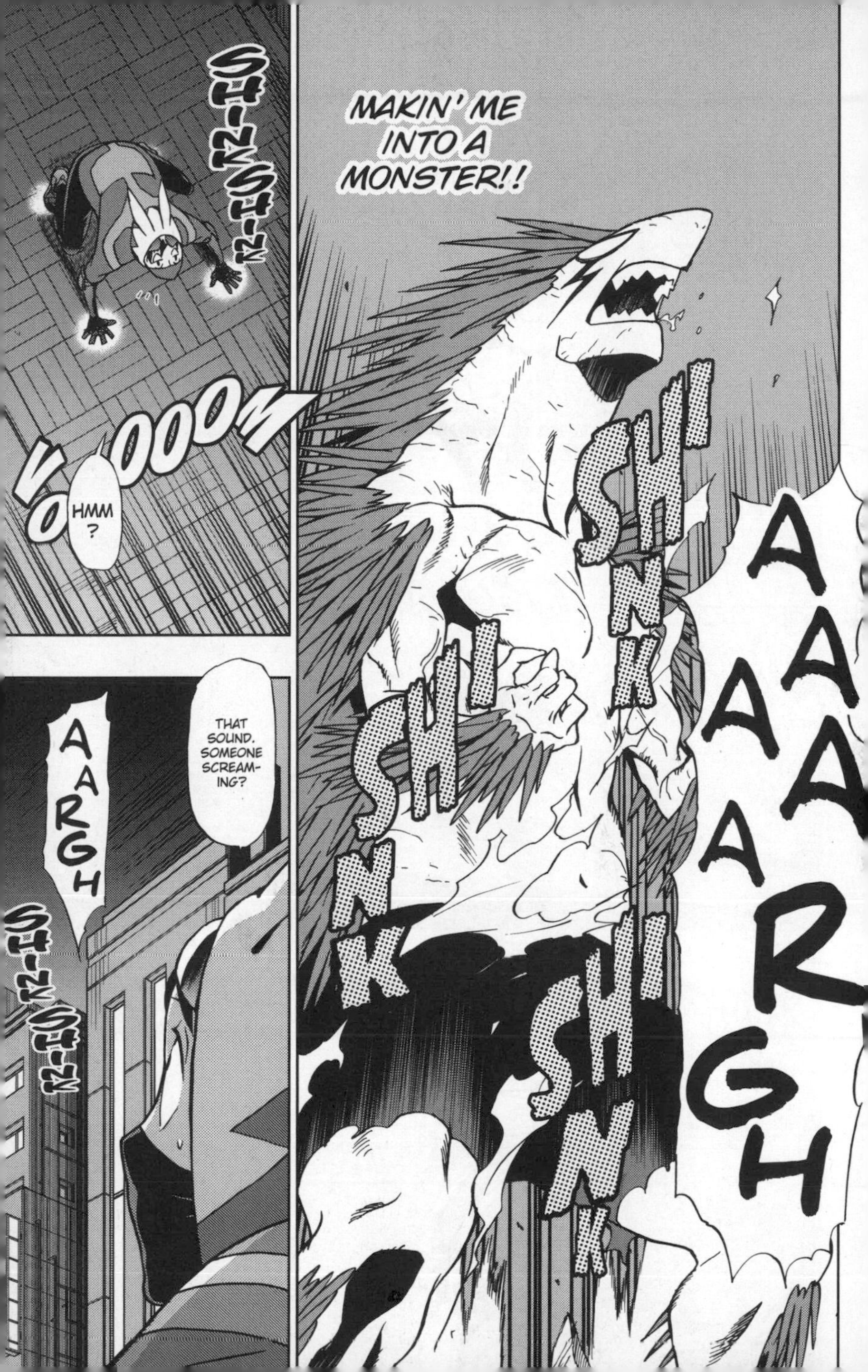
MAKIN' ME INTO A MONSTER!!
AAAAARGH
SHINK
SHINK
SHINK
VOOOOOM
HMM?
THAT SOUND. SOMEONE SCREAMING?
AARGH

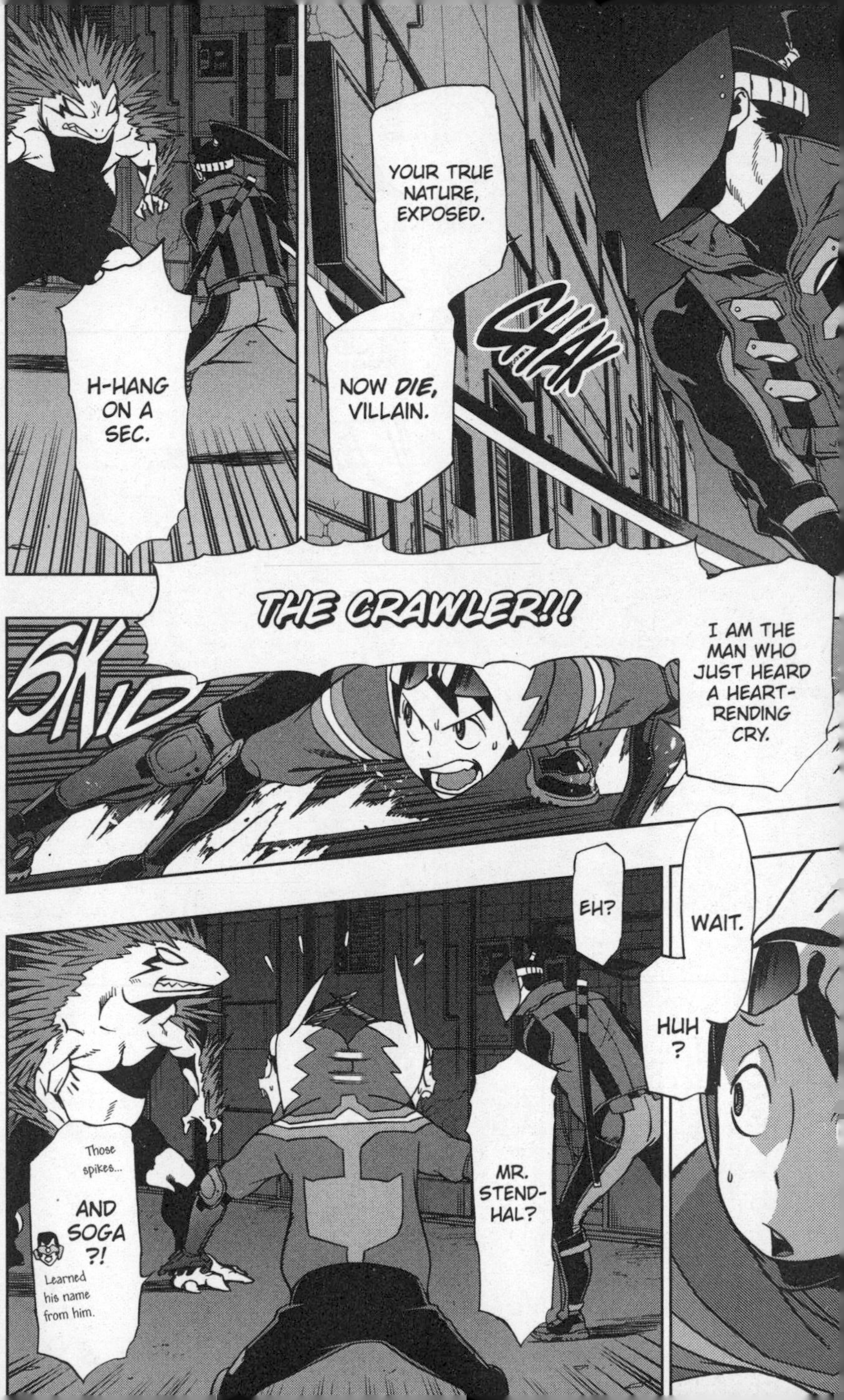
YOUR TRUE NATURE, EXPOSED.
NOW *DIE*, VILLAIN.
CHAK
H-HANG ON A SEC.
I AM THE MAN WHO JUST HEARD A HEART-RENDING CRY.
THE CRAWLER!!
SKID
WAIT.
EH?
HUH?
MR. STENDHAL?
Those spikes...
AND SOGA?!
Learned his name from him.

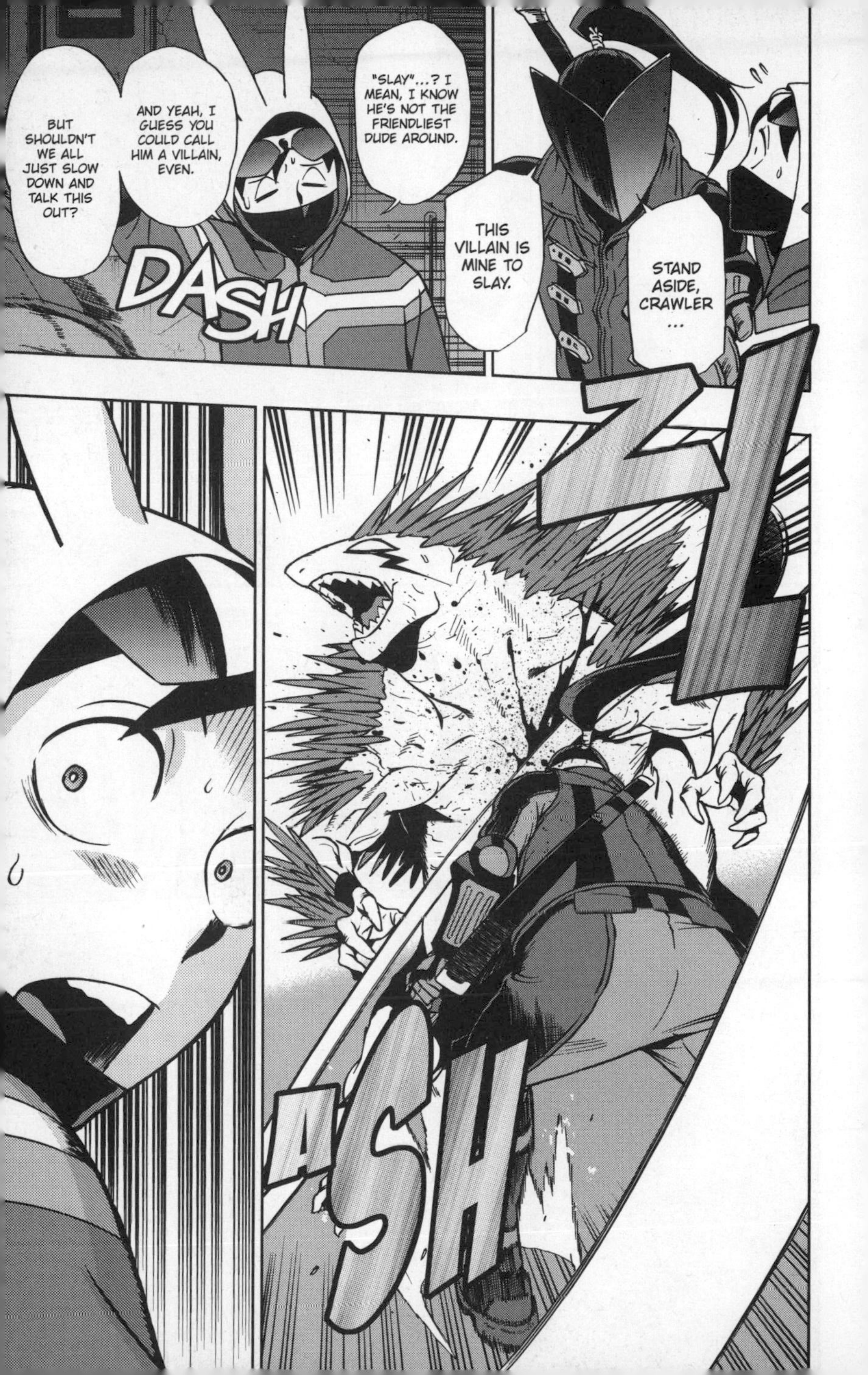
STAND ASIDE, CRAWLER...
THIS VILLAIN IS MINE TO SLAY.
"SLAY"...? I MEAN, I KNOW HE'S NOT THE FRIENDLIEST DUDE AROUND.
AND YEAH, I GUESS YOU COULD CALL HIM A VILLAIN, EVEN.
BUT SHOULDN'T WE ALL JUST SLOW DOWN AND TALK THIS OUT?
DASH
ASH

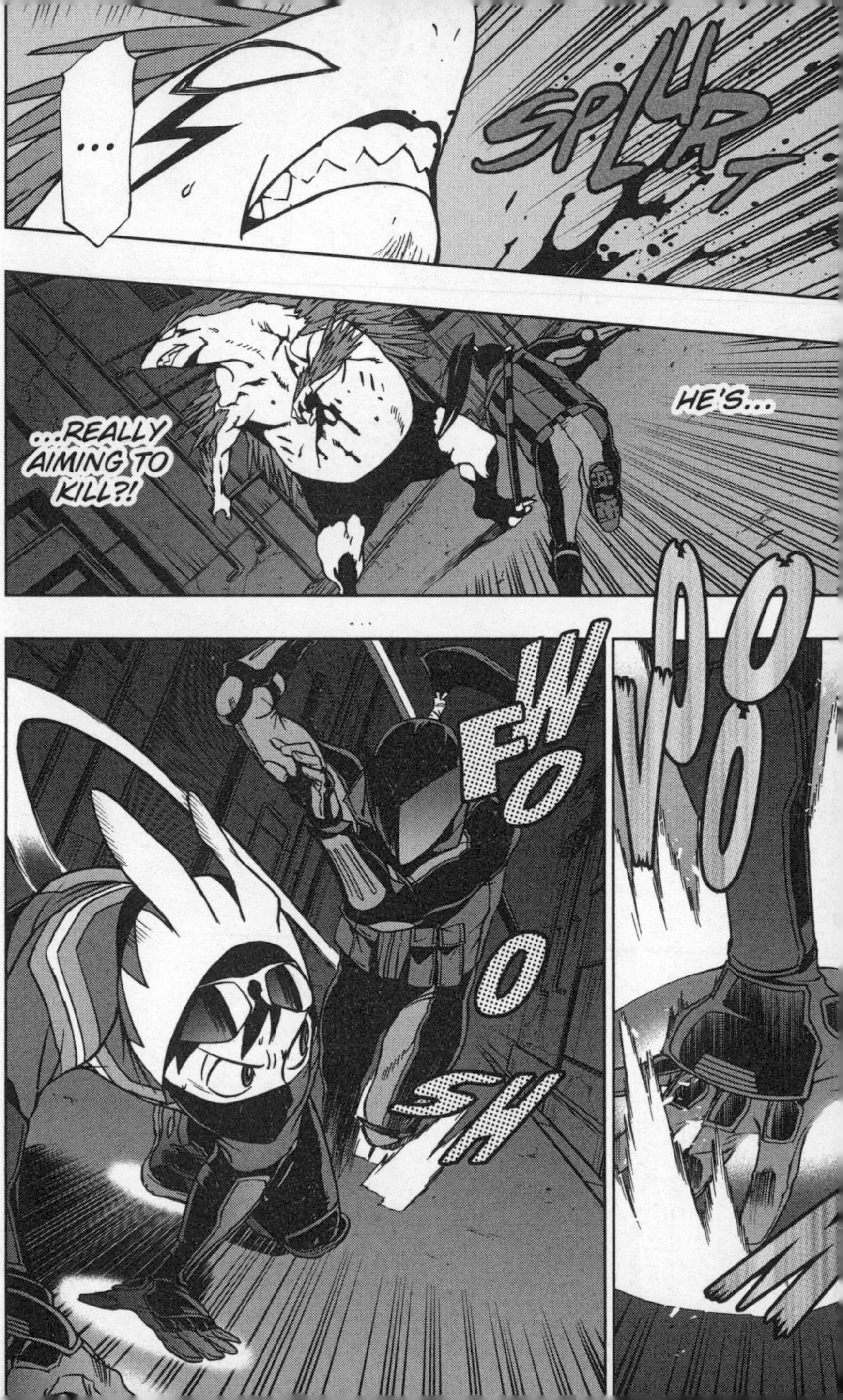
SPLURT
...
HE'S...
...REALLY AIMING TO KILL?!
...
VOOOO
FWOOOSSH

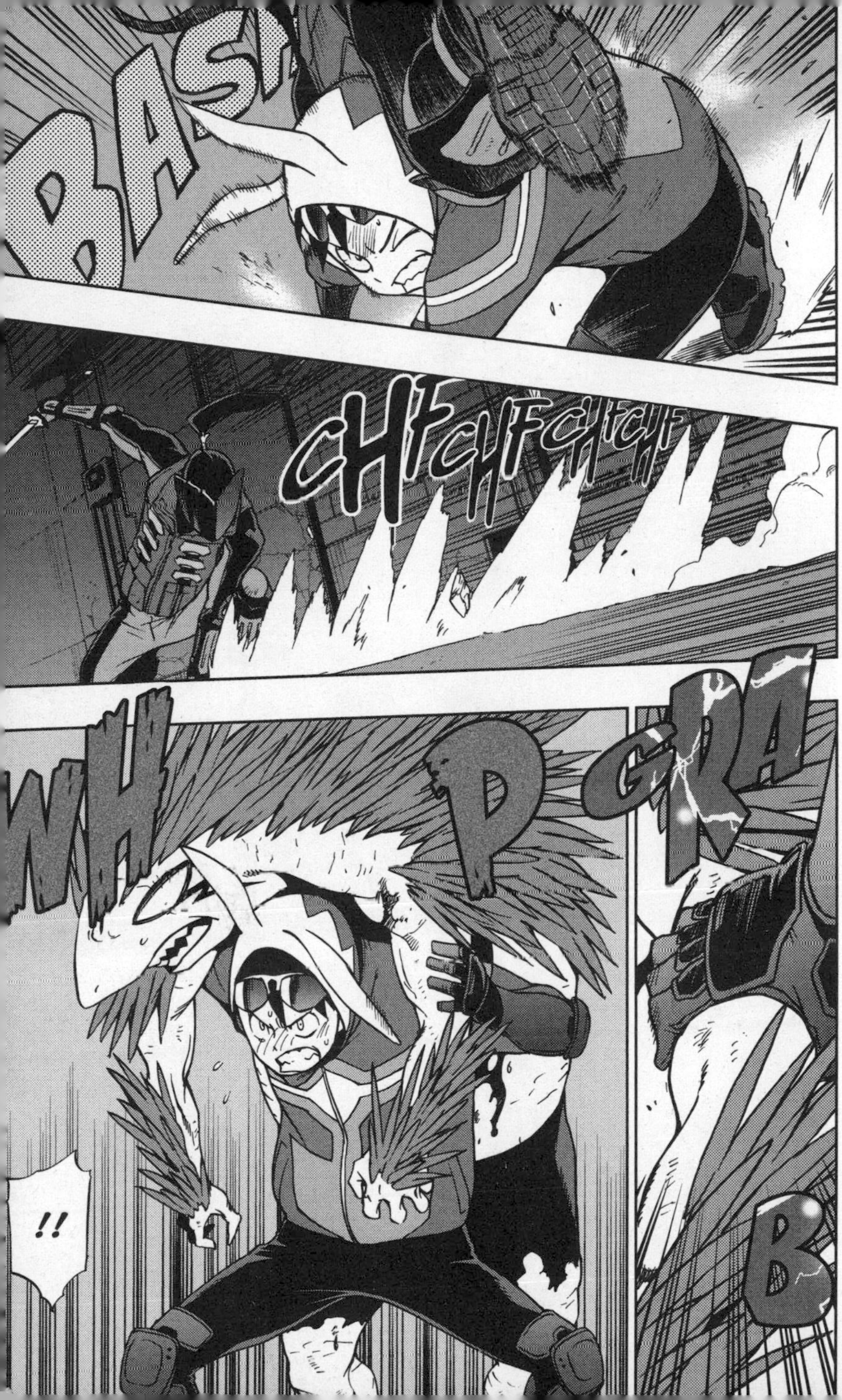
BAS
CHF CHF CHF CHF
GRA
B
WH
D
!!

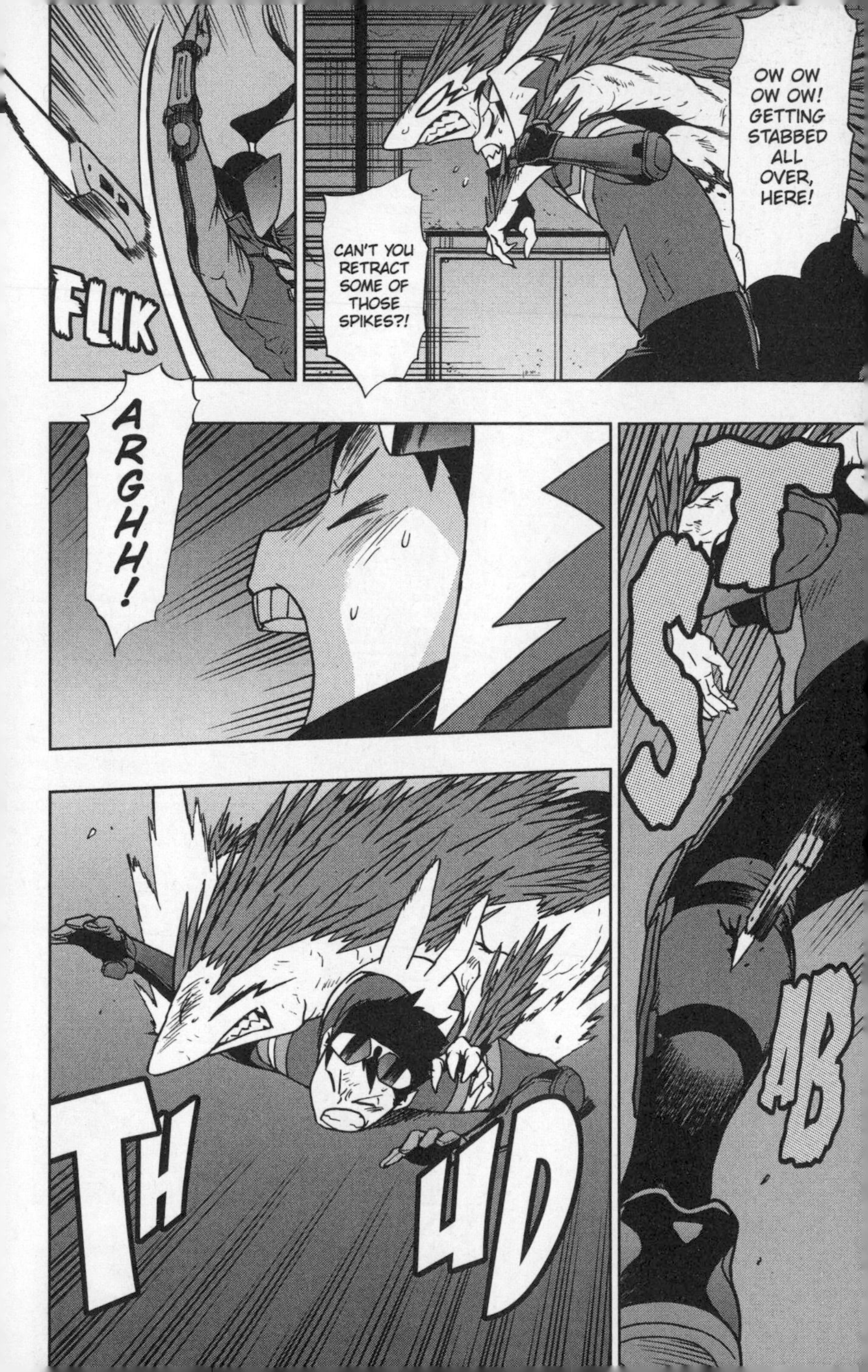
OW OW OW OW! GETTING STABBED ALL OVER, HERE!
CAN'T YOU RETRACT SOME OF THOSE SPIKES?!
FLIK
STAB
ARGHH!
THUD

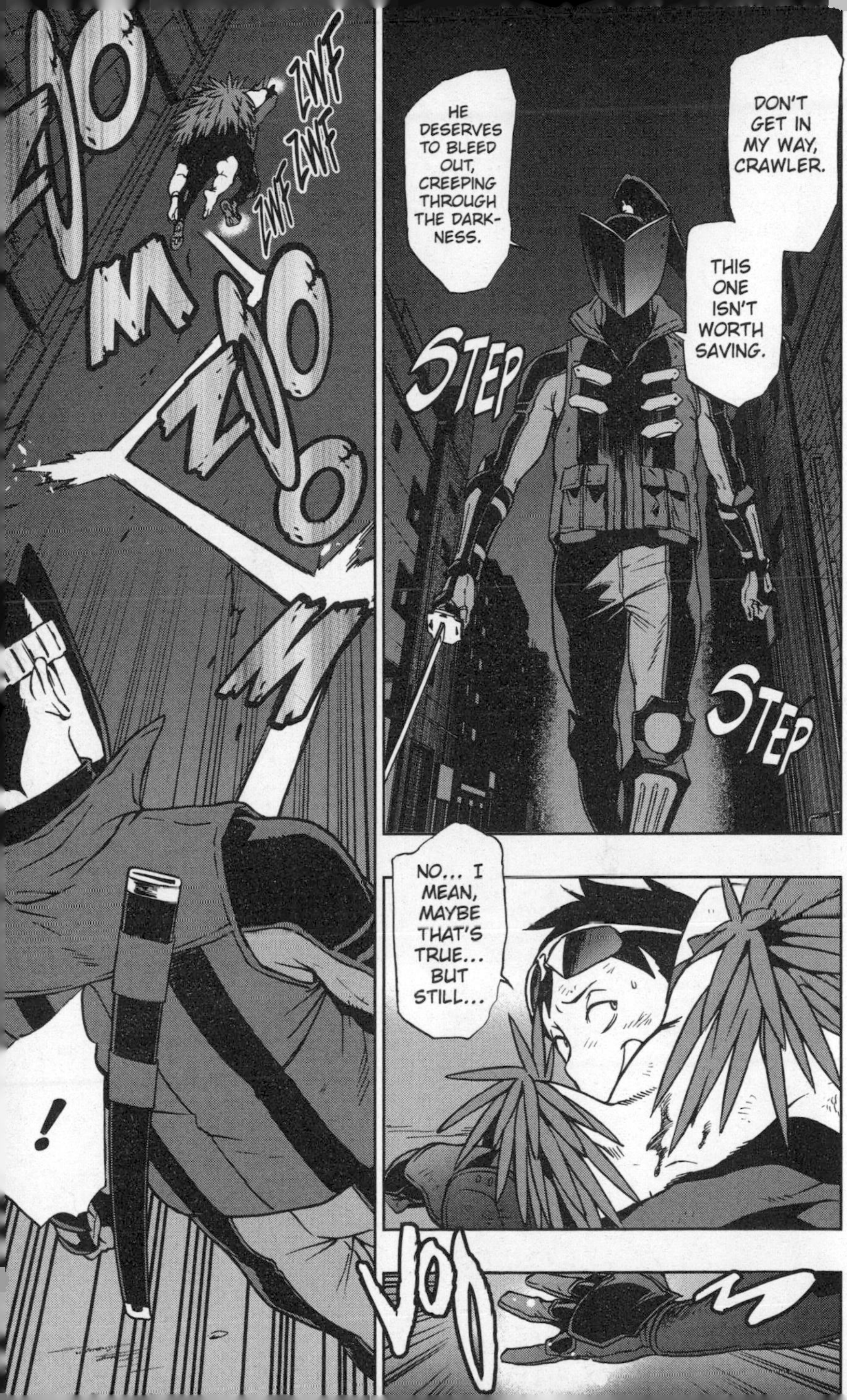
DON'T GET IN MY WAY, CRAWLER.
THIS ONE ISN'T WORTH SAVING.
HE DESERVES TO BLEED OUT, CREEPING THROUGH THE DARKNESS.
STEP
STEP
NO... I MEAN, MAYBE THAT'S TRUE... BUT STILL...
VOOM
ZWF ZWF ZWF
ZOOM
ZOOM
!

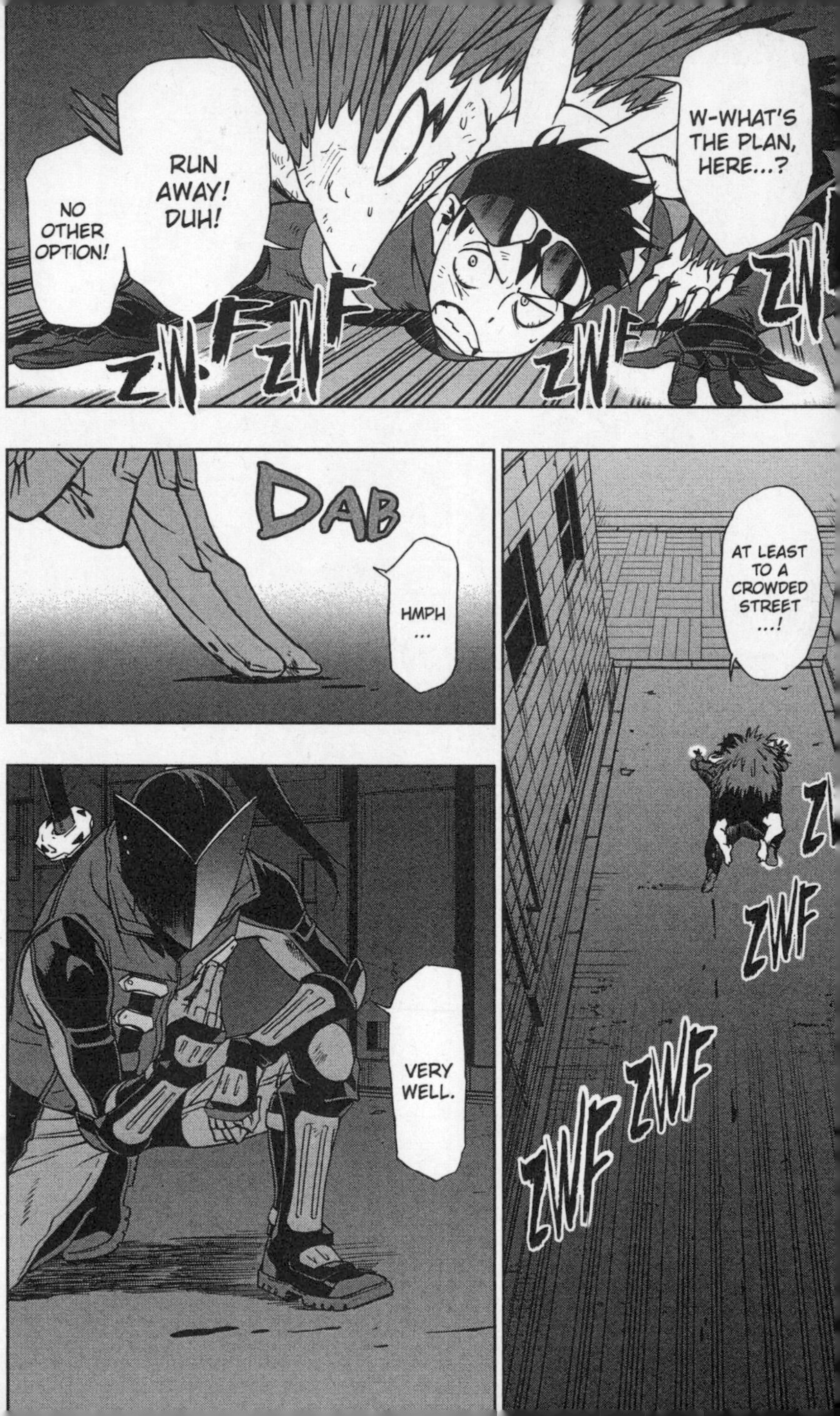
W-WHAT'S THE PLAN, HERE...?
RUN AWAY! DUH!
NO OTHER OPTION!
ZWF
ZWF
ZWF ZWF
AT LEAST TO A CROWDED STREET...!
ZWF
ZWF ZWF
DAB
HMPH...
VERY WELL.

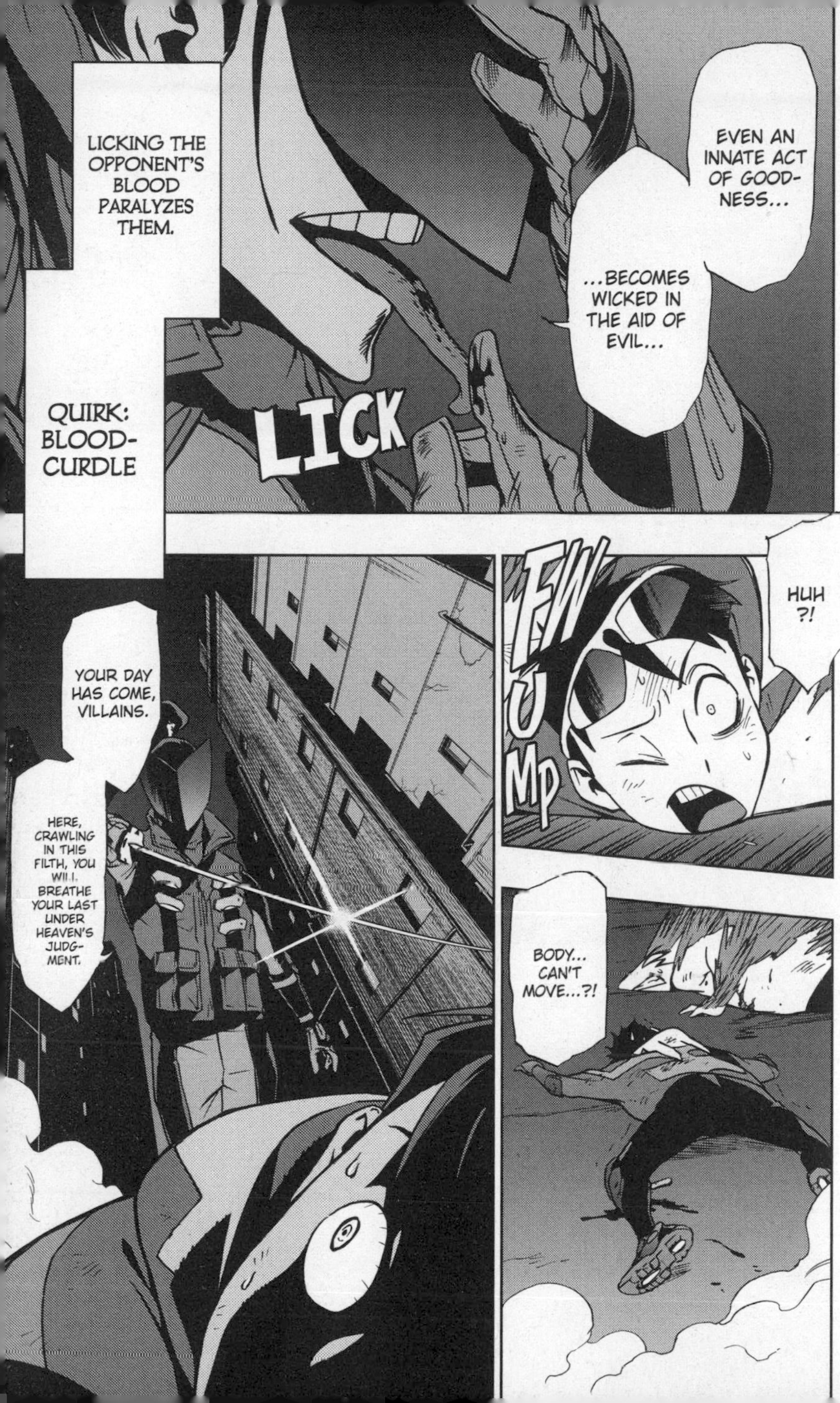
EVEN AN INNATE ACT OF GOOD-NESS...
...BECOMES WICKED IN THE AID OF EVIL...
LICK
LICKING THE OPPONENT'S BLOOD PARALYZES THEM.
QUIRK: BLOOD-CURDLE
HUH?!
FWUMP
BODY... CAN'T MOVE...?!
YOUR DAY HAS COME, VILLAINS.
HERE, CRAWLING IN THIS FILTH, YOU WILL BREATHE YOUR LAST UNDER HEAVEN'S JUDG-MENT.

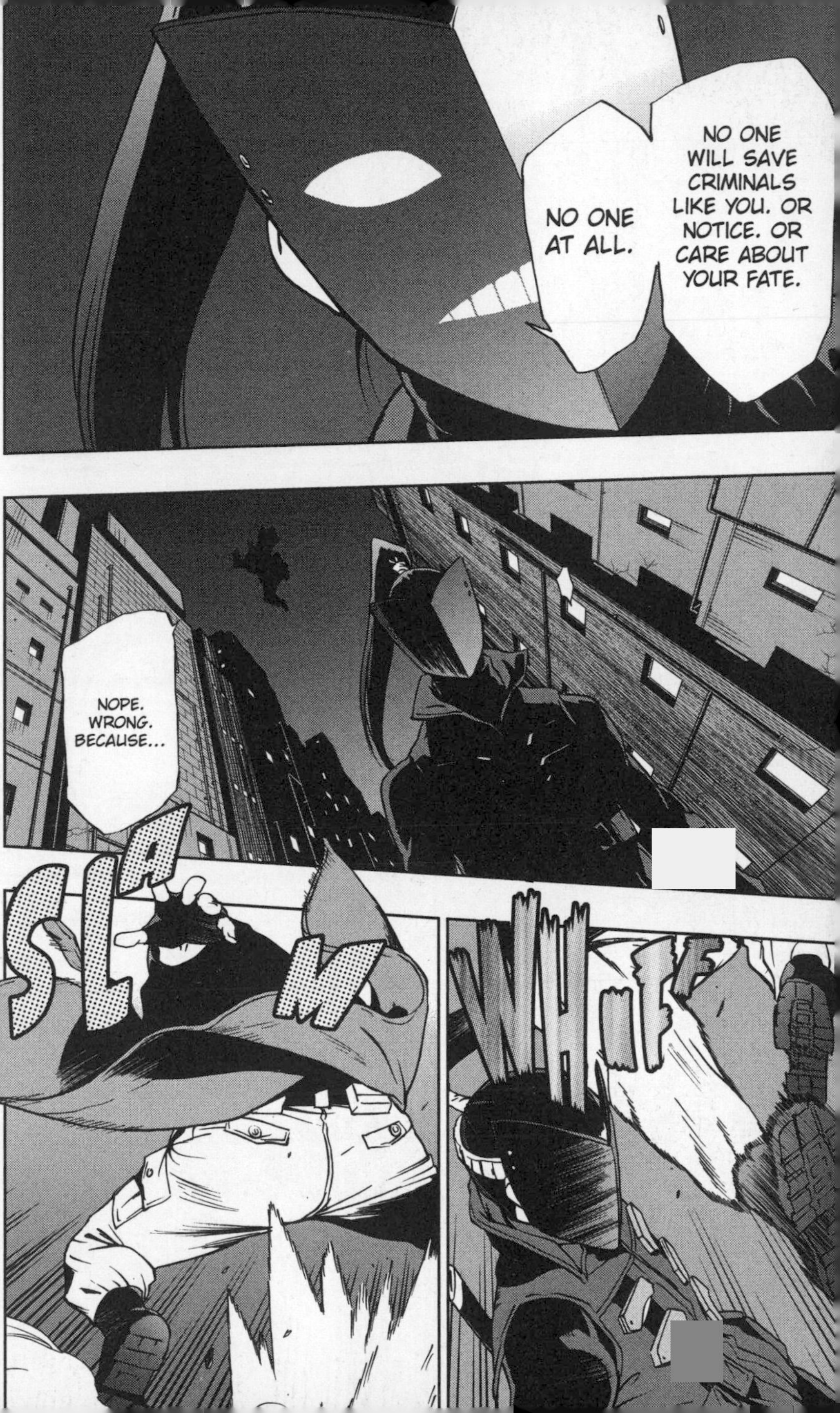
NO ONE WILL SAVE CRIMINALS LIKE YOU. OR NOTICE. OR CARE ABOUT YOUR FATE.
NO ONE AT ALL.
NOPE. WRONG. BECAUSE...
WHIFF
SLAM

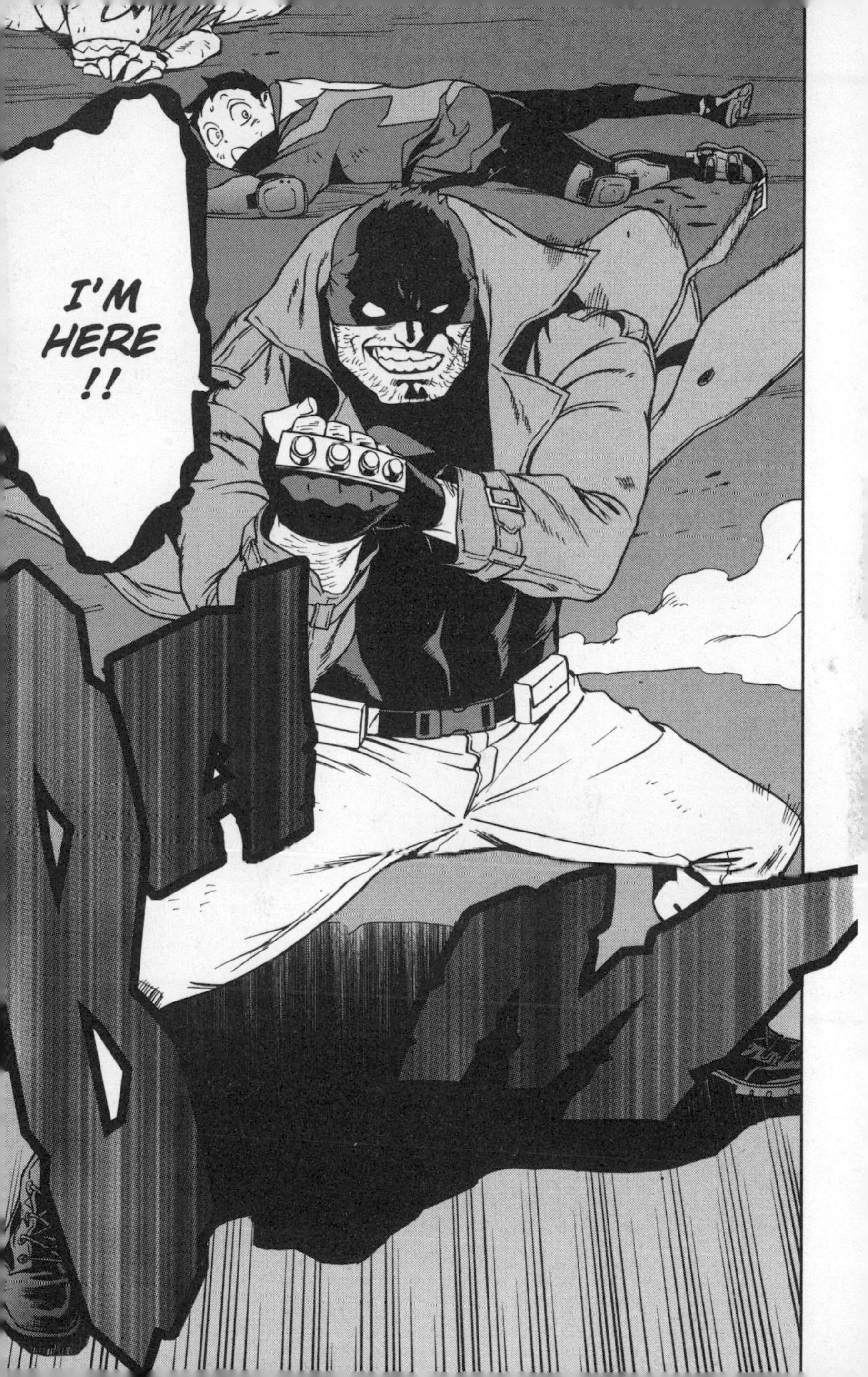
I'M HERE !!

SPIKE VILLAIN

THE ROUGH DESIGN

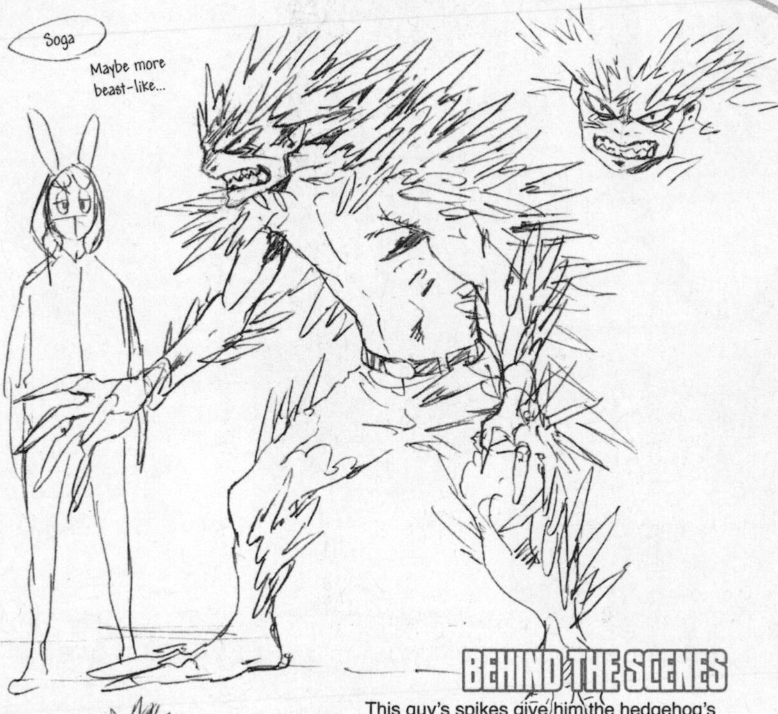
Soga
Maybe more beast-like...

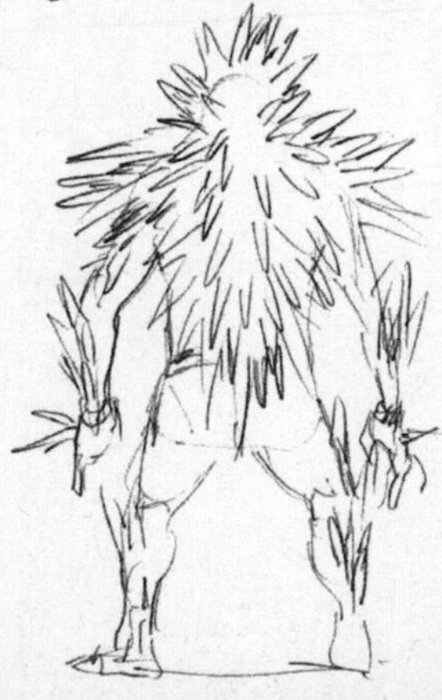

BEHIND THE SCENES

This guy's spikes give him the hedgehog's dilemma.

Out of the three friends, he's actually the most serious, the most complicated, the most prone to snap... That was the personality I came up with.

—Furuhashi

Very different design than what we wound up with (LOL). I must've gone through some trial and error, trying to make him look more like an actual porcupine. I like Soga, but it's hard to draw him in a convincing way.

—Betten

★ See page 204 for more on the three delinquents.

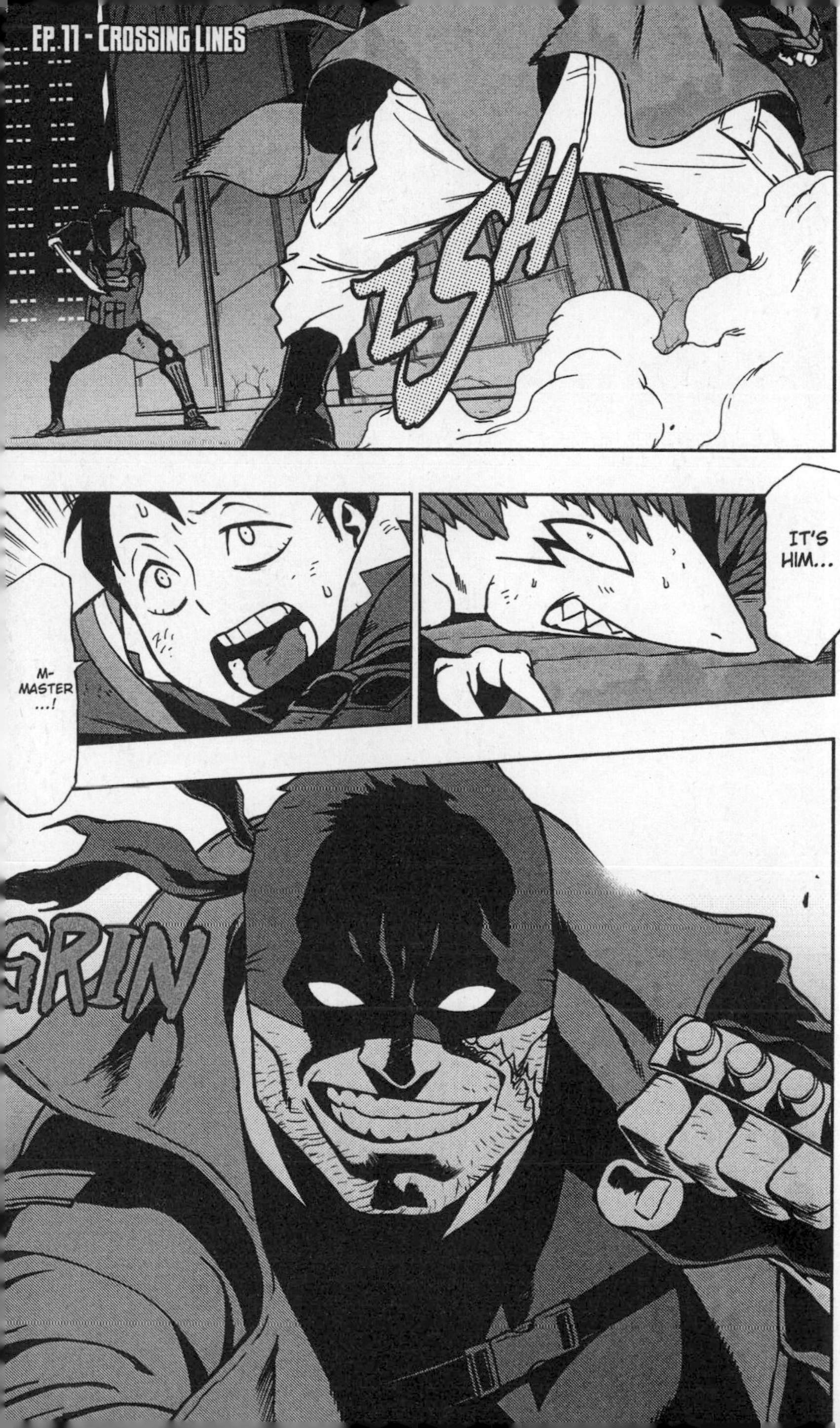
ZSH
IT'S HIM...
M-MASTER ...!
GRIN

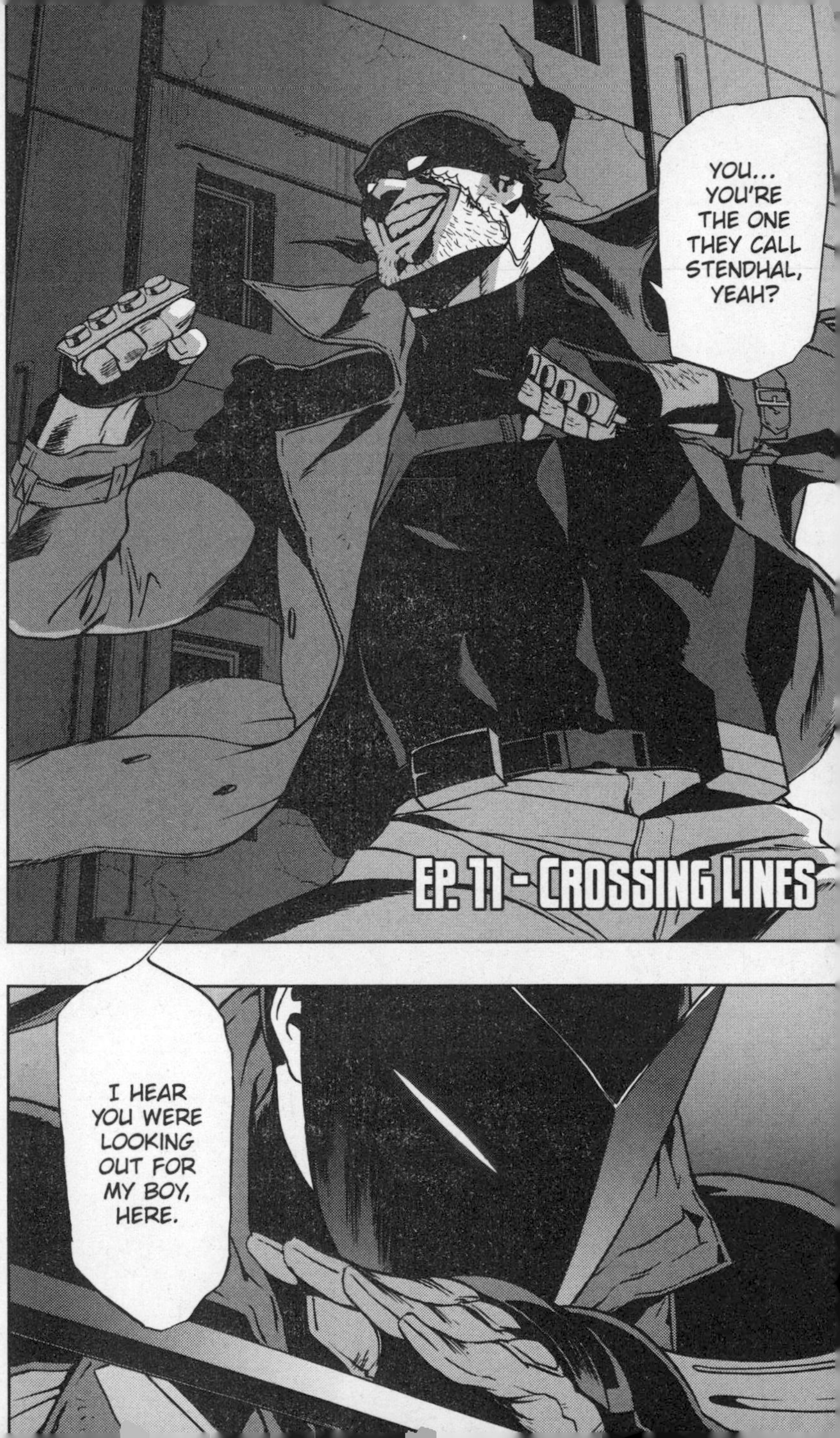
YOU... YOU'RE THE ONE THEY CALL STENDHAL, YEAH?
EP. 11 - CROSSING LINES
I HEAR YOU WERE LOOKING OUT FOR MY BOY, HERE.

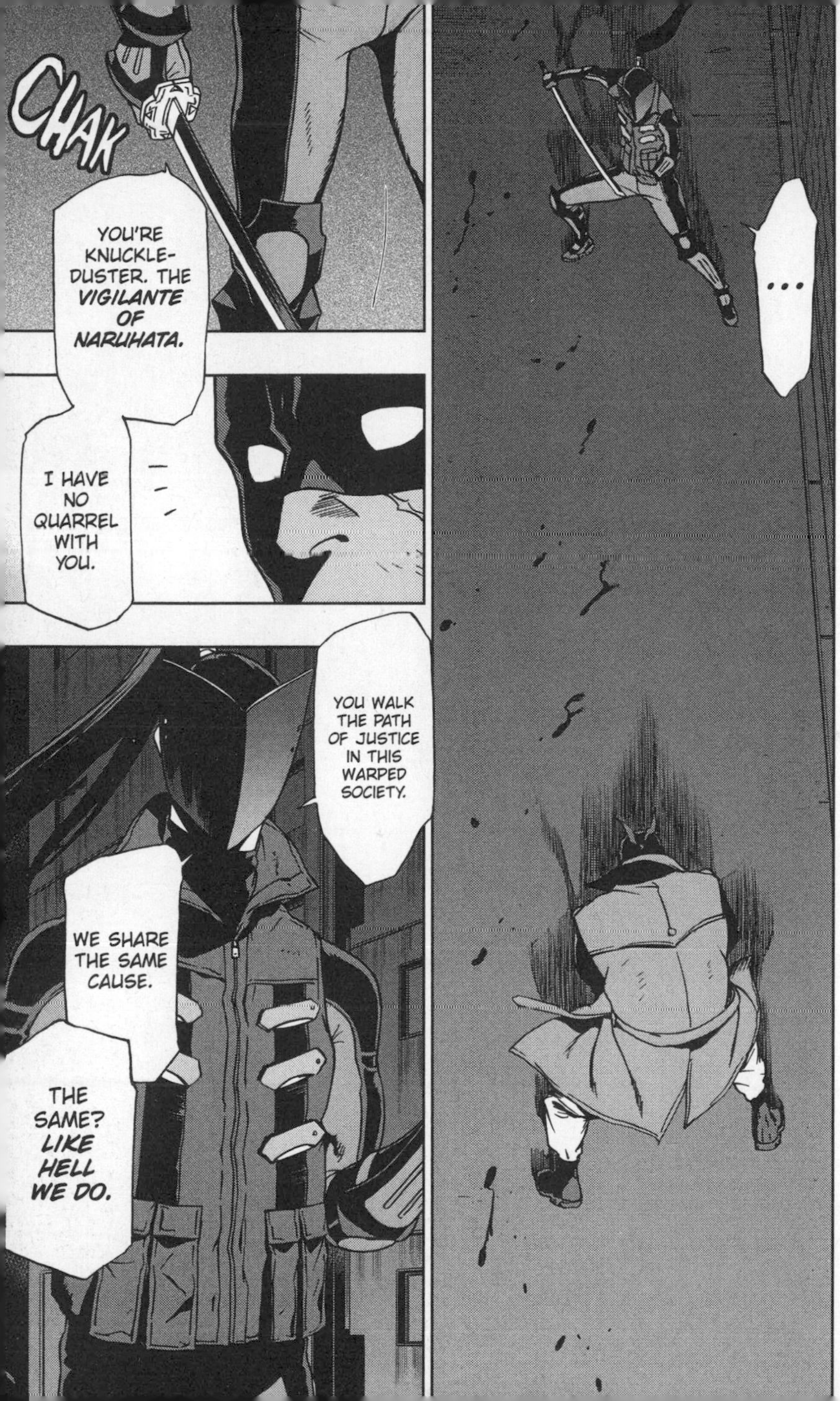
...
CHAK
YOU'RE KNUCKLE-DUSTER. THE VIGILANTE OF NARUHATA.
I HAVE NO QUARREL WITH YOU.
YOU WALK THE PATH OF JUSTICE IN THIS WARPED SOCIETY.
WE SHARE THE SAME CAUSE.
THE SAME? LIKE HELL WE DO.

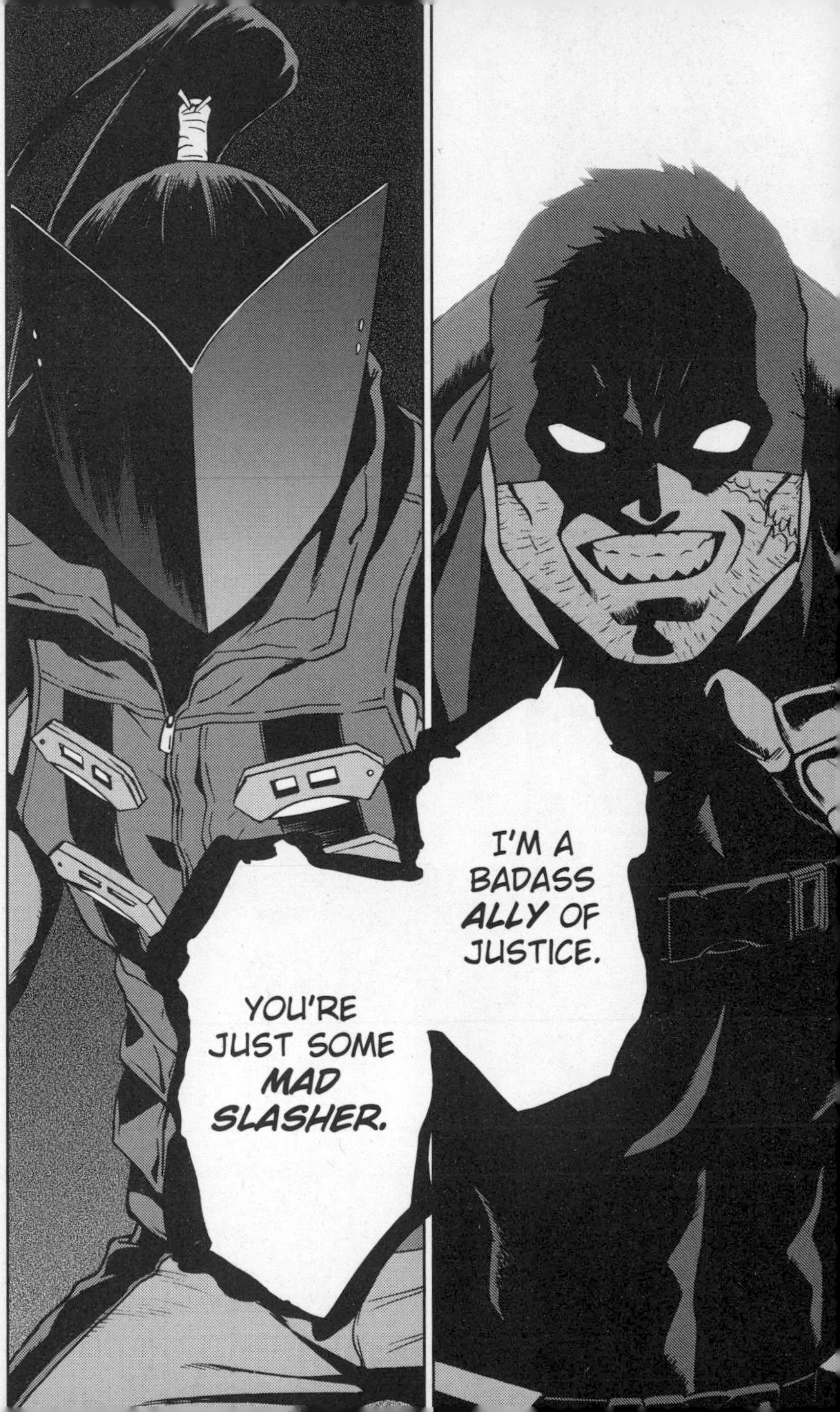
I'M A BADASS *ALLY* OF JUSTICE.
YOU'RE JUST SOME *MAD SLASHER.*

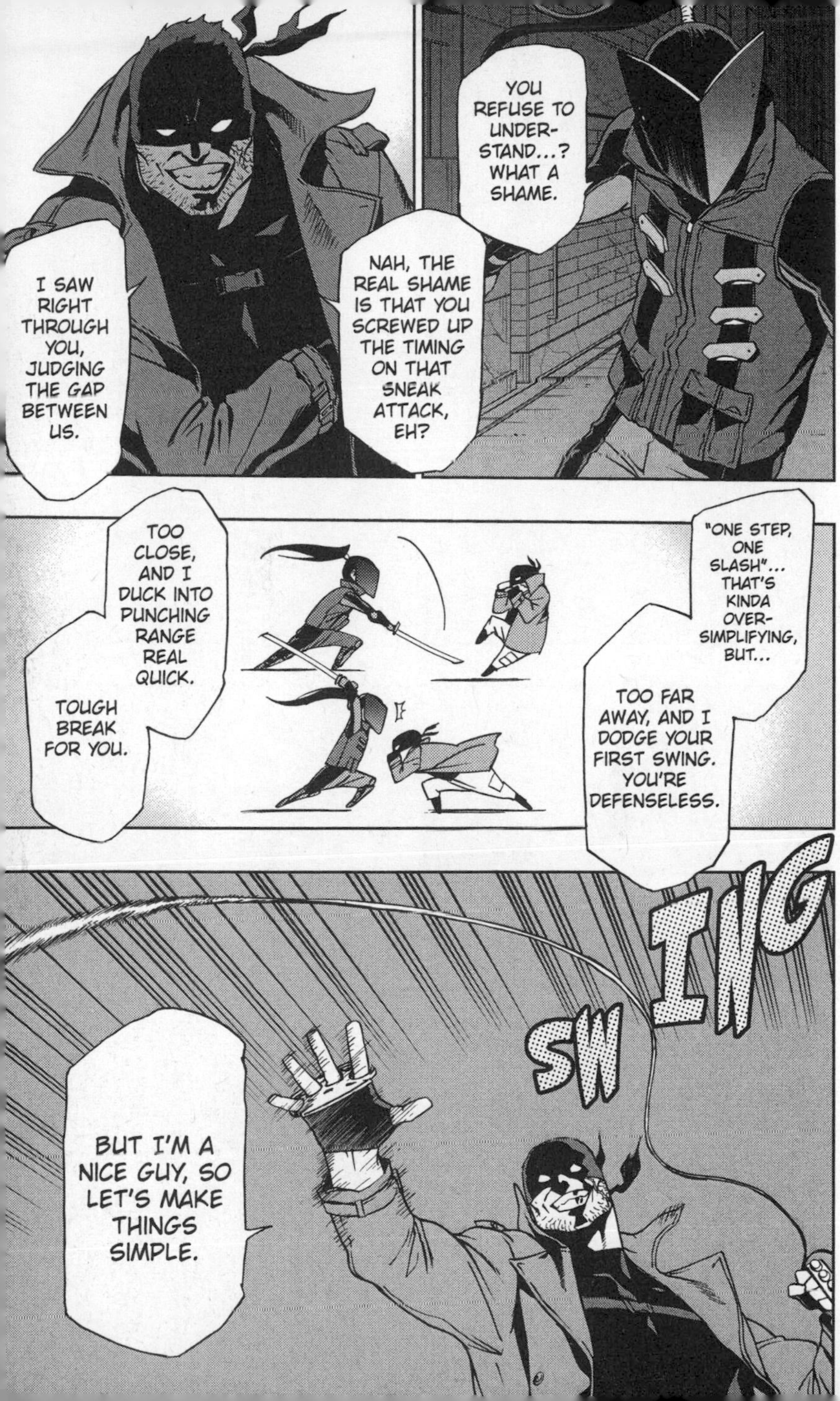
YOU REFUSE TO UNDER-STAND...? WHAT A SHAME.
NAH, THE REAL SHAME IS THAT YOU SCREWED UP THE TIMING ON THAT SNEAK ATTACK, EH?
I SAW RIGHT THROUGH YOU, JUDGING THE GAP BETWEEN US.
"ONE STEP, ONE SLASH"... THAT'S KINDA OVER-SIMPLIFYING, BUT...
TOO FAR AWAY, AND I DODGE YOUR FIRST SWING. YOU'RE DEFENSELESS.
TOO CLOSE, AND I DUCK INTO PUNCHING RANGE REAL QUICK.
TOUGH BREAK FOR YOU.
SWING
BUT I'M A NICE GUY, SO LET'S MAKE THINGS SIMPLE.

A ROPE ...?

FWISH

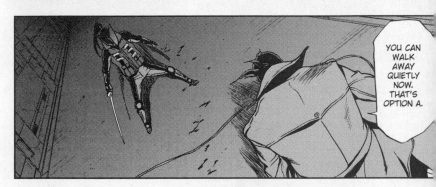

YOU CAN WALK AWAY QUIETLY NOW. THAT'S OPTION A.

CLINCH

OR YOU CAN CROSS THAT LINE.

AND THAT'S WHEN YOU'LL EAT A **KNUCKLE SANDWICH** !!

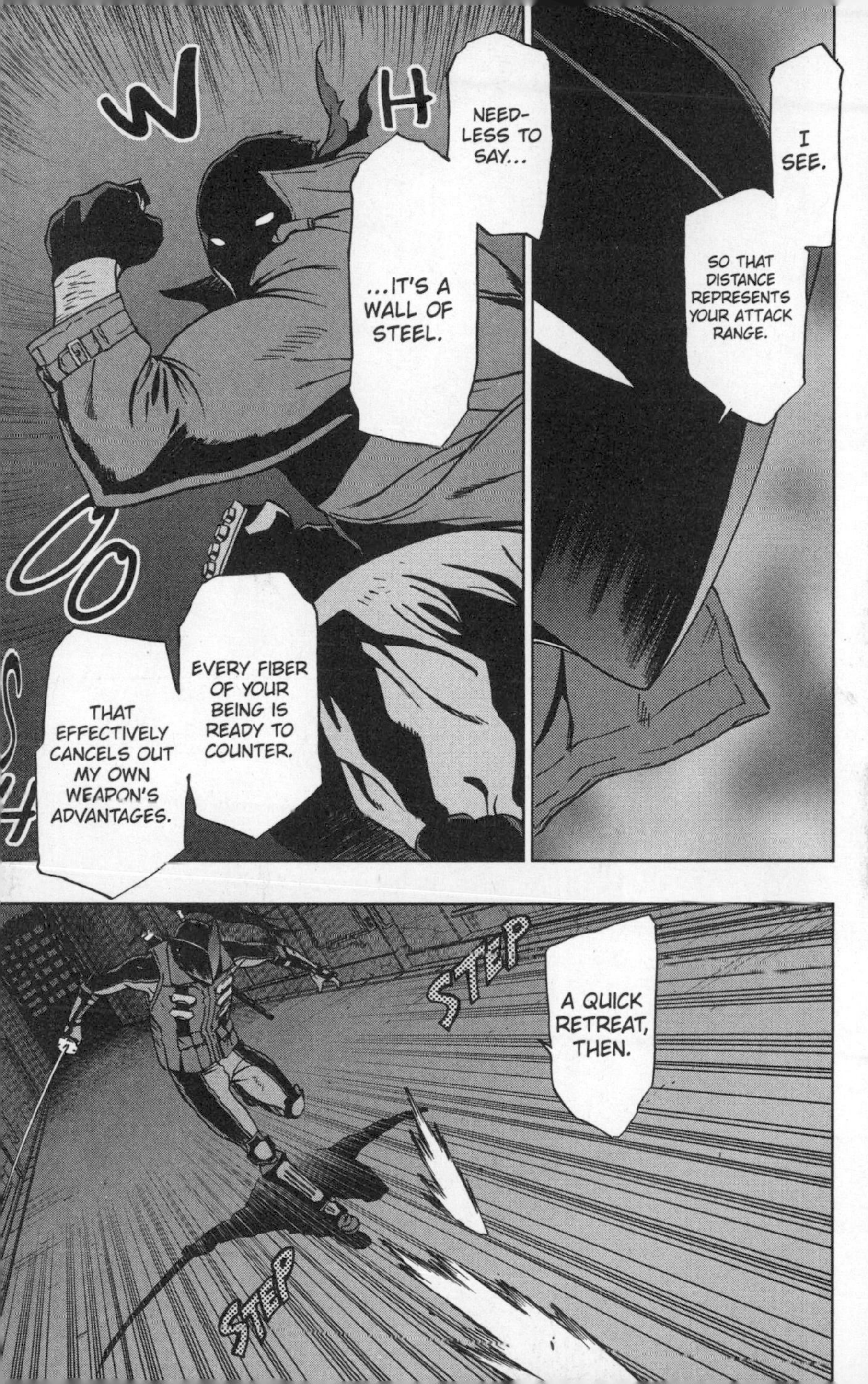
I SEE.
SO THAT DISTANCE REPRESENTS YOUR ATTACK RANGE.
WHOOSH
NEED-LESS TO SAY...
...IT'S A WALL OF STEEL.
EVERY FIBER OF YOUR BEING IS READY TO COUNTER.
THAT EFFECTIVELY CANCELS OUT MY OWN WEAPON'S ADVANTAGES.
A QUICK RETREAT, THEN.
STEP
STEP

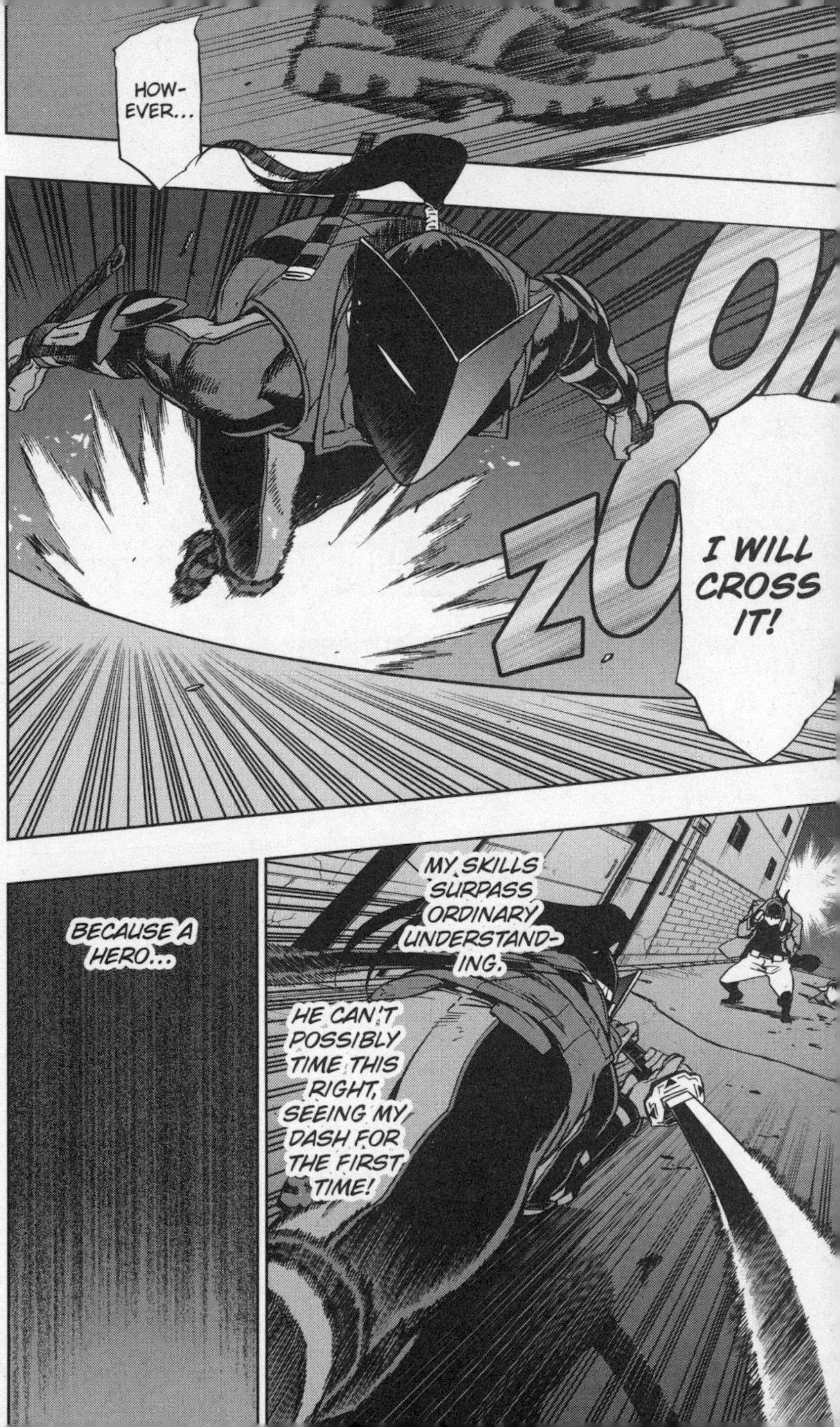
HOW-EVER...
ZOO
I WILL CROSS IT!
MY SKILLS SURPASS ORDINARY UNDERSTAND-ING.
HE CAN'T POSSIBLY TIME THIS RIGHT, SEEING MY DASH FOR THE FIRST TIME!
BECAUSE A HERO...

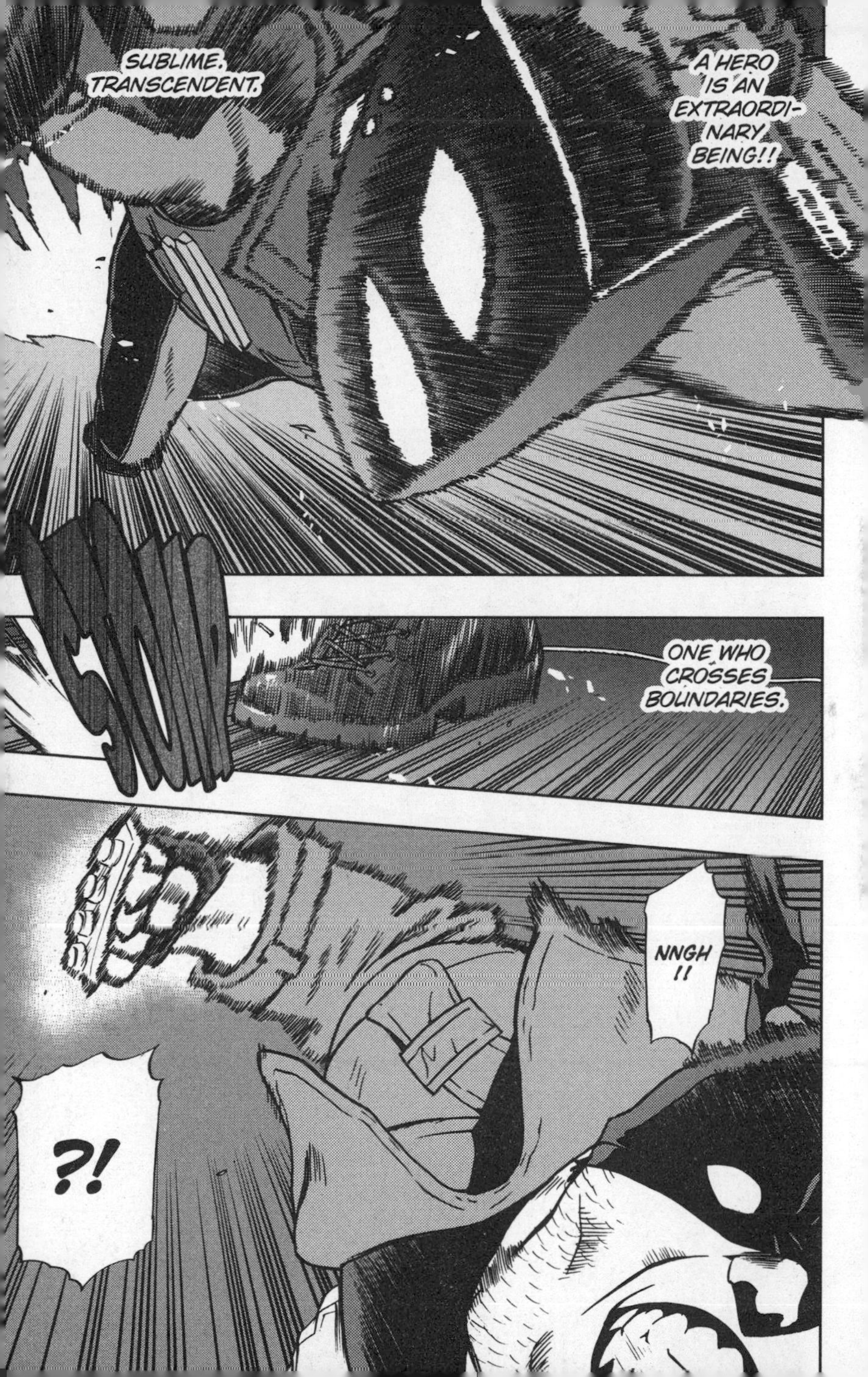
A HERO IS AN EXTRAORDI- NARY BEING!!
SUBLIME. TRANSCENDENT.
ONE WHO CROSSES BOUNDARIES.
NNGH !!
?!

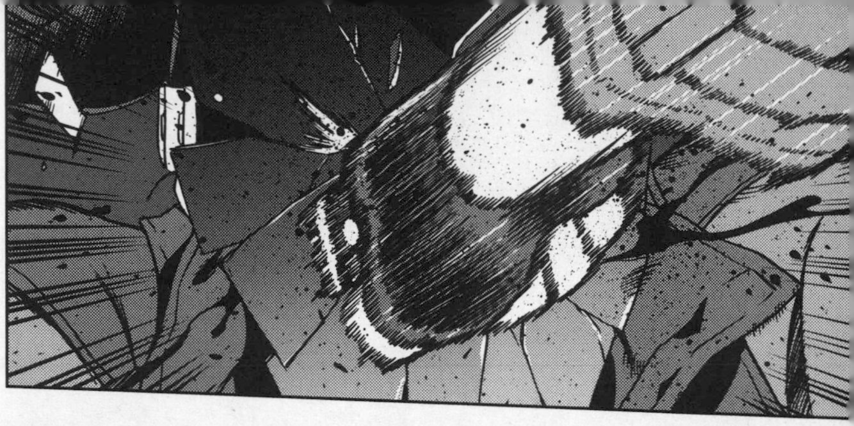
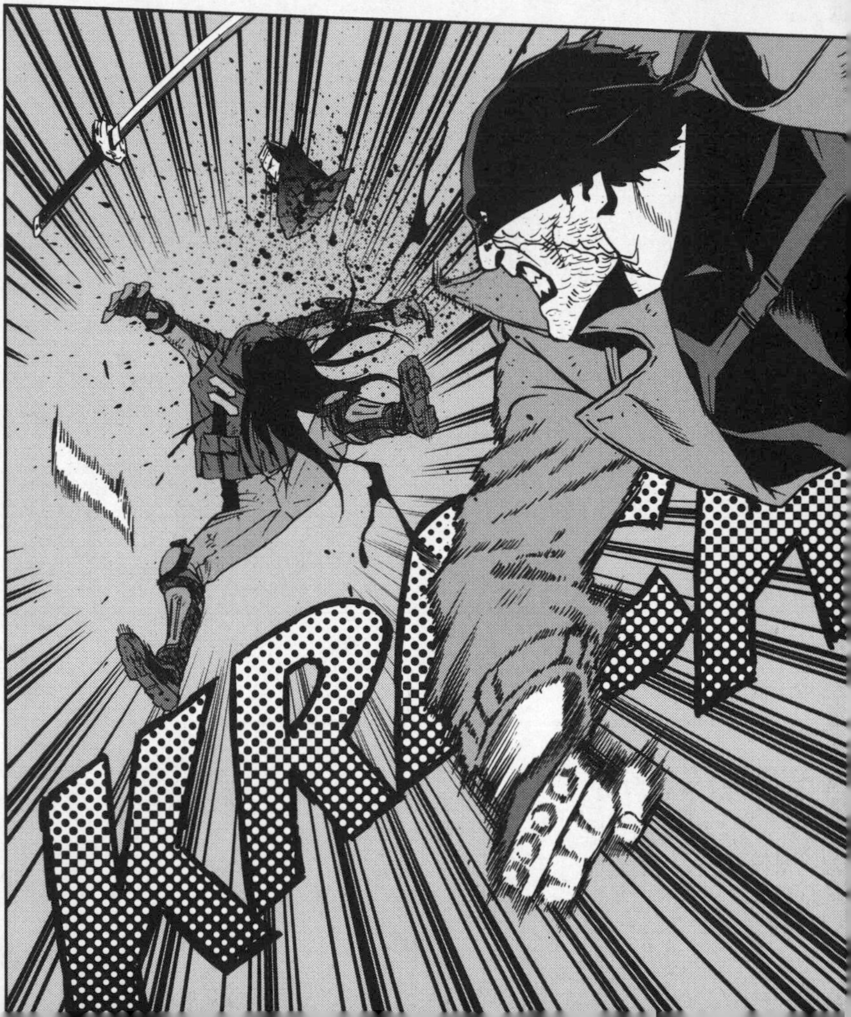

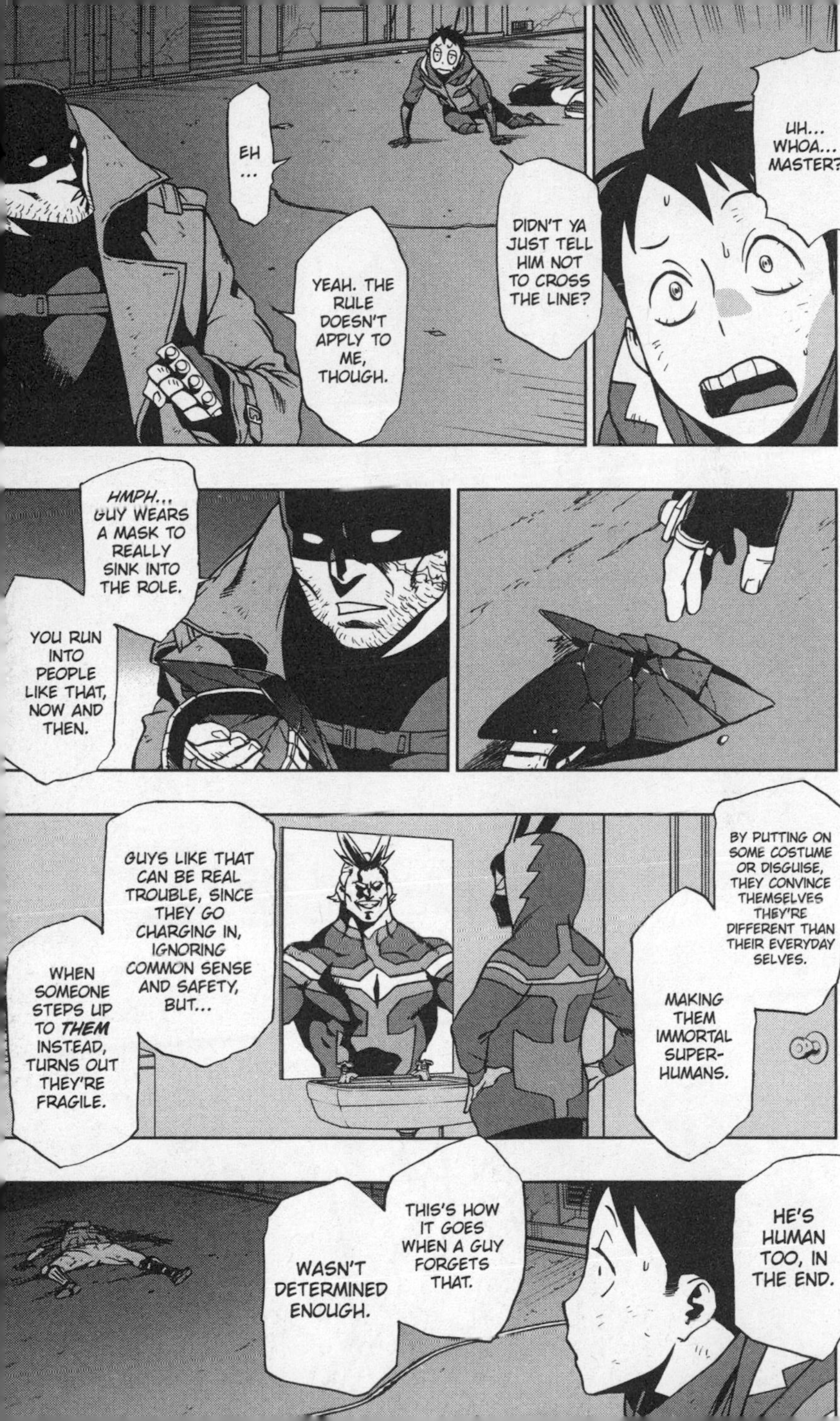
UH... WHOA... MASTER?
DIDN'T YA JUST TELL HIM NOT TO CROSS THE LINE?
EH ...
YEAH. THE RULE DOESN'T APPLY TO ME, THOUGH.
HMPH... GUY WEARS A MASK TO REALLY SINK INTO THE ROLE.
YOU RUN INTO PEOPLE LIKE THAT, NOW AND THEN.
BY PUTTING ON SOME COSTUME OR DISGUISE, THEY CONVINCE THEMSELVES THEY'RE DIFFERENT THAN THEIR EVERYDAY SELVES.
MAKING THEM IMMORTAL SUPER-HUMANS.
GUYS LIKE THAT CAN BE REAL TROUBLE, SINCE THEY GO CHARGING IN, IGNORING COMMON SENSE AND SAFETY, BUT...
WHEN SOMEONE STEPS UP TO *THEM* INSTEAD, TURNS OUT THEY'RE FRAGILE.
HE'S HUMAN TOO, IN THE END.
THIS'S HOW IT GOES WHEN A GUY FORGETS THAT.
WASN'T DETERMINED ENOUGH.

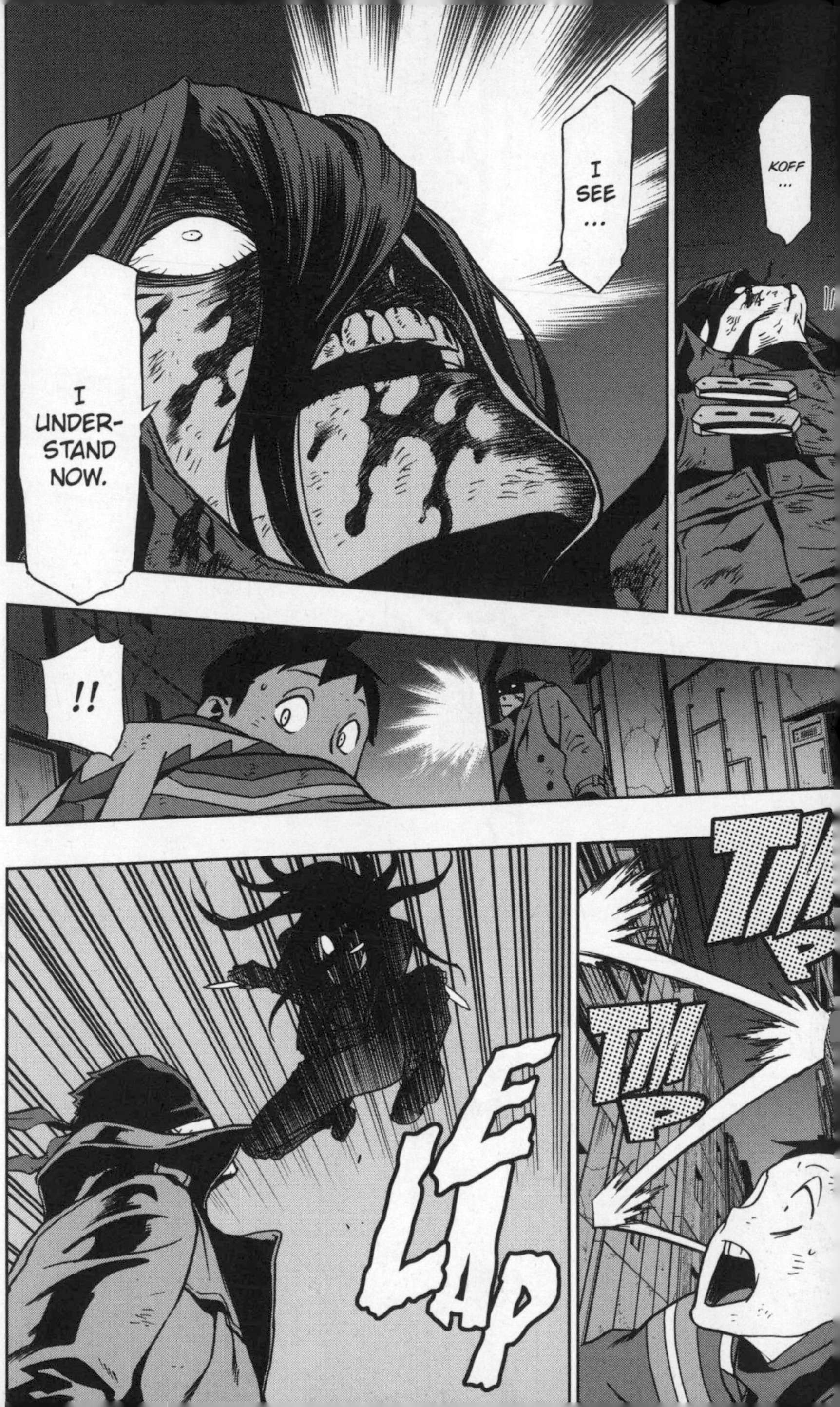
KOFF ...
I SEE ...
I UNDERSTAND NOW.
!!
THP
THP
FLAP

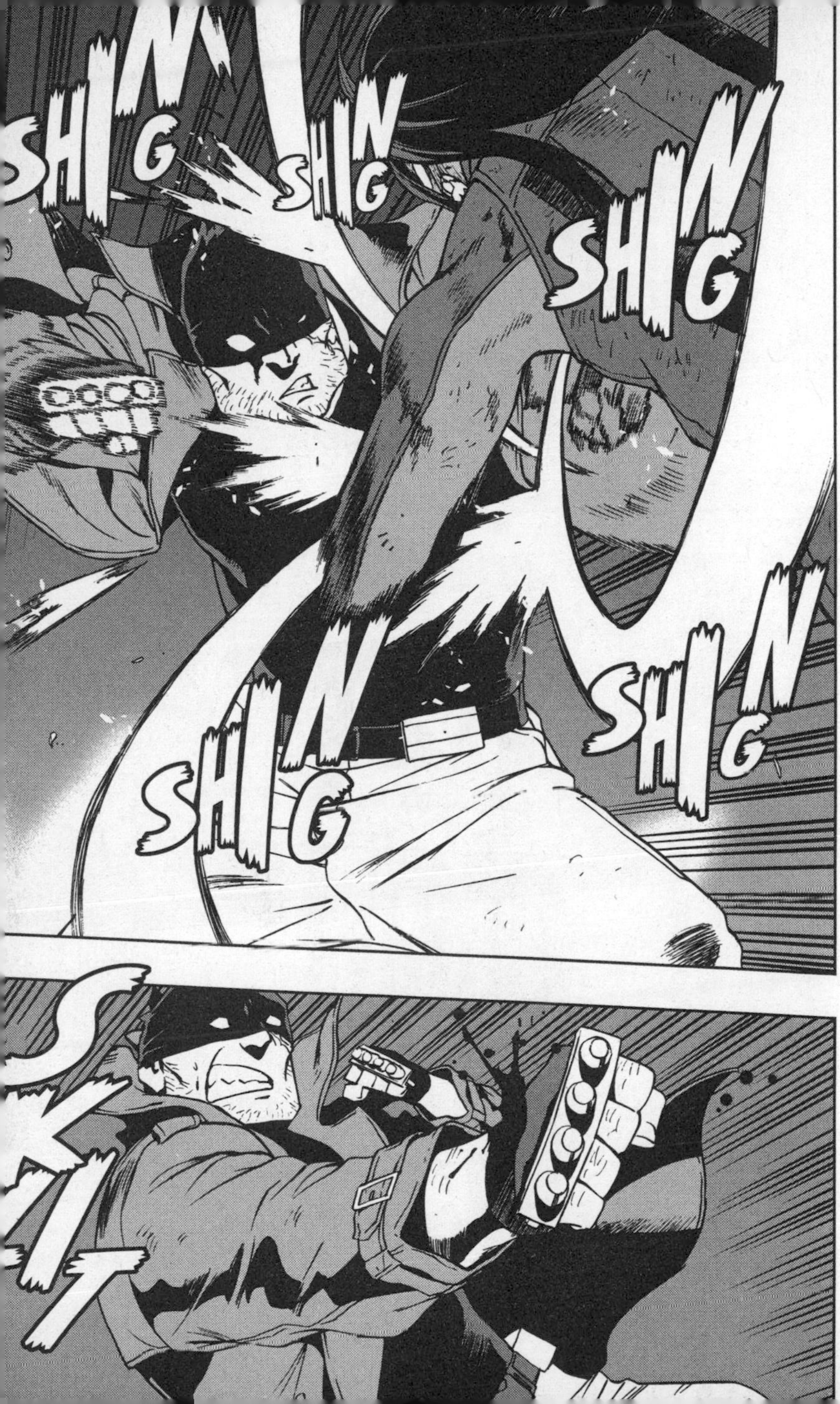
SHING
SHING
SHING
SHING
SHING
SHING

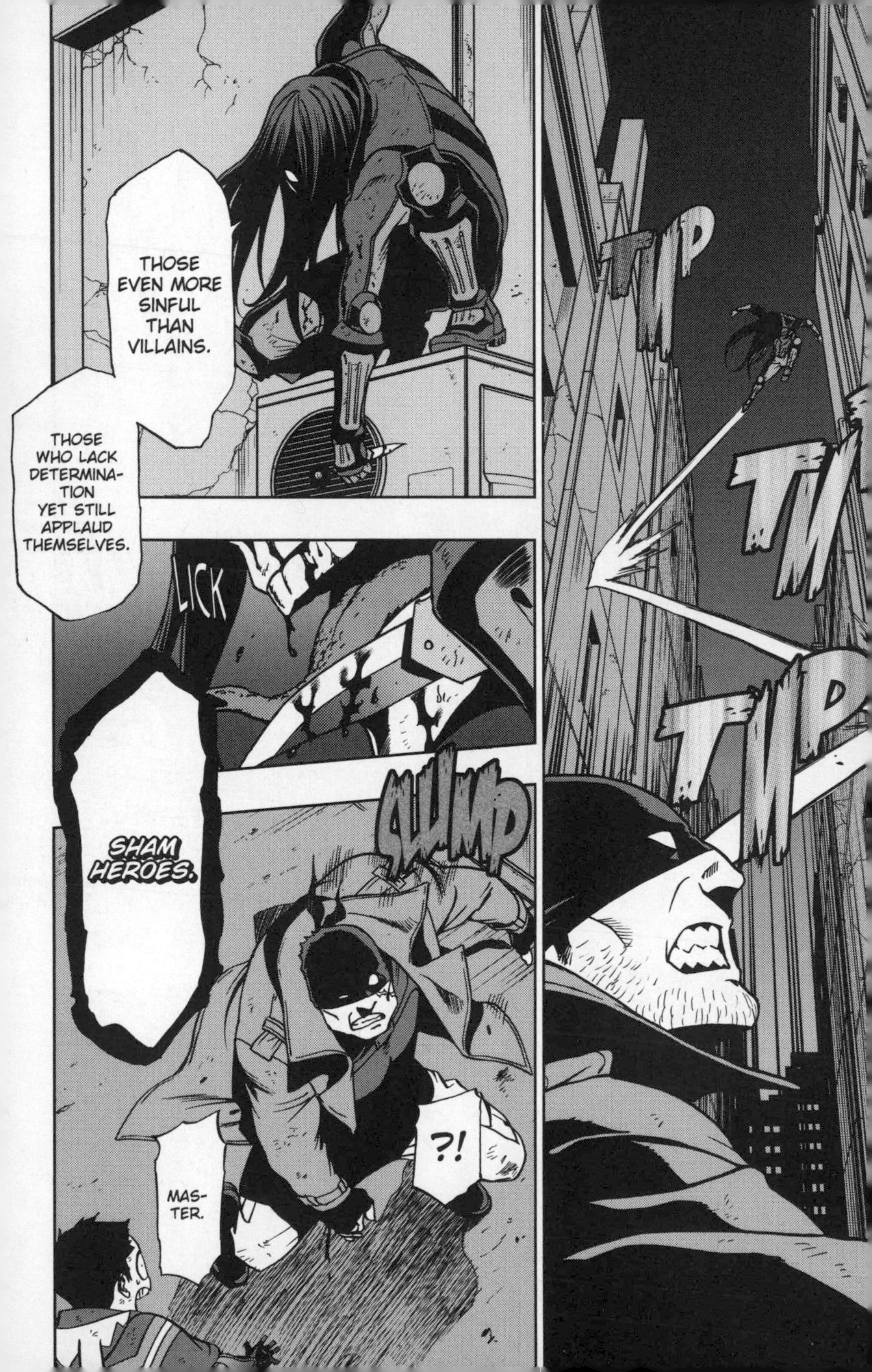
TIP
TIP
THOSE EVEN MORE SINFUL THAN VILLAINS.
THOSE WHO LACK DETERMINATION YET STILL APPLAUD THEMSELVES.
LICK
SHAM HEROES.
SLUMP
?!
MASTER.

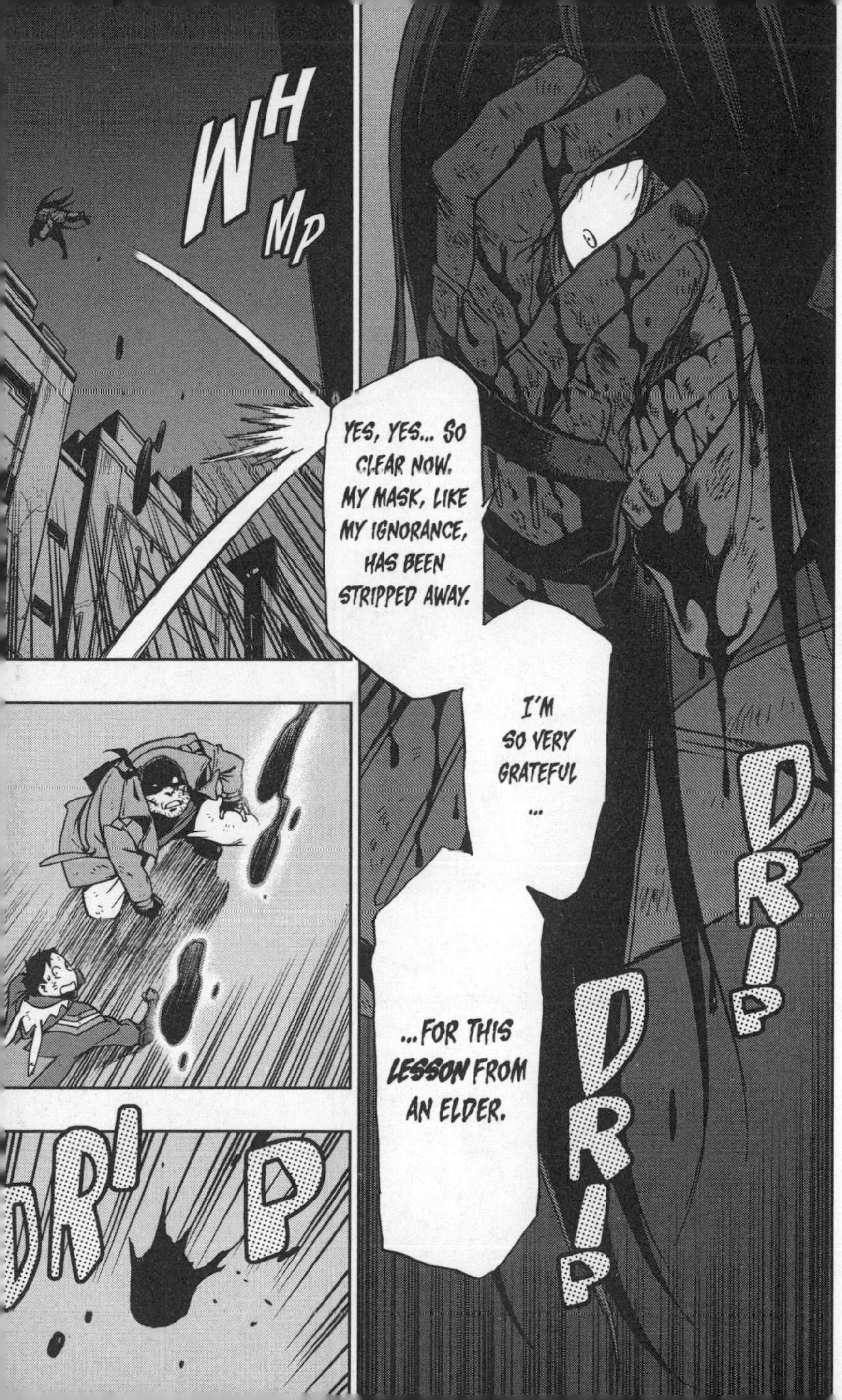
YES, YES... SO CLEAR NOW. MY MASK, LIKE MY IGNORANCE, HAS BEEN STRIPPED AWAY.
I'M SO VERY GRATEFUL ...
...FOR THIS LESSON FROM AN ELDER.
DRIP
DRIP
WHMP
DRIP

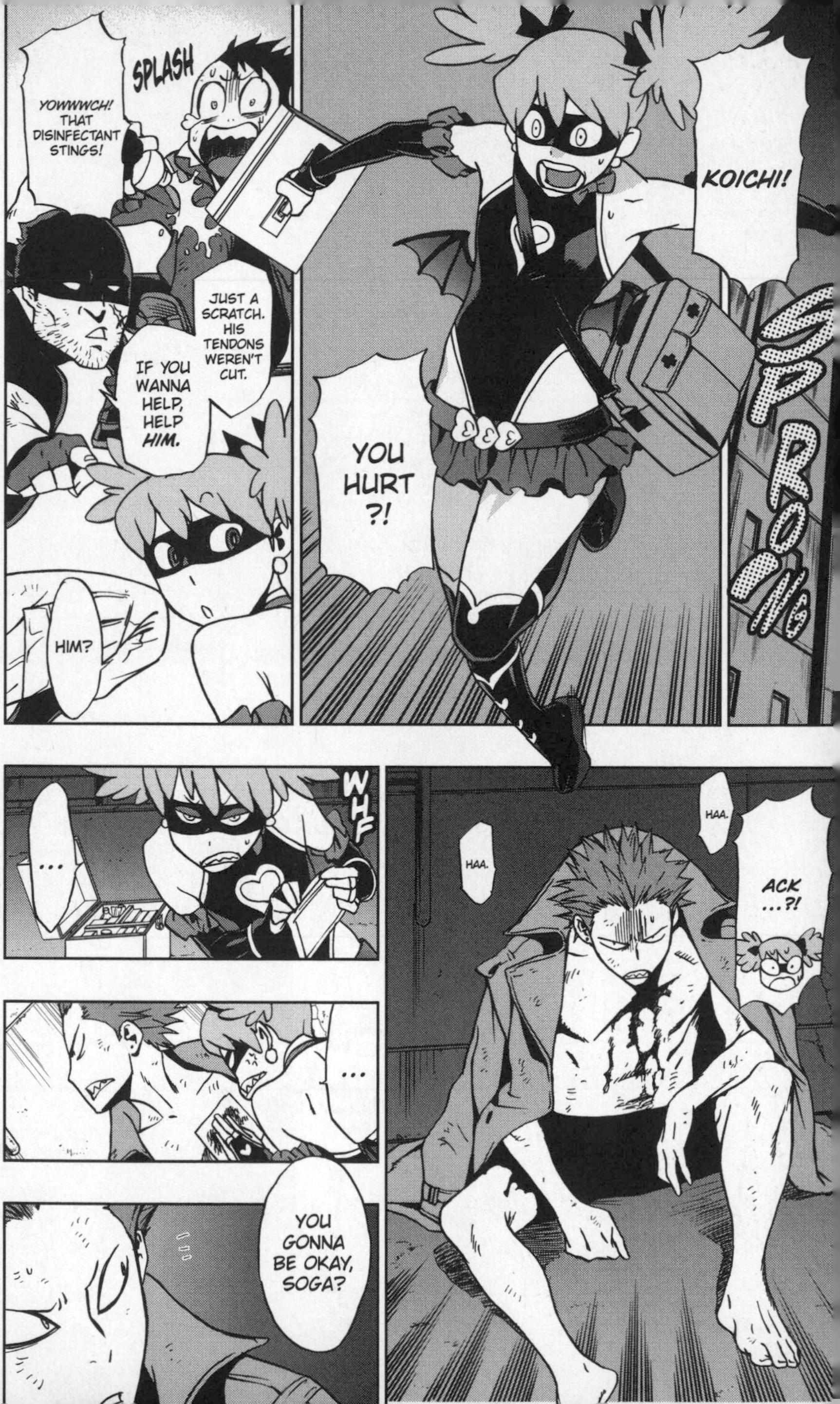
KOICHI!
SPROING
YOU HURT?!
SPLASH
YOWWWCH! THAT DISINFECTANT STINGS!
JUST A SCRATCH. HIS TENDONS WEREN'T CUT.
IF YOU WANNA HELP, HELP *HIM.*
HIM?
ACK ...?!
HAA.
HAA.
WHF
...
...
YOU GONNA BE OKAY, SOGA?

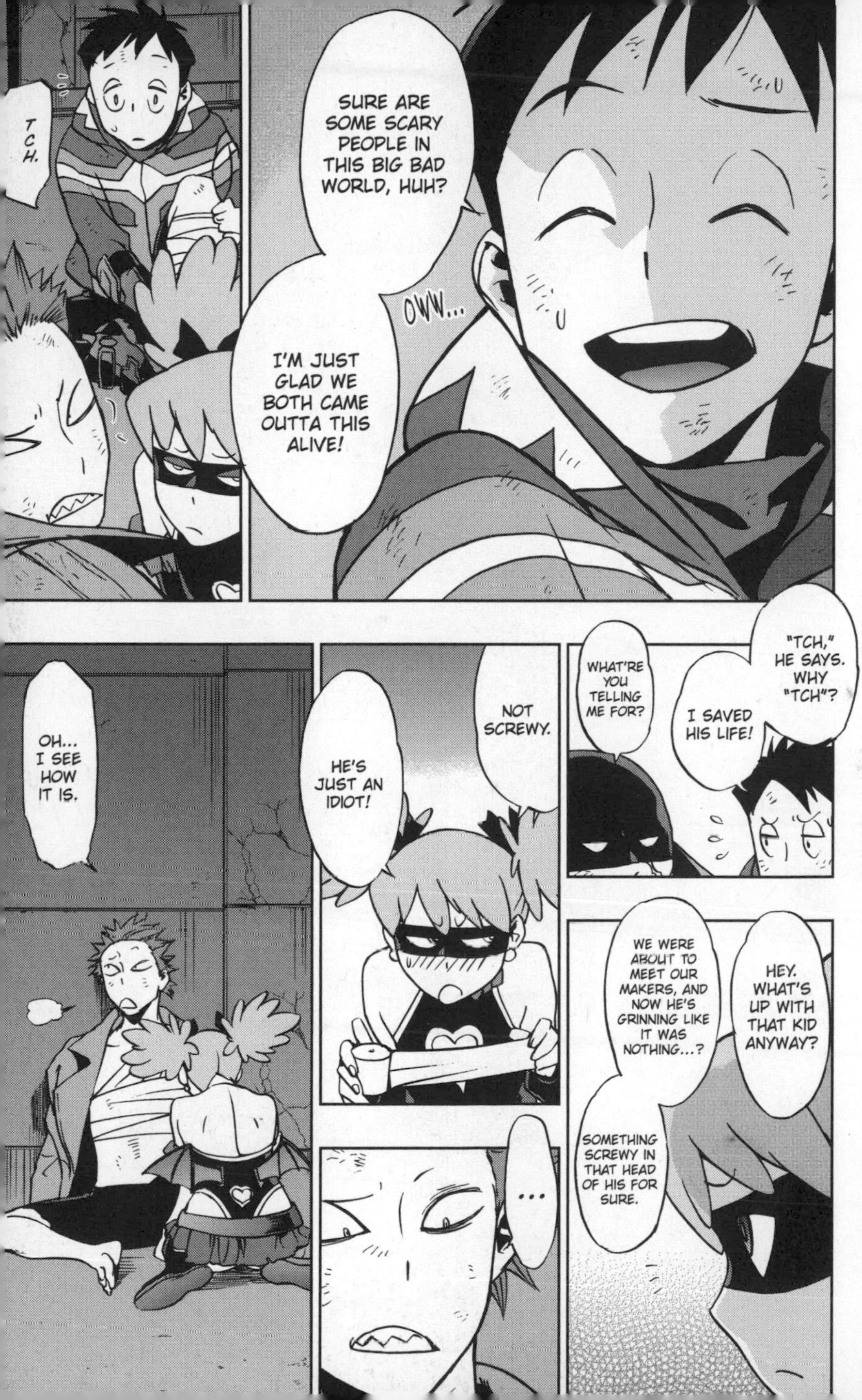
SURE ARE SOME SCARY PEOPLE IN THIS BIG BAD WORLD, HUH?
OWW...
I'M JUST GLAD WE BOTH CAME OUTTA THIS ALIVE!
TCH.
"TCH," HE SAYS. WHY "TCH"?
I SAVED HIS LIFE!
WHAT'RE YOU TELLING ME FOR?
HEY. WHAT'S UP WITH THAT KID ANYWAY?
WE WERE ABOUT TO MEET OUR MAKERS, AND NOW HE'S GRINNING LIKE IT WAS NOTHING...?
SOMETHING SCREWY IN THAT HEAD OF HIS FOR SURE.
NOT SCREWY.
HE'S JUST AN IDIOT!
...
OH... I SEE HOW IT IS.

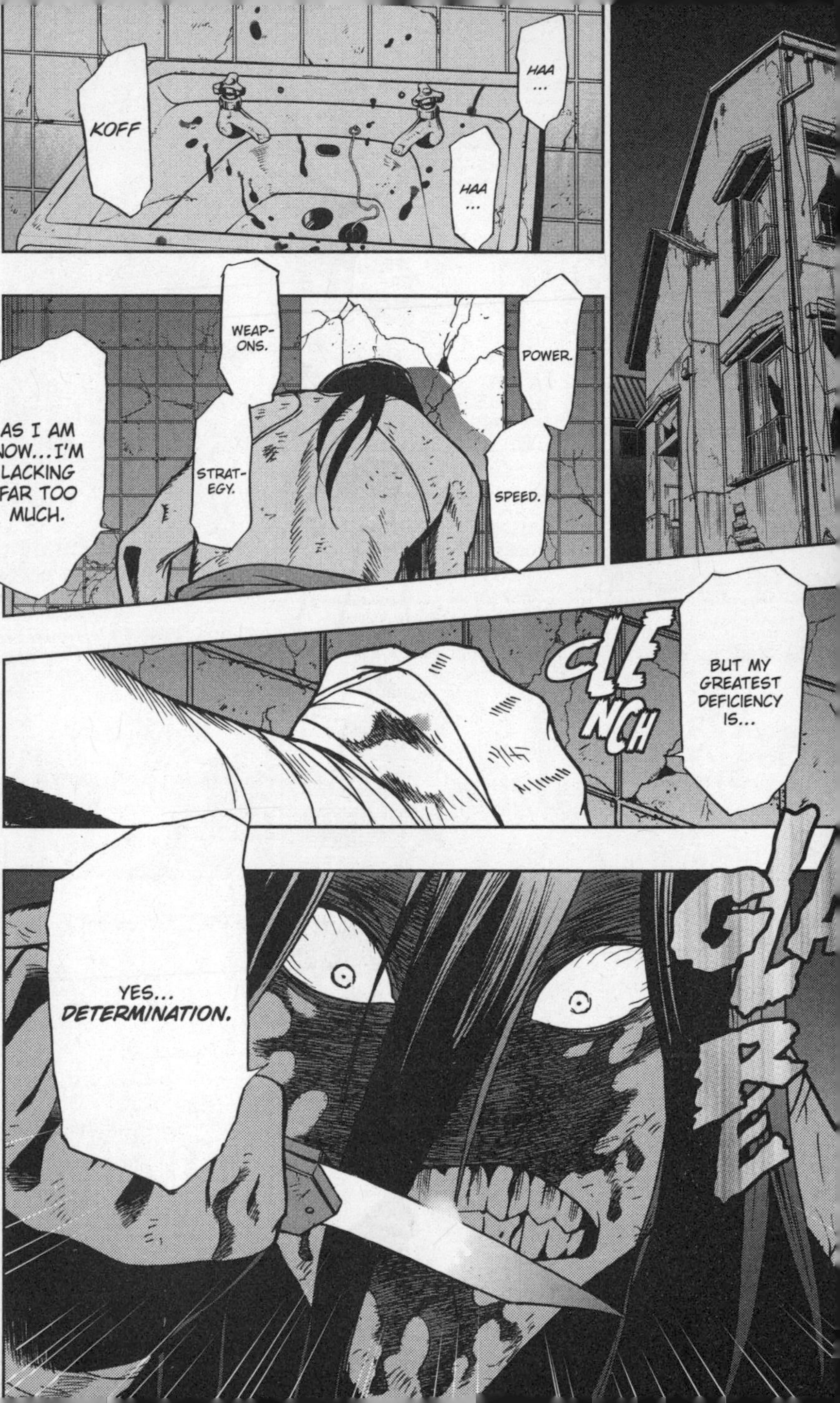
HAA...
KOFF
HAA...
POWER.
WEAP-ONS.
SPEED.
STRAT-EGY.
AS I AM NOW...I'M LACKING FAR TOO MUCH.
BUT MY GREATEST DEFICIENCY IS...
CLENCH
GLARE
YES... **DETERMINATION.**

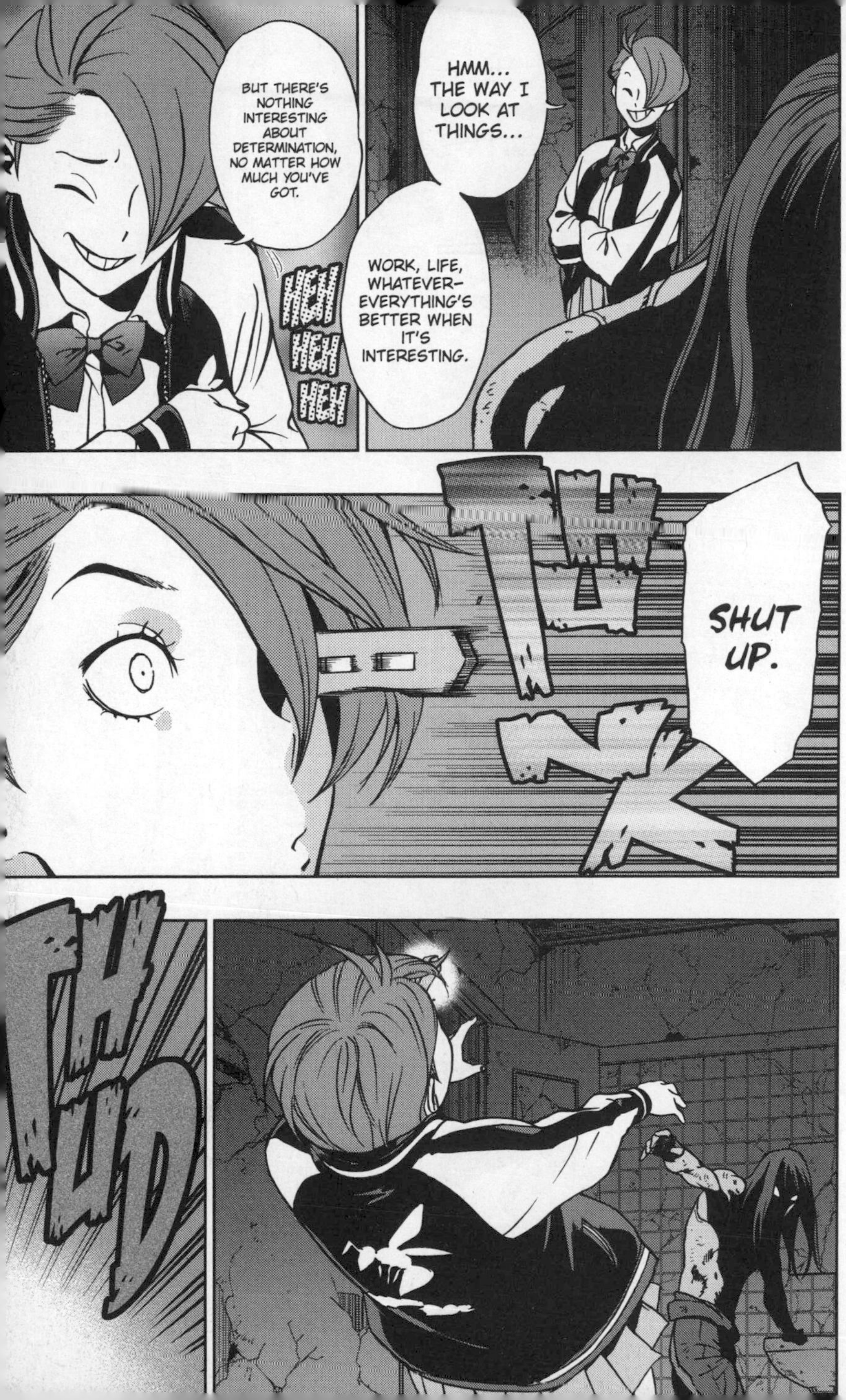
HMM... THE WAY I LOOK AT THINGS...
WORK, LIFE, WHATEVER— EVERYTHING'S BETTER WHEN IT'S INTERESTING.
BUT THERE'S NOTHING INTERESTING ABOUT DETERMINATION, NO MATTER HOW MUCH YOU'VE GOT.
HEH HEH HEH
SHUT UP.
THUNK
THUD

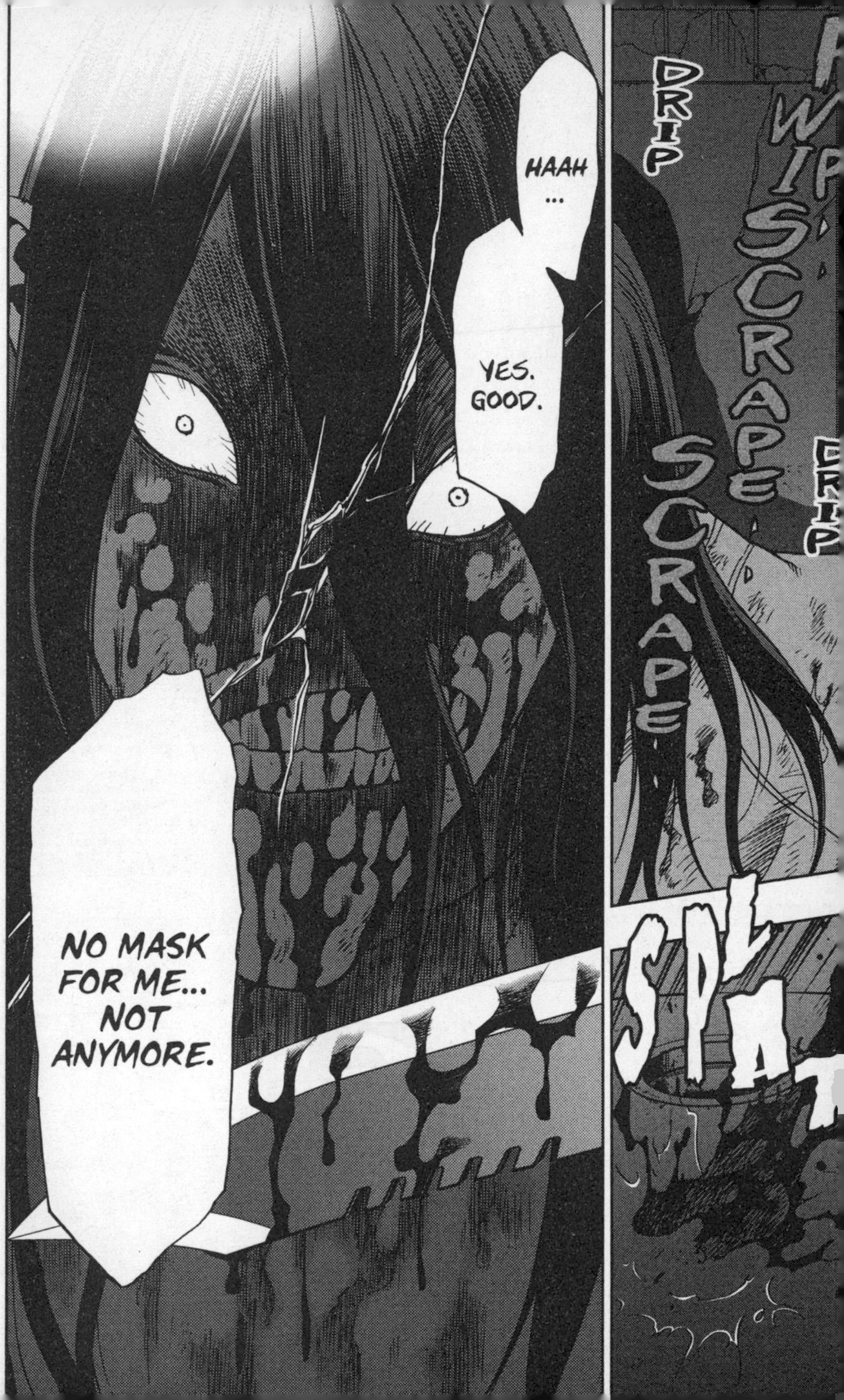
DRIP
SCRAPE
DRIP
SCRAPE
HAAH ...
YES. GOOD.
NO MASK FOR ME... NOT ANYMORE.

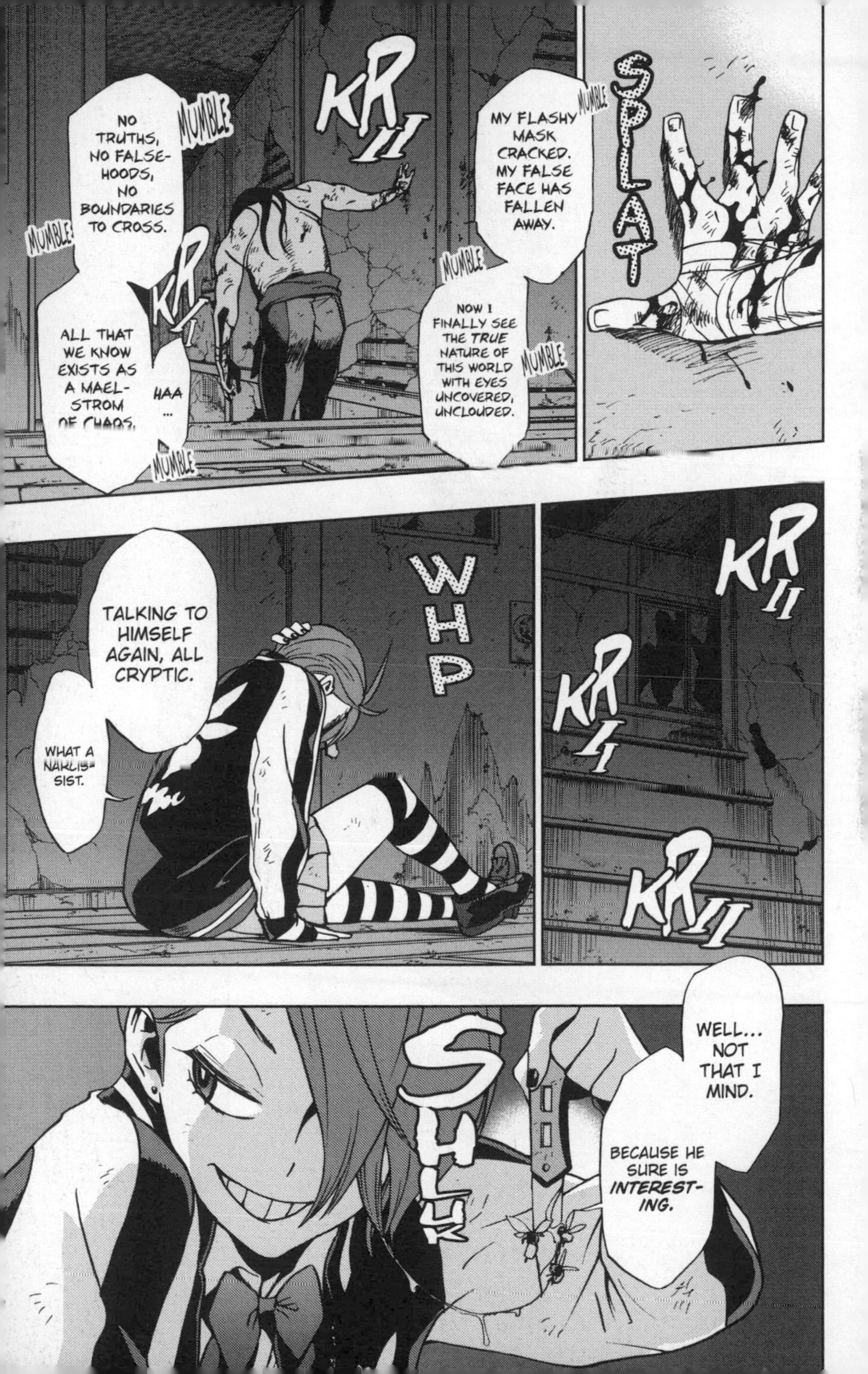
SPLAT
MUMBLE
MY FLASHY MASK CRACKED. MY FALSE FACE HAS FALLEN AWAY.
MUMBLE
NOW I FINALLY SEE THE TRUE NATURE OF THIS WORLD WITH EYES UNCOVERED, UNCLOUDED.
MUMBLE
KR II
MUMBLE
NO TRUTHS, NO FALSE-HOODS, NO BOUNDARIES TO CROSS.
MUMBLE
KR I
ALL THAT WE KNOW EXISTS AS A MAEL-STROM OF CHAOS.
HAA ...
MUMBLE
KR II
KR II
KR II
WHP
TALKING TO HIMSELF AGAIN, ALL CRYPTIC.
WHAT A NARCIS-SIST.
WELL... NOT THAT I MIND.
BECAUSE HE SURE IS INTERESTING.
SHLUK

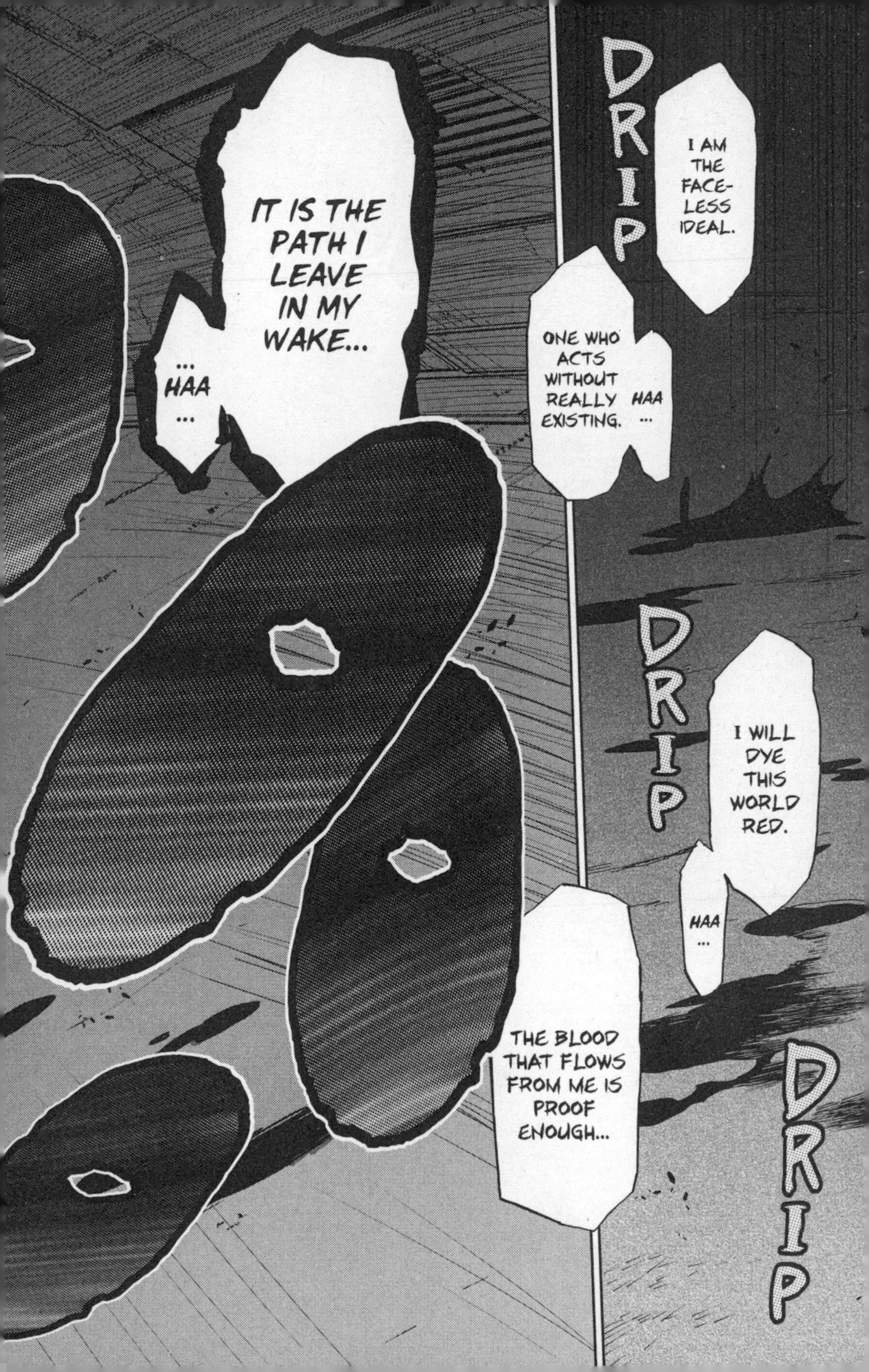
DRIP
I AM THE FACE-LESS IDEAL.
ONE WHO ACTS WITHOUT REALLY EXISTING.
HAA ...
DRIP
I WILL DYE THIS WORLD RED.
HAA ...
THE BLOOD THAT FLOWS FROM ME IS PROOF ENOUGH...
DRIP
IT IS THE PATH I LEAVE IN MY WAKE...
... HAA ...

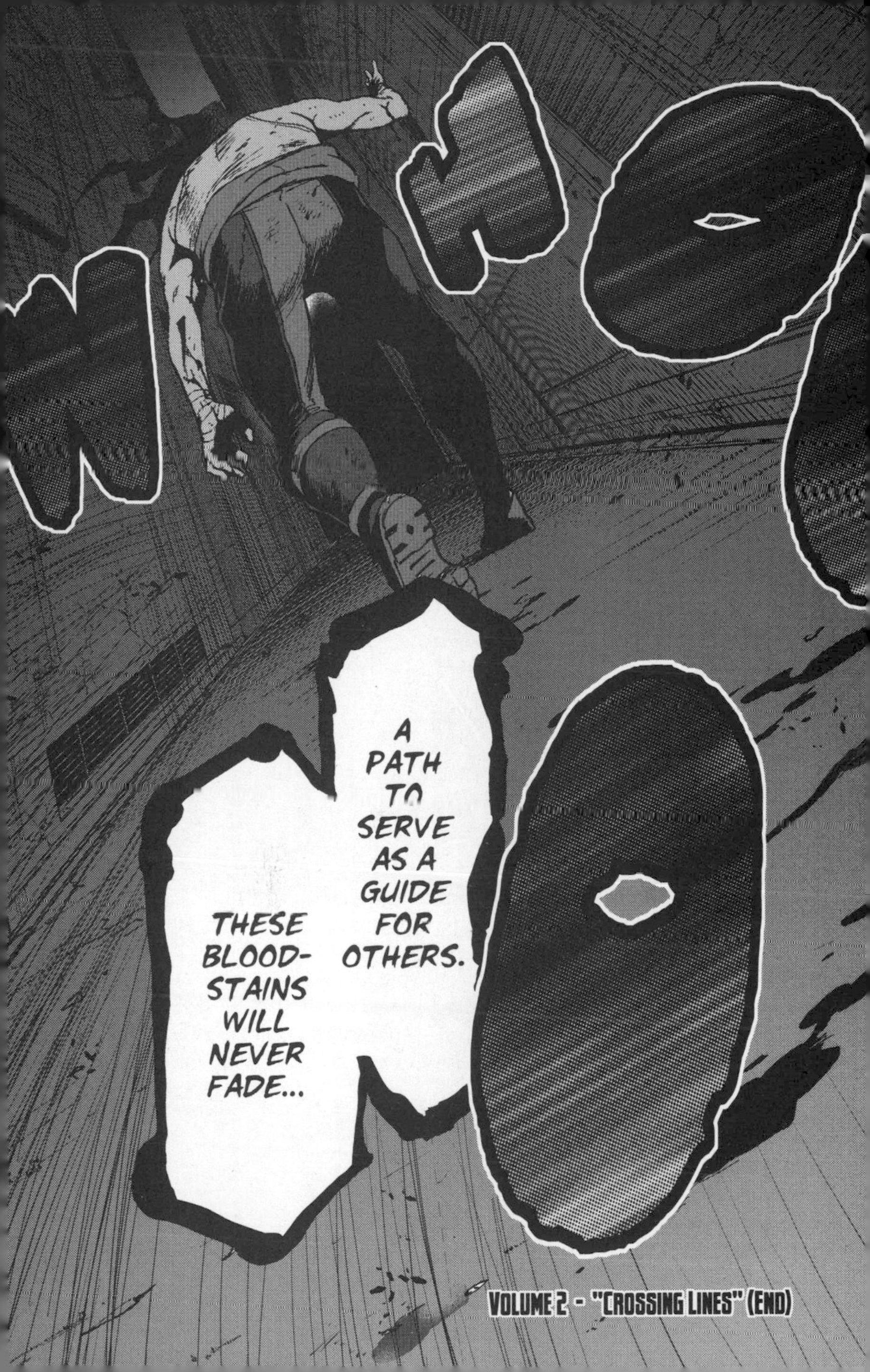
THESE BLOOD-STAINS WILL NEVER FADE...
A PATH TO SERVE AS A GUIDE FOR OTHERS.
VOLUME 2 - "CROSSING LINES" (END)

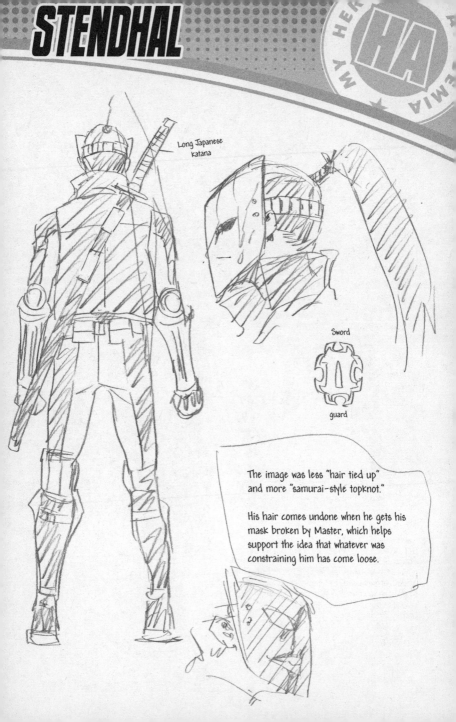

Long Japanese katana

Sword

guard

The image was less "hair tied up" and more "samurai-style topknot."

His hair comes undone when he gets his mask broken by Master, which helps support the idea that whatever was constraining him has come loose.

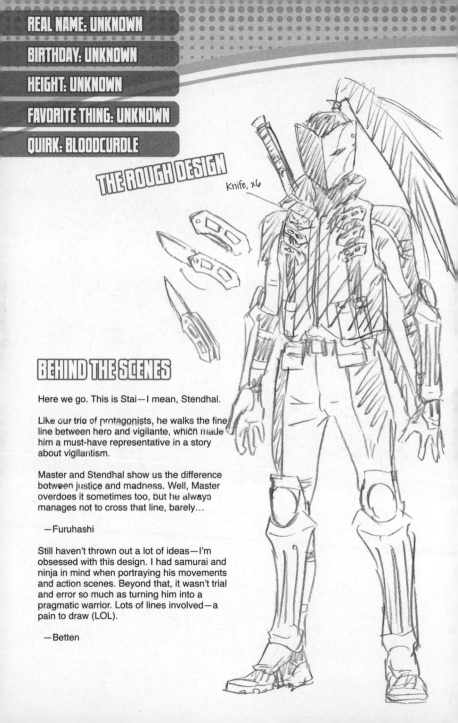

REAL NAME: UNKNOWN

BIRTHDAY: UNKNOWN

HEIGHT: UNKNOWN

FAVORITE THING: UNKNOWN

QUIRK: BLOODCURDLE

THE ROUGH DESIGN

Knife, x6

BEHIND THE SCENES

Here we go. This is Stai—I mean, Stendhal.

Like our trio of protagonists, he walks the fine line between hero and vigilante, which made him a must-have representative in a story about vigilantism.

Master and Stendhal show us the difference between justice and madness. Well, Master overdoes it sometimes too, but he always manages not to cross that line, barely…

—Furuhashi

Still haven't thrown out a lot of ideas—I'm obsessed with this design. I had samurai and ninja in mind when portraying his movements and action scenes. Beyond that, it wasn't trial and error so much as turning him into a pragmatic warrior. Lots of lines involved—a pain to draw (LOL).

—Betten

INGENIUM

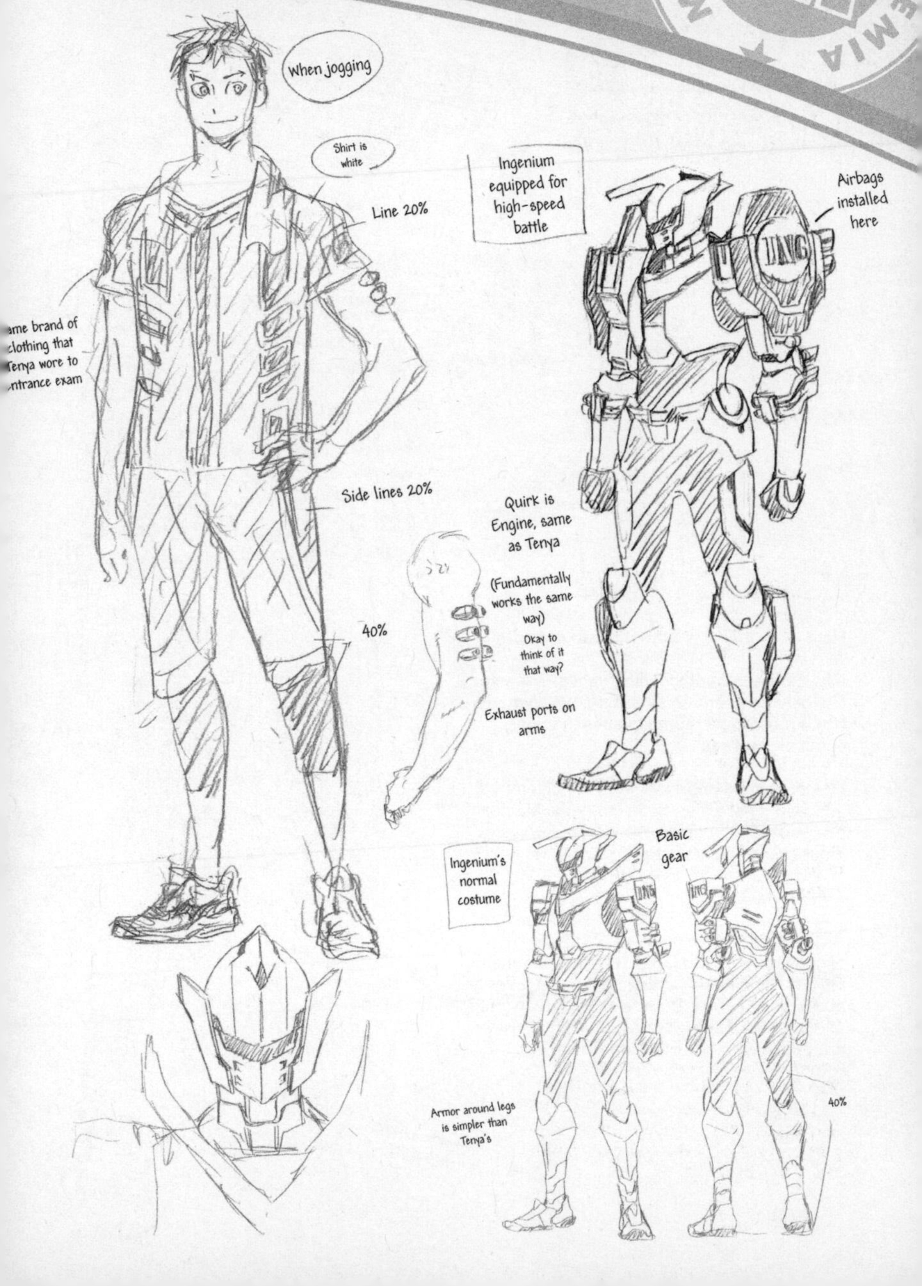

When jogging
Shirt is white
Line 20%
ame brand of clothing that Tenya wore to ntrance exam
Side lines 20%
40%
Ingenium equipped for high-speed battle
Airbags installed here
ING
Quirk is Engine, same as Tenya
(Fundamentally works the same way)
Okay to think of it that way?
Exhaust ports on arms
Ingenium's normal costume
Basic gear
Armor around legs is simpler than Tenya's
40%

REAL NAME: TENSEI IDA

BIRTHDAY: 7/22

HEIGHT: 183 CM

FAVORITE THINGS: SPORTS, HAYASHI RICE

QUIRK: ENGINE

THE ROUGH DESIGN

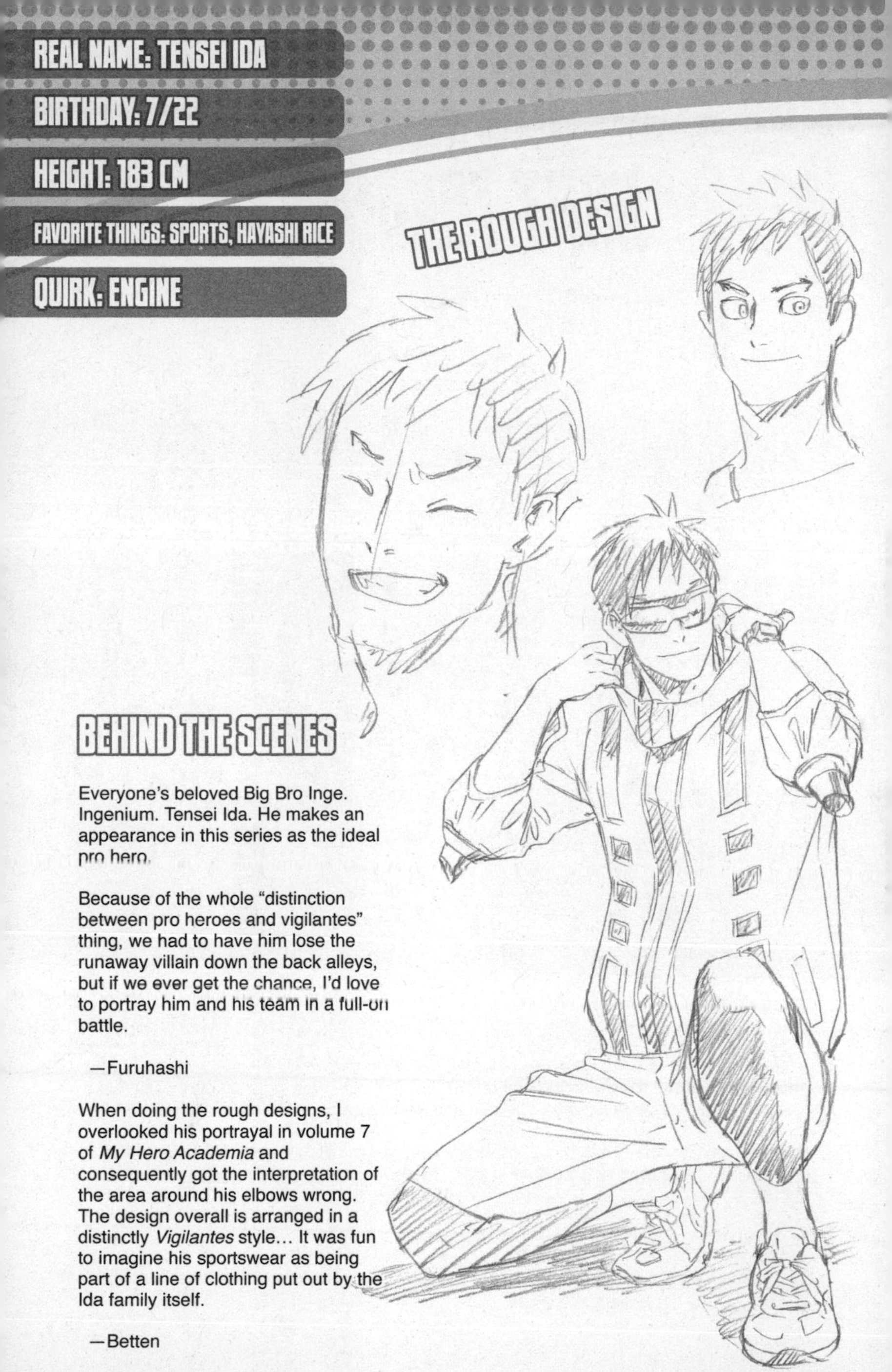

BEHIND THE SCENES

Everyone's beloved Big Bro Inge. Ingenium. Tensei Ida. He makes an appearance in this series as the ideal pro hero.

Because of the whole "distinction between pro heroes and vigilantes" thing, we had to have him lose the runaway villain down the back alleys, but if we ever get the chance, I'd love to portray him and his team in a full-on battle.

—Furuhashi

When doing the rough designs, I overlooked his portrayal in volume 7 of *My Hero Academia* and consequently got the interpretation of the area around his elbows wrong. The design overall is arranged in a distinctly *Vigilantes* style… It was fun to imagine his sportswear as being part of a line of clothing put out by the Ida family itself.

—Betten

SOGA KUGIZAKI / MOYURU TOCHI / RAPT TOKAGE

Hoodlums

Ⓐ

Thinking of something like this for now

—Betten

Ⓑ

The down vest and tent cap are so that his body temperature doesn't fall too much.

Winter clothes...for example

Ⓒ

Fire here is always burning

Skin is dark

BEHIND THE SCENES

In keeping with the trope of "the punks who serve as the first opponents in a battle manga and become allies," there was internal talk of having these three show up again, but their reappearance was delayed when Samazu and Namimaru became series regulars.

It doesn't look like they'll ever be allies at this point but rather those guys who came this close to being villains, which fits the theme of *Vigilantes*. In that sense, they serve an important role.

—Furuhashi

I fell in love with them during their second appearance. I need to practice drawing them better!

—Betten

THE THREE PERVY BROTHERS

THE ROUGH DESIGN

The Three Pervy Brothers

BEHIND THE SCENES

These villains, who rationalize their selfish desires, paired with Koichi, who can't help but ask, make their scenes important to the themes of *Vigilantes*, so we might bring them back someday. They don't seem like the types to reflect on their actions much.

—Furuhashi

All three had the same body type in Furuhashi-san's rough storyboard, but I made the third one on the chubby side to make it even worse when he wears panties (LOL). Incidentally, #2 must have some serious skills to pull off what he does! So I see them as representing mind, technique and body, respectively (that's just my personal interpretation).

—Betten

Rear view

Afterword

Hi there. I'm the storywriter, Furuhashi.

Vigilantes is a series that's riding on the coattails of the original *My Hero Academia*, so a constant part of planning it out is wondering how to make it align with *MHA* and how to have it diverge.

Before starting, some of the broad directives were to avoid things that would impact the main series' plot and to not introduce any villains stronger than those in the original *MHA*. But as we got going, I found myself being allowed to incorporate most of the ideas I came up with, as long as they weren't out-and-out violations (it's been really fun).

…So, I plan to continue using threads from the main series, especially elements that'll make readers go, "Eh? Can they really do that?" Basically, I'll keep exercising the freedom I've been given. Thanks to everyone for your continued support.

August 2017

Message from Kohei Horikoshi

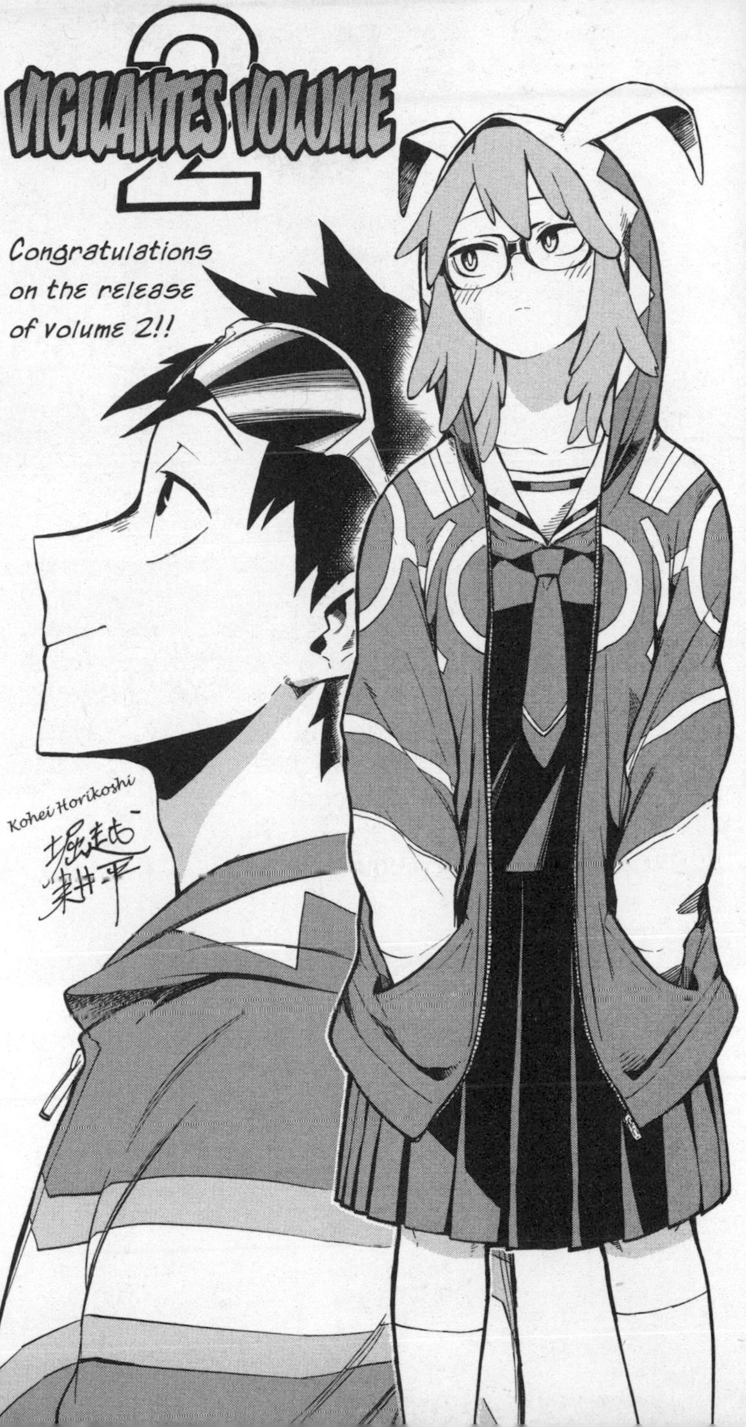
VIGILANTES VOLUME 2
Congratulations on the release of volume 2!!
Kohei Horikoshi
堀越耕平

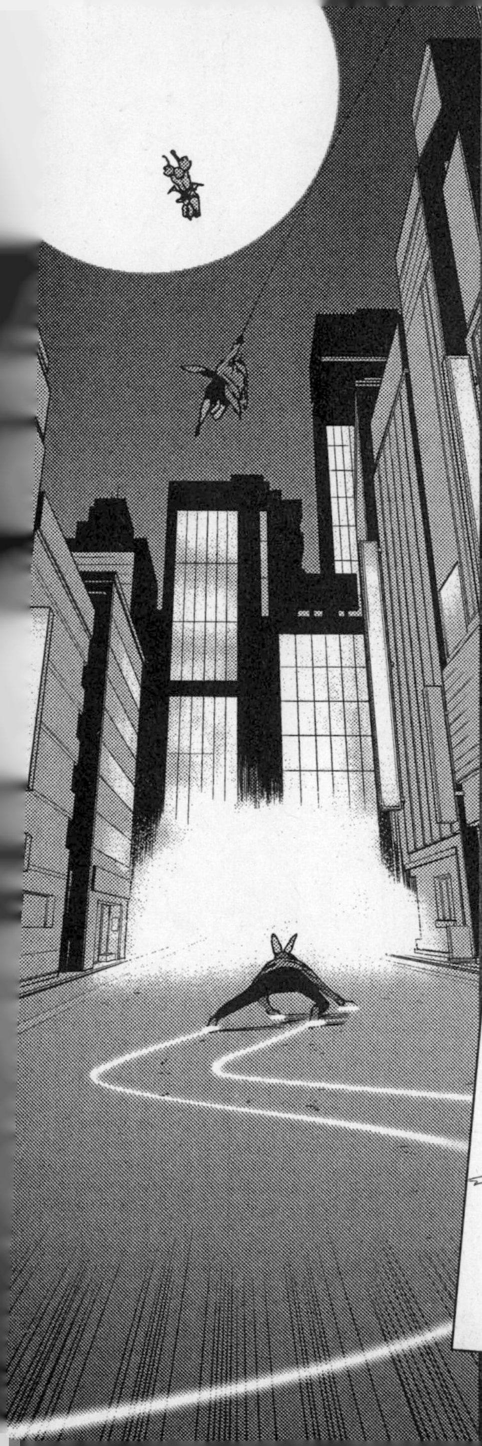

YOU'RE READING THE WRONG WAY!!

MY HERO ACADEMIA VIGILANTES

reads from right to left, starting in the upper-right corner. Japanese is read from right to left, meaning that action, sound effects and word-balloon order are completely reversed from English order.

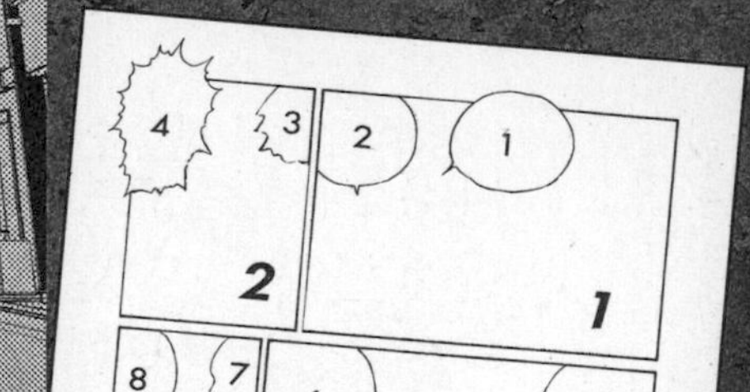

1
2
3
4
1
2
5
6
7
8
3
4
9
5
142

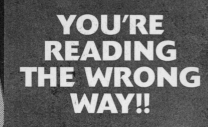

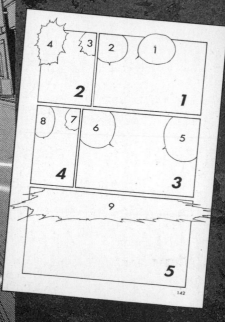